Constance de Markievicz

Constance de Markievicz

IN THE CAUSE OF IRELAND

—————

by Jacqueline Van Voris

THE UNIVERSITY OF
MASSACHUSETTS PRESS

1967

To Christy
a Fianna boy

Contents

List of Illustrations

April 30, 1916

At eleven o'clock on April 30, the Sunday after Easter in 1916, Michael Mallin and his second-in-command, Countess Markievicz, prepared to surrender the rebels who had occupied Dublin's College of Surgeons to the British forces in Ireland. A mile to the north, across the Liffey, was the burned-out General Post Office, headquarters of the Easter Rising. Rifle, machine gun and artillery fire, particularly incendiary shells, had made that position untenable and the leaders had given surrender orders the day before to all Irish Republicans in arms. The rebellion had involved about 1500 insurgents; the Irish Republic which they had proclaimed had lasted less than a week.

From the point of view of the British foreign office, the Easter Rising was merely a nuisance. It came when America was being encouraged to join the allies of World War I in the defense of small nations. A nationalist rising for Irish sovereignty was embarrassing, but it changed no major plans.

From a strictly military point of view, the Rising seemed a fiasco, though like most military fiascos it was distinguished by acts of great personal courage. The rebels had received little help from the countryside; most of the fighting was confined to Dublin. In order to deal with the rebellion, a comparatively large force had been detached from England, but this deployment of troops in no clear way affected the murderous balance of trench warfare on the Continent. The rebels were known to have had dealings with Germany, but if any of them hoped to defeat England by dividing its troops they were mistaken. In all of its history England had never had so many men in arms as it did in 1916.

The strategy of the rebellion seemed better aimed to exasperate than to win any immediate victory. The rebels had divided their small forces and disposed them about Dublin. When the British were foolish

enough to march down the street into one of these pockets, they
suffered many casualties. However, the rebels had only light arms,
and if the British troops stayed under cover, the rebel pockets could
be isolated with machine gun fire. At such times the rebellion turned
into fitful sniping. This is what had happened at the College of
Surgeons.

The rebels originally planned to establish a key outpost at St.
Stephen's Green, a lovely Victorian park at the south end of Dublin's
fashionable shopping district. From the Green they could control many
of the main roads from the south. For a day they had dug trenches
by the flower beds and set up barricades by the wrought iron gates
of the park. Due to some confusion in orders about whether or not
there was going to be any rebellion at all, only about 120 insurgents
had shown up at the Green, an insufficient number to take the large
hotels and clubs that border it. When the British mounted a machine
gun on the roof of a hotel at one end of the park, the insurgents
sought shelter in the dignified, greystone medical school at the other.
At first they were short of food, but eventually they managed to tun-
nel into a pastry shop. They were sealed off from the Green and the
streets by machine guns but returned the fire from the roof of
the building, treated their wounded with the generous supplies of the
College, and ate sweets from the shop until orders came from the
Post Office to surrender.

By eleven o'clock on Sunday morning the British captain had drawn
up his troops outside the College and the insurgents filed out. The
Countess Markievicz approached him with her usual brisk flamboy-
ance. She was wearing a green uniform with breeches; like her heroine
St. Joan, she had worn men's clothes to battle. She came up to the
British captain with the confidence of one whose ancestors had owned
the land for four hundred years, took her pistol from her holster,
kissed it, presented it to the astonished officer, then stood at attention.
"I am ready," she said. The captain gallantly offered her a ride to jail
in his car. She was indignant, she would march.

This was the Countess's most famous moment. At first glance it
seems a theatrical gesture in an outworn style. Most of the press of
the time treated her as absurd and thought the Rising was mad
fanaticism. But the leaders believed that death was a small price to
pay if it won popular support for their cause and secured recognition
of an independent Ireland at the post-war peace conference. For all

her histrionics in surrendering her revolver, the Countess was seriously offering her life for her convictions.

Due to British policy which she could not foresee, the Countess was not put before a firing squad with her friends. She and a young rebel born in America, Eamon de Valera, were the only two leaders allowed to live. She experienced the indignity of prison and deliberate terrorism, then held high political office as the Republic later grew in strength; afterwards came civil war, loss of power, and patronizing tolerance. She died eleven years after the Rising from peritonitis following a ruptured appendix. Had she been executed in 1916, she would have taken her place among the martyred saints of nationalism.

Although she was always, in a sense, a second-in-command, an instrumental but not a determining figure in Irish politics, she was bound into the rebellion by connections with art, literature, theater, labor, suffrage, and youth movements. Consequently she is one of the best representatives of the whole course of rebellion. She is also a representative of the class and circumstances which made rebellion necessary.

I

A Child of Lissadell
1868–1887

Constance Georgina Gore-Booth was born on February 4, 1868, at No. 7 Buckingham Gate, London. Her mother was an English aristocrat. The street was, as its name suggests, an elegant one, flanked by luxurious town houses and leading up to one of the Palace gates. When Constance was still an infant her mother and father took her to Lissadell, the Gore-Booths' great house in Sligo. It was in Ireland she lived the rest of her life, except for trips abroad, for lengthy visits to London during the social season when she was the proper age, and for two years spent in English jails for her zeal in the cause of Ireland.

Constance was born into a charmed circle of privilege, wealth, and power where she formed habits of leadership and service. In her middle years when she wished to extend privilege to others less fortunate, she rebelled against the class that nurtured her.

She always thought of herself as belonging to the west of Ireland and considered her London birth, when she thought of it at all, a mere accident. "We lived on a beautiful, enchanted Western coast," she wrote of her childhood, "where we grew up intimate with the soft mists and the coloured mountains, and where each morning you woke to the sound of the wild birds, the sad wintry cry of starvation that came like a keen from the throat of the phillabin driven from its haunts by the storm winds or the ascending triumphant song of spring that dropped down from the sky.

"Ranges of mountains lay like a great row of sphinxes against the sky and shut us out from Ireland. Trees and glades sloped down to the bay, across which Knocknarea rose, crowned by the great queen's cairn. The bay slipped into the Atlantic, somewhere behind black cliffs, and the Atlantic was the end of the world."[1]

The Gore-Booths lived in County Sligo, parish of Drumcliffe, in an imposing limestone house which had been built by Constance's grandfather thirty years before her birth. The house site had an old history and the new house inherited the sibilant name of its predecessors, Lissadell. The Irish form of the name has a startling translation, "The Fort of the Blind Man." Local legend tells that the land was once the prize in a victory of eloquence over economics. A blind thirteenth-century poet, Murray O'Daly, battle-axed a tax collector whom he thought too demanding and persistent. From self-imposed exile the poet wrote extravagant eulogies to be sung to his chief by a minstrel. The chief was so pleased that he forgave the murderer and granted him land and patronage. Lyricism and violence are as often associated with Lissadell's history as with Constance's career.

Lissadell is now best known outside Ireland as part of the Yeats country. It lies on the north shore of Sligo Bay, separated from the Atlantic by the sharp outlines of Ben Bulben. To the east is the lovely Loch Gill with its wooded Church and Cottage Islands, and the more famous Innisfree. Running from the lake to the sea is a short river, the Garvogue, whose Irish name is given to the town at its mouth as well as to the county in which it flows, Sligo (the Shelly River). To the west, and easily seen from Lissadell, is the hill of Knocknarea, whose summit is topped by Misgan Maeve, reputedly the burial mound of Maeve, the great Bronze-Age Queen whose name in Welsh became Maud, and in English, Mab. Under the influence of Yeats, Arthur Symons in 1896 saw the area as the distillation of the Celtic twilight: "a place of dreams. . . . On one of those luminous gray days, which are the true atmosphere of the place, it is like being in an eternal morning of twilight to wander over the undulating green lands, fringed at the shore by a soft rim of bent, a pale honey-coloured green, and along the delicate gray sands."[2] Residents there also know the fury of the gales that sweep off the Atlantic. The Gore-Booths often tried to paint the subtle changing light of Sligo, but they never lost sight of the land as most desirable real estate.

The family had come to Ireland in the Reformation and shown the ruthlessness and intrigue which characterized Renaissance soldiers of fortune. During the vicissitudes of Tudor and Stuart rule they had managed not only to hold on to their lands but to increase them. According to family history, a soldier of Henry VIII was the first of their ancestors in Ireland. Sir Paul Gore is first mentioned in writing in 1598. In 1608 he was with a small English force ordered to take Tory Island, occupied by a larger number of Irish. Sir Paul set the Irish fighting among themselves, then massacred the victors.

The eldest of Sir Paul's six sons, Ralph, inherited the title and stayed in Donegal; his successors were the Earls of Ross, those of the second son, Arthur, the Earls of Arran. The third son was Henry; the fourth, Francis, the direct ancestor of the Gore-Booths of Lissadell. They managed to be on the winning side through luck and intrigue in wars, and added to their fortunes by astutely choosing rich wives. A propitious marriage in the eighteenth century added the name Booth.

The modern history of the family begins with Constance's grandfather, Sir Robert Gore-Booth, who between 1837 and 1839 built the great house. Sir Robert had the disposition of a cultivated, sociable squire with a taste for living on an ample scale and a passion for acquiring land. He held a seat in Parliament for years but cared little for public life. He liked London society in season, hunting, riding, and improving his land in Sligo the rest of the year. In 1830 he married Caroline Goold, an heiress, second daughter of a Master in Chancery; she was as famous for her beauty and parties as Sir Robert was for his horses and hounds, the Lissadell Harriers. He was a musician as well, played the cello, and installed a handsome organ in Lissadell. His daughter Augusta inherited his musical talent, but his grandchildren showed ability in other arts. To all his heirs he bequeathed a passion for horticulture; Sir Josslyn, Constance's brother, made Lissadell a forerunner of scientific experimentation in improving the production of bulbs, potatoes, and fruit. His alpine gardens were internationally famous. Constance even planted a garden in Mountjoy jail, and her daughter became a landscape designer. Riding was so important to Sir Robert's pleasure and administration of his estate that he built a riding school at Lissadell for his children. He lived until Constance was eight, personally supervising her first riding lessons and giving her his love of the hunt.

In later years she remembered her grandfather's house as "a barracks." Actually it was the working center of a complex plantation society. There were endless comings and goings of family and friends, with servants to attend them. Some of the family sang, some played instruments, others painted or wrote. They all gardened and rode. Everyone did something at Lissadell, and through it all was the smell of farm animals, mud, and the sea. And always there was a bustle about administrative details for the land that made the Protestant Anglo-Irish establishment profitable.

It is questionable whether Lissadell under the Gore-Booths could have proved quite so profitable without the Act of Union in 1800. By that Act Ireland lost its own Parliament and Irish M.P.'s became a small minority in Westminster. Ireland shrank to a province and Dublin to a provincial capital in the hands of a few lawyers, physicians, and a small, often ineffectual administration in Dublin Castle. Except in the north, capital drained out of the country and what little Irish manufacture there was decayed. During the first half of the century the most influential politicians in England advocated laissez-faire economics as an article of faith. Those in Ireland who stood to lose the most were the tenant farmers, that is, the majority of the Irish. Those who stood to gain most were enterprising landlords with large holdings such as Sir Robert, especially if they had a flair for successful agricultural experiment. Sir Robert and Sir Henry, Constance's father, were in turn faced with the problem of preserving an almost medieval system while bringing its production up to date.

"The soft rim of bent" which Arthur Symons saw as the fitting fringe at the shore was an example of Sir Robert's husbandry rather than his poetic expression. He and others who owned land near the sea followed the continental practice of planting agrostis around the edges of the exposed land to stop the encroachment of the sand. Eventually thousands of acres in the area were saved and restored to tillage and pasturage. He was one of the first to experiment with planting oysters as a source of food and income, and also in methods of harvesting and efficiently utilizing the vast quantities of seaweed that grew on the rocky coast. For the owners of Lissadell the will had extraordinary power: it could change their landscape and the lives of everyone in it.

Since raising beef to sell to the English markets had proved to be the most profitable use of Irish land, whatever could be used for grazing was important to the prosperity of the landlord although it did not necessarily help the tenants. Salvaging a few acres from the sea was a slower process than wholesale evictions. In 1834 Sir Robert added about 800 statute acres by annexing Ballygilgan, locally known as the Seven Cartrons.[3] By this act he took advantage of poverty and bestowed on his son and grandchildren a strong social conscience and a sense of family guilt. Folk memory is long, and to this day one can hear in Sligo a tale about Sir Robert's coffin ship. It is said that he evicted his tenants from the Seven Cartrons and hired a fiendish captain to take them to sea in a ship with a false bottom and drown them. Jack Yeats even used this bit of lore in a play. Why the captain contracted to drown himself along with his passengers is not explained. Nor does the teller know what good it would have done Sir Robert to have his erstwhile tenants drown at all. The date of the story is usually put fifteen years after the episode which prompted it, the emigrant ship being absorbed into other stories of the Bad Times of the 1840's.

What actually had happened was that Sir Robert decided that thin tenants were less desirable than fat cattle. When Sir Robert bought the Seven Cartrons in 1834, he offered land elsewhere or passage money to America to the tenants (although he was legally entitled to turn them out with no compensation). Most chose to emigrate. They were paid at the rate of £2 a person for passage and £4 an acre for improved land. A ship was chartered, an unseaworthy hulk it proved to be, and it sank when barely out of sight of Ireland. All aboard were lost.

Father O'Rorke, a Sligo historian, thought the event encouraged the Gore-Booths to try to be model landlords, particularly during famine years, which were part of the economic pattern of western Ireland throughout the nineteenth century.

The Irish tenantry had been forced by circumstances and by law to rely on the land. England always watched closely any growing manufactories that would rival her trade, taxing exports or declaring them illegal so that it was impossible to establish an independent economic foundation apart from the land. A population explosion raised rents and forced the tenants onto ever smaller plots. The rents had to be paid in cash; every product of the often tiny farms that could be, was sold. The usual diet of the small farmer was potatoes and buttermilk (the butter itself was marketed). Depending on weather conditions, some years were better than others, but hunger was a constant threat. The potato crops were anxiously watched from May on every year. When blight ruined the potato crop for several years in succession, as it did in the 1840's, starvation, disease, and emigration raced to decimate the population. In 1845 it was estimated that there were 8.3 million people in Ireland; in six years nearly 2 million had disappeared. To add to the horror, the dispossessed wandered through fields of fat cattle and grain grown for export.

Humane landlords did what they could for the tenants during the lean years; most cared little for their tenants as long as the rents were paid. The absentee landlord was common. He drew his income from Irish estates while he lived in London or Paris, not knowing or caring what was happening in Ireland. He is a common villain of the time and place, the Sir Kit Rackrent or Lord Clonbrony of Maria Edgeworth's novels. Sometimes he fitted the stock character of the pleasant hunting and drinking incompetent like Sir Condy Rackrent or the protagonists of Somerville and Ross. Sometimes he was the land-grasping agent of Kickham's *Knocknagow* who ruined the homes of Tipperary.

Through the terrible famine of the 'forties, 1845, 1846, and 1847, Sir Robert and Lady Gore distributed food from Lissadell to keep what tenants remained from starvation. A prized possession still at Lissadell is a letter from the parish priest of Drumcliffe in 1847 saying that prayers were offered "every night in every home" for her ladyship's "extensive and unostentatious charities." The Gore-Booths collected the rents, at least the ones they could, but there is evidence that much of their income was turned back in the form of food. Eventually Sir Robert borrowed money to feed his tenants, although he retained the conviction that emigration was the more humane solution.

Sir Robert's second son, Henry, was married April 27, 1867, to Georgina Mary Hill of Tickhill Castle, Yorkshire.[4] Constance, their first child, was born the following year; the first son, Josslyn, was born in 1869; a second daughter, Eva, in 1870. A second son, Mordaunt, was born when Constance was ten years old, and a third daughter, Mabel, two years later. Sir Robert died in 1876, and Henry's elder brother having been drowned (and he nearly so) in a boating accident near Lissadell, Henry became the 5th baronet.

Sir Henry did not share his father's zest for acquiring land. As he saw it, the wealth of Lissadell carried with it a grave paternal obligation to tenants and family, and he was happiest when he could escape from it as far away as possible in arctic explorations. Sir Henry had inherited one of the family characteristics that appeared in a few individuals each generation, an almost inexhaustible energy. His eldest daughter had the same quality. They both showed a quickening of responses, a taut eagerness in the midst of danger and difficulty.

Sir Henry was one of those wealthy Victorians who were amateur scientists and explorers. In 1879 he and Captain A. H. Markham in the Norwegian schooner *Isbjörn* made one of the early explorations of the polar cap. They sailed along the west coast of Nova Zembla to its most northern point, passed through the Matotchkin Shar to the east coast, and examined the ice in the direction of Franz Josef Land as far as 78°24′ North. They studied the animals and currents and made useful observations on the drift and nature of the ice in the Barents and Kara Seas. For many years Sir Henry sailed on other arctic explorations in his own yacht, named the *Kara* in memory of this first expedition; he was justifiably proud of his master's certificate.

He was interested in harbor development and improving the fishing industry off the west coast to help better the economic conditions of the people. In 1890, in the hope of reviving fisheries off Galway, he undertook a ten-week trip off Buffin Island to explore the possibilities of taking the basking shark commercially and left a lively account of harpooning the 25 foot monster.[5] Lissadell is still full of trophies of his luck and skill with rod, net, and harpoon.

Brave and well-intentioned as Sir Henry might be, he was somewhat opaque about people. "It is quite possible that the small boats about Buffin and Shark [Islands] might still have taken a fish occasionally, had it not been for an unfortunate accident by which a fish upset the boat and three men lost their lives. In Ireland a catastrophe of this sort has a very damping effect."[5]

Sir Henry did not like upset boats of any kind. He was never tempted into Irish politics. His only public office was that of High Sheriff of the county in 1872. He dutifully served on Grand Juries, as the president of the annual Agricultural Show for years, and on the Board of Guardians of Sligo most of his life, but he had no wish to change laws or influence voters. He was a staunch supporter of the status quo, the way of his world.

The crucial winter of 1879–80, when Constance was twelve, fixed in her mind an image of public distress to which she later referred. Famine had returned, the worst in thirty years. The virus had remained in the soil and there was no longer hope that the blight would disappear as mysteriously as it had come. The winter was hard, evictions were sending the dispossessed wandering through the countryside. The editors of *The Sligo Champion* were loud in bitter charges against most landlords of the area. During the fall and winter of 1879 they printed full accounts of evictions. A quick little ritual accompanied each: the sheriff handed the bailiff a portion of the thatch of the vacated cottage and said, "On the part of the plaintiff I give you possession." The words meant misery, often exile, and sometimes death to the evicted. From her privileged position as the eldest child of a great house, Constance watched her father try to be a model landlord. Nearby, another attempt to solve the problem on a more permanent basis was being made by the Land League.

At a meeting in Irishtown in nearby County Mayo on April 19, 1879, Michael Davitt had inaugurated land reform to change the economic pattern that made recurring famines possible.[6] Through public agitation he wanted to reduce excessive rents and to force the government to make it possible for farmers to purchase their own land with the aid of subsidies. The Irish National Land League was organized in Dublin six months later under the leadership of the young Protestant landlord, Charles Stewart Parnell, recently elected leader of the Irish Parliamentary Party. The Land League proposed action through Parliament but also advocated limited civil disobedience to start the sluggish legal machinery and keep it moving. The tenants were to be organized for their mutual strength, and the League undertook the defense of those who might be threatened with eviction for refusing to pay unjust rents. Parnell's advice to the tenants set the tone: "Keep a firm grip on your homesteads."

The Land League's first meeting in County Sligo was held at Gurteen, part of the Gore-Booth estate, on November 2, 1879. There were 8000 men and women present, many of them wearing green rosettes and broad, orange-trimmed, green scarves across their chests. There were flags and banners and five bands. The three speakers, Michael Davitt, James Daly, a newspaper proprietor, and James Boyce Killeen, barrister-at-law, were subsequently arrested for sedition in Dublin. They were returned to Sligo for trial which opened November 25, 1879. Parnell was one of the many spectators because the Land League was using the trial to publicize the reform movement.

John Monroe, the law adviser of the Castle, in his concluding statement summed up the arguments for the sedition charge against Davitt. "After pointing out its [rent-paying] immorality, and that it was a tax on the people and must be swept away, Mr. Davitt invites the people of Ireland to spring to their feet and say they will tolerate this system no longer . . . If language like that is to be tolerated I am at a loss to conceive how any government could be carried on, or the peace or prosperity of the country maintained."[7] There was no prosperity to be maintained. Pressure from the Land League compelled the dropping of the charges and later passing of the Land Act of 1881 which secured tenure at fair rents and paved the way for state-aided purchase by the tenants.

Sir Henry's response to famine was individual. He personally investigated the conditions of his tenantry and inspected their crops. There was jubilee in Ballymote one evening that winter when he announced a 40 per cent reduction in the rents. "The tenantry got the bellman to go round, and request the townspeople to illuminate their windows and there was not a window from the largest business one to the smallest cottage in town that was not brilliantly lighted." The local band played and "through the country bonfires blazed on every hill."[8] Both Sir Henry and Lady Gore were in the tradition of the Victorian philanthropist. They went to each house to ascertain the need, then supervised distribution of food and clothing. They even saw to the carting of the straw from the haggard at Lissadell to contrive beds for those who needed them. The three oldest children, Constance, Josslyn, and Eva, helped with the food distribution from the storehouse set up at Lissadell. Constance was first known outside Ireland as the Countess Markievicz who was running a kitchen for Dublin's striking workers in 1913; providing food for the hungry was a skill she learned in childhood. She also learned from her parents the rare art of helping without patronizing.

The laws of the land often made it difficult to help the hungry. When the laws and his conscience were at variance, Sir Henry reconciled them to his own satisfaction. The kind of astounding compromise he was able to make is revealed in the records of a Board of Guardians meeting in December, 1879. Under the laws then in force, "extern relief" (outside the almshouse) was forbidden to anyone holding a quarter of an acre of land, unless he first surrendered his holdings. One of the Guardians thought it would be common sense to circumvent the law and was convinced that the government would have to provide outside relief; otherwise "these poor people would have to sacrifice their homes." To this Sir Henry made the generous but amazing statement: "They won't, as far as I am concerned. I will undertake that nothing will happen to their homes, or their cabins during any little time that it may be necessary for them to come in here [the workhouse]. All they will have to do will be to close their doors and lock them and their cabins will be safe for them when they return. I will be responsible for that. Besides, you see, we have no power to do anything else."[9]

Throughout their lives, Sir Henry's three oldest children, particularly Constance and Eva, showed the same single-minded commitment to the action they thought right. If they or others suffered in consequence, that was regrettable, but their integrity permitted no alternatives; they had "no power to do anything else." At twelve, Constance was unaware of the superiority of the Land League's effectiveness to Sir Henry's conscientious paternal care. Such awareness came much later when she and her colleagues aimed at the much broader goal of independence and extended the theory of civil disobedience to its logical conclusion, insurrection. By then she had articulated her main policy, one illustrated by the League: when you want to change anything, "organize and make a row."

Meanwhile, her mother disapproved of rows. Lady Gore-Booth enjoyed society in the narrow sense of the word, and when not in London or Dublin, there was much entertaining at Lissadell. When Constance was a child, the household included her grandmother, Lady Hill, and her Aunt Augusta, sister of Sir Henry. Another aunt was married to Owen Wynne, who lived at the neighboring estate, Hazelwood, and there were cousins who were constantly visiting each other. Living on the shore the children were naturally keen sailors, and spent much time boating and fishing on Sligo Bay. There were uncountable picnics. They learned early to shoot well, a skill that was to prove useful to Constance in her Dublin years. Above all, the family enjoyed riding and hunting, and they were skilled in driving as well. They showed horses and ponies at the annual County Sligo Agricultural Show and sometimes at the great Dublin Horse Show in August. Occasionally Lady Gore would ride the ten miles into Sligo town on horseback, accompanied by her son and daughters. They were a handsome, horsey, county family.

But there was something very special about Constance's riding, some grace, verve, and reckless precision that dazzled. Even as a young girl of fourteen, it was clear that she was the best rider ever seen by a county of enthusiasts. At home with her mother, young Constance often seemed merely one of the pretty Gore-Booth girls, but when they saw her flashing over walls on her hunter, local historians recalled a long line of fearless Gore-Booth women with furious wills. Among the legends of Sligo is that of an early Lady Gore who ordered her coachman to drive her around the edge of Derk, at Knocklane, a semi-circular chasm of seething, roaring waters. He demurred at first but changed his mind when Lady Gore drew a pistol and gave him his choice. Deciding that the chasm was less perilous than the lady, he whipped up the horses and galloped them along the edge of the cliff.

Constance won her first pony race when she was fourteen at the annual County Sligo Hunt, and from that time on she was famous for her riding. The County Sligo Harriers met every Tuesday and Friday during the winter and she rode with them nearly as often. For years she and her favorite horse "Max" were given the deference of prize athletes until finally he burst a blood vessel while racing for his mistress. The local paper awarded her bouquets of florid prose even when she lost a race: "Her gallant and daring horsemanship, as she led the field almost from the start, was the subject of universal admiration; and at the conclusion of the race she was accorded a most enthusiastic reception, being warmly cheered again and again. When it is considered that she decided on riding only the morning of the races, that she rode a strange horse, not properly trained, that the animal baulked when in the finishing lap, thereby losing several lengths, and also the disadvantages a lady has to undergo in a competitive race, her performance must be regarded as simply marvelous."[10] After she went to live in Dublin, her interest in horses waned, but Yeats remembered. When she was a political prisoner after the 1916 rebellion, he wrote:

> When long ago I saw her ride
> Under Ben Bulben to the meet,
> The beauty of her country-side
> With all youth's lonely wildness stirred,
> She seemed to have grown clean and sweet
> Like any rock-bred, sea-borne bird.[11]

Riding side-saddle at breakneck speed across difficult terrain was the only socially acceptable activity that would satisfy her vast energy and daring. It also satisfied her vanity, which was almost childishly simple. She loved being the center of attention and praise. What was remarkable about her is that she made very little use of charm. Once she had decided how she wished to be distinguished, no pains or careful planning were too great for her. She was born with the temperament to be a fine horsewoman, but it was her disciplined will that trained herself and her mount those early years to give her local fame.

Another trait, and equally strong, was her altruism—her compulsive generosity and quick empathy for those in distress. For all her vanity, she could be selfless in her attention to others. This was a quality shared with her less flamboyant sister, Eva, the member of the family with whom Constance had the strongest bond of affection.

Constance and Eva wandered over the estate, visiting tenants in their homes. Many of Constance's early drawings were of them: an old man sitting by the fire, leaning pensively on his stick; a poor woman before a huge pot hanging in the fireplace; a lonely young girl at a cottage window.

The son of a studgroom at Lissadell always remembered the time when his mother, who was near her confinement, was washing clothes in a tub in the kitchen. "Miss Con came in and she just put her away from the tub and washed out the clothes herself." Another time his father "had a terrible tussle with a divil of a horse, and, in the long run, he had to turn him into a loose box and leave him there, kicking and squealing. He was quite worn-out and down-like about it, and sat on a big stone in the yard to recover himself, and, heated and all as he was, he got a terrible chill that turned to pneumonia, and he all but died. He would have died if Miss Con hadn't sat up with him night after night and nursed him through it."[12]

She and Eva were educated at home in the manner of their time and class. They were taught the proprieties and the genteel arts of music, poetry, and sketching. Adjoining the large gallery and the dining room they had a sitting room they called their "glory hole," usually a girlish jumble of books and Constance's painting and carving. They would often sit there, Eva reading aloud while her sister sketched.

Constance later said their learning had been inadequate and claimed they had been denied an education. "No one was interested in politics in our house. It was rare that anyone mentioned them. Every one accepted the status quo, almost as if it had been the will of God. It was there, just as the mountains and the sea were, and it was absurd to try and alter it for that led nowhere and only made trouble. It was unlucky that landlords had been so bad, for if only they had done what they ought, everything would have been all right now. Anyhow you could not go back, and everything would soon be all right. Irish history was also taboo, for 'what is the good of brooding over past grievances?' But history was written on every fence and boundary wall. You saw the landlords in their big demesnes, mostly of Norman or Saxon stock, walled in and aloof, an alien class, sprung from an alien race."[13]

This was the bitter judgment of her later years when she was alienated from a class she was helping to destroy. It is very doubtful that she felt aloof as a child. She was extremely attractive, admired by all who knew her; she lived in a world where to be amused and amusing were goals enough. Until she was nearly forty years old she had only the most casual interest in any other world, being too absorbed in her own of parties and hunting, in painting and carving, in plays, in growing up, in traveling, in loving, in enjoying life. But as she matured she was constantly seeking some activity which would completely absorb her extraordinary vitality; there were to be many years of search before she finally found fulfillment in the cause of Ireland's independence.

The socio-economic history of Ireland was not part of her curriculum at Lissadell. The Gore-Booths felt themselves too wealthy and well born to concern their daughters with such matters. When Constance came to study the cause of labor and economics in Ireland, it was after long liberalizing study of painting and the theater. Her developing artistic sensibility awakened her social awareness. Lissadell did lay the groundwork for her interest in art, not as ostentatious culture but as part of a way of life.

Many long, dark winter days, with "a great storm from the ocean shouting o'er the hill" and the pounding rain shutting off Sligo Bay only a few hundred yards away, were spent in the chaos of amateur theatricals.[14] It was an amusing way to entertain a houseful of guests. The whole family played, and sometimes they were persuaded to take the entertainment to Sligo for some charitable purpose. Sir Henry was an admirable stage manager but usually could not be persuaded to act. Aunt Augusta and Lady Gore-Booth formed the orchestra of violin and piano, sometimes supplemented by a musically-inclined guest. Often the visitors were willingly pressed into stage appearances, usually in a comedy or farce, whether by a local or a well-known author did not matter. From the time she was able to talk, Constance liked to recite, and one of her first treasured books was *Twenty Minutes,* by Harriet Childe Pemberton, a collection of "drawing room dialogues" carefully pencilled by the young actress. Her love of theatrics was lifelong, but she was always better off the stage than on, as her later performances in Dublin proved.

The year she was eighteen, Constance went on the grand tour with her governess, Miss Noel, whom the girls called Squidge. She especially loved and always remembered Florence, where they had stayed in a pension in the Piazza Cavour. Squidge was well-informed about the city—Constance thought she knew all about everything. "How she loved Savonarola, too!" Constance wrote years later to her sister who was vacationing in Italy, "I never quite forgave his bonfires of Vanities, so much beauty must have been burnt." And in another letter, "I wonder do you love all the places I loved. I'd love to see the front of the Duomo & go up to San Miniato & look down at the sunset. I remember catching butterflies wildly across hedges & ditches at Fiesole, & distressed Squidge quite unable to follow. Young ladies hadn't found their legs in those days; & mine would have been quite up to the mark even in these days."[15]

Constance appeared to be at one with her world. She was nearly nineteen years old, eldest daughter of a leading landowner, a member of the ascendency class. The Gore-Booths were well established on extensive lands, Protestant, with mores modeled on those of their English counterparts; they typified the class called Anglo-Irish. High spirited, energetic, graceful, and beautiful, Constance was now ready for the excitements of the London and Dublin social seasons. On her return to Lissadell from Europe, final plans were made for her presentation to Queen Victoria which was to take place during the next season, appropriately, on St. Patrick's day. Outside of Sligo she appeared to be a properly-brought-up Victorian young lady. At home they knew her better, they had seen her ride. To the tenants of Lissadell she was "a wild, kind girl."

NOTES TO CHAPTER I

1. *Eire,* August 18, 1923.

2. Arthur Symons, *The Savoy,* No. 7 (Nov. 1896), 56–61.

3. Cartron was an ancient unit of land measurement, corruption of *quaterons,* i.e., quarters. Each quarter or cartron must contain sufficient ground to pasture 400 cows, and 17 plough-lands. A knight's fee was composed of eight hydes, which amounted to 160 acres, generally figured to be about a plough-land.

4. Tickhill Castle was one of the seats of Georgina Hill's uncle, the 9th Earl of Scarborough. His daughters were married to the 4th Baron Bolton, the 4th Earl of Bradford, the 1st Marquess of Zetland, and the 2nd Duke of Westminster (Grosvenor). The Gore-Booths were connected with so many of the leading families of England and Ireland that Constance's husband said that if her death sentence in 1916 had not been commuted, half of Debrett's would have been thrown into mourning.

5. H. W. Gore-Booth, "The Basking Shark," *Longman's Magazine,* XIX, No. CIX (November, 1891), 59–70.

6. Michael Davitt was born in 1845 in a tenant cabin in Co. Mayo. When he was six years old the family were evicted. They walked to the east coast and managed to get passage across the Irish sea. In Lancashire the father found work, and when Michael was eleven he himself went to work in a cotton mill. A few years later his right arm had to be amputated as the result of an accident while he was working at a dangerous and unprotected machine. Luckily he found a job as a newsboy and printer's devil and an opportunity for the

schooling he had not had. He joined the Irish Republican Brotherhood in his late teens. From 1869 to 1878 he was imprisoned on a treason felony charge. The years spent in the usual prisoner occupation of picking oakum ten hours a day were particularly torturous for a one-handed worker. On his release from prison he met Parnell and began his career with the Land League.

7. M. McDonnell Bodkin, *Famous Irish Trials* (Dublin, 1928), p. 137.

8. *The Sligo Champion*, December 27, 1879.

9. Ibid.

10. Ibid., April 20, 1895.

11. W. B. Yeats, "On a Political Prisoner," *The Collected Poems of W. B. Yeats* (London, 1952), pp. 206–207.

12. Katharine Tynan, *The Years of The Shadow* (London, 1919), pp. 281–282.

13. *Eire*, August 18, 1923.

14. The line is from Eva's best known poem, "The Little Waves of Breffny."

The National Museum of Ireland has a manuscript copy of Mabel's handwriting of one of Eva's plays, a burlesque sketch produced at Lissadell in January, 1891, called "A Daughter of Eve, or Alphonso's Bride." They called themselves "The Company of Angels" and Eva, "one of them," dedicates her play to them. Constance played the lead, Fatima Fitz Higgins. It is a light, humorous sketch roughly based on the Bluebeard story and with many family references:

> Either Gore Jones or Gore Booth—
> Gore Jones that's Gor-geous but there's a
> terrible suggestion of the Salvation Army
> about Gore *Booth*.

A few couplets carried political allusions:

> Anne [Eva]: Let's go and listen at the door
> If it was a monster, you know it would roar.
>
> Fat: If it was Gladstone you know he would talk
> So would the Hon. Member from Cork.
>
> Anne: Yes, supposing its Mr. Parnell himself
> He mightent enjoy being put on the shelf.
>
> Fat: It its Mr. Healy he'll rage and shout
> No! we certainly wont let Timothy out.
>
> Anne: Fatima! Now at last I have it
> I believe its poor old Michael Davitt.
>
> Fat: If its Mr. Balfour, he darent come out
> Because theres not one policeman about.
>
> Anne: If its Mr. O'Brien there will be a row
> For they'll put him in gaol if they catch him now!
>
> Fat: Yes, if its Mr. O'Brien you'd better beware,
> For he's as cross as a polar Bear.
>
> Anne: If it is Potheen we'll drink it neat
> Old Irish Whiskey is not to be beat.

15. Letters to Eva Gore-Booth, October 5, 1920, and May 3, 1921. Except as noted, the letters of Madame Markievicz are in the manuscript collection of the National Library of Ireland.

II

In Castle Society
1887–1904

Eighteen eighty-seven was Queen Victoria's Jubilee Year, and vast preparations made in London for its proper observation were matched in hundreds of meetings throughout the kingdom. The year before, Gladstone had joined with Parnell to urge Irish Home Rule as a national issue. Sligo, the most planted town in Ireland, where the pro-English element was very strong, hastened to show its devotion to the old Queen.

In February, Lady Gore-Booth presided over a well-attended meeting of Sligo ladies who unanimously resolved to make a general collection for the Jubilee gift. No one had decided just what they were collecting for, but it was believed that the presentation would be worthy. Under Lady Gore-Booth they set about with a will. When one old woman complained that she needed her penny for bread, she was curtly told to enforce her pledge of love and allegiance with a coin.

That was Constance's first publicly recorded meeting and nothing could be more indicative of her political and social leanings in those days than its aims. The meeting to uphold the proprieties and the proprietors of the land set the tone for the next several years of her life. She became increasingly bored and restless under the social trivialities as she grew older and more confident in her self-expression. But for the time being Society was exciting and her presentation to Queen Victoria the most important thing in her life.

A few weeks after the meeting in Sligo, on March 17, 1887, at three in the afternoon, Constance was presented to Queen Victoria by the Countess of Erroll, who was a cousin of Lady Gore-Booth and a lady-in-waiting to Her Majesty. The Queen was dumpy but impressive in a dress and train of black satin and a white tulle veil surrounded by a diadem of diamonds and pearls. She wore four rows of large pearls as well as pearl and diamond ornaments; the Riband and Star of the Order of the Garter, the Orders of Victoria and Albert, Crown of India, Royal Red Cross, Bulgarian Red Cross, and the Saxe-Coburg and Gotha family Order. One wonders there was room for it all.

Constance wore white satin with a regulation train three yards long, three white feathers in her fair hair. To be presented at a Drawing Room at Buckingham Palace was an ordeal. To curtsey gracefully, to walk backwards a few steps without stumbling over one's train, to seem composed in that huge room crowded with dignitaries would have tried the confidence of the most assured matron. Constance maneuvered it well.

Her formal debut into society made and her eligibility for marriage acknowledged, Constance spent four months at balls, parties, shopping, visiting, riding. She was young, full of vitality, very rich, and very popular. On June 22 came the climax of the season for the Anglo-Irish and the culmination of all the meetings and collections. After a long squabble about whether to wear the disloyal green or the blue of the Order of St. Patrick, a committee of ladies, headed by Lady Londonderry (in blue), presented the Queen with 150,000 signatures of loyalty in a casket of Irish bog oak. The list is now lost but there is no reason to doubt that the signatures from Sligo were headed by those of Lady Gore-Booth and Miss Gore-Booth.[1]

Constance and her mother returned to Ireland late in July, in time for the August Horse Show week in Dublin, where Sir Henry was persuaded to come to accompany the ladies to the great garden party at the Viceregal Lodge and to various dances and dinners. Then back to Lissadell where the hunting season started in November and lasted until March. Christmas was festive, followed by the Dublin season, modeled on London but on a much smaller scale, short and hectic. It lasted only a few weeks and culminated in the St. Patrick's night ball. Then to London. So the years went. The proper man was an unconscionable time in appearing. Meanwhile it was one's duty to be amusing, amused, and well-chaperoned. Constance was accepted as a desirable ornament in a small circle of the powerful and the lucky. For a time it seems to have held her full attention.

Lady Fingall described the dressing room in the Castle: "The ball is already beginning. We can hear the music as we put last touches to our hair and our frocks in one of the bedrooms upstairs. The windows of that room look out on an appalling slum, a fact characteristic of the life of those days. But the windows are curtained, and one need not lift the curtains and the wailing voice of a weary child only comes faintly through the glass. There is the waltz music to drown it."[2] It would be several years before Constance Gore-Booth lifted the curtains.

When Constance moved outside the circle it was only on a lark prompted by her quick sympathies. This anecdote about her was told by Lady Fingall, who, although only a few years older than Constance, was married and thus a suitable chaperone one evening when Lady Gore-Booth was unwell.

"Constance then was a wild, beautiful girl, and all the young men wanted to dance with her. She was lovely and gay and she was the life and soul of any party. She was much loved as well as admired. I chaperoned her and stayed the night with her and her mother." They were staying in a house in Harcourt Terrace which had once sheltered Lord Edward Fitzgerald. The viceregal carriage had delivered the two ladies safely to their door but had moved off when they were disconcerted to find a very drunk soldier in uniform clutching one of the doorposts. "Constance said, 'You must not make that noise. You will wake my mother.' To me she said briskly, 'I can always manage drunkards.' She took him by the arm and led him down to the gate, put him outside and shut it. She had sympathy with him even then and wanted him to get back to his barracks without trouble.

"We closed the door behind us and tiptoed upstairs. We had just got into our dressing-gowns when the peace of the quiet terrace was rudely disturbed by drunken singing. Our friend had returned. Constance never hesitated. And I could do nothing but follow her. We just stopped to throw coats hastily over our dressing-gowns, then went downstairs and out again. 'Now we'll have to take him to the canal,' said Constance. She took the man by one arm and I by the other, and we walked him down to the canal bank and set him on his way to the barracks. We returned then to the house in Harcourt Terrace. Only when, upstairs again, we saw ourselves in a mirror, did the full humour of our appearance reach us. I was still wearing my tiara and with it my dressing-gown and bedroom slippers! Constance seized paper and pencil at once, to make a sketch of me in this strange attire."[3]

In 1889 Lord Zetland was appointed Lord Lieutenant of Ireland. Lady Zetland was a cousin of Lady Gore-Booth's so they were even more welcome at the Castle during the three years of the Zetland regime. Those were the years during which the sordid Parnell scandal split Ireland into two hostile, bitterly-opposed camps, Parnellite and Healyite. The repercussions perhaps penetrated even the fort of the

blind man, and its occupants might have felt some stirring of political feelings in 1891 when the fight came nearer home.

In those days, Dublin Castle, "the best machine . . . ever invented for governing a country against its will,"[4] was the administrative center for the Chief Secretary for Ireland, its most powerful official. Through him, High Sheriffs, County Court Judges, Resident Magistrates, Crown Solicitors, and a host of other officials were appointed. The Constabulary was at his disposal. Castle government had evolved from the army of occupation and had lost little of the quality of its origins. The Lord Lieutenant usually acted on the advice of the Chief Secretary but under the Crimes Act of 1887 he was empowered to proclaim any Irish association illegal. Under some circumstances he could suspend trial and levy heavy fines against disaffection. Michael Davitt reported the case of a boy charged with looking at a policeman with a "humbugging sort of a smile."[5]

Parnell had great popular power between 1880 and 1890. Constance saw him once in 1891 shortly before his death, when his power was nearly gone. As Chairman of the Irish Parliamentary Party, Parnell had managed to unite those who wanted to solve Ireland's problems by peaceful, legal means, and those, such as the Fenians, who thought they could be solved only by force. English liberals and Irish clergy had recognized his power, but the Conservatives and the Castle longed to discredit him. By 1891, they had succeeded.

When Constance saw him in Sligo in March of that year, a divorce court had branded him an adulterer, the Catholic bishops had denounced him, the liberals had said there was no hope for Irish Home Rule as long as Parnell remained a leader. The majority of his party had become his enemies. Parnell went to Sligo to campaign for the Dublin solicitor Valentine Dillon, who was contesting the Parliamentary seat left vacant by the death of Peter McDonald of North Sligo. His opponent was Alderman Bernard Collery of Sligo, who had the advantage of being known locally and who had the support of the press. Michael Davitt and Parnell's former lieutenant, T. M. Healy, also supported Collery.

For weeks Parnell had sailed back and forth across the Irish Sea and to friends in exile in France, trying to hold together the remnants of his party. Sligo was the second of the three last by-elections in which he was defeated.[6] He had managed to secure a small audience at the Sligo Town Hall. Prominent among the audience was a Protestant minister and the Misses Gore-Booth. Parnell appeared as a tragic

hero before "popular rage, *Hysterica passio* dragged this quarry down."[7]

There was gossip about Eva and Constance riding at the head of the procession which escorted Parnell through the streets of Sligo. Their friends professed to be thoroughly shocked. The story has been embroidered by successive tellers. It is often predated by more than a decade, and the child Constance threatens to horsewhip (sometimes she threatens to shoot) her father unless he reduces the rents or stops the evictions of his tenants. The fabric of truth is that Constance and Eva were among the Parnell enthusiasts in Sligo in 1891, whether through political convictions or through a romantic interest in seeing the lover of Kitty O'Shea can only be guessed. Perhaps they just wanted to see the hullabaloo of a contested by-election. There were torchlight processions and grand fights with blackthorns. During that week Lady Zetland was a house guest at Lissadell and had to be escorted through the Male and Female National Schools and to the County Infirmary. It is possible that the girls' interest in the election was whetted by a surfeit of formality and that they wanted to shock their distinguished relative. There is no evidence of any deep political interest for years.

The diary which Constance kept the following year, 1892, is notable for its indifference to government or public policies or personalities of any kind.[8]

That Christmas, houseparty guests stayed until her birthday in February, shooting, hunting, fishing, playing theatricals and parlor games, "& fooling all around." When they left there were some adolescent squabbles with her mother about not getting up in the morning. By the 16th she was off to London to more visiting, hunting, going to balls, and shopping.

Her diary shows her occasionally restless and distracted, but not quite cloyed with the good life. "I must try & remember something of what I have been doing & thinking about all this long time. The hunt to begin with was great fun. . . . Jumped. Providence was kind enough to bring us to the hills just about lunch time so I got off and eat mine in comfort on a sunny bank in a wood while hounds ran round & round. . . . The Ball was A.1. I met an old friend & danced a good deal with him."

Sometimes she moons to find her "real true Love" and writes pages in a vein which shows a surprising lack of maturity for a woman twenty-four years old. Maturity is glimpsed only intermittently: "Tonight I write rubbish because I have nothing to do to occupy my heart and mind." A few days later her mood of depression was gone,

"Eva seems heaps better which had an elating effect! I am proud of that girl." (Both girls were nearsighted and when they were older wore glasses most of the time. Eva's girlhood headaches may have resulted from eyestrain, but in general she never enjoyed the robust health Constance did, although she never let it interfere with long years of hard work for the poor in the north of England.)

Riding continued to be Constance's physical and emotional outlet. She usually preferred her horse to her family. On her return from the London visit, she arranged to be met at the station by her horse, "Max," so she would not have to miss a drag race by going home. Alongside a clipping from a Sligo paper about the race she pencilled somewhat defensively, "Since ridings a joy for me I ride."

In April she went to Dublin for the races and stayed at the Vice-regal Lodge in Phoenix Park with "Mr. Mrs. W. Jameson, Ld & Lady Alwyn Compton, Sir W. & Lady Eden, Ld & Lady Longford & Miss Sutton, Lds Carlow & Romilly, Mr. Ramsden, Capt. Mathews etc." She moved frequently with famous people but did not record their talk. "After dinner we played Butter the Board." There were dances ("very cheery"), one at Lady Iveagh's. This house contains some of the most delicate examples of 18th century modelled plaster work in Ireland. She admired the "lovely plaster things on the walls & ceilings" but complained that "the dancing room was rather small."[9]

Like many Irish, she enjoyed the natural scene more than architecture, and at home in Sligo she could describe the Atlantic with the eyes of a young, romantic artist. "The sea was coming in, almost full—& the colours something marvelous—emerald green-peacock blue, but modified, mixed & blended by the fingers of nature till blue & green were lost in one undefineable shimmering mass."

In May her father was off on another Arctic expedition. He brought the *Kara* from the west of England and anchored off Lissadell for two weeks before sailing north. Constance spent several days and nights aboard the yacht, but she expressed no wish to join her father. She was amused at the astonishment of the crew when she sailed out past Raghley Point into the Atlantic to meet the *Kara*. "Crew met us in their whaling boat & were much astonished at our 'Courage.' Certainly we were nearly swamped. We came in from Rachly [Raghley] on the ship & stayed on board till dinner time." The next day, "Spent the afternoon on Kara. *All* the country side came on board." The *Kara* sparked much entertainment, including an elaborate dinner after which "the crew entertained us with songs & dances & we were much amused notwithstanding Mama came on board to sit in judgement which stiffened our marrow & wet our spirits." Relations between the chaperoning Lady Gore-Booth and her high-spirited, unmarried daughter were increasingly strained, and Constance began to turn her attention with more seriousness to art.

It took her a long time to persuade her parents to let her study art, first in London and then in Paris, but from the time she could hold a pencil she took every opportunity to draw. She sketched on anything handy, and at any time. Even in the margins of the Bible she owned as a child are a few surreptitiously drawn sketches of horses, her most successful subject. In later years when she spent many hours every week at meetings, she made thousands of pen and ink sketches of her colleagues around a committee table, or, irreverently, a swift caricature of a frowning judge, a soured jailer, or a pompous official when she or a friend were on trial.

When the Gore-Booth women went off to London again later in May, Constance had finally persuaded her parents to let her study art. She took her work seriously. She felt strongly that she must get away on her own, but she did not yet have enough confidence in herself to break with her family. In the 'nineties it was unthinkable for a girl to do anything without the full approval of her parents. There was an agonized wail in her diary at her inability to solve her problem, and she finally decided she must wait until she was sure of herself and her abilities. It was all part of the slow maturing process.

"If I could only cut the family tie & have a life & interest of my own I should want no other heaven & I see an opening daylight & freedom if I can only persevere & drudge & get my parsimonious family to pay! All the season I have worked my 4 hours daily with Miss Nordgren & Miss Griffin & have got on beyond my wildest dreams, & am encouraged to see success at the end if only if if. . . . Success & Art walled round with Family Pride stinginess & conventionality. What is one to do? How am I to coerce them? How break away? If I was sure of myself & knew I could succeed for sure & make a name or more to the point money I would bolt, live on a crust & do. But to do all that with the chance of having to return & throw oneself on the charity of ones family a miserable failure is more than I can screw up my courage to face. So many people begin with great promise & greater hope & end in nothing but failure & the poor house or improper."

But Lady Gore-Booth decided an excursion was more proper than self-expression; in July, she, Eva, Constance, and two friends went to

Germany for the opera at Bayreuth. They visited Cologne where Constance was impressed with the cathedral but embarrassed and cross with her mother. "Mama kept saying in a loud voice, 'Prof. Owen says all the Bones are those of inferior animals.' " Constance continued, "I think Faith is a very pretty quality & am greatly interested to know if it can be combined with knowledge & common sence." Her choice of adjective is curious and her spelling erratic, but she was searching for a meaningful pattern in religion.

The five ladies dutifully listened to *Tannhäuser, Parsifal,* and *The Mastersingers,* and visited Wagner's grave and house. Constance's favorite way of sightseeing was to take her sketching things and to draw the scene. She sometimes attracted crowds of children. "I sketched Liszt's grave for Squidge & made great friends with a small boy who sketched it too, I supplying him with paper etc." After three weeks of sightseeing she was thankfully home at Lissadell August 18. But she did not stay inactive for long; the next week she was in Dublin. "Went to the Horse Show & for Economy went by slow train. Damn Economy say I." In later life she always insisted on riding third class in spite of its discomfort. This, however, was not so much for economy's sake as part of her attempt to break down barriers of her birth and to identify herself with the poor of Ireland.

After the horse show she was home for a few months, did a lot of sketching and painting, and went to wood-carving classes in Sligo every week. The hunting started again in November; in December she went visiting. A clipping from a society paper was pasted in the diary with no comment from Constance: "The most difficult thing in the world since the days of Paris has been the judging of the fairest where many are so fair. One of the Attaches in the suite of the German Emperor declared that the three most beautiful women he saw while in England actually came from Ireland. They were the Duchess of Leinster, Lady Carew, and Miss Gore-Booth."

In January Eva and Constance went to a house party at Adare in County Limerick, home of the Earl of Dunraven. Lord Dunraven, a cousin of Sir Henry, was a famous yachtsman and big-game hunter. He was involved in Irish politics and later advocated a Commonwealth of Nations as a solution to England's colonial problems. Among the guests at Adare was Lord Randolph Churchill, whom Lord Dunraven had urged to return to public life after he resigned the Chancellorship of the Exchequer in 1886. Other guests were the Duke of St. Albans and his daughter, Lord Wolesley and daughter, Sir C. Barrington, Mr.

Weldon, Captain Dean, Mr. Gaisforth, the Morrises, and several others. Lord Randolph Churchill was then a sick man, and within six weeks made his last parliamentary speech. "The Irish Question lies in a nutshell," he said. "It is that a quick witted nation are being governed by a stupid party."[10] There was certainly much talk of the Irish question at Adare, but Constance was concerned with only one kind of party. She was full of indignation when, although their ball had gone on until 5 o'clock, the following night at the servants' party, although Lord and Lady Dunraven had said the dance might go on as long as they liked "that mean little rat Mr. P. stopped them at 12."

In March and April there are two brief political notes which are interesting in the light of her later views. They recorded attendance at two anti-Home Rule meetings, and although always against the plan, she was then as far on the right as she would later be on the left. On March 10, 1893, there was a great Unionist demonstration in Sligo against the Home Rule Bill which Gladstone had introduced in the House of Commons on February 13. Constance's own entry for the day was, in total, "Anti Home Rule Meeting in Sligo Town Hall. Declined to be among the aristocracy & sat in the hall & drew caricatures of the speakers. Went to Hazelwood to see Mabel."

In April she was staying in England at Aske, the home of the Zetlands. All the guests went to a meeting at Richmond, Yorkshire, protesting the Home Rule Bill. Lord Zetland, who presided, floridly announced that the Bill was the most marvelous piece of experimentalism that had been conceived by the ingenuity of man for the special purpose of satisfying the insatiable thirst of the political agitator, utterly and entirely regardless of the best interests of the Empire. He predicted it would lead to a social revolution in the country which would be "absolutely and entirely impossible for the power of man to stem." Lord Ashbourne, the principal speaker at the meeting, was unreported except by Constance, who succinctly, and apparently in agreement, wrote, "Lord Ashbourn a real angel, speaks splendidly." His position was very clear, however; he was on record as warning that "All must nerve themselves to realize what the position would be if this calamitous Bill had a chance of passing."[11]

The meeting decided home rule would be detrimental to the interests of Great Britain and ruinous to Ireland. In spite of the great Unionist demonstrations and dire predictions, the second reading of the Home Rule Bill was carried in Commons. There was a torchlight procession in Sligo, but it was premature. The Bill was defeated in the House of Lords.

The diary trails off after this and then stops. This was the only diary she kept, unfortunately, because her life became increasingly interesting as she matured and became less conscious of herself. Her progress from the Big House and the Castle to Surrey House and Liberty Hall parallels her growth in awareness of Ireland and of her own destiny.

During the winter, 1894–95, Yeats visited the Gore-Booths at Lissadell. He stayed with them on two occasions, met them throughout the winter, and has left his impressions of the family in letters and poems. The only record of the Gore-Booths of his visit is Constance's sketch of his lean, eager face as he sat talking with Eva one evening about poetry.[12]

The Reverend F. S. LeFanu was then the vicar at Lissadell.[13] He was young and enthusiastic, played cricket on the Lissadell team, helped Lady Gore-Booth with her home industries schemes, assisted with the annual school fêtes when several hundred children were entertained on the estate, advised on the education of the younger Gore-Booths, encouraged the older ones with their art, poetry, and various projects, in short, did all that was expected of the vicar at a country house. He was of a family of ministers and writers and was himself interested in encouraging young writers. When Yeats was visiting his uncle during the winter of 1894–95, the Reverend LeFanu invited him to give a talk on Irish folklore to his parishioners at the schoolhouse at Lissadell. He knew also that Constance and Eva were particularly interested in drama and poetry and would like to have him at Lissadell.

Yeats's amused account of the lecture was brief. He wrote to his sister Lily, "I lectured in the schoolhouse on Fairy lore chiefly to an audience of Orangemen. It was a novel experience. I found that the comic tales delighted them but that the poetry of fairy lore was quite lost on them. They held it Catholic superstition I suppose. However I had fortunately chosen nothing but humorous tales. The children were I believe greatly excited. Mr. Jones of Raughley said afterwards that now there should be another lecture to put my lecture 'on a sound religious basis' for he feared it may have sent away many of the audience with the idea that the fairies really existed."[14]

Although Yeats wrote that folklore was a new experience to the Gore-Booths—"They had not thought it existed"—he was referring less to knowledge of the lore itself than to the rush of enthusiasm about it generated by Douglas Hyde's Gaelic League in 1892 and his own concern with turning such narrative into art. Yeats acknowledged that he got a good bit of folklore at Lissadell; the Gore-Booths knew which tenants could be of most use to him. He used some of these Irish stories of the supernatural and uncanny in his *Mythologies,* a better designation than "folklore." His first stories had been published in 1893 under the title *The Celtic Twilight,* a name which became attached to a literary and art movement in Ireland that blurred into concurrent political and economic movements. He gave this volume, as well as his other books, to the ladies at Lissadell during his visit, including a large paper copy of *The Countess Kathleen,* which he had written in 1892 and dedicated to Maud Gonne, later a friend and coworker of Constance's. Yeats recorded no particular impression of Constance. He thought that Eva showed some promise as a writer of verse; although her work was very formless, it was full of telling little phrases. "She has some literary talent, and much literary ambition, and has met no literary people."

Eva's poetry reflected the family's interest in mysticism, the seen and the unseen. Throughout their lives there was a bond between her and Constance which transcended time and space, and they were interested in every manifestation of the apparently inexplicable, from ghost stories to the most esoteric and formless spiritual experience. Many years after this, Yeats told Lady Gregory that he had been interested in psychic things when he was about seventeen but had been frightened of the "influences" seizing him, and gave it up. Later, when Constance took him to a séance in London, he found he need not fear them.[15]

Indeed, most of the family accepted supernatural visitors with the same aplomb they accepted a house guest. Lady Gore-Booth once told W. H. Myers, who was Hon. Secretary of the Psychical Society, of her very matter-of-fact younger son seeing in the hall at Lissadell a houseboy who, unknown to Mordaunt, had died some hours previously.[16] In her cell at Aylesbury Constance felt the presence of a former prisoner, and she was curious to know if he was Irish, but he never spoke, though he often kept her company.[17] There was a lady in grey who used to appear at Belcamp, but Constance was the only one who saw her and generally only when the Fianna boys were being unusually noisy. At any rate, the family were receptive to Yeats and his stories, and indeed had never heard them told so well. He told them first to one, then another, and then told them over again to the ailing Aunt Augusta upstairs.

Yeats also turned a perceptive but not always accurate eye on the family and their house. He found old Miss Gore the strongest-willed of them all. She was an invalid and "mostly invisible but is always more or less behind the scenes like an iron claw. She is very much of a Tory and cares for nothing but horses."

He thought that Lissadell itself was an exceedingly impressive house inside and all things in good taste. He was particularly struck with the great sitting room which was as high as a church. This was the room with the bow windows he always carried in his memory. It was the room with "great windows open to the south" in which he remembered "that table and the talk of youth."[18] "These people are much better educated than our own people," he wrote to Katharine Tynan, "and have a better instinct for excellence."[19]

He was less understanding of the men of the family. He dismissed Sir Henry with a flippant, he "thinks of nothing but the north pole, where his first officer to his great satisfaction has recently lost himself and thereby made an expedition to rescue him desirable." The elder son, Josslyn, received a little more consideration, but Yeats underestimated his organizing ability. "The eldest son is 'theoretically' a home ruler and practically some kind of a humanitarian, much troubled by the responsibility of his wealth and almost painfully conscientious. He and the clergyman LeFanu are full of schemes. He is not however particularly clever and has not, I imagine, much will." It would be more accurate to say that Josslyn's imagination, interests, and talents lay in a direction different from the poet's. Both young men were reformers; Yeats wanted to invigorate Ireland with knowledge of its past, Josslyn wanted to instill hope and a sound economy through technology.

Josslyn was interested in the livestock and the farm production at Lissadell, in agronomy rather than riding and hunting. He liked to improve methods of production and was inventive and imaginative in trying new things, not always with complete success. The family laughed for years at one of his experiments to increase his chances of shooting wild geese. He concocted a blind in the form of a hollow cow, so the hunter could stalk them from behind and within. At the sight of the wonderful monster the geese fled honking for miles and were unapproachable for weeks. After completing his formal education, Josslyn had spent two years studying farming methods in the United States and Canada. When he returned home he was convinced that cooperation among the small farmers of Ireland would provide the only economic salvation, and in June, 1895, he organized the Drumcliffe Dairy Society, the first of several cooperative creameries in Sligo.[20]

That winter Colonel Campbell, Master of the Sligo Hounds, gave a great fancy-dress ball in the Sligo County Court House. Appropriately, Eva and Constance went costumed as Drumcliffe Cooperative dairy maids, but it was not until years later that Constance recognized the significance of the occasion. "At home we had been interested in Sir Horace Plunkett's movement and my brother had taken an active part in the establishment of creameries, but certainly I did not then recognise the full significance and importance of the movement, but I suppose it appealed to all that was Gaelic in one's subconscious self. Sir Horace always declared that the movement was non-political, and he and all concerned believed it to be so, and no one suspected, when it was first started, that it was perhaps the greatest political movement of the time, and that he had struck a vital note that would help bring the country back to the ideals of a Gaelic State."[21]

During this year, 1896, when Josslyn was engrossed in the cooperative movement, and the year of the first conference in Sligo of The Irish Agricultural Organization Society, the young ladies at Lissadell showed their first political awareness. They became suffragettes. Constance presided over a meeting at the Breaghway Old School at which it was decided to try to awaken in Irish women a sense of their responsibilities and encourage them by every means to fulfill their public duties. Further, they wanted to create a national demand for the extension of the Parliamentary franchise to women, on the same grounds as it was then held by men. Constance was elected president, Eva, secretary, and Mabel, treasurer. The Dublin Women's Suffrage Society had been founded in 1874, but the movement was slow to spread, and twenty-two years later, the Society in Sligo was only the third in Ireland.

Just before Christmas a public meeting was held at the Milltown National School in Drumcliffe to promote the suffrage movement. The women had spent the day decorating the room with evergreens artistically draped and framing appropriate mottoes: "Who would be free themselves must strike the blow"; "No taxation without representation"; "Liberty, justice, and equality." Notice of the meeting had occasioned considerable amusement among the men who decided to go and see the fun. The room was crowded, about one-third of those present were women.[22]

Constance opened the meeting promptly at 7:30 with a plea for action. Her first recorded speech foreshadows many of her later attitudes. It was typical of what she was to say and do ten to thirty years later. "Now in order to attain to any Political Reform, you all know that the first step is to form societies to agitate and force the government to realize that a very large class have a grievance, and will never stop making themselves disagreeable till it is righted. John Stuart Mill said thirty years ago that the only forcible argument against giving women the suffrage was 'that they did not demand it with sufficient force and noise.' Silence is an evil that might easily be remedied, and the sooner we begin to make a row the better." For the first time her prose is clear and sure. She had found her true vocation as an agitator, but did not yet know it.

Mabel spoke, and Miss Young, then the women were supported by Mr. E. Rowlette and a cycling tourist who was in the crowd. They were heckled by a man who feared that if his wife went to vote she would never come back. The president rode him down as she would a hedgehog in the path of her hunter: "She must think very little about you then."

Eva reminded the audience of the good done in the county by co-operation. "I should like to call on Irishwomen to follow the example of the farmers of Drumcliffe, and to insist, in spite of opposition in taking their affairs into their own hands." She expressed her own attitude to community service, one she was to spend her life putting into practice. "All of us, men and women alike, besides our immediate duties to our families, have duties to our neighbours, and to our country, and to society at large. Charity begins at home, but it should not end there." From this beginning Eva went on to spend fifteen health-shattering years organizing the mill girls in the north of England to cooperate with each other in fighting intolerable working and living conditions.

Eventually, after all the usual things for women's suffrage had been said by the women, and all the stock arguments mouthed by the men, the resolution demanding the franchise was put to the meeting. Considering that the attendance at the meeting was two-thirds men, the results were amazing. On a show of hands the resolution was declared carried by the President, and the meeting ended amidst much noise, cheering, booing, and applause.

The following year Eva attended a suffrage meeting in London as the Irish delegate. The Sligo Women's Suffrage Society limped along for several years but had an unspectacular career. Within twelve

months of the Drumcliffe meeting, Constance was at last in Paris
studying art, and notions of reforming the world by making a row
were temporarily forgotten.

The year 1897 started well for Constance and ended triumphantly.
She rode with the Sligo Harriers, went to Dublin, Punchestown, and
was a great success at the St. Patrick's day races at the Springfield
course. These evoked memories and encomiums of her grandfather
and extravagant praise for herself. Her most notable asset was the
ability to throw herself completely into the activity at hand, with an
efficient gusto that made everyone else enjoy it too. "Miss Gore-Booth
entered into the spirit of the day's doings with a heartiness that made
us all feel comfortable."

She went off to London for the season as usual. In July she was
bridesmaid with Lady Rachel Wyndham Quin at the wedding of her
cousin Gray Wynne to Maud Morris. In August she was back in
Dublin for the Horse Show.

That year at the Horse Show there was an exhibit of textiles and
Irish cottage industries which included entries from Lady Gore-Booth's
classes at Lissadell. She had been appalled that so few girls knew how
to sew and at her own expense had hired a teacher to teach plain
sewing, drawn linen work, and lace crocheting. She had found the
girls eager to learn and soon had about fifty pupils. Lady Gore-Booth
also undertook to sell their needlework, and was convinced that with
good hard work a girl could earn ten shillings a week.

The greatest triumph for Constance was that she finally won her
parents' reluctant permission to go to Paris to study art. Sir Henry had
been in indifferent health, he and Lady Gore were going to Europe to
seek a cure, and it would be as easy to keep an eye on Constance in
Paris as in Ireland or London. Her parents were victims to her successful plan of agitating and making herself heard, as she had advised
the women at the suffrage meeting.

Julien's was the popular and approved studio for young English
girls in those days, and it was there she went. Unlike the Slade, where
she had studied in London, the students were not segregated and all
worked together. George Moore had studied at Julien's in 1873, and
it had not changed much in the twenty-five years since he described
it: "In the studio there were some eighteen or twenty young men.
There were also some eight or nine young English girls. We sat round
in a circle and drew from the model. And this reversal of all the
world's opinions and prejudices was to me singularly delightful; I

loved the sense of unreality that the exceptional nature of our life in this studio conveyed. Besides, the women themselves were young and interesting, and were, therefore, one of the charms of the place, giving, as they did, that sense of sex which is so subtle a mental pleasure, and which is, in its outward aspect, so interesting to the eye—the gowns, the hair lifted, showing the neck; the earrings, the sleeves open at the elbow."[23] Lady Gore-Booth had never read George Moore on Julien's when she consented to her daughter's going there.

Constance worked hard at her painting and enjoyed herself thoroughly, spending hours drinking gallons of coffee from tiny cups at the sidewalk cafés, talking to her friends, watching Paris, and visiting the art galleries and museums by herself, not under the watchful eye of her governess. Her many friends called her "Teuf-Teuf" because of her always bubbling energy. For over two years she worked and played in an ecstatic and sustained burst of her incredible vitality.

She had some money of her own and an allowance from home, though not enough to live extravagantly. She knew only what she chose to know of the crust-and-garret bohemianism the words "studying art in Paris" conjured, although certainly some of her friends were living on the traditional two francs a day.

She lived in a respectable, moderately expensive English pension on the rue de Rivoli. One of her friends who also lived there was the distinguished writer, Violet Hunt, who later married, or supposed she had, Ford Maddox Ford. It was Miss Hunt who recalled Constance at Worth's. Lady Gore-Booth was visiting in Paris, and Constance had ordered a green dress with a high upstanding ruff at the back of the neck. At the final fitting she turned from the mirror and wailed, "I look just like a rabbit sitting in the heart of a cabbage." Miss Hunt and the vendeuse collapsed in laughter. Miss Hunt described her as very tall, very tense, and very fair; her short-sightedness gave her face a peering, puzzled look which was at variance with her perfect boyish frankness and camaraderie. She remembered Teuf-Teuf lying on the floor of her room after a party early one morning and putting herself to sleep with a recitation of Swinburne's "Triumph of Time."[24]

Daisy Forbes-Robertson was sometimes a guest of Miss Hunt and the three shared many hours of good talk and laughter. Miss Forbes-Robertson was a tiny woman, a militant suffragette and fighter. She was one of the rebels in that large, active, talented family of actors, painters, writers, and intellectuals. Constance agreed with many of her ideas and methods, particularly in later years. It was her artist brother,

Eric, who took Constance to the students' ball at which she met Count Casimir Dunin-Markiewicz.

Casimir Dunin-Markiewicz[25] was the second son of a Polish land-owner. He had been born in 1874 at the estate of Denhoffowka, in the Government of Kief, in the Ukraine. The family, like many others in Poland and the Ukraine entitled to use the prefix "Dunin," traced their ancestry to a twelfth century Peter Dunin, "the Dane," who settled in Poland. Casimir's boyhood home was similar to Constance's, that of the landed gentry, with hunting, riding, and affairs of the estate the primary concerns. He had studied law at the University of St. Vladimir in Kief, then, against his parents' wishes, had gone to Paris in 1895 to study at the State School of Art. There he married a girl from home to whom he had been secretly engaged. As a second son, he had no great expectations, but he had an allowance which was to continue. In 1896 their first child, Stanislas, was born. Their second son was born the following year, but the mother was ill and she took the two boys home to her people in the Ukraine, where she died early in 1899, her second son surviving her by only a few months. Stanislas stayed on with his mother's family and Casimir continued with his art studies in Paris.

Casimir was tall, well over six feet four, strong, broad shouldered. His hair was black and his eyes grey-blue with a bright, roguish twinkle. He had the same boyish gusto and enthusiasm for living that was characteristic of Constance. He took his art seriously, and was at that time working on what he considered his first masterpiece, "Amour," which subsequently was awarded a Medaille d'Honneur at the Paris Salon. He had a charming manner and ready wit. He was gregarious, popular, and loved.

Constance was a young woman in love with a handsome man with whom she could share all her interests in art and drama. They both were enthusiasts of the new and fashionably popular pastime of cycling and pedalled miles observing the green Seine valley. There were even reports of a duel in the Bois de Vincennes with a Frenchman who had made a disrespectful remark to Constance at a costume ball. Casi was not wounded. They spent a young romantic's dream of a year in Paris, working and playing hard. "He fills me with a desire to do things," Constance wrote to Eva. She was sure Casi would accomplish great things, and she felt she might get something done, too.

Constance spent Christmas of 1899 in Switzerland with her mother and ailing father. For a time Sir Henry seemed to be improving, but on January 13, 1900, at St. Moritz, he died from influenza. Constance accompanied her mother back to Lissadell where her father was buried on the 23rd.

After the death of her father, Constance did not return to Paris. Her engagement to Casimir had been approved by her family, but not yet announced. He had met Sir Henry and Lady Gore, Josslyn, Mabel, and Eva at various times in Paris, and in May he went to Lissadell for the first time. It was too soon after Sir Henry's death for much entertaining, but he met the rest of the family and many relatives and friends who lived near by. For the most part he and Constance painted or rode or walked; she was anxious to show him every bit of the country she loved.

He stayed two months at Lissadell and they made plans for their wedding. The engagement was formally announced in July, not that it was news to anyone by that time. The whole countryside had been buzzing for weeks about the enormous Polish Count with the unspellable name Miss Gore had met in Paris. There had been many excuses made for calling at Lissadell to get a glimpse of the handsome young man. There were scores of stories about him, some of them with a basis of truth. One was that before his Paris days he had been called to the bar in St. Petersburg. He was entrusted with the defense in a particularly brutal murder case, got his man off, and immediately achieved a reputation. However, he loathed his profession and abandoned it in favor of art. Casimir was a charmer, and in general the engagement had Sligo's approval. It was only to be expected that the unconventional and beautiful Miss Gore would marry a man who was exotic.

Casimir and Constance planned to go to Europe after their marriage, and eventually to live in Dublin. They would not, of course, be living at Lissadell, her brother's home. In July, Constance sold her nineteen horses and ponies at a very successful sale. She loved them and it was an unhappy day, but she did not brood over their loss. Constance, her mother and sisters headed immediately for Bond Street. Dresses and hats could not be taken lightly and they had only two months to prepare. Casi left for a visit to Poland, meeting them again in London in September and bringing with him his cousin from St. Petersburg who was to be his best man.

Owing to the recent death of Sir Henry, the wedding was quiet, with only four bridesmaids and no more than fifty guests. The religious ceremony took place at the Parish Church, Marylebone, in London,

September 29, 1900. It had been preceeded by civil formalities at the Russian Legation and at a London registrar's office. The groom was spectacular in his Russian court uniform. He wore a close-fitting black tunic with gold-braided collar and cuffs, white trousers, long rapier and a three-cornered hat. The bride wore white satin and from her shoulders flowed a transparent train of old Brussels lace lined with silver tissue. She carried orange blossoms and myrtle, wore a tulle veil and the pearl necklace with a diamond pendant that was her mother's gift. Eva and Mabel wore violet satin, and the other two bridesmaids, Rachel Mansfield and Mildred Grenfeld, were in green satin. Sir Josslyn gave his sister in marriage and the Rev. Mr. LeFanu came over from Dublin to officiate at the ceremony.

Afterwards Lady Gore-Booth received the guests in Devonshire Place, near the church. Count and Countess Markievicz were leaving immediately after the reception for a trip to the continent. With much fuss and flurry they were put on the train for Paris. There were the usual tears, goodbyes, false departures, and reminders. Finally the train started. The bride and groom rode to the next station, got off, and went back to London to spend the night at a party given by some of their livelier friends who had not been included in the respectable wedding party. They went on to Paris the next day.

The rainy autumn and the cold winter were spent with the Count's family on their estate near Kief. They loved their daughter-in-law and she them. She found much in Poland to remind her of Ireland, though the poverty was even more apparent and distressing. The roads were worse, and she had never been so cold in her life. Mud was halfway up the wheels of the carriages during most of the autumn and travelling was difficult. She and her husband rode and hunted when they could, painted, visited the peasants on the estate, entertained and were entertained. It was all very much like home.

There were some beautiful autumn days, and it was on one of them that they went to his father-in-law's house, twenty-five miles away, where his son lived. Stanislas, then between four and five years old, was a thin, fragile little boy, with a crop of golden hair and a pathetic face. His new mother seemed to him a goddess from another world. "She was tall, slim, exquisite, with a crown of soft wavy golden-brown hair, the rays of the Southern sun playing upon it." Soon he was to know that "she was as kind as she was beautiful."[26]

One of her best pictures was painted in the Ukraine. Titled simply "The Conscript," it shows a young peasant sitting at the table in a clean but bare cottage. He obviously does not want to leave this life for the hard unknown. The artist's strong sympathy for the unwilling soldier is vividly expressed.

In the spring of 1901 they went to Paris for a few months. It was then that the Count's friend, B. Szankowski, painted the life-size portrait of Madame which hangs in the National Gallery in Dublin. She has a rather wistful, Slavic expression, like a Chekovian heroine yearning for Moscow, that her friends do not recognize. Like so many women whose mobile faces and quick movements are a strong part of their personalities, it was extremely difficult to express her beauty with brush or camera. In one or two formal portraits the elegance of her clothes gives the impression of a confident beauty, but nothing expresses her grace and vitality.

She was pregnant that spring and had decided to go to Lissadell for her confinement because she wanted her child to be born in her own country. By July they were back at Lissadell where they spent a quiet summer. There were a few social occasions, the wedding of a cousin, the annual school fête to help with, some family dinner parties, but most of the time they walked, painted, read.

Their only child, Maeve Alys, was born at Lissadell November 14, 1901.[27] The choice of name for their daughter indicates the direction of the reading and thinking Madame had been doing during the long waiting months. The reputed burial mound of the great Queen Maeve was visible from Lissadell, so it was not an unusual choice. However, her decision had also been guided by a play of Edward Martyn's which the Irish Literary Players had performed in Dublin the year before. The play was named for its heroine who symbolized Ireland's choice between English materialism and her own natural idealism, as well as the choice of every individual soul. Madame Markievicz's own natural idealism was quickening.

Count and Countess Markievicz had planned to move to Dublin after Maeve's birth. They were anxious to be where there was more society, more scope for their interests in people, in drama, in art. George Russell, who knew Sir Josslyn through his cooperative work, visited Lissadell for a few weeks. They painted and talked about poetry and art. The young couple decided to go to Dublin in the summer. AE was delighted; they were both clever and he hoped they would help create an art atmosphere. "We might get the materials for a revolt, a new Irish Art Club," he wrote to a mutual friend, Sarah Purser. "I feel some desperate schism or earthquaking revolution is required to wake up Dublin in art matters." In the same letter AE announced a new genius, Padraic Colum, and thought that Ireland would get a good lift when Miss Gonne appeared as Kathleen ni Houlihan in Willie Yeats's little one act play which was to be produced with his *Deirdre* during Easter week.[28] Easter was always a favorite time for projects to lift Ireland.

But they stayed on at Lissadell that year. During 1902 Sir Josslyn inaugurated a new kind of cooperative in Sligo. With the applause of the Trades Union Council he organized the Sligo Manufacturing Society. Over a hundred persons representing every creed and class in the town and district responded to his appeal and became shareholders in the new association which proposed to start a shirt and clothing factory. This was a pioneer effort in industrial cooperation and its development was watched approvingly by the *United Irishman* and other nationalist papers. The first shirts were made in July and the factory operated with success for some years.

The following spring Count and Countess Markievicz went to Poland. This was Madame's last trip; she never again saw her husband's people, though she often wondered and worried about them, especially during the war. When they returned to Ireland in October, 1903, they brought Stanislas who lived with them for the next several years. Madame had a way with boys. There was something in her own nature, free, imaginative, boisterous, indifferent to furniture, to which they responded. She was always more successful with boys than with girls and made her singular contribution to Ireland, Fianna na hEireann, through her understanding and love of them. Stanislas always remembered the look of joy on Madame's face when she told him his grandparents had at last agreed he was to go to Ireland with them. It was a wildly exciting trip for him, trains, hotels, cities, toy shops, and finally Lissadell. Lady Gore-Booth was kind, gracious, and loving to the new grandchild and he remembered her with affection.

At last came the long-talked-of move to Dublin. By winter, 1903, Count and Countess Markievicz were at home at St. Mary's, 1 Frankfort Avenue, Rathgar. It was the right time and place for energetic, generous, gregarious artists, especially if they did not have to live by their art.

It was becoming increasingly obvious that political and economic changes were long overdue in Ireland. The core of inspired nationalists[29] who had celebrated the centenary of the 1798 rebellion had sparked national feeling in many directions. Ireland was ready for increasing participation in her own government. It was time to break the present drought by drawing on the wellsprings of the past. In art, in speech, in poetry, in music, in economics, in government, in dress, in drama, the past must be tapped to give life to the present. "We need a national theatre," James Connolly wrote in 1903, "not for the purpose of enlarging our national vanity but of restoring our proper national pride."[30]

On January 2, 1904, shortly after the Markieviczs moved to Dublin, Arthur Griffith began in the *United Irishman* a series of articles called, "The Resurrection of Hungary—A Parallel for Ireland." In a few years his suggestions for achieving economic and political independence for Ireland had grown into a national movement with a catchy name, Sinn Fein.[31]

Sometime after her move, Madame Markievicz was on her way to Dublin Castle with her husband when a small beggar girl put her dirty hand in the window of their carriage. The child was so overwhelmed by the magnificence of the diamonds worn by the beautiful lady that she forgot her begging formula. The carriage rolled on. The Countess looked back and saw the child being slapped hard across the face by her furious mother. Madame never forgot that slap. It filled her with a vague doubt and she dated her disenchantment with rich display from that time.[32] The days of dressing for the Castle or Palace were almost over.

NOTES TO CHAPTER II

1. The Queen wrote in her diary, "Drove to St. James's Palace . . . & Ly. Londonderry presented me with that [key] of another very fine coffer, containing the signatures of the Women of Ireland. I saw a number of people I knew." Letter from The Librarian, Windsor Castle, who reported that neither he nor the Lord Chamberlain's office knows now where the casket is.

2. Elizabeth, Countess of Fingall and Pamela Hinkson, *Seventy Years Young* (London, 1937), p. 66.

3. Ibid., pp. 191–192.

4. Lord Morley at Manchester, May 12, 1902, quoted by Dorothy Macardle, *The Irish Republic* (Dublin, 1951), p. 53.

5. Michael Davitt, *The Fall of Feudalism in Ireland* (London, 1904), p. 526.

6. *The Sligo Champion,* April 4, 1891, has lengthy accounts of the election. The results were: Mr. Collery 3,261; Mr. Dillon 2,493. Parnell died six months after this, in October, 1891.

7. W. B. Yeats, "Parnell's Funeral," *Collected Poems,* p. 319.

8. The diary is in the National Museum of Ireland, Dublin.

9. Iveagh House, on St. Stephen's Green, now the Department of External

Affairs, was designed by Cassels and built about 1730. Constantia Maxwell, *Dublin Under the Georges* (London, 1956), pp. 179 ff., briefly discusses some of the notable examples of modelled plaster in the city.

10. Robert Rhodes James, *Lord Randolph Churchill* (London, 1959), p. 362.

11. *The Times* (London), February 27, 1893. After her marriage, Constance was to know the younger Lord Ashbourne in Dublin. He was frequently at the Arts Club and he was an enthusiastic nationalist at about the time she became interested. He spoke Irish well and when he took his seat in the House of Lords he addressed that assembly in his native tongue, and wore his favorite costume, the saffron kilt.

12. The drawing was carefully preserved in a photograph album by Constance's friend, Maud Morris, daughter of the Lord Chief Justice of Ireland. Maud married Constance's cousin, Gray Wynne, and was a lifelong neighbor and friend of Lady Gore-Booth. The album is now in the Sligo County Library and Museum.

13. About 1900 the Rev. Mr. LeFanu went to St. John's, Sandymount, Dublin, and during his first years there was the center of violent and bitter debates among his parishioners on the subject of just how high the service could be and still remain within the bounds of Anglicanism.

14. Allan Wade (ed.), *The Letters of W. B. Yeats* (London, 1954), p. 242. The comments on the Gore-Booths which follow are also from this letter.

15. Lennox Robinson (ed.), *Lady Gregory's Journals* (London, 1946), p. 261.

16. Frederic W. H. Myers, *Human Personality and Its Survival of Bodily Death* (London, 1903), II, 63–65.

17. Letter to Eva Gore-Booth, May 14, 1917.

18. W. B. Yeats, "In Memory of Eva Gore-Booth and Con Markiewicz," *Collected Poems*, pp. 263–264.

19. *Letters of W. B. Yeats*, p. 254.

20. During the Black and Tan terror, 1919–1921, when the British reverted to their ancient tactics of striking at the economic heart of Ireland, 55 creameries were destroyed. This one escaped, but others in Sligo were burned. The strategy was grim testimony to the effectiveness of the project.

21. *Eire*, August 25, 1923.

22. Fully reported under subheading "Amusing Proceedings" in *The Sligo Champion*, December 26, 1896.

23. George Moore, *Confessions of a Young Man* (London, 1926), pp. 18–19. Passages from this work are reprinted by permission of J. C. and R. G. Medley.

24. "Ireland's Joan of Arc," *The Literary Digest*, 53 (July 15, 1916), 147–151.

25. The Count and his son spelled their name Markiewicz. The Countess always wrote her name "de Markievicz" although usually the "de" was dropped in speaking of her.

26. Count Stanislas Markiewicz, "Memories of My Father," *Irish Times*, December 2, 9, 17, 1937, and January 6, 1938, is the most complete source of information on the Markiewicz family background. In January and February, 1938, he wrote two articles for the *Irish Press*, "Memories of Countess

Markiewicz"; the Christmas issue of the *Kerryman* (Tralee), December, 1938, included some of his reminiscences of his stepmother.

27. The spelling of the name varies, Maeve or Meave usually, although sometimes the final "e" is dropped. Madame was not consistent about her daughter's name. The former is the spelling she used in her will in 1927 when she left to her daughter her total estate (which by then had dwindled to £329).

28. Alan Denson (ed.), *Letters from AE* (London, 1961), pp. 38–40.

29. Throughout this book the word "nationalists" refers to the Irish men and women who were working towards independence for Ireland, not to the political party which called itself Nationalist.

30. *The United Irishman*, October 23, 1903. This was in an article defending Synge's *In the Shadow of the Glen.* Arthur Griffith and Maud Gonne (who denounced it), and W. B. Yeats (who wrote in defense) were among the contributors to the controversy in *The United Irishman* over this play, which was first produced by the Irish National Theatre Company at the Molesworth Hall on October 8, 1903. The objections were generally levelled against the unflattering view of the Irish peasantry. Dudley Digges, Maire Quinn, and a few others left the company in protest against its being produced. On the opening night Yeats made a speech against the attacks.

31. Pronounced, approximately, *shinn fain.* For years language purists have argued over the correct translation, but it is generally recognized that "We Ourselves" is fairly accurate. "Sinn" is the first person plural of the personal pronoun, "fein" is an emphasizing affix. The connotations of the name "Sinn Fein" stress the doctrine of national self-respect and self-reliance which the policy implied. A basic tenet was that the Irish parliamentary members should not attend Westminster but set up their own Council in Ireland.

32. Anna Kelly, "The Rebel Countess," *Sunday Express,* November 10, 1957.

III

The Call of Cathleen ni Houlihan

1904-1910

Dublin at the turn of the century may have been the dreary, dirty city Joyce remembered, but Dublin society was gay for those who were young and active. Society lived in rose brick houses on Merrion Square, near St. Stephen's Green, or built ample homes for itself south of the city. Bicycling was fashionable, motors were just beginning, there was yachting along the green coast. Young Count and Countess Markievicz moved in places Joyce's Bloom could only dream of. The Count with his good looks and good humor and willingness to enter into any kind of joke was particularly popular. The Markieviczs had moved to Dublin not merely to be close to families Madame had always known, they were attracted to that growing circle of artists who were making the city their home. It was through that group that Madame met and eventually joined the tight militant organizations that were opposed to the ascendency in their rose brick houses.

Horse Show Week in August was then, as now, a time for many important exhibitions, concerts, and plays. The first year the Count and Countess lived in Dublin they exhibited paintings with their friend, George Russell. On August 23, 1904, the showing they called "Pictures of Two Countries" opened, continued through the week, was well attended and favorably reviewed. Each of the three young artists had in common a delight in the changing world as seen under Polish and Irish skies. The Countess painted as she did everything else; her work was intuitive rather than intellectual, the result of a swift artistic impulse rather than a deliberately plotted creative effort. Afterwards she often justified her work intellectually, but a sure impetuosity was characteristic. She also had an instinct for selection that rarely failed. The Count's work showed a greater mastery of the craft of painting and reflected a stronger analytical mind and a more flexible personality. The painting of Russell, who was well known as a writer of limpid lyrics, showed iridescent figures in silver mists, landscapes of the mind half-felt, half-remembered.

George Russell, generally known by his literary signature AE, was a gentle, energetic man whose interests and talents were concerned with every part of Irish life. He was a mystic who could speak in a melodic, persuasive voice of Celtic ideals and the aristocracy of the spirit, but he could be thoroughly practical. "We may believe in fairies," a Denis Johnston character says, "but we trade in pigs."[1] AE considered both. Politically his greatest contribution was his work with Sir Horace Plunkett and the Irish Agricultural Organization. He was for years the editor of the cooperative journal, *The Irish Homestead,* and before that he had traveled throughout Ireland advising and organizing cooperatives. Madame had first met him at Lissadell through her brother's work.

One of AE's great gifts was his ability to see talent in even the most diffuse writing or the roughest lines. For Irishmen such as he, emigration, which had seemed to Madame's grandfather the humane solution to poverty, had become an unhealed wound on the land. Men and women of imagination, enterprise, dedication, and wit were always leaving Ireland. Indeed, much of the chauvinism of the period reflects the concern of those who realized that the constant drain of population debilitated the country. AE did what he could to keep men of talent in Ireland. Sunday nights at AE's were famous in Dublin for years, and it was there that many friendships were made and many careers begun. There Madame first met Arthur Griffith and found the cause she had been seeking. AE also encouraged, advised, and published young writers. He claimed that he was able to publish the popular *New Songs* from manuscripts lying about in his room. Two of Eva Gore-Booth's poems appeared in that collection, but AE thought those of Padraic Colum the best of the lot. That year, 1904, AE also announced the presence of a young scamp named Joyce, who wrote with a more perfect art than anyone except Yeats. Joyce was about to publish a book of lyrics.[2] The night after the opening of their art exhibition, the Count and Countess went to the Antient Concert Rooms to hear John F. McCormack, "the pride of Sligo." Also on the program was the literary "scamp," who had a sweet tenor voice.

The art exhibits with AE continued for the next several years, until Madame became too involved with politics to continue painting seriously. In the early years art was the focus of her life, although she soon developed her long-time interest in the theater as well.

About 1906 a small group in Dublin decided to form an Arts Club to bring together all those who were interested in art in its widest sense. The Arts Club was a meeting place for all those who were interested in life and recording its experiences: the Markieviczs, the Orpens, the James Duncans, Padraic Colum, Jack and W. B. Yeats, John Millington Synge, Percy French, Conor O'Brien, AE, Page Dickinson, and many more. The daily lunch hour and occasional cheerful evenings developed a camaraderie among a diverse group of people unified only in their broad attitudes towards self and national expression. Some of the members were interested merely in encouraging art; others, such as Yeats, wanted to create a national art so excellent that the world could not ignore Ireland.

Nationalism was a vortex into which art and social reform groups were being drawn. When the United Arts Club brought the first post-impressionist pictures to Dublin in a memorable exhibit, the applause of the nationalist *Irish Freedom* indicated the concurrent artistic-political attitudes: the paintings had "their special message for Ireland, where we are making a beginning with so many things, in the determination of the artists to achieve self-expression, no matter what hoary conventions suffer in the process."[3]

The painters in the Arts Club ran a life class two or three nights a week. Page Dickinson, the artist and architect, remembered that all sorts of people turned up for it, not many of whom he thought were much good at self-expression. The Markieviczs were the best draughtsmen, he said, and what was learned was mainly from them. Madame was the soul of good nature, always ready to help and advise others with less knowledge. "As a matter of fact," he wrote, "they were both painters of considerable merit, and could both have been really first-rate if they had worked. They never did, however, their energies were too diffuse to concentrate on painting."[4] This was high praise from their fellow-artist, and generous, since it was written after Madame's politics had diverged completely from his.

Much of the Markieviczs' energy went into drama. Madame had been interested in the new theater movements in Dublin even before she left Sligo. In 1898, when Lady Gregory, W. B. Yeats, and Edward Martyn had appealed for three hundred pounds to guarantee an experiment to build up a Celtic and Irish school of dramatic literature, Constance Gore-Booth was one of the first to respond to the call for funds for what later became the Abbey Theatre.

Always in love with theatrics on and off the stage, it was in 1907 that Madame played her first part in Dublin. There were many theater groups in those days, as there are now. The Irish Literary Theatre was one of the first, the Theatre of Ireland another. On December 13, 1907, the Theatre of Ireland opened the season auspiciously with a revival of AE's three-act play, *Deirdre,* at the Abbey. The house was full and the audience enthusiastic, insisting that the author come forward at the conclusion of the piece. He had himself played the small part of Cathmha, a Druid, the same role he had taken in the first production five years before. Countess Markievicz imparted suitable mystery and weirdness to her portrayal of the Druidess, Lavarcam.[6]

A few months later, another theater company was formed which gave its first production on March 9, 1908, at the Abbey. They called themselves the Independent Dramatic Company, and their first play, *Seymour's Redemption,* was also the first written by Count Markievicz, the producer and director of the new company. It was the height of the Dublin social season, and since Count and Countess Markievicz were still very much in Castle society, the production was more a social than a theatrical event. One night's proceeds were given towards the purchase of a Corot presented by the women of Ireland to the newly-opened Municipal Art Gallery.

The theme concerned the point at which an illicit act becomes acceptable; it was a problem play, a type more popular on the continent than in Ireland. The plot was based on the familiar triangle: a successful M.P., Seymour; a former love, Daphne (played by the Countess); and his wife whom he had married because she was the daughter of his own political chief. Seymour comes under Daphne's influence and to the conclusion that being successful in his public life is incompatible with his emotional needs. He makes a sensational parliamentary speech in which he pleads for the legitimatizing of children of unmarried mothers and for which he is condemned by his party. Daphne is persuaded to give Seymour up, but when he has a nervous breakdown she is called back to help persuade him to go to a hospital for rest. Her strength of will breaks down, and she agrees to go away and start a new life with him.

The characterizations were clear and the dialogue clever. The reviewers marveled that a foreigner who could hardly speak English when he married and still often conversed with his wife in French, could have managed the task so well. They were generally kind to the performers, although they found too little variation in intensity in the Countess's performance. Her speech, too, was a problem; she was not always clearly understood. She had a strong, Anglo-Irish clipped drawl which at first aroused suspicion among Irish nationalists. Also, her voice was shrill, good, no doubt, for hallooing in a chase or haranguing a crowd, but grating on the stage. She was vital and emotional, but lacked the control and restraint necessary to be a first-class actress. She was responsive to the words and situations and later showed a sense of comedy, but most of the plays she acted in and later wrote were intense and didactic. She was always direct, honest, and sincere, on stage as well as off, but her most successful performances were off stage.

In May, 1908, Madame acted with her old friends in the Theatre of Ireland company, of which she was a member. At the Abbey they revived Edward Martyn's *Maeve*. Martyn himself was pleased with the production. Madame was appropriately dignified as Queen Maeve. She was working hard to improve her voice.

During this period Madame became aware of the cause of Ireland's independence. Many of the artists and writers she knew in the Arts Club and in Dublin generally, and many of the actors in the Theatre of Ireland and in their own Independent Dramatic Company were strongly nationalistic. It was part of the reviving pride in things Irish. Madame herself said it was two newspapers that opened her eyes, *The Peasant* and *Sinn Fein*. She happened upon a bundle that someone had left lying around the rehearsal hall in Harcourt Street. The first article that attracted her attention was something about Robert Emmet, whose face was familiar to her from prints she had often seen on cottage walls around Sligo. She vaguely thought he had been a Fenian. She read then of his speech from the dock and death, of what a few were actually trying to do at that moment, and like a flash she made up her mind she must join up.[7]

And there it was, conversion to anti-British militarism. It sounds like jingoism, almost too easy, the sudden identification with the romantic revolutionary idealist while his famous words from the dock rang through her mind: "When my country takes her place among the nations of the earth, then, and not till then, let my epitaph be written." Her decision has puzzled many. Why should such a girl make such a choice? Even as she made it, she must have realized that such a commitment would mean some personal neglect of her husband and their two children, direct opposition to her class and her family in Sligo, the eventual corrosion of her interests in art, perhaps the loss of life. It is doubtful that she had any clear program for rebellion. On the other hand, she had a heritage of service, and luxury had begun to pall.

Among the ways she could serve her nation, the cooperatives, followed by her brother and AE, were slow, technical, and ultimately required an effacing of the self not in her nature. She was clearsighted enough about her limitations in art; and although the Parliamentary Party under Redmond had made gains, it was steadily losing the confidence of the Irish and promised her no vote. Above all, she yearned for action and something gallant and dangerous to ride.

One Sunday night at AE's, Madame met Arthur Griffith, the brilliant, taciturn, cautious leader of Sinn Fein. His suspicious response to her interest and desire to join in helping the movement was typical of the coldness she received from many nationalists, men and women, before she convinced them of her integrity. "I told Mr. Griffith quite frankly," she wrote, "that I only just realised that there were men in Ireland whose principles did not allow them to take an oath of allegiance to the foreign King, whose power they were pledged to break and overthrow. Mr. Griffith was very discouraging to me and very cautious. I first thought that he merely considered me a sentimental fool; later on I realised that he had jumped to the conclusion that I was an agent of the enemy. Many years afterwards, it was after my release from Holloway [Prison] in 1919, I chaffed him about it. He did not deny it, but laughed heartily, and said something to the effect that no one could ever say it again."[8]

Madame next met Bulmer Hobson. He had been a Belfast journalist, became editor of the I.R.B. periodical *Irish Freedom* when it was founded in 1910 in Dublin, and was rising in the nationalist movement. When Madame met him, he had not yet been discredited. There was something enigmatic about Hobson, but he trusted Madame, or professed to trust her, and certainly proved very helpful. He was on the Executive of Sinn Fein at the time, and through him she joined the Drumcondra branch where the smouldering young railway worker, Sean O'Casey, was also a member. Soon after that night at AE's, Madame went to a meeting at the Rotunda at which Arthur Griffith was speaking. Helena Molony, a dedicated nationalist, spotted her in the audience. This was not difficult: Madame was one of the few women at the meeting and the only one in an elegant dress. Miss Molony was looking around for possible recruits for the women's organization, Inghinidhe na hEireann (Daughters of Erin). Bulmer Hobson introduced them and Miss Molony invited Madame to an Inghinidhe meeting scheduled for a few nights later. She went. It was a memorable night for the women present and for herself.

The Inghinidhe na hEireann played an important role in artistic and nationalist Dublin for years. It had an interesting history as an early feminist as well as patriotic organization, particularly because of the people involved in it. Arthur Griffith, in his new weekly *The United Irishman,* had urged as early as 1899 that the women of Ireland should perpetuate a true national spirit in the country by seeing that their homes were kept sacred from the contaminations of the British press and the music hall jokes. He did not ask them to go so far as to step into the open and air their views before the multitude but did urge them to look to the preservation of their children's national faith. But there were women like Maud Gonne, Helena Molony, and later Madame Markievicz who wanted to have their views aired, who wanted to do more than keep English newspapers and songs out of their homes.

In 1900 Maud Gonne, who had worked with the Land League through the 1880's and '90's, presided over a ladies' meeting called to organize an excursion for Dublin school children who refused to attend the Queen's breakfast, an expression of loyalty on the occasion of the Queen's visit to Dublin. Deputations from the Daughters of Erin, the Ladies Foresters, and the Ladies' Wolfe Tone Committee attended Miss Gonne's meeting. The result was that on July 1, 1900, a Patriotic Children's Treat proved so successful that the ladies formed themselves into the permanent organization Inghinidhe na hEireann. Their immediate program was the starting of free evening classes for children over nine years old. The boys and girls were taught Gaelic, Irish history, music, art, and drama. There were also entertainments. In June, for example, the children were taken on a pilgrimage to the grave of Wolfe Tone. They carried Irish flags and Boer flags, loudly booed and hissed every English soldier they passed, and had a very pleasant day.

Inghinidhe na hEireann was closely allied in aims with the Celtic Literary Society (which did not welcome women) and later with Sinn Fein. They continued to work with children's classes and entertainments, with drama and concerts, and later started a monthly paper for women. There were women on the Executive of Sinn Fein and its predecessor, Cumann na nGaedheal, but Griffith was never a strong feminist.

One of the ways the Inghinidhe could effectively educate was through the theatre. In St. Teresa's Total Abstinence Hall in Clarendon Street, Dublin, April 2, 1902, the intensely patriotic *Kathleen Ni Houlihan,* by W. B. Yeats, and AE's *Deirdre* were first produced by

W. G. Fay's Irish National Dramatic Company. This was a new society which had been formed by his Ormond group and the Inghinidhe dramatic class. The success of the productions, which ran three nights under the auspices of the Inghinidhe, encouraged Yeats and Lady Gregory to found the Abbey Theatre.[9] Kathleen ni Houlihan was Maud Gonne's single, unforgettable role; many nationalists were inspired and sustained by her performance and its memory. Madame took one of the lines as her personal motto, "If a man would help me, he must give me himself, give me all." This was the most significant contribution the Inghinidhe made to theatrical history, but they continued with plays and play production as a favorite fund-raising and teaching device. Many nationalists wrote plays and were part-time actors.

The Inghinidhe had been active for about eight years when Madame found her way into it. The night she went to her first meeting was cold, drizzly and dank. It was a night to be home by the fire, not in a gloomy, unattractive meeting room with a deal table and splintery chairs. The dedicated ladies went dutifully to the meeting, feeling a bit grim and wishing they were someplace else. Suddenly the door flew open, and in burst a beautiful woman in a long, flowing, blue velvet cloak. She was wearing a satin dress with a train, and diamonds flashed in her hair. Madame had come straight from some Castle affair. Miss Molony introduced her to the women who were suspicious, perhaps a little jealous. But she unceremoniously walked over to the fireplace, took off her wet shoes, placed them on the hearth, sat at the unpainted table, and listened attentively as the meeting went on.

The Inghinidhe were not convinced of her sincerity and were doubtful of her motives. They were cool, nearly rude to her. She was of the ascendancy class, and they did not know why she wanted to be there with them and not at the Castle. Typically, she later told Miss Molony it was because of the way they snubbed her that she liked them from the beginning. It was the first time she had been anyplace she was not "kowtowed to as a countess."

The year 1908 was a lively one for Madame. She was finding varied and sometimes violent outlets for her vast energy—the theater, art, Sinn Fein, Inghinidhe. She even found time in April to visit her sister, Eva, in Manchester to help in a fight there. Asquith had just become Prime Minister, there was a general move up in the Cabinet, and the Ministers who had changed their posts were obliged to vacate their seats and face re-election.

Miss Gore-Booth had been in the north of England for several years.

She had been instrumental in forming the Manchester and Salford Women's Trades Council whose purpose was to do battle for the representation of women's labor. In 1908 a Licensing Bill was an important issue in the North-West Manchester election. Among other things, this would have made it illegal for women to serve as barmaids. The Women's Trades Council saw the attempt to abolish barmaids as an insidious plot to restrict women's sphere of labor. Although one candidate, Winston Churchill, had urged the suffragettes to trust him as their friend, they doubted that he would try to make votes for women a reality. They supported his opponent, William Joynson-Hicks, who was on the women's side on the Licensing Bill.

On Easter Sunday, April 19, there was a blizzard in Manchester. In spite of the unseasonable cold, the days before election on the 24th were noisy with frenzied speech making. Motor cars, traps, and carriages sped around town carrying speakers and banners. Madame herself expertly drove a four-in-hand through the crowded streets for Miss Gore-Booth. Madame was heckled by the query, even today dear to the domesticated male, "Can you cook a dinner?" She flung back, "Yes, I can. Can you drive a coach-and-four?" The crowd's sympathies were with her.

The barmaids and Mr. Joynson-Hicks won the election; Mr. Churchill was defeated.

Madame found time to paint during that busy year, and on August 20 she, the Count, Mrs. Baker, AE, Dermod O'Brien, and Mr. Leech opened an exhibition of their pictures at Leinster Hall. Her art was improving and her "Tinker's Honeymoon" and "Old Man in Connemarra" were particularly praised. She exhibited with the Count and AE again the following year, and in the Sinn Fein Aonach in December, 1909, but that was the last time. Although she continued to paint, she never again exhibited.

It was indicative of the important place politics was assuming for her that on the night the exhibition opened, she went to a Sinn Fein meeting[10] and the following day met with the Inghinidhe about starting a journal for women. Mrs. Dryhurst, Miss Ella Young, Miss S. Varian, Miss C. Doyle, Miss Day, and Miss Molony were appointed with Madame Markievicz to form the committee to get on with the project. After many meetings and letters appealing for funds and contributions, the first issue of *Bean na hEireann* (*Woman of Ireland*) was published in November, 1908. It was the first and only journal devoted to Irish women's nationalist activities. Each member of the

Inghinidhe was asked to canvass her own friends for one shilling a month to pay the printer, the only expense. The paper sold for a penny a copy, Miss Molony was the editor, and Roger Casement, Arthur Griffith, James Connolly, AE, and Seamus O'Sullivan were among the contributors.[11]

Among her other contributions to *Bean na hEireann,* Madame wrote the garden notes with the zeal of a new convert. She turned any phase of gardening to her single line of thought—Irish independence. The result was humorous but bloodthirsty horticulture. "It is very unpleasant work killing slugs and snails, but let us not be daunted. A good Nationalist should look upon slugs in a garden much in the same way as she looks on the English in Ireland, and only regret that she cannot crush the Nation's enemies with the same ease that she can the garden's, with just one tread of her fairy foot. True the garden's enemies are as hard to find, and as subtle in their methods as the Nation's." In a less aggressive mood, she wandered through a twilight garden: the crimson roses "remind us that we must live so that our martyrs' blood shall not have been shed in vain." Again, "Ireland—like the garden—lies sleeping and resting, recouping her vital powers for the struggle that will come." And, in the same vein, "What is Ireland but a poor wee bulb buried away in the dust and dirt of English rule and English influence and struggling to gain the light and air."

A lecture delivered by Madame on March 28, 1909, to the Students' National Literary Society, Dublin, was published through the Inghinidhe.[12] This was loudly applauded by the *Bean na hEireann* as striking a new militant and hopeful note. It was an appeal to the young women of Ireland to take part in politics and in the national movement, not as women fighting for the franchise only, but for Ireland. " 'A Free Ireland with no Sex Disabilities in her Constitution' should be the motto of all Nationalist women. And a grand motto it is," Madame said. She anticipated the stand of the Inghinidhe (by then incorporated in the Cumann na mBan) in the bitter 1920's with an appeal against compromise. "Fix your minds on the ideal of Ireland free, with her women enjoying the full rights of citizenship in their own nation, and no one will be able to sidetrack you, and so make use of you to use up the energies of the nation in obtaining concessions that for the most part were coming in the natural course of evolution . . . our national freedom cannot, and must not be left to evolution." As a firm believer in collective action, she made the Sinn Fein appeal to buy Irish goods only, as individuals and through organizations. She urged the women to talk and talk and talk "publicly and privately, never minding how they bore people—till not one even of the peasants in the wilds of Galway but has heard and approved of the movement." She knew from experience that this could be tedious. "I daresay you will think this all very obvious and very dull, but Patriotism and Nationalism and all great things are made up of much that is obvious and dull, and much that in the beginning is small, but that will be found to lead out into fields that are broader and full of interest." She urged them to take an active part in public life. "You will go out into the world and get elected on to as many public bodies as possible. By degrees through your exertions no public institution— whether hospital, workhouse, asylum or any other—and no private house but will be supporting the industries of your country."

In summary, Madame outlined all of the nationalist forces at work. She urged the young women to "regard yourselves as Irish, believe in yourselves as Irish. Arm yourselves with weapons to fight your nation's cause. Arm your souls with noble and free ideas. Arm your minds with the histories and memories of your country and her martyrs, her language, and a knowledge of her arts, and her industries. And if in your day the call should come for your body to arm, do not shirk that either." Her lecture concluded with a call to arms: "May this aspiration towards life and freedom among the women of Ireland bring forth a Joan of Arc to free our nation!" This was the first time she publicly articulated her vision of herself and her destiny.

The reference to the fight for women's suffrage mirrors her feelings about that movement. Since 1896 and the Sligo Women's Suffrage Society meetings, Madame had changed her mind. "Surely it's illogical to stop at a mere vote, for myself I demand and expect a great deal more."[13]

In the early months of 1909 the Irish Women's Franchise League had gained momentum and was holding regular, well-attended, and fully-reported meetings. The IWFL grew in numbers and prestige over the years, and although Madame was always sympathetic and helpful, especially when her very good friend, Hanna Sheehy Skeffington, was its president, she always felt that they were not going far enough in their demands. She often attended IWFL meetings to urge that the women of Ireland would be better employed working along national lines at home rather than in sending members to advocate their claims in the English Parliament. Eva Gore-Booth continued her interest in the suffrage movement in England, however, and in 1910 spoke to the question in Sligo. Lady Gore-Booth expressed her approval by being on the platform with her daughter. She did not sit on platforms with her eldest child.

In addition to her growing interest in Sinn Fein and in the Inghinidhe, Madame continued to be active in the theater in Dublin. In December, 1908, a few months before her lecture to the Students' National Literary Society, Count Markievicz's Independent Dramatic Company had presented his second and third plays at the Abbey. Countess Markievicz, billed as Miss Constance Gore, played Lady Althea in his *Dilettante,* a comedy about the selection of excellence.

Althea, although in love with a young poet (J. M. Carré), is married to an old man. He conveniently dies and Althea prepares to marry the poet, but in the meantime he has discovered Ella Watt (Maire Nic Shiubhlaigh), daughter of Althea's estate steward. Althea has a fine sense of honor, and gives him up. She takes him to Ella's cottage to make arrangements for a wedding. But Ella and Althea have a congenial chat, decide the poet is not good enough for either of them, and go off together. The poet meantime has bought for £50 from Ella's mother a Gainsborough worth £10,000 (why this was in the estate steward's possession is not explained), so he is happy in spite of losing two loves. The second play of the evening was a one-act farce, *Home Sweet Home,* on which Nora Fitzpatrick and the Count collaborated. It was all very gay and light. The Count had discovered Dublin's insatiable appetite for amusement, and the audiences that filled the Abbey for the three performances were very appreciative. But Yeats was indignant that the Abbey would be rented to a company doing such frivolous plays which did nothing to further Irish drama and merely entertained.[14]

Three weeks later the company took the two plays to Sligo for benefit performances. They were a feature of a Christmas Carnival organized to pay off the debt on the Gillooly Memorial Temperance Hall. The Count and Countess were spending Christmas at Lissadell, but the other sixteen members of the company went to Sligo for the two days. In spite of a blizzard, flooded streets, and a fierce wind, large and fashionable audiences filled the hall on both nights and gave a hearty reception to both the play and the farce. Miss Gore received gracious notices on her spirited acting.

The Count, who was nearly as popular in Sligo as he was in Dublin, had already made one public appearance this trip when he spoke at a Gaelic League meeting. Although he was not interested in the national question at any level, he captured the hearts of his audience with burning words affirming the necessity for making Gaelic compulsory in the new National University. Amused friends in Dublin regarded this as typical. With all sincerity he often lectured convincingly on a subject in which he had little interest and less knowledge (temperance was a favorite topic).

The Christmas Carnival activities concluded in Sligo with a concert at which Madame accompanied her husband on the piano while he sang the Polish National Anthem. In response to a tremendous ovation he sang "The Wearin' o' the Green" in capital style. The Count, who came as near to being a perfect stage Irishman as anyone in Ireland, was a perceptive, sharp-witted internationalist in the middle of nationalist fervor; clowning was a way to make his difficult position bearable.

In April, 1909, Seumas O'Kelly gave the Theatre of Ireland his most memorable play, *The Shuiler's Child.* This is a harshly naturalistic story about a child abandoned by his mother, a shuiler. He is taken from the workhouse by a prosperous farmer, but his itinerant mother reclaims him, then finds herself unable to support him, and leaves him again at the farmhouse. Maire Nic Shiublaigh was brilliant in the leading role, and Madame played a government inspector with great vigor. Her acting was gaining in steadiness and conviction. Portraying another official was the young writer, James Stephens, billed as Stephen James, who was thought to be a comedian of great promise.

In August the company, including Madame, played in Kilkenny with indifferent success. That same month she was elected a vice-president of the Theatre of Ireland, along with Arthur Griffith, AE, and Padraic Pearse. In November *The Shuiler's Child* was repeated in Dublin, and this was Madame's last performance with the Theatre of Ireland. Although she continued to be interested in the group, her work with the Count's company took all the time she had for the stage in those busy years.

By this time she had started a project of her own, the Fianna na hEireann, which was her unique contribution to Ireland and perhaps her greatest achievement. Indeed, many people in Ireland today think of her only as the founder of the Fianna. She did much more, but if she had done only this she would have contributed significantly. Padraic Pearse said that if the Fianna had not been founded in 1909, there would have been no Volunteers in 1913. The Easter Rising of 1916 would have been impossible.[15]

The Fianna was unique in its purpose and method. There had been boys' brigades for years, but this was the first time that an organization had been formed with the openly-avowed purpose of training boys to take arms against the English in the cause of Irish independence. The Fianna aimed to train boys in the old traditions of the Gaels. They took their name, as had the 19th-century Fenians, from the ancient brotherhood of Irish warriors, the tough and idealistic commandos.

Madame conceived the idea, saw the best way to organize it, hovered over Fianna meetings, paid the rent of halls, gave her enthusiasm, vitality and idealism. "We have heard the imperious demand of Cathleen ni Houlihan," she told them, "her call to those who would serve her, to give her all, to give her themselves. It will take the best and noblest of Ireland's children to win Freedom, for the price of Freedom is suffering and pain. It is to the young that a nation must look for help; for life itself. Ireland is calling you to join Fianna na hEireann, the young army of Ireland, and help to place the crown of freedom on Her head."[16] To her sister she said, "I have great faith in the young."

Madame said the idea had occurred to her in the spring of 1909 when she read of the Lord Lieutenant reviewing a number of Boy Scout organizations. The only boy she knew well was her stepson Stanislas, but she had a working psychology that was new to Ireland in 1909. "The early impressions that a young mind receives become part of his subconscious self. These impressions create the instincts that guide him and make him; the driving forces, that, quite unrealised by him, goad him into action, make him voice opinions. . . . I could see these children growing to manhood and gaily enlisting in the British army or Police forces, and being used to batten their own class into submission."[17] She was quite right. Part of the effectiveness of the Royal Irish Constabulary came from the fact that the Castle recruited it from the people it controlled.

For weeks she talked with her friends about the right way to organize the boys. Helena Molony was actively sympathetic from the beginning. The first written suggestion for forming an Irish army through training the boys was by Madame in *Bean na hEireann* as early as May, 1909. In June the formation of a National Boys Brigade was announced. Through a Unionist schoolmaster friend of hers, she met a nationalist sympathizer who taught in a school near Westland Row. Madame had a difficult time convincing him, but finally he was persuaded of her sincerity and introduced eight boys to her. Because she was serious and of good social standing, he knew their mothers would not object. The boys went to Madame's house in Rathgar, where she explained her ideas to them. Awed at being singled out, they agreed, and formed themselves into "The Red Branch Knights."

She remembered their first campout with bemused affection: "We knew nothing whatever about camping; but that did not matter. Someone very opportunely gave me a little garden tent. I bought a scout tent. The Fitzgerald boys volunteered a pony and cart—which since those early days did many a journey for the Fianna. We filled up the cart with tents, rugs, cushions, food, saucepans, books, etc., and off we started for the Dublin mountains—Miss Molony, myself and six boys. . . . After long hours of pushing, pulling, lifting, resting and pushing again we arrived at the last gate at the end of the track. A few minutes more saw us in the valley, kneeling on the soft green sward and bathing our dusty faces in the little stream. We dawdled over a most delicious tea and dragging out poetry books and sketching things we lazily drowsed away the evening. Twilight woke us to the necessity of fixing up things for the night. We started to pitch the tent on a grassy slope where the hill slid down to the stream. It took a long, long time. Tents are very hard to pitch if you don't know how, especially at night. Whenever you trip over a rope in the dark the peg comes out, you probably fall on to the tent, and it collapses. Anyhow the peg flies out and is lost. Next comes the task of trying to disentangle jam from the blankets . . .

"We woke very early to find a bright, pleasant morning, with a cheerful sun shining in through the flaps of the tent. Early as we were, the boys were still earlier, and one was already improving his mind with W. B. Yeats' poems. The others were mostly blacking their boots, and quite ready for breakfast. I didn't wonder that they looked so fresh when at last I found my soap and towel—a brown dripping rag, wrapped round a sticky mess. It was the only towel in the camp. After long experience I have come to the conclusion that the only thing that you can be quite sure that every boy will bring to camp is boot polish.

"After breakfast the boys went to Mass, we put things straight and settled ourselves snugly to read. Suddenly some heavy drops of rain sent us scurrying to the tent. We hastily grabbed all the blankets, coats, rugs and cushions that we had spread around in the sun to air. We piled them up into a snug nest, from which we defied the elements. Down came the storm, the thunder crashed above us, sharp blades of lightning cut through the rain beside us, menacing our fragile shelter. The boys came rushing up—and then—oh horror!—we had not thought of digging a ditch round the tent, which was pitched on the side of a hill. The rainshed poured right through the fragile wall over the ground sheet. Our snug nest was one soppy sponge.

"Luckily the rain stopped as suddenly as it began. The sun came out and did its best to dry our things. When it had to set, we took up the job, and, lighting a primus stove, we held the damp blankets to it, and watched the steam gradually growing less. The boys anyhow slept in dry coverings that night, and no one took cold. The next evening saw the end of our holiday. . . .

"I have taken some time in describing this camp, as it is one of the things I like to dwell on. It convinced me finally that a boys' organisation could be made a success in Ireland. But I saw that the English loose system of organisation by sections and patrols would not work here. It would have to be run more on the lines of a Boys Republic and an army. There would have to be a hall taken and an organisation formed more on the lines that Irishmen were accustomed to work in."[18]

Meanwhile she continued to try to interest other nationalists in her idea. Throughout the early summer in Dublin there were open-air propaganda meetings on behalf of Sinn Fein policy at which Madame was one of the speakers. She put her ideas about the boys' organization to the audiences and was unhappy when she got little response and no offers of help. The Sinn Fein Executive, to which she was co-opted in August, refused to sponsor the rebel Boy Scout organization. "Sinn Fein could not undertake this work, it would be most unwise for it to do so," she was told, "but of course the members would all help me individually if I decided to start myself." Sinn Fein advocated abstention from the English Parliament and building up the Irish economy through trade and manufacture but did not condone violence or physical force. It was naive of her to expect their support.

There were, however, advocates of physical force and members of the secret Irish Republican Brotherhood (I.R.B.) in all the nationalist organizations in those days. One of those in Sinn Fein was her friend, Bulmer Hobson. One night in early August he and Madame discussed it at the home of Helena Molony's brother, Frank, just before Frank Molony and his wife went to the United States. By this time Madame realized that the Red Branch Knights were a false start. They would have to be reorganized, and she knew she did not have enough experience working with boys to carry it through on her own. She knew that Hobson had formed an organization in Belfast for boys several years before, and had considerable understanding of them. The pur-

pose of his group had been to serve as a junior hurling league, to promote the study of the Irish language, and to teach the boys to be sound
nationalists. They wore no uniforms, and there was no provision for
drilling or military organization or training of any kind. He and
Madame decided to work together on the militant organization she had
in mind. His scouts had been called Fianna na hEireann[19] and the new
group took the same name.

Madame undertook to pay the ten shillings weekly rent for a hall
for meetings, and continued to do so for years. The hall at 34 Lower
Camden Street was the same one in which she had often visited and
watched rehearsals of the National Theatre Society a few years before.
Sinn Fein of August 14, 1909, announced that a meeting would be
held Monday, August 16, to start a national Boys Brigade to be managed by the boys themselves on national and party lines. The announcement appeared in other nationalist papers the same week. About a
hundred boys showed up. Hobson took the chair, Madame served as
secretary. Her excitement was suddenly checked when one of the bigger
boys got up and pointed out, "This is a physical force organization,
and there are two women in the room. This is no place for them, they
must be put out." Hobson explained who thought up the idea and
who was paying the rent, so she and Miss Molony were allowed to
remain, on sufferance, of course. Some of the boys never got used to
the idea of having a woman in the organization, and there were occasional mutterings. But to most of the boys she was an inspiration, and
the younger ones particularly idolized her.[20]

The local branch of Sinn Fein and that of the Gaelic League were
quick to disclaim any connection with the affair. A notice pointing this
out was published in *Sinn Fein* August 21. However, *Bean na hEireann*
was, naturally, full of its praise and gave complete coverage to Fianna
activities during the next few vital years. Within a month the hall at
Lower Camden Street was busy nearly every night: soon it was identified as the Fianna Hall. In those early weeks there was drill on Mon-
days and Thursdays, on Tuesdays and Fridays games, and on Wednes-
days language and history classes. One of the future Easter Week
heroes, Con Colbert, compiled a course of drill commands in Gaelic
and soon Gaelic became the language in which all commands were
given. Another Fianna, Joe Reynolds, remembers that they took turns
standing in uniform beneath a large flag outside the hall to attract
recruits.

A series of lectures was given, the first by Dr. Patrick McCartan who spoke on "The Boy Heroes of '98." Seamas Deakin lectured on "A Boy's National Duty," and another week Madame Markievicz talked on the "Women of '98," a favorite subject of hers. She illustrated her lecture with limelight views depicting British atrocities committed during that memorable year. She concluded by telling the boys how the Irish of that day lost all sense of honor and chivalry by serving under the English flag and urged the need of a much stronger anti-enlisting movement in Ireland.

Madame also taught the boys how to shoot, how to take care of guns, and safety in using them. At this she was expert. Out near Sandyford, at the foot of the Dublin Mountains, Madame had rented a small cottage where she used to go at odd times to paint and walk. The air is sweet there on the easy slope of the hills, and one can see Dublin city and the bay below. Like many raised in the country, she had to get away from the city from time to time into the quiet beauty of the countryside. The cottage was about eight miles from Dublin, a convenient cycling distance, and less than a mile's walk to the city tram. There was a large field in front of the cottage and it was there the boys camped, played games, learned about guns. The only legal place to shoot was on one's own property, so the instruction took place there. First she taught Helena Molony to shoot, and together they taught the boys. The only time Madame was cross with the boys was when they mishandled the guns. She was thinking of future insurrection in practical terms: this was their most important business and they had to learn it right. She raged at one of the boys who pointed a gun at another. None of them ever forgot her fury at his feeble excuse, "It isn't loaded."

At about the time the Fianna was getting under way, she decided to move from St. Mary's where she and the Count had been living since they had come to Dublin. She stayed briefly on Garville Avenue and then hit upon the idea of establishing a cooperative community near Dublin. It would be self-supporting, the boys would have agricultural experience, and expenses would be met by a farming program. This would also serve as a healthful change from their city lives. The value of cooperation was the only thing on which she fully agreed with her brother. A boys' cooperative would meet two needs: it would solve some financial problems and it would provide a place to train a boys' army. She knew about a successful commune at Ralahine over seventy-five years before, the history of which was widely read in Ireland by landlords like Sir Josslyn who were interested in the cooperative movement. James Connolly further popularized the commune in *The Harp* in the spring of 1909, and in 1910 included a chapter about it in his *Labour in Irish History* called "An Irish Utopia."[21]

Inspired by Connolly's account in *The Harp,* Madame decided to establish a cooperative at Belcamp Park and moved there in 1909. Belcamp was not to be a true commune with schools, shops, churches, and resident families. The idea was simply to have a self-supporting farm which would give some agricultural experience and outdoor exercise for the Fianna boys. It would provide food for them while they were there, and it would give them a place for camping and drilling. The help of an agricultural expert was enlisted, but the mainstays were Bulmer Hobson, Madame, and Helena Molony. Miss Molony and Madame lived at Belcamp but cycled into Dublin nearly every day to attend meetings and carry on their nationalist activities. Madame had recently been elected to the Sinn Fein Executive to fill a place vacated when Mrs. Frank Molony went to America, and this work became more demanding on her time. She was helping Miss Molony with *Bean na hEireann,* working with the Fianna, and painting. She remained interested in the theater, was a vice-president of the Theatre of Ireland, and acted with her husband's Independent Theatre Company. So Belcamp never really got started properly. There was no one to give it the time and the attention to administrative details that would train city boys to become farmers.

When the Count came back to Dublin after one of his periodic trips to Poland, he was appalled at the mess, disapproved of the whole scheme, and it was disbanded after only a few months. However, through 1910 and into 1911 the Markieviczs continued living at Belcamp Park, the 17th-century house where the Irish parliamentarian Grattan had been born. At Belcamp Park, as at Surrey House, to which they moved in the fall of 1911, there was always talk and activity. Madame loved the excitement of having people around, Fianna boys coming and going, and friends visiting. Someone was always there.

On August 21, 1910, the first annual conference of the Fianna was held at the Mansion House. Madame was elected president, Councillor Paul Gregan and Bulmer Hobson, vice-presidents, Padraic O'Riain, secretary, Michael Lonergan, assistant, and James Gregan, treasurer. The secretary reported that seven *sluaghte* (as they spelled the Irish word for troops) were affiliated, five in Dublin, one in Waterford, and one in Glasgow. The membership of each sluagh ranged from twenty to sixty. This organization of young nationalists was quickly becoming national. An address at the convention set the tone: "We have laid the foundation of a very important work—the raising of a disciplined army. We will go to fight praying to God for victory and we will fight, please God, with a right good will. Now it is quite clear that we are preparing for a hot time . . ." The boys cheered enthusiastically.

While other boy scouts worked at good deeds, the Fianna were busy with war games. A typical occasion was in November, 1910, when on a very wet Sunday they held their inter-sluagh scouting games. On that occasion An Chead Sluagh and Sluagh Wolfe Tone jointly defended the citadel against the north side sluaghte who were the attackers. The citadel consisted of 400 square yards of Mr. Jolly's fields in Scholarstown, and the object was for the attackers to enter the citadel without being captured. A natural rivalry between sluaghte on the north side of the Liffey and those on the south side added interest. Seventy eager boys shouted their way through the noisy afternoon to a non-decisive conclusion.

It was characteristic of Madame's uncompromising integrity and unstatesmanlike attitude towards political compromise that almost immediately after her election to the Sinn Fein Executive she was in the middle of a controversy. Her political education had been guided by Bulmer Hobson. He had introduced her to Sinn Fein, to the Inghinidhe, and had worked with her in organizing the Fianna. "When I first knew him," she acknowledged in later years when political differences had created bitter personal antagonism between them, "he was associated with Dr. McCartan and Mr. Sean McGarry. These three were constantly together, and always to be found at certain times at Tom Clarke's shop. They now took me under their wing and educated me, giving me books on Ireland to read, and explaining to me all the intricacies of such simple things as organizations and committees. Hobson next arranged for me to be chosen as delegate to the annual convention of Sinn Fein for the Drumcondra branch, and there elected as a member of the executive [August 1909], much to the annoyance of Mr. Griffith [who was not a feminist]. The executive was another great disillusion to me. Here were a crowd talking high ideals and love of Ireland, and stultifying the useful work they might have been doing by splitting into two camps behind two jarring leaders."[22]

This split was over a matter of principle in a critical election in

January, 1910. William O'Brien, T. M. Healy, and seven other members of the Home Rule Party had withdrawn from Redmond and as a group of independent Nationalists had formed the "All for Ireland Party," recommending a policy of "Conference, Conciliation and Consent."[23] Just before Christmas, 1909, a special secret meeting of the Sinn Fein Executive was summoned. There were dozens of rumors as to why the meeting had been called. All of Gaelic Dublin were at the annual Christmas fair, the Aonach, an ideal occasion for rumors to multiply. At the United Arts Club Madame heard that Griffith was going to join up with Tim Healy and bring Sinn Fein and the All for Ireland League together with a new policy. The first activity of the joint party would be to fight Redmond's candidate in the South Dublin election. This rumor proved accurate.

When the merger was proposed at the secret meeting, Madame spoke against it as a bold scheme of William O'Brien's to capture the Sinn Fein organization and employ it on behalf of his friends and against Redmond's party at the coming General Election. Griffith saw the scheme as a shrewd compromise that extended Sinn Fein power. It provided for the running of Sinn Fein candidates in Dublin division; O'Brien would supply the necessary funds, in return for which his candidates in the South and West and elsewhere were to receive the active support of Griffith's organization. Madame and others thought it treachery even to have listened to the proposal and to have admitted the possibility of working with a parliamentary party of any description. After an angry meeting, the proposal was defeated.

Madame went to Lissadell for Christmas immediately afterwards. When she returned to Dublin a fortnight later she found a freezing and suspicious atmosphere at the regular weekly Sinn Fein Executive meeting. Finally her friend, Mrs. Wyse-Power, told her outright what the trouble was. The *Irish Nation* had printed a special edition dated December 23 to report in detail the secret meeting which had been held December 21. "I want to ask you something that none of the men have the courage to ask you," Mrs. Wyse-Power said. "You are being blamed for giving an account of the secret meeting to the press." Madame was dumbfounded, especially when told she was alleged to have given it to Mr. Ryan herself, since at that time she had never had any conversation with him and had met him only once. Her friend, Dr. McCartan, thought the accusation was just an attempt to bully her into signing an incomplete report of the meeting as it had been published in *Sinn Fein*. She and one other refused to be intimidated; Denis McCullough and Bulmer Hobson signed only on the condition that it would not be used for newspaper controversy. But discussion of the affair continued for several weeks in the paper. Men who had not trusted Madame before admired her integrity in refusing to be bullied into signing a misleading, incomplete report. The source of the *Irish Nation*'s accurate information was never revealed.

Dr. McCartan wrote of the affair to John Devoy, thinking that he would be able to see things more clearly from a distance. McCartan himself saw that the main issue dividing nationalists into two major groups was "to fight or not to fight." The militarists were gaining. "Would it be better," he asked Devoy, "for the few who mean business to clear out or stick on and fight as best they could."[24] At any rate, McCartan told Devoy, "There will be wigs on the green at the next [Sinn Fein] convention." He concluded his letter with another prediction which proved correct, "I think Count Markievicz's drama on '98 will go well."

The Memory of the Dead, a rousing, patriotic melodrama, opened at the Abbey on April 14, 1910. It was the most successful of the Count's plays and was revived several times in the next few years. James Stephens was favorably impressed with the Count's writing, thought that the language moved with ease and flexibility and that the playwright had complete control of his craft and materials.

Briefly, the plot concerns Nora Doyle (Madame), daughter of a gentleman farmer (Sean Connolly).[25] She marries Dermod O'Dowd (George Nesbit) who with his friend James M'Gowan (Edward Keegan) goes to Killala to fetch arms when they hear of General Humbert's landing. In the second act, Nora, becomingly dressed in men's clothes, sets out to guide a fugitive French officer (J. M. Carré) to Donegal to prevent the landing and capture of General Napper Tandy. By chance Nora meets Dermod and M'Gowan, and Dermod undertakes to fulfill her dangerous mission. By the third act, which takes place twelve months later, popular feeling has grown against Dermod, who is unjustly believed to have acted the part of a traitor. His faithful wife trusts in his loyalty to the cause and stands by him. Dermod has been imprisoned but escapes and makes his way home to Nora. He is in rags, dying, and almost unrecognizable. The play ends with Nora comforting him and the others stricken with remorse for doubting him.

Madame played her part with gusto, reading her lines with a passionate earnestness and feeling which showed she was not merely acting. Clearly the play was written for her, a gift of theatrical propaganda from her husband. Backstage was somewhat cluttered by Fianna boys who had come along to help. A month later it played a full week at the Gaiety with equal success. Some of the Fianna boys managed to be out in front this time, which lessened the backstage confusion and added mightily to the applause.

Count Markievicz's fifth play *Mary* was produced the night following *The Memory of the Dead*. *Mary* was a romantic comedy of a middle class family in an English provincial town. Madame was not in it.

NOTES TO CHAPTER III

1. "The Moon in the Yellow River," *Three Irish Plays* (Baltimore, 1959), p. 26.
2. *Letters from AE*, pp. 55–56.
3. *Irish Freedom*, February, 1911.
4. P. L. Dickinson, *The Dublin of Yesterday* (London, 1929), p. 67.
5. In 1906 the Theatre of Ireland had been formed by the actors who had broken away from the Irish National Theatre Society. It consisted of nearly all the original company who resented usurpation of their control of the society. This was one of many internal squabbles that the Abbey, successors of the Irish National Theatre Society, survived. The Theatre of Ireland's president was Edward Martyn, and included on its board of officers during the next few years were Padraic Colum, Thomas Keohler, George Nesbitt, Dermot Trench, James Cousins, Helen Laird, Padraic Pearse, Thomas Kettle, Arthur Griffith, AE, and Madame Markievicz. "Its members were all amateurs, young men and women, typical of the period, who strove first for a national ideal; secondly for a theatrical one. It began to decline in 1912 only because its members were absorbed into the wider and, at the time, more important work of the Irish Volunteer Movement" (Maire Nic Shiubhlaigh, *The Splendid Years*, Dublin, 1955, p. 77).
6. Maire Nic Shiubhlaigh played the title role; Seamus O'Sullivan and Padraic Colum also had parts. It was followed by the first performance of Seumas O'Kelly's *The Matchmakers*, a favorite comedy which was frequently revived.
7. *Eire*, August 18, 1923.
8. Ibid.
9. Maire Nic Shiubhlaigh was in both plays and never forgot the night. "Yeats wrote *Kathleen ni Houlihan* especially for Maud Gonne, and there were few in the audience who did not see why. In her, the youth of the country saw all that was magnificent in Ireland." After the show, Lady Gregory went backstage to offer congratulations. "Later we saw her talking earnestly with the

Fays and AE. Although we did not know it, we were witnessing the conception of The Irish National Theatre Society and the real beginning of the movement that was to bring us into the Abbey Theatre" (*The Splendid Years*, pp. 19–20).

Maud Gonne said that the only reason she acted in the play was that Yeats made it a condition for giving them the right to produce it, and she felt it would have great importance for the national movement.

10. This was the public meeting which followed the annual convention of the National Council at which Edward Martyn resigned and John Sweetman was elected president.

11. The editor's statement of purpose was deceptively modest: "The women of Ireland do not ask for votes for the men of Ireland have no parliament for them to use it in. They are therefore not Suffragettes, but they ask to have a voice and influence in matters concerning the economic welfare of their country, in the industries and the arts, the health and the wealth of Ireland; and above all, in the education of their children."

12. Constance de Markievicz, *Women, Ideals and the Nation* (Dublin, 1909). The lecture was reprinted in 1918.

13. Rough text of what seem to be notes for a lecture criticizing the IWFL, in Madame's handwriting in a notebook now in the National Museum, Dublin.

14. Joseph Hone, *W. B. Yeats 1865–1939* (London, 1962), p. 286, notes that Madame was "no longer a particular friend to Yeats . . . she was one of several who ran a rival dramatic company." The poet's disapproval was deeper than mere rivalry. The more fundamental difference was one of theatrical aims. The Count wanted to avoid the parochial and bring to Dublin a variety of European drama; Yeats insisted on plays which he thought elevated Irish art.

15. The Irish nationalists influenced future rebellion against British rule, notably in Israel. In his autobiography, *For the Life of Me* (London, 1958), p. 264, Robert Briscoe wrote of a visit of the Zionist Vladimir Jabotinsky in 1938: "[He] came to Ireland to learn all he could of the methods we had used in training our young men and boys for the Revolution against England in order to form a physical force movement in Palestine on exactly the same lines as Fianna Eireann and the I.R.A." Although Jabotinsky's biographer, Joseph B. Schechtman, found no evidence of direct influence of the Fianna on Brit Trumpeldor (Betar), he wrote: "There is, however, no doubt in my mind as to the impact of Ireland's revolutionary struggle on the thought and action of the 'maximalist' groups in Revisionism, both in Palestine and in the Diaspora countries. The Irish rebels and martyrs were a powerful source of inspiration for the leadership of those groups. This applies not only to the Betar, but also to 'adult' formations" (letter to the author, January 29, 1965).

16. *Fianna Handbook* (Dublin, 1914), p. 8. Madame reiterated this appeal in writing and in speeches the rest of her life.

17. *Eire*, June 9, 1923.

18. *Fianna*, Christmas, 1914.

19. *United Irishman*, December 1, 1906, carried an account of the inaugural meeting which had been held in Belfast the previous month. Over 100 boys

had been enrolled and Bulmer Hobson elected president. The name had also been used in 1901 by a Gaelic Athletic Association hurling club which met at 32 Lower Abbey Street, Dublin.

20. The officers elected at the first meeting were: Bulmer Hobson, president; Patrick Walsh and Countess Markievicz, Hon. Secs.; J. Robinson and J. Dundun, Hon. Treas.; P. O'Riain, Treas., Camping Fund. The committee members were S. MacCaisin, Con Colbert, G. Harvey, R. Harding, G. Sherry, S. McGarry, and Helena Molony. Michael Lonergan and Eamon Martin were among those who joined that first night. On Tuesday, Con Colbert drilled the first squad.

21. Connolly read the history as the framework and basis of a free Ireland. The conclusions he drew from the experiment were, typically, that "when Ireland does emerge into complete control of her own destinies she must seek the happiness of her people in the extension on a national basis of the social arrangements of Ralahine, or else be but another social purgatory for her poor."

22. *Eire,* August 18, 1923.

23. Macardle, *The Irish Republic,* especially pp. 67–78, has a detailed discussion of this election and its issues. She notes that the new policy was at once more militant than Redmond's towards English Liberals and more conciliatory towards the Irish landowning class. Redmond had modified his demands, he now would be content with an Irish Parliament subservient to the Imperial Parliament. He knew and admitted that he was not speaking for all Nationalist Ireland when he framed so modest a demand, but he believed the section which desired separation to be insignificant.

24. William O'Brien and Desmond Ryan (eds.), *Devoy's Post Bag, 1871–1928* (Dublin, 1953), II, 390–393. John Devoy was born in County Kildare in 1842, moved with his family to Dublin after the Famine, and joined the Fenians when he was nineteen. After a year with the French Foreign Legion, which he regarded as an apprenticeship to his chosen career of fighter for Ireland, he returned to Dublin and served as organizer for the Fenians. (In the United States at this time the leaders of the Young Ireland movement of the 1840's who fled to America after the collapse of their insurrection formed fighting organizations, one of them the Fenian Brotherhood [1855], another the Irish Republican Brotherhood [1858]. The I.R.B. was later supported by a strong Irish-American organization, the Clan na Gael. The name "Fenian" quickly appealed to the newspaper men and caught on, as the name Sinn Fein was to catch on later, with disregard for distinctions the members made among themselves. "I.R.B." and "Fenians" are commonly used interchangeably.) Devoy was imprisoned in Ireland and England for five years, from November, 1865, until December, 1870, when he was amnestied under terms of self-exile. Among the prisoners who arrived with him in New York in January, 1871, was O'Donovan Rossa, another Fenian whose name was to be well-known in both countries. Devoy joined the four-year-old Clan na Gael, one of whose purposes was to continually influence Irish-American opinion against Anglo-American rapprochement. Devoy made his living as a journalist, and after a few years on New York and Chicago newspapers, started his own paper, the *Irish Nation.* In 1903 in New York he founded the weekly *Gaelic American* which he edited

until his death in 1928. For fifty-seven years Devoy was the personification of the Irish freedom movement to his exiled compatriots.

25. Both Sean Connolly and Helena Molony, who was also in the cast, were with the Irish Citizen Army contingent at the City Hall in 1916. Sean Connolly was the leader of the small group, and was subsequently killed in action.

IV

Fianna and Labor

1910-1912

Madame had found her way into the nationalist movement and had thrown herself into its activities. Now she had finished her apprenticeship in rebellion and had become a figure to watch.

Desmond Ryan, a student at Padraic Pearse's school, St. Enda's, remembered going to a meeting of the Drumcondra Branch Sinn Fein about this time. "Two strange figures" remained in his memory: "Sean O'Casey sits in silence at the back of the hall during the lecture, a dour and fiery figure swathed in labourer's garb, for he works on the railways just then. . . . He speaks first, and very fluently and eloquently in Irish, then launches out into a violent Republican oration in English, stark and forceful, Biblical in diction with gorgeous tints of rhetoric and bursts of anti-English Nationalism of the most uncompromising style. . . . Madame de Markievicz sat in the middle of the room, pensive and beautiful with a costly lace collar draping her shoulders, ready to explode into the most unconvincingly blood-thirsty sentiments as the lecture and debate developed, but speaking with a gentle charm to any one who approached her in private. She was, although her fury expressed in such polite accents had a comic aspect, a very courageous woman, for she had broken with all her friends and immediate circle to champion an obscure movement."[1]

Her courage was soon tested by her first brush with the police, and a month later, her first arrest. The events began on March 4, 1911, during the Robert Emmet birthday commemorative meeting at the Rotunda. It was sponsored by the Wolfe Tone Memorial Committee, the organization under which the I.R.B. held its public functions in those days. The speaker was Padraic Pearse, and Major MacBride presided. In the course of his speech Pearse touched on one of his favorite themes: the political guilt of the past is visited on the present. "Dublin will have to do some great act to atone for the shame of not producing a man to dash his head against a stone wall in an effort to rescue Robert Emmet."

Hearing the line, Dr. Patrick McCartan, sitting next to Madame, decided to dash his head against the stone wall of I.R.B. discipline. He had been fretting about ways of getting the Committee to pass a resolution against the forthcoming royal visit of George V to Ireland, but Tom Clarke had told him that the I.R.B. had decided against any resolution on political grounds. Dr. McCartan scribbled a resolution on the back of an envelope, showed it to Madame and told her he was going to propose it. "For God's sake do and I'll second it," she said. Dr. McCartan advised her not to unless nobody else did; he knew that she was not popular with the heads of the I.R.B. Just as the St. James Band concluded their last number, Dr. McCartan jumped up on the platform and proposed his resolution. Tom Clarke, the old Fenian fighter, seconded it, and it was passed with a whoop.[2]

The royal visit was intended to reaffirm the union of Ireland and England. Dr. McCartan's resolution used the visit to unify, temporarily, the quarrelsome groups of nationalists. In the next issue of *Irish Freedom,* all those who were against loyal addresses to the King of England were asked to communicate with Dr. McCartan with the object of forming a Committee to oppose addresses during the royal visit. On March 23 the National Council of Sinn Fein formed the United National Societies Committee, headed by Arthur Griffith. Mrs. Wyse-Power represented the women of Dublin. The committee's first resolution called on the members of the Dublin Corporation not to depart from the stand they took in 1903 when they declined to recognize Edward VII as the accepted sovereign of Ireland. The resolution was supported by Madame and others.

Irish labor also joined the nationalists on the issue. At Foster Place James Connolly and Helena Molony addressed a public meeting of workingmen who adopted resolutions calling for the rejection of the loyalty address. *Sinn Fein* happily commented, "There has not, perhaps for years, been an occasion on which such unanimity has been exhibited by organisations and individuals usually found in opposition to each other."

The United National Societies Committee sparked four months of meetings, deputations, writing, talking, resolving, interfering with canvassers for signatures on loyal addresses, and making any protests in whatever form their ingenuity could contrive. The nationalists were too few in number to prevent the royal visit, but they had the opportunity to practice the technique of a militant minority, publicizing their aims by embarrassing the official representatives of the majority. Madame had a chance to carry out her advice to the Sligo suffragettes: "The sooner we begin to make a row the better. Form societies to agitate and never stop making ourselves disagreeable."

There were always those who disapproved of these tactics, of course. Madame remembered a heated argument over a proposal to hold meetings at street corners all round Dublin, speaking from chairs or egg boxes. Arthur Griffith nervously opposed the idea on the grounds that it was lowering the dignity of Sinn Fein, that they might create trouble, and that they would only be laughed at. He turned to The O'Rahilly, that wise, urbane aristocrat, and said, "Really, O'Rahilly, we must stand on our dignity." With a kindly and persuasive smile The O'Rahilly replied, "Well, if we go on standing on our dignity much longer, we soon won't have anything else left to stand on." The point was carried.[3]

June 22, 1911, was the date of George V's coronation in London. It was also the deliberately-chosen date of a huge nationalist meeting in Dublin when upwards of thirty thousand people crowded Beresford Place and overflowed far up Lower Gardiner Street. The speakers included The O'Rahilly, Major MacBride, Dr. McCartan, Laurence Ginnell, M.P., The Honorable James O'Sullivan of New York, Madame Markievicz, Arthur Griffith, Cathal Brugha, James Connolly, and Alderman Kelly. Although the huge crowd could not have heard all the speeches, they did hear two words shouted again and again that night, "Insurrection" and "Republic." These flaming sentiments were to become more and more commonly heard in Ireland; after the Rising one sometimes felt them to be mere mouthings without feeling, but in 1911 they were fresh and stirring. To preach Republicanism openly then was daring and farsighted. One of the men in the crowd who was close enough to hear what was being said was Eamon de Valera. He later told Dr. McCartan that it was the first time he heard an Irish Republic advocated and that he went home thinking it was a fine ideal but one not likely to be attained.

It was The O'Rahilly who had the idea for what turned out to be one of the National Societies' most successful ploys, a banner calculated to embarrass officialdom. This is Madame's memory of the occasion: "The O'Rahilly took the well known line 'Thou art not conquered yet, dear land,' and suggested that we should inscribe the line on a huge white scroll, and that we should apply to the Paving Committee of the Dublin Corporation for permission to erect poles at the foot of Grafton Street and float the scroll across from side to side of the street." To the ironic delight of nationalist Dublin, the required permission was given and Corporation workmen lifted the pavement and made the holes. "We were busily engaged on the scroll; there was an immense amount of work in it. The O'Rahilly was one of the neatest and best dressed men in Ireland, yet there he was down on his knees on a dusty floor, pencilling out the gigantic letters on the calico for us to fill in with printing ink. When he had finished he started cutting stencils out of the lines and printing from them on strips of white calico, to be cut into badges for distribution. The scroll was finished at last, and dry.

"At 11:30 P.M. a lorry arrived, and we loaded up our burden, and started off in a drizzling rain. There were very few people about; two or three policemen looked at the strange little convoy and then followed us, but they did not interfere. After some trouble the men got the poles firmly planted and the scroll into position. It made a splendid show.

"Of course, the enemy pulled it down, but not till quite late next morning, and it had done its work. Half Dublin had seen it; it had been photographed, and the papers had howled."

Sinn Fein printed and circulated postcards captioned "The Battle of the Poles" which caricatured two overfed policemen carrying away the banner, poles and all. At least one man was arrested for selling the postcards. Bureaucracy has never been noted for its sense of humor.

That evening, July 4, at one of the demonstration meetings held throughout Dublin, Madame invited her first real skirmish with the police. While Sean MacDermott was finishing a speech at Foster Place, she slipped down from the brake they were using as a platform, taking with her a Union Jack they had "captured" from Leinster House lawn. "I had cut it in two," she wrote, "as it was too large to handle. I pushed out into the middle of the crowd, who had made a little circle round me, and struck a match. Breathlessly we waited for the blaze, but bunting won't burn, and though we tried again and again the flag seemed like a thing bewitched, and the matches burned out sadly one by one. Meantime the police had marked me down, and came hurtling through the crowd at me. I hastily tied the flag round my waist as they came up. Then the fun began. The police wanted to get their precious flag; the people thought they wanted to get me. The police seized one end of the flag and began to pull; some of the crowd caught me and pulled as hard as they could, thinking that the police wanted to arrest me. The flag began to slip and slip through my fingers, and at last went with a bang. The police fell back on their side, and the crowd rolled back with me. A mighty cheer went up from the crowd thinking that they had rescued me, and, for a moment, there was a wild scrimmage, and Jack McArdle was arrested. This sobered the crowd, and everything grew suddenly quiet again. I climbed back into the brake and we moved on in an orderly fashion."

"Orderly" is a curious and not very accurate description of what happened next. Madame gave a boy some coins and asked him to buy some paraffin oil. By the time the procession had reached Queen Street he was back with it. Madame soaked the remaining half of the flag, went into the crowd again, and this time succeeded in making a blaze. "It made a fine show, and nobody was left in any doubt as to what we were doing. The police could not get at me, marching in the centre of a wild and excited crowd, and the flag burnt itself out amidst wild shouts of applause." The charred bunting was cut into tiny bits and distributed during the meeting at Smithfield which followed.

Helena Molony was with her and helped with the flag burning. Remembering her brother's stories of breaking windows of shops displaying Union Jacks during the '98 centennial celebrations, Miss Molony had then slipped away, filled her handbag with stones from a building site, and had distributed them to young men she knew in the crowd. She later learned that they did not throw them because the I.R.B. had issued orders against creating a disturbance at that time. After the Smithfield meeting, the procession was reformed and the crowd marched back to the city, keeping time by singing rousing nationalist songs.

They intended to go to Dawson Street and protest in front of the Mansion House, the official residence of Dublin's Lord Mayor. However, when the speakers' wagonnette passed through College Green they found the police had formed a cordon across Nassau Street. At the corner was an optician whose advertising sign was a large pair of spectacles. Each huge lens now displayed a picture of the king and queen. The temptation was too strong for Miss Molony. She happened to have one stone left in the bottom of her handbag and on an impulse she heaved it at the sign. It missed, but made a terrible racket on the corrugated metal which covered the shop windows.

Madame took immediate advantage of the confusion, seized the reins from the hesitating driver, and galloped the horses, speakers' platform and all, up Grafton Street to the corner of St. Stephen's Green. There they found the way blocked again, but she turned into the police cordon, hoping the crowd would break through the line of policemen and sweep down to the Mansion House. Her strategy was sound but she acted too swiftly for the crowd to follow. Only a couple of young men and some boys got through after them. Miss Molony got off the wagonnette and stepped into a doorway. She felt a hand on her shoulder and heard, "I've got her, Chief." She was then escorted to the College Street Police Station. By the time Madame had bailed her out, most of the crowd had gone home.

The following day there were four prosecutions in the police court arising from the nationalist meetings. Seamus O'Duffy, Secretary of the National Council of Sinn Fein, was charged with selling postcards (The Battle of the Poles) without a peddler's license. James McArdle was sentenced to one month's hard labor for setting fire to a flag and assaulting the police. Madame testified she was the one who burned the flag, but the police insisted that he had helped and that in any case he had resisted arrest. James Pike, "late of the *Nation*," was fined 40s. or one month on a charge of disorderly conduct. Madame stated she was close to the defendant who was holding her arm part of the time. She testified that "he only spoke to me and asked me to come away [from St. Stephen's Green]."

To Helena Molony went the honor of being the first woman of her generation to be jailed in Ireland's cause. She was convicted of throwing stones in Grafton Street and fined 40 shillings, or, alternatively, one month's imprisonment. "You will get no money from me, Sir," she said defiantly. This brought a great outburst of cheering from the crowded gallery. Despite this bravura she was deeply ashamed to think she had disgraced the Inghinidhe until Maud Gonne telegraphed congratulations to her from Paris telling her she had been splendid. Miss Molony was enormously pleased at this view of her arrest.

That same day the problem of presenting an address declaring the loyalty of Dublin was settled. The meeting called by the Lord Mayor to reconsider the matter was not held. The council adopted an easy escape from turmoil and by general agreement, there was no quorum. This do-nothing attitude infuriated Madame and others of her temperament, although the result was the one they were agitating so violently for. She wanted to win by positive action rather than by default. However, in 1911, as in 1903, the Dublin Corporation did not present an address of loyalty to the new king.

July 8 was the day the royal visit actually began, and in spite of
the violent scenes the preceding few weeks, the King's actual arrival
in Dublin was comparatively calm. The I.R.B., not yet ready to show
its strength, had decided to postpone the annual pilgrimage to the
grave of Wolfe Tone from the Sunday nearest June 23, until July 8,
which this year would also be a holiday. By this means several hundred
potential firebrands enjoyed songs, speeches, and recitations at Bodenstown instead of creating a row in Dublin.

Madame heartily disapproved of the whole idea, as did the rest of
the Inghinidhe. The men might take orders from the I.R.B., but the
women thought this policy of abstention was quite futile, those absent
were too few to be missed. The most positive action they felt themselves capable of handling on their own was to distribute handbills
along the route of the procession at the moment it was passing. Some
of the Fianna boys helped and they sat up all night printing the handbills on a small press that Madame owned: "Today another English
Monarch visits Ireland. When will Ireland regain the Legislature which
is by everyone granted to be her mere right? Never! as long as Irish
men and women stand in the streets of Dublin to cheer the King of
England and crawl to those who oppress and rob them. God save
Ireland!"

Madame reported that the row created by this wordy protest was
tame, but at least they had done something. "The most adventurous
among us were distributed around Trinity College, the Unionist stronghold, inside the railings of which platforms and seats had been erected;
I was on the corner of Nassau Street with a young man. Most of the
crowd held Union Jacks and were very loyal. We had a black flag, and
as soon as the procession was audible to our listening ears we produced
it and began to hand out our bills to the crowd. We timed it well, for
just as the first carriage came along the row started. An irate old
'gentleman' started whacking me on the back with the stick on which
his flag was mounted, but my back is pretty stiff and the stick broke
almost at once.

"However, it created a disturbance, and the same sort of little disturbances occurred all down the line of the route; so we congratulated
ourselves, for anyone with a spark of national consciousness reading
our bills was startled into seeing the real significance of this Royal visit
and felt ashamed of being where they were. The Unionists were quite
tolerant and quite amused at our audacity. Everything had been so
quiet for so many years that they had come to believe that they had

succeeded in pacifying Ireland. They never dreamed that there was anything more in it than a little spark from the ashes of a dead idea."

The talk at the Castle and among the Countess's society friends and relatives was anything but tolerant and amused, however. There was much clucking and speculating over just what had come over Constance. Why was she acting this way? No Gore-Booth had been a traitor to his class before. It was one thing to show independence and courage on the riding field, quite another to diverge socially, and unheard of for a countess to concern herself with politics. And such politics!

On a hot Sunday afternoon in August, the Inghinidhe and the Socialist Party of Ireland sponsored a demonstration (that favorite entertainment of Dublin) in Beresford Place to welcome Miss Molony and Mr. McArdle on their release from Mountjoy Jail. Miss Molony had actually served only a few days of her month's sentence. (Much to her annoyance, her fine had been paid by someone unknown who turned out to be Anna Parnell, sister of Charles Stewart Parnell. She thought Miss Molony was more valuable out of jail than in. Miss Parnell belonged to an older generation of nationalists and did not understand the tactics of the new breed.) However, when Mr. McArdle was released, the welcoming meeting was held as planned. Madame presided, and about fifty police were placed around the crowd of one thousand. Sean Milroy and Sean McDermott[4] spoke to the resolution of welcome proposed by Francis Sheehy Skeffington, the pacifist. Madame then said that in organizing in the future they should learn how to use their fists; physical force must be met with physical force. The meeting took on an even less pacific tone when Miss Molony began to speak her thanks. She was reported as saying, "There is one man who is not here today. That is Mr. Walter Carpenter. He was sent to gaol for saying that King George was descended from one of the worst scoundrels in Europe. I will go further than that. Not only was King George the descendant of a scoundrel, but he himself is one of the worst scoundrels in Europe."[5]

Immediately a police officer directed his men to advance to the platform. A couple of them seized Miss Molony and one of them tried to arrest Madame. She resisted, and when the constable applied further force, she struck out with her foot, which caught him in the stomach. Another constable grasped her by the left shoulder, and she and Miss Molony were taken to the Store Street Station.

Madame's version of the affair was that when the police took exception to something Miss Molony said, she stood up, and a policeman who was standing in front of the lorry grabbed at her ankles. She shuffled back and another seized her from behind, picked her up and literally threw her into the arms of a policeman standing on the ground in front who luckily caught her, so she was not hurt. She said she was never so taken by surprise in her life, the whole thing was so sudden and unexpected. She remembered only the flashing of batons, the stampeding crowd, some girls who stood firm and spoke to her as she was dragged by two enormous policemen across Beresford Place towards Store Street Station, and one great little Fianna boy, who followed the whole way kicking wildly at the legs of her captors and shouting, "Ah, you devils, ah, you brutes."

Madame was puzzled by her arrest. She thought she had been quite passive and quiet, as indeed she had, for her. The charges against her were resisting arrest, and throwing gravel and dust at the policemen. How she had found enough gravel on the lorry platform to fling was never explained. Miss Molony was ecstatic "with delight, pride, and vanity." She thought she was being charged with high treason and had achieved the same rank as Wolfe Tone. She was sadly deflated when the charge was reduced simply to having made derogatory remarks. Madame and Miss Molony spent a dull and hot afternoon in the police station, encouraged by friends who remained outside cheering. The gallant Sean MacDermott sent the ladies a bunch of grapes and some roses. Nancy Wyse-Power sent in tea. In the evening they were released on bail.

Madame did not want to employ counsel, but was persuaded to do so by Arthur Griffith, who wanted to make it a test case on the question of freedom of speech. Prophetically, he wrote in *Sinn Fein:* "If today a policeman can arrest a speaker because as he alleges the speaker is disrespectful to a monarch, tomorrow the same force will be empowered to attack a meeting and arrest a speaker because in their opinion he is disrespectful to a British Ministry. A very grave issue is involved . . . if the policeman on the spot is to constitute himself the judge of whether a speaker may or may not proceed, then the right of public meeting is lost to people of this country."[6] This was exactly what did happen with increasing frequency in the next several years.

The question was begged in this case, however, and both ladies were released. Madame always thought that the magistrate had decided to give them a sentence but that at the last moment a higher and wiser authority intervened and ordered their release. For once someone may have realized the folly of giving them the publicity that would have resulted from a month in jail.

Nevertheless, the meeting and hearings had considerable publicity in the Dublin papers, and the issue was widely discussed in the nationalist press. *The Sligo Champion* reported the case in full, to the consternation of the Lissadell family. It was the *Champion's* last account of Madame's activities (except for brief mention in 1916) until 1917 when she was given the freedom of the city and hailed as an illustrious daughter of Sligo. The Sligo papers, whether sensitive to the delicate feelings of her family or under pressure of some sort, pulled the curtain on her activities for the next few years as she became more and more articulate and publicly involved with the active freedom movement.

Throughout these busy spring and summer months Madame had continued her work with the Fianna. By this time it was well established and proving the worth of her idea of training boys on military lines. Primarily through Bulmer Hobson and Sean McGarry, the I.R.B. had watched the Fianna's growing strength with interest and from that year on secretly directed Fianna policy. In 1911 a separate Circle of the I.R.B. for Fianna members, known as the John Mitchel Circle, was formed with Con Colbert as Centre and Padraic O'Riain as Secretary. (Both had joined the Fianna that first night in Lower Camden Street.) The Fianna officers from the country who were members attended this Circle when they came to Dublin. The practice was to hold a meeting of the Circle with Hobson as the "Visitor" on the eve of every Ard Fheis (Convention), at which all matters of Fianna policy were decided. The agenda for the Ard Fheis was discussed and decisions were made. Certain resolutions of no great import were left open for free voting, but apart from the discussions arising out of these the convention voice was that of the I.R.B. They were really responsible for policy and administration; any proposals which ran counter to their directive were either outvoted or over-ruled.

Madame continued to be the president, or chief scout, for the rest of her life. She travelled about the country speaking to boys, but it was no longer her Fianna. Officially she was told nothing of the takeover by the I.R.B., but she was aware of it almost at once. She had grown somewhat more astute since the days she had asked Sinn Fein help in establishing the revolutionary boy scouts. But she disapproved strongly of secret societies because she thought they were very bad for a nation's morals and felt that everyone should be brave enough to express his opinions openly. She felt that mediocre men could rise to power in secret societies and control talented young members who were fascinated by the complicated machinery and mystery. She deplored this possibility because the young I.R.B. men whom she admired most were Fianna boys; she accepted it because there was nothing she could do about it. Tact was never one of her weapons, however, and she expressed her disapproval on every possible occasion.

Even the most hidebound of the anti-feminist I.R.B. acknowledged that without her the Fianna would never have been founded successfully. She alone had the vision and she freely gave her money, enthusiasm, and unbounded energy. To the younger boys who knew nothing of the caucus control, she was still the chief, and even to many of the dissembling officers she remained a symbol of courage.

In the autumn of 1911 she went to Cork to organize the Fianna there and to Belfast to inspect the first girls' company. She was re-elected to the Resident Executive of Sinn Fein at the 7th Congress in October, regularly attended the weekly meetings, and somehow had time to find a new house and move to it. She had left Belcamp Park in the early summer and taken a flat for a few months in Lower Mount Street. That fall she and the Count moved to Surrey House on Leinster Road. This was in the suburb of Rathmines, at that time not incorporated in the city of Dublin but very close in, and much more convenient than Belcamp.

Surrey House became synonymous with hospitality and insurrection. It was always open to Fianna boys, any of Madame's republican or labor friends, visiting journalists, plotters of revolution, and convalescents from the rigors of prisons. She rolled up the rugs to simplify housecleaning, and there was always bread and tea and talk. There was a small-platen model printing press on which all kinds of seditious posters, slogans, and handbills were printed to be distributed around town. Some of the Fianna boys were there so much they were called "the Surrey clique" by the others. It was in the garden at Surrey House that they tested a Howth rifle they had acquired. They were satisfied that it worked well, but Madame was not keen on their shooting in her garden. As Madame's work in the movement became more and more public, Surrey House was undoubtedly the best guarded house in Dublin, by detectives on the outside and by Fianna boys on the inside. Later, as the date for the 1916 Rising neared, one French journalist reported that the salon of Madame Markievicz was not a salon, it was an army headquarters.

In the middle of all this activity she still continued her work in the theater with the Count. In April there had been two more performances of *Memory of the Dead,* but their first new play that year was a very successful comedy, *Eleanor's Enterprise,* first produced at the Gaiety on December 11, 1911. Its author was George A. Birmingham (James Owen Hannay). One day when the Count's company was playing at Westport, Madame visited Canon Hannay at the rectory and in the course of the conversation asked him to write a play for her. He professed no interest in the theater, but happened to have a play laid away in a drawer which Madame could have if she liked. The gentle Canon gave it to her with certain reservations, which he later recorded:

"Madame Markievicz was brilliant but most erratic. I was not at all sure that I wanted her to take the leading part in my play. There was a scene in which the heroine, the part which Madame Markievicz played herself, had to emerge from her bedroom in the middle of the night. I was anxious that my name should not be associated with anything *risqué* and I feared that Madame Markievicz would be inclined to wear as little as possible when making her appearance. I wrote her several letters urging the wearing of a dressing-gown, bedroom slippers and other similar garments. She wanted to reduce her clothing to a minimum.

"The correspondence went on for some time. I forget how it ended. But when Madame Markievicz was arrested after the 1916 rebellion her rooms were searched and her papers seized by a young officer who happened to be a son of a parishioner of mine in Westport. He found a bundle of letters tied up and labelled with my name. He was greatly upset about this, for he feared I had involved myself in some treasonable correspondence. I do not know whether anybody in authority read those letters, but can imagine a Chief Secretary being a little puzzled by the correspondence between Madame Markievicz and me entirely about underclothes."[7]

The play is a delightful froth about a visiting do-gooder in the West of Ireland, Eleanor Maxwell, whose idea of helping the peasants is to live with a family, the Finnegans, and teach them cleanliness and economy. Unknown to her, a friend, Dr. Reilly, pays the Finnegans a pound a week for the inconvenience, and undertakes to provide food, furniture, and furnishings for the time she is there. She gradually realizes that everything in the cottage has come from the big house. Thinking it is stolen, she is disenchanted with her whole idea and leaves in disgust. In the last act she accepts Dr. Reilly's marriage proposal and the Finnegans are left happily alone and dirty again.[8]

Alternating with *Eleanor's Enterprise* throughout the rest of the week was *Rival Stars,* written by the Count. Madame and the play were damned with faint praise, "Not wholly to have failed in it is in itself something of an achievement." However, it is of particular interest for its theme, the story of an affectionate husband and wife gradually drifting apart through conflicting interests. The rival stars are Robert Ellis (John Raeburn), a successful artist in Paris, and his wife Dagna (Madame), a writer, Socialist, and philanthropist who has no interest or ambition beyond an overwhelming desire to ameliorate the woes of suffering humanity. The action stems from Robert's jealousy over the friendship of his wife with an intellectual journalist. After many misunderstandings she leaves her husband but her strong maternal feelings overcome her better judgment and she returns to him.

After eleven happy years of marriage it was obvious to both the Count and Countess that her interests were moving more and more definitely from the arts towards political revolution. Her energies were devoted to organizing young men and women for the armed rebellion she hoped was coming. The Count looked with some bemusement on the Fianna and Madame's escapades and went his own way. As a Pole whose family's lands had been annexed to Russia, he was more interested in his own national problems. Although Dublin often gossiped about the extraordinarily handsome producer and his relations in and out of Green Room and pubs, those who knew the Markieviczs scoff at the idea of any estrangement between them. Their lives simply went in different directions. Two years after *Rival Stars* the Count went to the Balkans as a correspondent, and later fought in the war. Like many other families, theirs was divided by the European slaughter.

After spending Christmas at Lissadell, the Count and Countess immediately went into rehearsal for a production of Edward Martyn's *Grangecolman,* which was produced January 25, 1912, at the Abbey. The Count directed the play, Madame played the lead, Catherine Devlin, a neuropathic heroine, a victim of higher education. In the author's stage directions she is described as having "a certain haggard and restless expression. Rather tall and commanding looking with refined features, and is dressed carelessly." It might have been written with Madame in mind. The plot is a melodramatic one in which Mrs. Devlin, jealous of her husband's secretary, disguises herself as a ghost to frighten the girl, and is shot by her rival. Madame was temperamentally suited to play neurotic types, but not even she could succeed in making Mrs. Devlin plausible. *Grangecolman* was followed by *Unseen Kings,* a mythological verse play in one act by Eva Gore-Booth. This was an interpretation of the closing episode of Cuchulain's life and was more a tableau than a play. The company then went to Cork, where, to the delight of the nationalists, it produced *Memory of the Dead,* February 12–17, 1912. The Count left on his regular trip to Poland soon afterwards, and Madame did no more acting for six or seven months.

After a violent and hectic year, 1912 was comparatively quiet for Madame. It was a year for appraising Sinn Fein policy, for taking stock of her own attitudes, and for continuing constructive work with the Fianna. Sides were being taken for a strong stand on labor issues; Home Rule within the next few years seemed almost a certainty; even the suffragettes seemed to be making progress. It was a year of guarded optimism, and hope which was to prove unfounded.

Sinn Fein was not happy with the latest Home Rule measure being debated in Parliament, and throughout the spring and summer there were many protest meetings. At the convention of the Sinn Fein branches held in Dublin in April to consider the proposed bill, Madame was one of the many speakers against it. The main objections were that the British Parliament would have veto power in the proposed Irish parliament, that the Irish parliament was denied mineral rights, that taxes were not collected by the Irish parliament, and that the British Parliament held the right to tax the Irish without their consent. The convention recommended wide publicity be given to their objections.[9]

At the other pole of political opinion there were those, particularly in northern Ireland, who were afraid that the Home Rule Bill was too liberal. They began to organize military opposition to it. In Ulster in September a solemn League and Covenant drawn up by Lord Londonderry, Sir Edward Carson, Captain Craig and others, was signed by thousands. They pledged to refuse to recognize the authority of an Irish parliament in the event the Home Rule Bill was passed. In December the Ulster Volunteers were formed and proceeded to train in the use of arms. These were not boy scouts, but a militia. The fact that the British authorities did not interfere with the Unionists ultimately necessitated the formation of similar citizen armies by the separatists in southern Ireland a year later.

The suffragettes in the south did not approve of the Home Rule Bill, either. On June 1, 1912, Madame lent her support at a mass meeting in the Antient Concert Rooms of Irish women, the first of its kind in Ireland.[10] They demanded the Home Rule Bill be amended to include the vote for women. Women had for some time been eligible for election as Poor Law Guardians or District Councillors, and now they were eligible to be elected County Councillors. The gains women were making were small and confined only to local government, but their spirits were high and they hoped that by continued protests they would eventually be recognized as full citizens. The suffragettes were becoming increasingly militant. Daisy Forbes-Robertson, Madame's friend from Paris days, was one who chained herself to the Parliament railings. She was just over four feet tall and her spirit delighted Madame, but she was incensed at the thought of a towering English bobby lifting her tiny friend and carrying her away. In 1914 Miss Forbes-Robertson's arm was broken in the melee which followed a meeting illegally addressed by Sylvia Pankhurst.

When Asquith visited Dublin on July 18, 1912, Mrs. Sheehy Skeffington and other Irish suffragists paraded with posters to protest his delay in giving votes to women. The women were attacked by a mob allegedly led by stalwarts of the Ancient Order of Hibernians, and several, including Madame, were hurt. There was much press criticism when two English suffragettes, Gladys Evans and Mary Leigh, set fire to the Theatre Royal where Asquith was to speak. Dublin followed the case avidly; the Irish suffragettes admired the English women's pluck. After a noisy trial, the two were sentenced to five years' penal servitude at Mountjoy.

In August, at the Fianna Ard Fheis, Madame succeeded in overriding the plans of the I.R.B. circle and in carrying a proposal to open the organization to girls. But it led to a hassle and much delay and obstruction on the part of the Fianna council. A girls' company had been formed in Belfast the preceding year, but their official affiliation was debated. Eventually the point was carried but was never enthusiastically put into effect, and there were never more than a few girls in the Fianna. Mr. Sheehy Skeffington, editor of the feminist *Irish Citizen*, commented: "We note with interest this display of anti-feminist spirit in the ranks of the most advanced Nationalists. We feel sure all our readers, whatever their opinions of Fianna na hEireann will wish success to Countess de Markievicz in her struggle to obtain equal rights for her sex in an organisation which owes so much to her efforts."

The Independent Theatre Company produced no more new plays that year, but in September and October, after the Count returned from a visit home, it took *Eleanor's Enterprise* to Tralee, Cork, and Liverpool, and played another week in Dublin. By the end of the year the Count had dissolved the Independent Theatre Company, and with Evelyn Ashley formed the Dublin Repertory Theatre. Its purpose was to bring to Dublin the best of the new European plays. They felt too much emphasis was being placed on strictly Irish plays and problems.

The first appearance of the new company was in April, 1913, in François Coppée's *For the Crown*. It was not new to Dublin, Forbes-Robertson had previously played it with success. The Count's influence in its choice is evident. The play is set in the fifteenth century when the Turks overran the Balkan peninsula and sought by atrocities to subdue the Christians. Madame played a minor role. The Count produced a more important play in May when the company made its second appearance with Shaw's *The Devil's Disciple*. The house was packed, and Breffni O'Rorke in the title role was vivid and spirited, but Madame played Judith Anderson with indifferent success. Her acting was not improving with experience. This was Madame's last appearance in the theater, although she retained an interest in drama and later wrote a few plays herself. By now she had moved onto the larger stage of Dublin labor strife, and it was here that she played her first really successful role.

Prophetically, the Dublin Repertory Theatre produced John Galsworthy's *Strife* the week before the Irish Transport and General Workers' Union opened its own version of labor conflict on August 26, 1913.

NOTES TO CHAPTER IV

1. Desmond Ryan, *Remembering Sion* (London, 1934), p. 82.

2. This incident and others in which he was personally involved were recorded by Dr. McCartan in memoranda now in the National Library of Ireland.

3. *Eire,* July 21, 1923. "*The* prefixed to a family name corresponds to the Gaelic designation to denote the senior living member in direct descent from the chieftain of the clan" (Macardle, p. 95). Yeats suggested that it should be merited before it was used: "Sing of the O'Rahilly,/Do not deny his right;/Sing a 'the' before his name;/Allow that he, despite all those learned historians,/Established it for good;/He wrote out that word himself,/He christened himself with blood" ("The O'Rahilly," *Collected Poems,* p. 354).

Madame's memories of the king's visit were published in a series of articles in *Eire* in 1923: June 16, July 14, July 28, and August 4. Miss Molony also recalled the occasion in conversations with the author in Dublin in 1963 and 1964.

4. Many of his friends thought that Sean MacDermott's attack of infantile paralysis soon afterwards was caused by his working for Ireland day and night. He recovered but always had to use a walking stick.

5. Miss Molony remembered her speech somewhat differently, something to the effect that, "We don't indulge in personalities, but as a symbol, he was the greatest scoundrel in Europe."

6. *Sin Fein,* August 12, 1911.

7. George A. Birmingham, *Pleasant Places* (London, 1934), pp. 170–172.

8. Sean Connolly and Helena Molony were extremely successful as the Finnegan father and mother, and a scene between them was played as a separate concert item for years. Nellie Gifford, who was with Madame in St. Stephen's Green in 1916, also had a small part. The play was revived in London in 1923 as *Send for Dr. O'Grady,* with Arthur Sinclair playing Connolly's part and Margaret Bannerman in Madame's. Under the latter title it was also published as a novel.

9. *Sinn Fein,* April 17, 1912. In an appeal for money to pay for the propaganda, signed by Arthur Griffith, president; Jennie Wyse-Power and Thomas Kelly, vice-presidents, Sinn Fein political policy was spelled out: "By its compliance with Mr. Redmond's appeal for a free hand in his present negotiations with the British Government, Sinn Fein has made it impossible for any critic to call it an obstructionist policy. On the contrary, all sincere Irishmen, whether they agree with us or not, must admit that Sinn Fein is qualified to do good and useful work for our common country in fighting the emigration evil, in supporting Irish manufactures, in extending the language of Ireland, and above all, in upholding the national ideal. Even on the very lowest grounds of policy, it is of the utmost importance that during the consideration of the Home Rule Bill there should be in Ireland a strong organisation prepared to consider this question from the Irish point of view, unhampered by treaties or negotiations with English statesmen and not crippled through lack of adequate financial resources.

"No measure of limited self-government for Ireland which is honest and workable will receive opposition from Sinn Fein, but on the other hand no such measure will be accepted by it as a national settlement. Sinn Fein is based on the inalienable right of the people of Ireland to national independence. That right it will continue to assert irrespective of the success or failure of the Home Rule movement" (*Sinn Fein,* January 18, 1912).

10. Miss Mary Hayden was the chairman, and on the platform were women whose names were familiar to all nationalists in Dublin: Dr. Kathleen Lynn, Miss Delia Larkin, Mrs. Cruise O'Brien, and Miss Gavan Duffy.

V

Strike

1913

There are reformers who, when faced with problems which prove insoluble by threats, argument, compromise, arbitration, or passive resistance, reluctantly turn to rebellion as the only practical solution. There are others, such as Madame Markievicz, for whom rebellion is a revelation of their own destiny. All their talents, impulses, and creativity thrust them towards violence. These, when they are sane, must labor to define the terms under which rebellion is viable. Often they are great publicists of rebellion. Even before their reasons are clear in their minds, they try to awake similar impulses in others.

By 1911, Madame was a woman feeling her way, looking for a policy, not a principle. She was ready for anything she personally might have to sacrifice or endure for Ireland's independence. Quite suddenly she realized that what was lacking in Sinn Fein policy was justice for the laborers.

Sinn Fein advocated Irish manufacture developed by Irish capital and Irish men but little cared that the industry might be built up with cheap Irish labor. Its models were the Dublin employers who used national material, but many of these were no better than rack-renting landlords and held nineteenth-century attitudes, hiring labor as cheaply as possible and ignoring the human misery involved. It came as a discovery to Madame that Irish labor could be organized along national lines and enlisted to work for Ireland's political independence from England at the same time workers were gaining their own economic independence. It was Jim Larkin whom she first heard voicing this revolutionary idea and James Connolly who clarified it.

Jim Larkin was a spellbinding speaker, the most dynamic ever heard in Dublin. He had the gift of stirring his audiences to action and of giving them confidence in him and what he was doing. Most important of all, he gave them confidence in themselves. A fighter by instinct and training, he inspired strong emotions in anyone who had any dealings with him. He was often worshipped by the workers and just as often hated by the employers. Some of the union officials mistrusted his every move, others followed his lead unquestioningly. But no one ever discounted his genius in giving the workers courage.

He flashed onto the Dublin labor scene in 1908 and was immediately the center of violent controversy. He was Liverpool Irish, had worked on the docks and in unions there, and then gone to Glasgow as an official of the National Union of Dock Laborers. In 1907 he went to Belfast to organize the dock laborers. With all the power of his gigantic personality he built the union, won a great strike which paralyzed Belfast for over two months, and became the idol of the slum districts. In 1908 Larkin was called to Dublin by the carters who were badly organized and shockingly underpaid.

A public health survey published in 1913 by Sir Charles Cameron shows that Dublin was overripe for labor agitation. The facts are shocking. The death rate in the city of Dublin in the previous decade was 24.6 per 1000, as compared to 13.6 in London during the same time. In Dublin 43.3 per cent of the deaths were in workhouses, hospitals, lunatic asylums, and prisons; in London 18 per cent were in those public monuments to poverty. "But the gravest cause of the unhealthiness of Dublin is its tenement houses," Sir Charles said. The estimated population of Dublin was 306,573: 21,000 families were living in single rooms (70,000 persons); 6,000 people lived seven to a single room; another 9,000 lived six to a room. Of their dwellings, 1,518 units housing 15,063 persons were unfit for human occupation. About the same number, 1,516 units housing 27,052 persons, were considered structurally sound, while 2,288 houses sheltering 22,701 persons were so decayed as to be on the border line of being unfit for human habitation.[1]

Men were working 70 hours a week for 14 shillings. (Day laborers often were paid in pubs, and by custom had to buy their foremen drinks in order to be assured of work the next day.) Women were even worse off, many working 90 hours for 5 shillings.[2] Whole families were living on 10 shillings a week at a time when 22 shillings bought minimum food and shelter. Dublin showed the signs of almost oriental poverty, tuberculosis was like a plague, and prostitution was flagrant but officially ignored. Even Larkin, who was raised in some of the worst slums in England, found those of Dublin "putrid."

In December, 1908, Larkin was dismissed from his position as organizer of the Dock Workers' Union. But having won the allegiance of the Dublin working class, he founded the Irish Transport and General Workers' Union. He was brought to court on a charge of misappropriating funds, but he argued that he had paid over money in hand to the Dublin headquarters instead of to the English headquarters of the Transport Workers Union for which it had technically been collected. Larkin was sent to jail for three months in 1910. Like many popular men jailed for fighting a good fight, he was hailed a hero, and the jail term immeasurably enhanced his power. He used it to build up his union. Since Dublin was a depot rather than a manufacturing city, most of its laborers were involved in the movement of goods, and hence were potential members of the union. Whether he was truly a socialist, a syndicalist, or simply a powerful, anarchic personality, no one was sure, but everyone looked on him as a force, which they called "Larkinism."

Madame had read about Jim Larkin. His idea that Irish labor must not be controlled from England was illuminating and filled her with "hope, admiration, sympathy and delight." Although she had not met him when she read of the meeting to celebrate his release, she made up her mind to bicycle in from Belcamp Park to join in the welcome she felt was due to him. It was an important day for her. It brought her firmly into the labor movement and friendship with Jim Larkin and later with James Connolly. It took her into the Irish Citizen Army, to St. Stephen's Green on Easter Monday, 1916, and in 1919 to the cabinet of the Irish Republic as Minister for Labour, the first woman cabinet minister in western Europe.

Characteristically, she remembered her feelings the first time she heard him better than anything he said. "It was a scorching day when I arrived, and Beresford Place was already packed, but, luckily, a friend of mine, Mr. McGowan, saw me hot and weary in the dense crowd and brought me up on to Larkin's platform, a lorry, where I could rest in peace.

"Sitting there, listening to Larkin, I realised that I was in the presence of something that I had never come across before, some great primeval force rather than a man. A tornado, a storm-driven wave, the rush into life of spring, and the blasting breath of autumn, all seemed to emanate from the power that spoke. It seemed as if his personality caught up, assimilated, and threw back to the vast crowd that surrounded him every emotion that swayed them, every pain and joy that they had ever felt made articulate and sanctified. Only the great elemental force that is in all crowds had passed into his nature for ever.

"Taller than most men, every line of him was in harmony with his personality. Not so much working man as primeval man. Man without the trickeries and finickiness of modern civilisation, a Titan who might have been moulded by Michaelangelo or Rodin, such is Jim Larkin, and this force of his magically changed the whole life of the workers in Dublin and the whole outlook of trade unionism in Ireland. He forced his own self-reliance and self-respect on them; forced them to be sober and made them class conscious and conscious of their nationality.

"From that day I looked upon Larkin as a friend, and was out to do any little thing that I could do to help him in his work, but it was only much later that I got a chance to do so."[3]

In the meantime she saw him frequently because a branch of the Fianna and his Union had separate rooms in the same house at 10 Beresford Place. He was very friendly to the boys and often loaned his bigger room to them. When the Union bought the large building, which he christened "Liberty Hall," a Fianna sluagh had a room there.

Madame was drawn even closer to the Union by James Connolly, who saw a relationship between women's rights and labor. He was Edinburgh Irish, had joined the British army when he was 14, and was stationed in Ireland for the next seven years. He then married a Dublin girl and worked in Edinburgh, where he joined the Socialist League and served his apprenticeship in socialism. He returned to Dublin in 1896 and founded the Irish Socialist Republican Party. It was not successful, and he went to America in 1903, where he worked with the growing labor movement, mainly in New York and New Jersey, and edited an Irish-American socialist paper, *The Harp.* He returned to Ireland in 1910 to work for the Socialist Party of Ireland, soon went to Belfast where he joined the Irish Transport Workers' Union, and did most of his work there until called to Dublin in August, 1913.[4] James Connolly was a man of deep sympathies, very articulate about them, skillful, and ultimately more important to Irish labor, women's suffrage, and nationalism than the tumultuous Larkin.

In September, 1911, Madame spoke at a meeting of the newly-formed Women Workers' Union. Also on the platform was her friend Mrs. Sheehy Skeffington, an active suffragette who was always interested in any organization to better women's lot. Madame's appeal was her old one, the reiteration of her conviction that only in organization was there strength. She said that the purpose of the meeting was to form the women workers into an army of fighters. By joining the

Union, they would add to their own strength and Ireland's, they would get better wages, and as an organization work towards getting the vote as well. When Union men interfered at the rowdy meetings in Dublin to protect the suffragettes from the hooliganism attributed to the Ancient Order of Hibernians, the women and the Union were brought closer together.

In November, 1911, Connolly organized the textile mill-girls in Belfast. *The Irish Citizen* called him "the soundest and most thorough going feminist among all the Irish labour men. When the Dublin meetings of the Irish Women's Franchise League were attacked he travelled especially from Belfast to speak to them in defence of the right of free speech."

In *The Re-Conquest of Ireland,* Connolly has a chapter titled simply "Woman" in which he correlates the cause of labor with that of women. He pays glowing tribute to the intelligence and capability of women. It is no wonder they adored him. "In Ireland the women's cause is felt by all Labour men and women as their cause." He saw the paradox that the militant feminist ultimately brought peace by disturbing it: "The militant women, who, without abandoning their fidelity to duty, are yet teaching their sisters to assert their rights, are re-establishing a sane and perfect balance that makes more possible a well-ordered Irish nation."

The year 1913 was one of action for Dublin labor, for the nationalists, and for the politicians. It was the year of the great general strike and lockout in Dublin. There were months of bitter labor strife, of ineffective resistance to police force, and eventually the formation of a Citizen Army. On the national and political scenes it was a year of resorting to the threat of force on the Home Rule issue. In the north the Ulster Volunteers were arming and preparing to fight against the separation of Ireland from England. In the south the Irish Volunteers were preparing to fight for the separation of Ireland. For Madame the year marked the completion of the break with her class and with many of her former friends.

The year started fairly quietly for Madame. She was carrying on with her usual nationalist activities, was busy with the new repertory company, and was following with increasing interest the course labor was taking. There was labor trouble all over Ireland. Even Madame's brother had been involved when the shirt factory in Sligo in which he took so much interest received goods carried by a non-union carter. The goods were eventually taken back to the quay and removed under union regulations to the factory. As a protest against being dragged into a dispute to which he considered himself no party, he paid all hands a week's wages in lieu of notice. Within the week he relented, reopened the factory, and the hundred girls employed there went back to work. Sir Josslyn had always been on good terms with the Trades Council in Sligo, often opening the grounds at Lissadell for outings and receiving delegates to conventions there. But he heartily disapproved of Jim Larkin and his methods, and particularly of the policy of the sympathetic strike which was the fundamental thesis of the Irish Transport and General Workers' Union. This policy was crystallized in the Union's affirmation, "An injury to one is the concern of all."

James Connolly articulated the Union's position. "It is the recognition by the Working Class of its essential unity. . . . In practical operation it means that when any body of workers is in conflict with their employers, that all other workers should co-operate with them in attempting to bring that particular employer to reason by refusing to handle his goods . . . he and his should be made 'tabu,' treated as unclean, as 'tainted,' and therefore likely to contaminate all others."[5]

In August began the great strike and lockout in Dublin that lasted through months of bitter street battles, near starvation for thousands of workers, and unimaginable misery from cold and illness during the winter for their families. Conditions in Dublin were incredibly uncivilized for thousands of her citizens at the beginning of the strike; it seems inconceivable that they could have become worse. Yet in many cases, before a fundamental will to survive forced them back to work on the employers' terms in the early months of 1914, their level of existence sank even lower.

During the early summer of 1913 the I.T. and G.W.U. had been active among the employees of the Dublin United Tramway Company, who were entirely unorganized. As a result, the Company dismissed any employee who was known to have joined the Union. The Tramway Company was one of many holdings of William Martin Murphy, a soft-spoken, determined financier who was probably Ireland's richest man and the acknowledged leader of its employers. Murphy made it clear that he would refuse to recognize or negotiate with the Union. On the basis of the clearcut, unequivocal issue of the right of the workers to organize, the great struggle began.

The Union chose the busiest time of the year in Dublin, the opening of the annual Horse Show, to demonstrate its strength. On Tuesday, August 26, at 9:40 A.M., the tram drivers and conductors stopped work, put on their union badges (the red hand of Ulster), got off and walked away, leaving bewildered passengers on the stalled trams. The Dublin Trades Council voted unanimous support of the I.T. and G.W.U., an affiliated union. Martin Murphy immediately locked out about sixty men and boys employed by him and Charles Eason, a wholesale newsagent. Retaliation was followed by counter-retaliation. Soon about 400 employers and much of Dublin's labor force were involved.

On the opening evening of the strike, Jim Larkin, in one of his almost nightly meetings at Beresford Place, announced that there would be a demonstration in O'Connell Street the following Sunday. He concluded this speech with the first call for a citizen army, though the idea was only germinal and would not flower for another ten weeks. Larkin said that police brutality had been shown against strikers and he advised his friends and supporters to take Sir Edward Carson's advice to the men of Ulster. If Carson would call on the people of Ulster to arm, he (Larkin) would call upon those present to arm.

For this speech Larkin was arrested and charged with sedition. He was in Police Court for a long hearing on August 28 and 29, along with P. T. Daly, Thomas Lawlor, W. P. Partridge, and William O'Brien, other union officials. They were released on bail and escorted by a procession of their friends to Liberty Hall, where Larkin spoke from a window on the right to hold public meetings. E. G. Swifte, Chief Divisional Magistrate, had issued a proclamation banning the meeting scheduled for O'Connell Street the following Sunday. While the crowd in Beresford Place cheered, Larkin dramatically set fire to his copy of the proclamation. Leaning over the crowd, his great arms thrashing the air, he shouted that he never attended an illegal meeting—the people were the law and the people were there, and he was glad to be with them. "I will be in O'Connell Street on Sunday next, dead or alive, and if I am dead, I hope you will carry me there."

After that Friday night promise to be on O'Connell Street on Sunday, Larkin disappeared from Liberty Hall, while Dublin waited edgily. Unknown to the police, he went to Surrey House, and there Madame and her friends prepared him for his appearance. The most feasible and most theatrical solution was to disguise Larkin in some way, get him undetected to O'Connell Street and to a vantage point from which he could address the crowd which would surely be there. They decided he would go to a leading hotel disguised as an aged clergyman from the country. He would be escorted by a young lady pretending to be a relation who could do all the talking so the old man would not have to speak. On Saturday night a reservation was telephoned to the Imperial Hotel, asking for rooms for Reverend Donnelly and his niece, Miss Donnelly, for the following night. The Imperial Hotel was in the center of the city at Nos. 22 and 24 O'Connell Street, the fourth building from the corner of Sackville Place (now incorporated in Clery's department store). The hotel had four stories, with four windows on each floor facing the city's busiest street, and a balcony across the second floor which was admirably suited to Larkin's purpose. To add zest to the enterprise, the Imperial was owned by his antagonist, Martin Murphy.

Tension had continued to mount as the employers pressed some of their office and administrative personnel into service as tram drivers and conductors and tried to maintain some sort of tram service. Attacks on the "blacklegs" brought savage counterattacks from both foot and mounted police, especially near Liberty Hall and in the tenement areas adjoining Lower Abbey Street on the north side of the river Liffey, and Great Brunswick Street (now Pearse Street) on the south side.

Anxiety seems to have made the police ferocious. Many alleged they "had drink taken" before the baton charges. Even people who were taking no part in the fighting were victims of the police frenzy. One Union member, James Nolan, on his way along Eden Quay to Liberty Hall to pay his subscription, had his head so badly fractured by police batons that he died from his wounds on Sunday morning. Robert Monteith was understandably outraged when his fourteen-year-old daughter was brought home from a shopping trip with her long golden hair clotted with blood. She had ducked into the doorway of a dairy shop when she heard the cry, "Baton Charge," but a tall constable pulled her out and clubbed her on the top of her head. "This became a personal matter," Monteith said, "and I managed to square accounts within a week." He was not alone; there were personal vendettas with police all over Dublin.

On that Sunday afternoon there were perhaps more than the usual number of people strolling up and down O'Connell Street, the main street of Ireland's capital city. On a fine Sunday in August there were many sightseers. Some were undoubtedly drawn to the vicinity to see how Larkin would keep his promise and strolled the street looking for him. However, William O'Brien had organized a march from Beresford Place to Croydon Park, the labor union estate in Fairview, three miles away, so a large percentage of the union members were not present. In the interests of peace, the officials had decided to abandon the O'Connell Street meeting and take their members out of the vicinity.

At Surrey House Helena Molony was busy making up Larkin for his role. Madame outfitted him in a morning coat, striped trousers, and black patent boots belonging to the Count. Fortunately, they were both large men and the coat was a fairly good fit. The Count entered into the spirit of the masquerade and advised on the costuming and makeup, which included a beard. They also dressed up the niece, played by Nellie Gifford, a friend of Madame's and one of a prominent Dublin family whose several daughters were all involved in the national movement.[6]

At 12:45 P.M. a taxicab pulled up in front of the Imperial Hotel and two passengers got out. The well-dressed young lady was very solicitous of the bent, shuffling, old man whom she was helping into the building. The hotel porter met the taxicab and carried in a lady's cabin trunk and a gentleman's portmanteau, both marked, it was noticed afterwards, with the initial "M."

One of the guests at the hotel was a member of parliament, Handel Booth, who was in Dublin with his wife for the Horse Show. As he sat with Mrs. Booth and friends in the dining room he noticed an elderly man, apparently a foreigner from the cut of his coat, who quietly walked to the window and stepped to the balcony. It was the last quiet moment in the hotel that day. Suddenly Larkin threw back his shoulders and began to shout to those in the street below that he had kept his promise. More than a dozen policemen who were in the near vicinity rushed into the hotel and converged on him before he had time to say more than a few sentences. But there was no doubt on O'Connell Street that Larkin was there and the passers-by stopped to look and listen. He was pulled back from the window by the policemen but made no resistance. Soon Larkin, bareheaded, smiling triumphantly, and still wearing the beard, was brought out of the hotel by twenty police, all with drawn batons.

The Count and Countess Markievicz had driven down with Sidney Gifford and Helena Molony to see what would happen. There were no unusual crowds, so they went down O'Connell Street and pulled the car up at Prince's Street, opposite the Imperial. They were there in time to see Larkin on the balcony before he disappeared into the hotel. A friend recognized Madame and called on her for a speech. She jumped down off the car and crossed the street just as Larkin came out of the hotel with his police escort.

At this point the comedy the Markieviczs were directing turned into mass terror. "I ran across in front of him and shook his hand, saying, 'Good-bye, good luck,'" Madame recalled. "As I turned to pass down O'Connell Street the inspector on Larkin's right hit me on the nose and mouth with his clenched fist. I reeled against another policeman, who pulled me about, tearing all the buttons off my blouse, and tearing it out all round my waist. He then threw me back into the middle of the street, where all the police had begun to run, several of them kicking and hitting at me as they passed."

What she saw was the beginning of the terrible baton charge. "I saw a woman trying to get out of the way. She was struck from behind on the head by a policeman with his baton. As she fell her hat slipped over her face, and I saw her hair was grey. She had a little book, which fell out of her left hand as she fell. I saw a barefooted boy with papers hunted and hit about the shoulders as he ran away. I shall never forget the look on his face as he turned when he was struck.

"I could not get out of the crowd of police, and at last one hit me a back-hand blow across the left side of my face with his baton. I fell back against the corner of a shop, when another policeman started to seize me by the throat, but I was pulled out of the crowd by some men, who took me down Sackville Place and into a house to stop the blood flowing from my nose and mouth, and to try and tidy my blouse.

"I noticed that the policeman who struck me smelt very strongly of stout, and that they all seemed very excited. They appeared to be arranged in a hollow square, and to be gradually driving the people into the street, and then closing in on them and batoning them. I tried to go up, down, and across O'Connell Street, but each time I was put back by them into the crowd of charging police. The people were all good-tempered and there would have been no row. They were also out-numbered by the police round about where I was."[7]

The ugly situation developed so quickly that it is difficult to establish a sequence of events. As Larkin stepped out onto the balcony and the police recognized him, police cordons in Abbey Street and Prince's Street rushed out into O'Connell Street and formed a long line extending from the post office to the O'Connell monument. Before anyone realized what was happening, a baton charge was in progress. People going home after mass at the Marlborough pro-cathedral were turning into O'Connell Street, and as the baton charge began, numbers of church goers who had unwittingly swelled the crowds were swept up into the wild scene. The grey-haired woman with the book in her hand was perhaps one of those returning home. Panicked crowds jammed into side streets where cordons of police had orders to let no one by. Screaming and pushing they were beaten by angry police.

Count Markiewicz, not entirely sympathetic with the cause of labor but an intelligent man, and, as an artist and author, a trained observer, saw it all. "There was no sign of excitement, no attempt at [Larkin's] rescue, and no attempt at a breach of the peace, when a savage and cruel order for a baton charge—unprecedented in such circumstances in any privileged country—was given to the police. It was equalled, perhaps, by the bloody Sunday events in St. Petersburg. Scores of well-fed metropolitan policemen pursued a handful of men, women and children running for their lives before them. Round the corner of Prince's street I saw a young man pursued by a huge policeman, knocked down by a baton stroke, and then, whilst bleeding on the ground, batoned and kicked, not only by this policeman, but by his colleagues lusting for slaughter. I saw many batoned people lying on the ground, senseless and bleeding. When the police had finished their bloodthirsty pursuit, they returned down the street batoning the terror-stricken passers-by who had taken refuge in the doorways. It was, indeed, a bloody Sunday for Ireland.

"Photographs taken by the Press representatives will bear irrefutable testimony to the truth of my statement. I at once sought out Sir James Dougherty (the Under Secretary for Ireland) and told him what I had witnessed. I felt it my duty also to inform the foreign Press. No human being could be silent after what I saw, and the public should insist on a sworn inquiry."[8]

Baton charges were not new in Dublin but had been part of the scene for thirty years.[9] The extraordinary force of police in Dublin, whose purpose seemed to be to intimidate, terrorize and assault the people they should serve, was often remarked by visitors of all nationalities. The O'Connell Street charge in 1913 was particularly nasty, involving as it did many persons unconcerned with the events provoking it. It publicized the cause of labor, however, and made obvious the distinction between classes; it haunted the memory of the workers and convinced them they should arm.

One of the few who took part in the drama on O'Connell Street who escaped unruffled was Larkin's "niece," Nellie Gifford. Her sister, Sidney, was outside and had avoided being clubbed by standing perfectly still. After the excitement had died down somewhat, she and Miss Molony decided to go back to the hotel to see what had happened to Nellie. A detective talked to them but they would give him no information and were persuaded to leave. Sidney was convinced that Nellie was still there, so she went back. She asked if the investigator would take her word about Miss Donnelly's real name. Assured that indeed he would, she said, "She's really Miss Murphy. Her father owns this hotel." Sensing disbelief, she quickly left. Still not knowing what to do she enlisted the aid of Francis Sheehy Skeffington and then herself went along to Surrey House. To her surprise, there was Nellie. The detectives had given up trying to find out her name, she had picked up her handbags and left. She gave the bags to a friend she happened to meet on the way so she could be freer to elude the detectives she thought were following her, and so made her roundabout way to Surrey House.

Four hundred and thirty-three civilians were treated in hospitals that weekend; how many were doctored at home is not recorded. About 45 police were injured.

That same Sunday James Nolan, who had been batoned Saturday night on his way to Liberty Hall, died. His funeral on Wednesday was the occasion for a huge demonstration of the workers, eleven thousand of whom walked behind his coffin to Glasnevin. Many of the men, women, and even children had bandaged heads. Among the prominent citizens who followed the coffin were the Lord Mayor, Keir Hardie (the long-time friend of the suffragettes and the first member of parliament for labor), Madame, Peter and Delia Larkin (Jim's brother and sister), Helena Molony, Councillor Briscoe, and P. T. Daly.

The following day, John Byrne died. His was the second death directly resulting from the Saturday night baton charge. The day before James Nolan's funeral, still another worker had died, not from batoning but in the collapse of the tenement house in which his family lived. One of the shames of Dublin is the regularity with which the neglected houses of its poor collapse. In this case two tenements in Church Street in which sixteen families lived fell down, causing at least five deaths. One of the victims was a seventeen-year-old boy, Eugene Salmon, who had saved six members of his family before being buried in the falling debris when he went back to get the last child. He was a union member locked out of Jacob's at the time. He was considered another martyr to the greed of the employers and landlords.

Liberty Hall was draped in black and displayed a sign "In Memory of Our Murdered Brothers."

James Connolly had been called to Dublin from his job as organizer in Belfast when the strike began. He was arrested on Saturday afternoon and sentenced to three months in jail because he was in Beresford Place when Jim Larkin burned the proclamation. He soon decided there was too much to be done outside to wait out his sentence, and on Sunday, September 7, he went on hunger strike. On the seventh day orders came from the Lord Lieutenant that he must be released under the terms of the recently-enacted "Cat and Mouse Act," which meant he was liable for imprisonment again when he recovered his health. The vice-regal car was sent round for him and he was taken to Surrey House where he rested for a few days.[10] Madame's home was becoming a sanctuary.

At a Foster Place meeting that Horse Show Week Madame denounced with spirit and conviction the Cat and Mouse Act as a barbarous piece of legislation unworthy of any civilized country. Her sister, Eva, by this time well-known for her work among the textile workers of Manchester, was in Dublin the following week and spoke at a meeting with Mrs. Sheehy Skeffington. By mid-September the regular meetings were largely attended, and to emphasize further the relations between the Irish Women's Franchise League and the I.T. and G.W.U., the gatherings were transferred from Foster Place to Beresford Place. Madame spoke there of the moral and educational value of the vote and reiterated what a large factor it was in the mental growth and social development of the men of the community. She pointed out that there were three great movements going on in Ireland at that time—the National Movement, the Women's Movement, and the Industrial Movement. They were all really the same movement in essence, for they were all fighting the same fight, for the extension of human liberty.

By September 5 the fight was not going well. A general lockout of Transport Workers had been effectively declared by the Dublin employers. The situation was worsening.

A Dublin society magazine complained that "as the industrial atmosphere has approached fever heat the social barometer has fallen to zero; Dublin is plumbing the lowest depths of the dead season." The only social event worthy of note was the opening of an exhibition of paintings by Frances Baker, Count Markievicz, and AE.

Meanwhile the Markieviczs were eased out of the theatrical company they had formed, and The Dublin Repertory Theatre was boycotted by labor after it "resolved to victimize our good friend, the Countess, for daring to identify herself with the cause of the locked out workers of Dublin." The story is told in a series of letters written by the co-directors, Count Markiewicz and Evelyn Ashley, who sided with David Telford, chairman of the Gaiety Theatre Company. The first, dated September 25, 1913, is from Mr. Telford to Mr. Ashley and spells out the attitude the company took toward Madame and labor: "Owing to the high feeling which prevails in the city at the present moment, and owing to the prominent part which the Countess has taken in the labour disputes, I honestly do not think that her appearance on the stage would be good for business." With this Mr. Ashley concurred, feeling that the Count and Countess could only "do the Repertory Theatre movement irreparable injury." The laborers did not have money enough to go to the theatre, the employers did. The salaries paid the actors were minimal and it would be a shame to let such a subversive influence as Madame contaminate them; they might even get the idea of asking for living wages themselves. This was never so bluntly stated, but seemed to underlie their disapproval of Madame and their stand against her. The Count had the final word: "As I am convinced that your policy must be fatal to the interests of the Repertory Theatre movement, as well as insulting to the people of this city, I feel it is impossible for me to retain my position as co-director of the Dublin Repertory Theatre Company."

The Count supported his wife throughout the strike, and although he was not himself embroiled in the struggle, he offered no obstacle to her taking part. The Count and Countess, although their ways and interests diverged, felt strong mutual respect and admiration. He remained in Dublin throughout the autumn and most of the strike but left in December for the Balkans as war correspondent.

It became immediately apparent that unless relief of some kind were provided, the locked out and striking workers and their families would starve. Madame led in the collection of food. With experience remembered from Lissadell and with help from many sources, she soon had kitchens going in Liberty Hall. There were other organizations helping to feed the poor, but the Liberty Hall operation was the broadest in scope, asked no questions about political or other affiliation, and began almost at once through Madame's energy and drive. Instrumental in its organization were Patrick Lennon and Sean O'Casey, the secretaries of the relief fund.

Mrs. Sheehy Skeffington, who contributed to the kitchens with as much zest as Madame herself, considered this Madame's finest achievement. In siding with labor, she espoused an unpopular cause, and flouted convention in her championship of the poor and lowly. "The children," remembered Mrs. Skeffington, "ever the hungriest and the most eager, used to file past with mugs, tin cans, porringers, old jam crocks, which she filled, and with a jolly word for all, for Madame had a personal contact and real sympathy with the poor that removed all taint of the Lady Bountiful and made her a comrade among comrades. One day a youngster came along, a boy of about ten, with his little soup-can, only to be recognized and pushed aside scornfully by the others with a taunt, 'Go away, your father is a scab.' Madame, seeing the hurt look in the child's face and the quick withdrawal, called him back. 'No child is going to be called a scab. He can't help his father. When he grows up he'll be all right himself, won't you sonny? And now have some soup.' "[11] There are many men and women in Dublin today who thankfully remember receiving food from Madame's hands.

Liberty Hall had been in the 1830's the Northumberland Coffee Rooms, later known as the Northumberland Hotel. In the basement were kitchens, large storage rooms, and space to set up dining rooms. There were plenty of locked out women and girls eager to prepare and serve the food. The men helped by stoking the fires, fetching water, and bringing supplies from the storeroom. Madame was in charge and was to be found there from early morning until late at night. The hungry must be fed. She even set up a special dining room for mothers when she discovered that when they took away their dinners they did not eat them themselves, but gave them to their families. Now they ate at the Hall so Madame could be sure they were getting something nourishing.

The British Trade Union Congress pledged itself to supply food to the Dublin workers for the duration of the strike, and the first of the food ships, *S. S. Hare,* arrived in Dublin from Manchester on September 26. She carried £5,000 worth of food bought through the Wholesale Cooperative Society. A great crowd of men and boys cheered as the ship tied up at the quay at one o'clock on Saturday and by four o'clock the first food had been distributed. The *Hare* brought potatoes, bread, butter, sugar, tea—all distributed directly to the workers. Food which took long cooking and consequently would use up their scant fuel supplies was cooked at Liberty Hall and distributed there. Madame continued her active supervision in the kitchens throughout the long months. She said she was prepared to keep it up indefinitely because she saw the workers engaged in a fight for freedom and this was her contribution.

Sinn Fein protested the arrival of the *Hare* from England on the grounds that the £5,000 should have been spent in Ireland.

A clothing shop was also set up in Liberty Hall to distribute to the women and children warm clothing which had been donated. Many unemployed girls and women who were trained seamstresses went to work to alter the clothing to fit. Nora Connolly, visiting Liberty Hall, was impressed by the kitchens and the workrooms and remembered one of the busy girls who was sewing saying with a smile, "We were astonished at first at the size of the families. Then we found that in most cases a child or two had been adopted for the purpose of getting it clothed. But we didn't mind. As long as we kept the youngsters warm, what does that matter?"[12]

The strike and lockout continued with each side growing more bitter and the antagonism increasing daily. Most of the press, the politicians with very few exceptions, Dublin Castle with its police and military forces, and some clergy were outspoken in denouncing the union. The brutality of Bloody Sunday and the extension of the lock-out to thirty-seven unions aroused some sympathy among Dublin's citizens and among workers all over Ireland and Great Britain. The nationalists, again with notable exceptions, remained silent. Professor T. M. Kettle organized a Dublin Industrial Peace Committee in early October, which had two public meetings before it became the Civic League. Thomas Dillon and Joseph Plunkett served as secretaries to the Peace Committee; W. B. Yeats and the Reverend R. M. Gwynn were among those on the platform at the second meeting.

The most outspoken in appreciation of the workers' resistance and in denunciation of the employers' action were a number of Ireland's leading writers. AE, gentlest of poets, wrote a famous invective to the *Irish Times* which was reprinted in all the newspapers. "An Extraordinary Outburst by AE" was the *Freeman's Journal*'s shocked headline. AE's open letter, accurately addressed "To the Masters of Dublin," accused the employers of "insolence and ignorance of the rights conceded to workers universally" and of depending on a "devilish policy of starvation" rather than accepting the recommendations made by a Board of Trade Inquiry.

This inquiry, under Sir George Askwith, Chief Industrial Commissioner, into the causes and circumstances of the industrial deadlock in Dublin presented its report on October 6. Rather than clarifying or helping the issue, it succeeded only in clouding and complicating it. The employers were criticized for demanding a pledge from the workers that they would not join the Transport Workers' Union. The workers were willing to accept the conciliation scheme outlined by the court as a basis of negotiation, but the employers complained of the manner in which the men's case was presented and the fact that they had no opportunity to rebut the statements made by Larkin. The employers would accept the union only if it were "reorganized on proper lines and with new officials who have met with the approval of the British Joint Labour Board." In other words, get rid of Larkin. In his letter to the masters of Dublin, AE criticized the employers for choosing "as your spokesman the bitterest tongue that ever wagged in these islands." T. M. Healy, the spokesman, complained to his brother that the whole situation was handled "by stranger-fools instead of by native resolutes."[13]

A much less widely-known but even more bitter letter from AE was published in *The Irish Worker* under the heading, "The Crime and the Punishment." In one of the most bitingly satirical pieces since Swift, AE accused the workers of spoiling an experiment of the employers. In the interests of sociology, the employers had long been trying to determine what was the least amount of food and space a human being needed for survival. It seemed they were getting close to an answer when the workers refused to cooperate any longer, and it would take years to get them down to a useful experimental level again: "It is quite possible that after exhaustive experiments had been carried out we could have produced the really economic worker who would be content with five shillings a week, which would suffice for his simple wants; we might have found out that human beings could be packed comfortably in rooms like bees in a hive, and could generate heat to warm themselves by their very number without the necessity for coal. Nothing is more annoying to scientific investigators than the unscientific, humanitarian-like James Larkin, who comes along and upsets all calculations and destroys the labour of generations in the evolution of the underman, which was getting along so well. [With his] fantastic notions of the unscientific mind, James Larkin was rightly locked up before he made matters worse. We can now without interruption retrace our steps backward in the direction of the cave man."[14] Other writers energetic in labor's cause were W. B. Yeats, Padraic Pearse, James Stephens, Seamus O'Sullivan, Padraic Colum, Joseph Plunkett and Thomas MacDonagh.

There was more clouding of the labor issue when, by the end of October, in spite of the kitchens at Liberty Hall and the supplies coming from England, the food situation was desperate. Three well-meaning but not very astute philanthropists proposed sending Dublin children to selected homes in England where they could be cared for until the end of the industrial strife, at which time their parents would be in a position to provide adequately for them. Some of the parents in Dublin were in such desperate straits by this time that they gave their permission. The Church, however, saw fit to step in and raise a cry against proselytizing, although the organizing ladies insisted the Irish children would be supervised by local Catholic priests in England. The Church propagandists referred to the scheme as a deportation, and then, after a week's emotional prodding, nearly hysterical crowds led by priests "rescued" the children in rowdy scenes at the train station. One of the lady escorts was Mrs. Lucilla Rand, twenty-one years old, the daughter of an American government official in Portugal, a former governor of California. She was arrested on a kidnapping charge. The other ladies involved were Mrs. Dora Montefiore, a trained social worker with an international reputation, and Miss Grace Neal, an organizer of domestic workers.

Whatever the demerits of the scheme and the mistakes made in trying to carry it out, it had the immediately beneficial effect of shocking the complacent middle class into action. A committee was set up to collect and administer funds for the relief of distress among the children. Within a few days Countess Plunkett had opened a large house at Sandymount for whatever poor children wanted to live there. Offers of help from convent after convent were reported by His Grace the Archbishop, William J. Walsh. In three parochial districts hardest hit by the strike, Marlborough Street, Westland Row, and City Quay, the breakfasts served to schoolchildren more than doubled, from 1,200 daily to 2,450. Dinners in the same districts nearly doubled from the normal 690.

On November 1, 1913 (the day AE's satirical comments applauding Larkin's arrest were published in *The Irish Worker*) a huge meeting, organized by the London Socialist paper, *The Daily Herald*, was held in the Albert Hall to demand the release of Larkin. George Lansbury presided, and AE spoke out against the employers again: "If the courts of justice were courts of humanity the masters of Dublin would be in the dock charged with criminal conspiracy. Their crime was that they tried to starve out one-third of the people of Dublin."

G. B. Shaw also spoke, pointing out that the citizenry would have to use force before it could expect justice. He reiterated the thought of some Dublin leaders on the necessity for some kind of citizen army: "If you put a policeman on the footing of a mad dog, it can only end in one way, and that is that all respectable men will have to arm themselves. I suggest you should arm yourselves with something which should put a decisive stop to the proceedings of the police." He added that he would like to be prosecuted for sedition so that he might have an opportunity of publicly explaining what he meant by the advice he had just given.

James Connolly also hinted at military force when he spoke to a crowded suffragette meeting in Dublin on November 11, which many of the locked out women attended. They were beginning to realize their potential strength and their present weakness. The two movements, for the right of labor to organize and the right of women to vote, seemed mutually strengthening. Connolly said that the women, like labor, had been played with and tricked by every party in turn. They, too, had learned the necessity of trusting to no party—if freedom were attained it must be by their own efforts. He declared that he had never heard of a militant action in their behalf which he was not prepared fully to endorse. Madame took part in the discussion which followed, heartily endorsing the militant sentiments expressed and the necessity for self-sacrifice and of subordinating everything, regardless of consequences, to the attainment of their object.

The same night another meeting was being held at Wynn's Hotel in Dublin. This was a smaller, more select one, consisting of eleven invited men: Eoin MacNeill, Bulmer Hobson, Padraic Pearse, Sean MacDermott, W. J. Ryan, Eamonn Ceannt, Sean Fitzgibbon, James A. Deakin, Piaras Beaslai, Joseph Campbell, and The O'Rahilly. The meeting had been organized by the I.R.B. and was the first to discuss the formation of the Irish Volunteers.

The following night, November 12, the Peace Committee dissolved into the Civic League at a small meeting held in the Reverend R. M. Gwynn's rooms at 40, Trinity College. At this meeting Captain Jack White proposed a drilling scheme for the strikers which was enthusiastically received. Captain White, a former officer in the British Army and son of the famous defender of Ladysmith in the Boer War, had recently come to Dublin, and through AE his sympathies with the workers were immediately aroused. He was hot-tempered, a commanding speaker, and an experienced military man who took charge of the drilling of the Citizen Army when it was formed. He contributed money for equipment as well as his knowledge, skill, and time. It is neatly ironical that the first practical plan of the Citizen Army was made in the stronghold of all that the Transport Union as well as the nationalists were fighting; less than three years later Trinity and its officer training corps were instrumental in physically dividing the rebel forces and in providing invaluable help to the British.

The night after the formation of the Civic League and Captain White's proposal, news came that Jim Larkin had been released from prison, having served only seventeen days of his seven months' sentence. The Transport Union regarded this as their first great victory and proof of their strength. At 7:30 that evening a rocket blazed up into the sky from the roof of Liberty Hall, and as the rockets and other fireworks continued for half an hour a crowd rapidly collected in front of the Hall. A drum and fife band arrived, followed immediately by a band of pipers, which led an unusually noisy procession estimated at ten thousand along the quays and part of O'Connell Street. About nine o'clock the procession returned to Beresford Place and Connolly shouted, "Listen to me, I am going to talk sedition." He raised the hopes of the crowd that night when he told them of plans for a citizen army. This was his first definite public proposal of what had been hinted at for weeks. First Connolly explained why he felt they were in a state of war in Dublin: every right had its duty, but when they were deprived of their rights they owed no duty to anyone.

"Listen to me, I am going to talk sedition. The next time we are out for a march, I want to be accompanied by four battalions of trained men. I want them to come with their corporals, sergeants and people to form fours. Why should we not drill and train our men as they are doing in Ulster?" He told them that when they came to draw their strike pay that weekend he wanted every man who was willing to enlist as a soldier with them to give in his name and address so that he could be informed when and where he was to attend for training. Connolly had been promised the assistance of competent chief officers who would lead them anywhere. He would say nothing about arms at present, but when they wanted them they knew where to find them. Their demands were the restoration of their rights, a general settlement, and release of every man, woman and child who was a member of the Transport Union and who was now imprisoned and wrongly imprisoned in Mountjoy.

Madame was on the platform and applauded the militant spirit. In her speech she praised one of the girls who worked in the kitchen at Liberty Hall who "when she stood in the dock the other day had the courage to say, 'God save Ireland.' " Madame was one of the first to join the Citizen Army.

The same night, November 13, the Civic League held its first public meeting at the Antient Concert Rooms, and the formation of the citizen army was announced there as well. Reverend Gwynn, Professor Collingwood, Francis Sheehy Skeffington and Darrell Figgis were on the platform. Madame went round to the meeting after she left Liberty Hall although it was nearly over by that time. The idea was as enthusiastically accepted at the Civic League meeting as it had been at Beresford Place, and the labor army got under way at once.

The Civic League met again a week later, November 19. This time the audience was swelled by a hundred young men from Trinity. They were there primarily because they had been forbidden to attend by the Provost Anthony Traill. The previous night at the opening meeting of the seventh session of the Dublin University Gaelic Society, Captain White had made a most unorthodox speech for a gentleman, calling upon those present to attend a meeting the following night on the subject of the police. Provost Traill had jumped to the conclusion that if Captain White were going to speak against the government, it must be a Home Rule meeting. Consequently, to the embarrassment of other Trinity authorities and to the amusement of everybody else, he forbade the students to attend Captain White's Home Rule meeting. The provost's interdiction and muddled conception of the issues increased interest, and over a hundred Trinity students marched to the Antient Concert Rooms singing their version of a popular song, "Oh, oh, Antonio." They were greeted with hilarity and enthusiasm at the Hall, and proceeded around the room and to the platform where they were seated with the speakers and other distinguished guests. The main purpose of the meeting was to protest against the employers' refusal to confer with Dublin workers about the pledge profferred to the employees and against the postponement of the police inquiry. A telegram was sent from the meeting to Jim Larkin who was in the Albert Hall addressing a meeting there.

Captain White used the opportunity to reiterate his preparations for meeting physical force with physical force. He read a concurring telegram from Sir Roger Casement offering support in the movement to drill and discipline Dublin workers. Sir Roger, who had been knighted for his exposés of worker exploitation in Africa and South America, hoped a citizen army would begin a widespread national movement to organize drilled and disciplined Irish volunteers to assert Irish manhood and uphold the national cause. Among other speakers, Madame spoke strongly in favor of an inquiry into the conduct of the police.

On Sunday, November 23, 1913, enough men to form two companies appeared at the Transport Union's Croydon Park and handed in their names to Captain White. There was no drilling or demonstration that day, but the name Transport Union Citizen Army was used for the first time. It was soon shortened to Citizen Army, and later called Irish Citizen Army. Two days later the organizational meeting of the nationalist Irish Volunteers was held at the Rotunda Rink. Dublin was preparing for resistance of force by force. The Citizen Army promised that when the men were trained, disciplined and drilled, there would be no more baton charges in Dublin. The object proposed for the Irish Volunteers was to secure and maintain the rights and liberties of all the people of Ireland.

Madame's friend and neighbor, Mrs. Sheehy Skeffington, was arrested the end of November for assaulting a policeman while he was on duty outside Lord Iveagh's residence in St. Stephen's Green. (This was the same house where Madame in her younger days used to dance and where she admired the "lovely plaster things" on the walls and ceilings.) When Bonar Law and Sir Edward Carson, Ulster militarists, had gone into the house for lunch, Mrs. Skeffington tried to give them some suffragette literature and was forcibly prevented by the police. She was in Mountjoy Jail when, at a meeting in Beresford Place presided over by her husband, James Connolly made another promise to the citizens of Dublin: in time the Citizen Army would become a well-drilled, disciplined body and they would not then have the occasion to fear police brutality. He said they would then see about getting arms for the men. Then they would be in a position not only to defend themselves but their city from the wanton attacks and brutality of the police.

Even *Sinn Fein,* ever suspicious of armed force, applauded the new Volunteer movement and spoke of getting guns. "Public feeling is strongly with the movement and if those who launched it now draft a practical scheme for arming the people there should be an efficient Volunteer corps in Dublin before spring. Drilling is gymnasium and boy scout work, possible at any time. The first essential of a Volunteer is a rifle, and the second is a rifle range, and these are the prime things for the new association to deal with." There was hotter blood in Sinn

Fein than four years before when they would have nothing to do with Madame's militant boy scouts.

Because the Citizen Army and the Irish Volunteers were developing simultaneously, some confusion in nomenclature was inevitable and has led to misstatements about the beginnings of the two movements in 1913. Captain White in his Gaelic Society speech on November 18, for example, exhorted his audience to raise again "the standards of the Irish Volunteers" referring to the Volunteers of 1782 who were instrumental in the setting up of Grattan's Parliament. Some careless reading of this has led to the assertion that Captain White was first to suggest what became the Irish Volunteers, when, in fact, he was talking about the formation of the Irish Citizen Army. Casement's telegram to the November 19 meeting of the Civic League also spoke of the movement of Irish volunteers rather than the citizen army. On the other hand, the Manifesto of Irish Volunteers distributed at the meeting on November 25, 1913, written by Eoin MacNeill, had a paragraph headed "Citizen Army" and acknowledged the appeal of the formation of a citizen army "from a population now at the mercy of almost any organized aggression." The rest of the manifesto refers to the movement as the Irish Volunteers, however, and this was the name by which it was organized and known. Later, some publicity, such as that announcing the inaugural meeting of the Cumann na mBan, the women's branch of the Volunteers, referred to the National Volunteer Movement. When the Irish Volunteers split in September, 1914, and part of them took the name National Volunteers, while the nationalists retained the name and aims of Irish Volunteers, confusion was compounded.

However, there is no question but that both the Irish Volunteers and the Citizen Army were militantly nationalistic from their inceptions. The Citizen Army was born of the need of the workers to have more than moral force to back their claims. It was not only British industrial slavery they were fighting against (indeed, some of the members of the Employers Federation who locked them out proudly displayed on their products the Sinn Fein seal of nationalist approval). It was exploitation they armed against at first, but there is no doubt that from the beginning they were concerned with the unity of Irish nationhood and the principle of equal rights and opportunities for the Irish people. They did not want to be exploited either by British employers, or, when the day of Ireland's freedom came, by Irish employers. The Irish Citizen Army saw itself as the protective arm of labor.

James Connolly expressed the whole idea very simply when he wrote to William O'Brien, "There is a magnificent chance for the Transport Union all over Ireland as the one Labour organisation aggressively active on the true nationalist side." He saw the importance of labor's support to the nationalist cause and of nationalist support to the labor cause; they were inextricably dedicated to the same end, the development of Ireland for the Irish. In both cases, secure freedom first, then maintain the rights and liberties. Definitions of these latter concepts differed, and therein lay the fundamental differences between the two groups. But first, freedom; on that they were agreed.

The immediate reaction of the Castle to these organizing activities was to declare an arms embargo. There had been a Royal Proclamation prohibiting the importation of military arms and ammunition into Ireland under the Customs Consolidation Act of 1876, but for the last few years only the ordinary restrictions of civil law had been enforced. The Ulster Volunteers had been arming for months, technically illegally. Two proclamations were signed December 4, 1913, by the King, one prohibiting the carriage coastwise of military arms and ammunition, the other prohibiting the importation of military arms and ammunition into Ireland. These did not deter anyone. The Volunteers soon had plans for bringing in both arms and ammunition.

The Citizen Army and the Irish Volunteers began drilling immediately and by December the Citizen Army was estimated at between 500 and 600 men, the Irish Volunteers at 3,500. The Volunteers, because it was nationalist and had no particular class affiliation, always outnumbered the Citizen Army. In the beginning the Citizen Army placed certain age and size restrictions on the members. They wanted no boys, only fully grown men. This stopped many of the eager young workers from joining the Citizen Army, and it was only those young men with the strongest labor views who resisted joining the Volunteers, who had no requirements except devotion to Ireland.

Another Commission of Inquiry, this one into the disturbances in Dublin in August and September, was being set up, but there was no labor representative on it. There were meetings protesting this omission, a typical one a public meeting held under the auspices of the Dublin Civic League. Captain White presided, W. B. Yeats supported the meeting by letter, W. P. Partridge, Louie Bennett, William Forsyth, Mary Hayden, and Madame protested that the membership of the commission was such as to insure the shielding of officials of the police and higher officials in Dublin Castle.

Madame was still working all day in Liberty Hall but had little amusements for the children in mind as well as the major issues. She spent much of her time in December preparing Christmas parties for some 20,000 children. The Manchester Cooperative Wholesale Society had provided small gifts and sweets for the children; Madame and some of the locked out girls prepared individual packets for each child. It was the only bright afternoon for most of the children that winter. Madame never overlooked personal details in providing for the children no matter how busy she was. Years of helping with the annual school fête at Lissadell stood her in good stead in planning and giving such parties successfully.

In *Drums Under the Windows* Sean O'Casey has a brilliantly venomous portrait of Madame in the kitchens of Liberty Hall. He shows her a "scintillating harlequin" whirling through the steam and columns of workers in a dress of green, gold, and purple lozenges, not doing a lick of work, indifferent to her own class and ignorant of his, beating at thin ideas in a shrill voice, sampling a bit of stew now and again, and rushing for a ladle whenever a photographer came by.[15] The portrait was drawn after Madame bested him in a bitter feud. O'Casey had the intellectual's, particularly the self-made intellectual's, arrogant contempt for the activist such as Madame who was most effective when repeating and exemplifying a few ideas that can be easily understood by many. He also liked his women gentle, long-suffering, and very admiring. Furthermore, he was a little jealous. At the time he fancied his own administrative abilities, which, considering his quarrelsome life, proved to be no part of his remarkable genius. Connolly, on the other hand, was one of the most resourceful executives in Dublin, and he appreciated the woman chosen to administer the kitchens. Liberty Hall was an arsenal of food for the strike, a warehouse piled high with goods, and much of it would have been useless if the kitchens faltered. Food for thousands every day had to be stored correctly and apportioned accurately. Delia Larkin was efficient but did not capture the imagination of the strikers. Someone with unusual talents and training was needed to keep up the spirits of volunteer workers peeling millions of potatoes in the damp old basement of the hall week after week during the Dublin winter. If Madame had an actress's affection for limelight, that was a foible she might easily be forgiven. Her altruism and dedication always equalled her vanity. Even when the strike faltered and the stores of food dwindled, she could keep up with gusto as she felt the pace towards armed conflict accelerate.

It was a desperately cold winter, unusually severe for Ireland, and by Christmas the ponds in Dublin were frozen and there was ice-skating in Phoenix Park. The first rifts in the solidarity of the strikers were appearing when on December 10 the London and Northwestern Railway Company workers announced the abandonment of the sympathetic strike and the Dublin port reopened after fourteen weeks.

The dreary winter dragged on for the workers and their families. Aching hunger, cold, and family necessity finally drove the men and women back to the factories, mills, docks, and stores, to seek their own individual reinstatement. In late January the British Trades Council stopped the flow of food supplies, the kitchens at Liberty Hall had to close, the number of men on strike diminished, and by the end of February the strike was over.

The Report of the Dublin Disturbances Commission which was published on February 9, 1914, was accepted by the press as an exoneration of the police, although admittedly "wilful damage was done without justification." It was noted that the police had done their jobs so well with batons that only in one case had it been necessary to call out military reinforcements against the unarmed workers. The admission of attacks on the people in Corporation houses on the first Saturday of the strike in August provoked the loudest protests. The Rev. R. M. Gwynn wrote indignantly, "For the officers of the law to commit a deliberate outrage on the homes of the poor, knowing that it can be done with impunity because they are poor and helpless leaves a sense of burning wrong."

The Commission was considered by many to be not impartial, and in spite of continued protests the public for the most part had been kept out of the hearings. The meetings which had been held in December to advocate having a labor representative on the Commission had not produced results, but Madame and others continued to speak at protest meetings through January as the hearings proceeded.[16] The Commission paid little attention to all the rumblings, went its own way, and issued its report in just over a month, and apparently the matter was forgotten by bureaucracy.

The strike had accomplished nothing in bettering the conditions of the workers although it had focused some attention on the wretched conditions under which many Dubliners were living, labor had begun to organize, and the Citizen Army had been formed. Sinn Fein recognized what Madame had felt when she had heard Larkin for the first time over three years before, that labor and nationalism should work together. *Sinn Fein* declared that in a self-governing Ireland every man would be able to live decently in his own country. It saw trade-union-ism as a monitor to remind capital of its duties and declared that no intelligent Irish nationalist dreamed of reproducing the sordid indus-trialism of England and calling it good. However, Sinn Fein intended to have nothing to do with "socialist humbug." Madame did.

NOTES TO CHAPTER V

1. *The Times* (London), October 22, 1913, was one of many journals which publicized the report.

2. C. Ferguson, "Larkin and the Union," *Workers' Union of Ireland 1924–1949 Silver Jubilee Souvenir* (Dublin, 1949).

3. *Eire*, June 16, 1923.

4. C. Desmond Greaves' *The Life and Times of James Connolly* (London, 1961) is the most recent and complete biography. Mr. Greaves establishes the place of Connolly's birth as Edinburgh, and in several ways attests to the fact of his army service, although direct documentary proof is lacking because he did not enlist under his own name.

5. James Connolly, "Labour in Dublin" in *The Re-Conquest of Ireland* (Dub-lin, n.d.), p. 207.

6. One of her sisters was married to Thomas MacDonagh, another was to marry Joseph Plunkett just before his execution in 1916. A third sister was active in the Inghinidhe and was a well-known journalist. Coincidentally, Nellie's married name, several years later, was Donnelly, but in 1913 the name had no special significance to her; it was chosen on the spur of the moment when the reservation was made.

7. *1913, Jim Larkin and the Dublin Lockout* (Dublin, 1964), pp. 34–35.

8. *Freeman's Journal*, September 1, 1913. Other eyewitnesses described the scene, always in terms of terror, of innocent civilians being batoned by uncon-trollably angry policemen, of side streets cordoned off to make escape im-possible, and of the defenselessness of the people. Sean O'Casey, the greatest of all evokers of emotions and images, who was active in the labor movement at that time, described it memorably in his autobiography (*Drums Under the Windows,* New York, 1947, pp. 291–302). Handel Booth, the M.P. who saw Larkin come into the dining room, had a view of the scene from the balcony recently vacated by Larkin, and made strong protests in Ireland and England. He later gave evidence at an inquiry to which he came at considerable incon-venience and at his own expense.

9. In February, 1909, disturbances at a nationalist convention resulted in a court case in March. Serjeant Moriarty had testified that the same precautions were taken at this meeting as had been taken at every public meeting connected with Irish nationalist politics for the past twenty-five years in Dublin—he was surprised that those on the side of his learned friend, Mr. Healy, should think that batons were used for the first time in this [1909] case.

10. Prolonged fasting was an ancient Irish political and religious practice.

Probably the first of the modern Irish to use it as a political weapon was John Daly who in 1896 had secured his release this way after he had been imprisoned for twelve years. The English suffragettes had been using it since June, 1909, when Marion Wallace Dunlop fasted for 91 hours to obtain her release. Since then they had extended the practice, even after forcible feeding became commonplace. It had become so effective that in the spring of 1913 a bill picturesquely called the "Cat-and-Mouse Act" had been passed by Parliament. It was officially the Prisoner (Temporary Discharge for Ill Health) Bill, and meant, in practice, that when a hunger striker weakened dangerously, she was released temporarily from prison. When her friends had had time to nurse her back to health she was rearrested and sent back to finish the original sentence. Under these terms, a three-year sentence could extend over sixteen years.

Madame was among many who had denounced the act at many meetings that summer. Among the speakers at a Mansion House meeting in June, for example, were Professor Oldham, Padraic Colum, Dr. Kathleen Lynn, and Madame. Letters were read from Mrs. Wyse-Power, George Birmingham (Canon Hannay), James Stephens, Padraic Pearse, Maud Gonne, and others.

The Cat-and-Mouse Act was used extensively in England and Ireland to fight women's suffrage and later in Ireland against the nationalists.

11. Hanna Sheehy Skeffington, "Constance Markievicz in 1916," *An Phoblacht,* April 14, 1928.

12. Nora Connolly O'Brien, *Portrait of a Rebel Father* (London, 1935), pp. 151–153.

13. Healy, *Letters and Leaders* (London, 1928) II, 536.

14. Two pages of *The Irish Worker,* November 1, 1913, indicate some of those who were speaking out in favor of the unions. Col. 1 of the second page has an account of Larkin's trial. He was sentenced on October 27 to seven months' imprisonment for sedition. In col. 2, James Connolly advocates political action; columns 3 and 4 carry messages from Ben Tillett, George Lansbury, Charles Lapworth, and Thomas Johnston in England, as well as comments on Jim Larkin by Madame de Markievicz. W. B. Yeats writes on "Dublin Fanaticism" in col. 5, and adjoining it Maud Gonne calls the employers "The Real Criminals." "The Crime and the Punishment" by AE is in col. 1, p. 3, and on the same page is a long poem by Susan Mitchell. Winifred Carney reports on the efforts of the Fianna boys and girls in Belfast to raise money to help Dublin's locked out workers.

15. Pages 314–316.

16. On January 11, for example, Madame spoke at an O'Connell Street meeting along with Bulmer Hobson, Captain White, and Mrs. Connery. Madame said they were there to condemn the Government which had made a farce of their lives by appointing an absurd caricature of an inquiry board. Handel Booth, M.P., was that same day protesting in Hyde Park, asserting he had left Dublin because he was threatened with violence.

VI

Neither King nor Kaiser

1914

In 1894 Maud Gonne had called Home Rule "the carrot dangled before the donkey's nose to keep the donkey quietly trotting along in the harness of the British Empire."[1] Twenty years later Prime Minister Asquith noticed that the donkey was of two minds about carrots and decided the beast would be happier cut in two. After nervously watching Carson's militant preparations against Home Rule in Ulster, Asquith suddenly accepted the principle of partition and advocated that any Irish county could reject Home Rule by a majority vote. Carson immediately began to urge that all Ulster be excluded from Home Rule. Nevertheless, nationalists in the south were still hopeful that Ireland could be whole, free, and prosperous. In the first issue of *Sinn Fein* for 1914 Arthur Griffith triumphantly predicted, "Nothing can prevent the Home Rule Bill becoming law before the summer has faded except treachery on the part of the English liberals."

In February, with the encouragement of James Connolly, Madame visited Belfast for three days during which she addressed several meetings of workers on cooperation as a national way of life. Sweeping aside any objections to the practicality of an idealistic solution to social, political, and economic problems, she saw only the benefits for Ireland. She was enthusiastic about what she saw as the revolutionary spirit of the Irish working class and praised the solidarity and heroism of the Dublin workers. She optimistically saw a great, unflinching, and undeviating forward march to a cooperative commonwealth of labor. Whether Madame actually thought the Dublin strike had won some social and political improvements or whether she was convinced that positive thinking and assertion would make it true is difficult to say. She was always a great believer in cooperation, organization, and talk as weapons to overcome all manner of apathy, pettiness, ignorance, and prejudice; her idealism blinded her to the more selfish motives of others. Her idea of a workers' republic assumed only the most altruistic motivations and admitted no concessions to human frailty.

The workers did not always understand her. At one of the meetings in Belfast at the I.L.P. rooms in Rosemary Street, she addressed a large meeting on "Strikes as a Revolutionary Weapon." She expanded her sentiments on the Dublin strike, sketched the social revolutionary movements in Russia, and added some impressions of her visits to her husband's home near Kief. But "questions and discussions on this subject were difficult to stimulate for the main reason that few of the audience knew anything of the subject."[2]

Other meetings were more successful. Madame addressed the women workers at the York Street mill gates during their dinner hour on the heroism of the Dublin women strikers, and that night the women crowded into the Falls Branch rooms to hear more. As usual, she urged them to organize and agitate. James Connolly carried her point further and suggested that if the Belfast workers resolutely opposed the division of Ireland, they could be instrumental in preventing the exclusion of Ulster in the forthcoming Home Rule.

Madame concurred and repeated this idea a few weeks later at a Dublin conference called by Sinn Fein. She, Mrs. Sheehy Skeffington, and Mrs. Wyse-Power moved that the women of Ulster should be able to vote on Home Rule. Although the sentiment of the meeting was in favor of their motion, the president, Arthur Griffith, ruled it out of order. Mr. Sheehy Skeffington wrote angrily in the *Irish Citizen:* "These women [of Sinn Fein] are now moved to great indignation at the action of their President in trying, after the approved Parliamentary fashion, to shirk a question which so closely concerns them, by putting it aside as a mere social question."[3] Within five months, however, the declaration of war shelved the entire Home Rule question until after the armistice, and by that time events in Ireland had taken her far past the stage where she would be content with the carrot of Home Rule.

After the first months of optimism in 1914, the nationalists began to show the quarrelsome bitterness of the frustrated. During this time Madame's ideal of cooperation was tested. She was one of those who helped hold the nationalists together. Although she gave less time to Sinn Fein, her work with the Fianna continued, and she kept her friendship with leaders of the Irish Volunteers. She was active in the women's organization connected with them, the Cumann na mBan, and continued to help Mrs. Skeffington with the women's suffrage movement. But her first concern was labor and the Citizen Army.

As the strike had waned, so had the numbers and enthusiasm in the Citizen Army. Its pretentious name became almost an embarrassment. Sean O'Casey thought its rather haphazard organization at fault and suggested that a constitution be drafted and submitted for approval to a general meeting; that a Council be elected to see to the revival of systematic drills and generally to take steps to improve, strengthen, and widen the scope of the Irish Citizen Army. Captain White thought the reason for the poor attendance at drills was that the men had only shabby and inadequate clothing and footwear. Frank Robbins, a sergeant in the Citizen Army at St. Stephen's Green in 1916 and a mainstay in the labor movement for years, thinks one cause was the deep depression which had set in among the workers as an aftermath of the 1913 struggle. Even more basic, he says, was the men's confusion about or lack of interest in the ideals which had led to the creation of a workers' army; the concept was revolutionary, and men with families to feed were more immediately interested in food than in learning new ideas.

It was apparent, however, that there was still a need for a disciplined workers' unit if they were to succeed in bettering their conditions since they seemed to be able to accomplish nothing through talk and their general strike had failed. In March, 1914, there was still considerable unemployment, and Captain White decided to parade the jobless men from Liberty Hall to the Mansion House to draw attention to their plight. Ironically, the Citizen Army men were for the most part those in the best physical condition and the first to be back at work. The men Captain White proposed to march to Dawson Street were undrilled, undisciplined, and untrained. Only four of them were Citizen Army men; these were in the front ranks, the other several dozen lined up in military formation behind them. They marched out from Beresford Place but got no further than Butt Bridge where they were met by a number of Dublin Metropolitan Police with drawn batons. Captain White showed himself skillful with his blackthorn, and his few Army men stood their ground, but most of the other hunger marchers ran away from the scene as fast as possible. Captain White had for months been tantalizing the police by marching his men in the Union's Croydon Park, just out of D.M.P. jurisdiction. Now the police took out some of their frustration on the captain. He was beaten and taken to the station under arrest.

Madame, who liked to be where there was action, was with the marchers, and Captain White described her part in the scene at the station in his autobiography: "My head was a bloody pulp, but my spirit remained exalted from the joy of battle. Madame Markievicz had hung on the flanks of the enemy throughout, darted in and tried to trip up a policeman when possible. Now she was magnificent at the station. She forced her way in and demanded that a private doctor should be sent for at once. The first time they flung her out, but she ducked between policemen's legs and got back again somehow. Madame insisted on getting a solution of Jeyes fluid and bathing my head at once for fear of its getting septic, and got her way in having a private doctor summoned at once."[4] He was convinced that her attentions saved his life. At his trial he admitted calling a certain Superintendent Quinn an ill-conditioned hound when he saw him pushing Countess Markievicz out of the police station.

On March 13, the day of the hunger march, the work of reorganizing the Citizen Army began with a preliminary meeting. Sean O'Casey as secretary had made out an agenda and drafted a Constitution. By March 22 the Captain was sufficiently recovered to chair a public meeting which the workers had been especially urged to attend. O'Casey explained that this was the initial effort to improve the affairs of the Army. His proposed Constitution affirmed "that the ownership of Ireland, moral and material, is vested of right in the people of Ireland; that the Citizen Army . . . shall support the rights and liberties of the democracies of all nations; that the Citizen Army shall be open to all who accept the principle of equal rights and opportunities for the people of Ireland; [and] that one of its objects shall be to sink all differences of birth, property and creed under the common name of the Irish people."

At the request of Jim Larkin, Madame proposed a fifth clause as a guarantee that the identity of the little unit would not dissolve in socialist ideology: "Before being enrolled, every applicant must, if eligible, be a member of his trade union, such union to be recognised by the Irish Trade Union Congress." Thomas Healy seconded Madame's proposal and it was included in the Constitution of the Citizen Army which was adopted unanimously. The curious phrasing allowed Madame, who was not a member of a union, to belong to the Army. The first Army Council was then elected as a Provisional Committee to hold office for six months. Captain White was chairman, Jim Larkin one of the vice-chairmen, Sean O'Casey, secretary, and Richard Brannigan and Madame treasurers.

After the meetng the *Irish Worker* urged its readers to hold themselves in readiness to join the Citizen Army which, the *Worker* emphasized, was prepared to explain and define its Constitution upon any platform in Ireland. The writer of the article took a passing swipe at the more popular Volunteers: "Let others who may prate about 'rights and liberties common to all Irishmen.' We are out for the right to work and eat and live." The unsigned article was probably by O'Casey. Certainly it reflects his antagonism towards the Volunteers and anyone else who was not in wholehearted agreement with him. The *Irish Worker* published several anti-Volunteer letters during the first few months of 1914 signed S. O'Cathasaigh which were also probably from O'Casey. They reflect his views that the Volunteers were bourgeois, hence the enemy in the class struggle. In the notes of March 28, O'Casey wrote: "Personally I hold the workers are beside themselves with foolishness to support any movement that does not stand to make the workers supreme, for these are the people, and without them there can be no life nor power. Soon all workers shall realise that it is good to die for one's friend but foolish to die for one's enemy." O'Casey's refusal to see the Volunteers and the Citizen Army as allies in the cause of nationalism prompted Captain White to leave the Citizen Army in May, and O'Casey to quarrel with Madame.

As the months went by, the two military groups cooperated in various demonstrations with only occasional signs of hostility, but there was increasing suspicion on both sides. In April, 1914, Captain White had written: "The principal activity I am now engaged in is a campaign to spread the Citizen Army. I think it will result in compelling the National Volunteers to cease from the suspicious aloofness from anyone connected with Labour and draw together the Middle Class and Labour National Movements, if it cannot succeed as a Labour National Movement alone." Optimistic as he had been in April, however, he soon complained that "to draw together the Labour and National elements in Ireland was not and is not possible. A common emotion of patriotism cannot reconcile a concrete and fundamental antagonism of interest and objective."[5]

In May, 1914, the Volunteer attitude was expressed in a letter written by Tom Clarke to John Devoy: "Larkin's people for some time past have been making war on the Irish Volunteers. I think this is largely inspired by a disgruntled fellow named O'Casey. By this attitude they have antagonized the sympathy of all sections of the country and none more so than the advanced section. Liberty Hall is now a negligible quantity here."[6]

However, for the time being, Captain White contributed his knowledge, energy, and money to the Citizen Army, while O'Casey and Madame worked in uneasy collaboration. One of the many causes of dissension between them was her militant feminism. She thought that if a woman was physically strong and temperamentally fit she should be allowed to march and fight with an army. O'Casey rumbled against her feminism, but there is no evidence that she paid any attention.

Beginning in April, 1914, efforts were made to recruit workers for the Citizen Army in the predominantly agricultural districts north of Dublin, in Swords, Lucan, and Clondalkin. One of these early meetings was on April 12, when Captain White drove Madame, P. T. Daly, and Sean O'Casey through a happy spring day to Lucan. O'Casey wrote that "everything in nature seemed to laugh quietly at the querulous efforts of man to solve the complex human problems with which he was surrounded. When we reached Lucan things looked far from promising, for we were silently and curiously received by a few stragglers, that stood here and there about the village, and seemed to be in no way desirous of helping in the promotion of anything that Labour stood for."[7] To a shy and timorous group they spoke of the importance of safeguarding one's own position. "Much interest was evinced in the passionate and nervous eloquence of the Countess Markievicz." It was probably more the novelty of a woman speaking in public than any concern with organized labor that drew these countrymen, but whatever aroused them, about twenty men signed up with O'Casey and were authorized to hold a subsequent meeting to elect officers and arrange for drills.

They drove on to hold another meeting at Clondalkin where O'Casey read in the awe shown for the Captain's car a fear that it was "some dangerous machine calculated, if approached too closely, to upset for ever the quiet rhythm of the pastoral life of Clondalkin's inhabitants." The results of the day's efforts convinced O'Casey that "the work of building up the Irish Citizen Army would be a long, arduous and painful task." There were one or two other attempts at organizing outside Dublin, but soon all efforts were concentrated in the city.

News of the Citizen Army began appearing in the *Irish Worker* on April 4, headed "By The Camp Fire" and signed "S.O'C." The first notes announced a general meeting the following day at which fifty men were to be selected to receive the first set of uniforms. The uniforms were dark green with wide-brimmed hats which many of the men turned up on one side and fastened with the Transport Union badge. Those who did not have uniforms wore armlets of blue; the commissioned officers wore red arm bands. The men paid for all equipment and uniforms themselves, a large item considering their wages. Later when a miniature rifle range was set up at Liberty Hall it was used extensively during the winter nights by those who could afford the charge of 1d. for three shots. Often many of them did not have the penny to spare.

At the April 5 meeting which had been announced in the first Citizen Army notes, the starry plough flag made its first appearance. (It was later flown over the Imperial Hotel on Wednesday of Easter Week, after the Tricolor had been hoisted over the post office.) O'Casey read the whole Labor movement into its symbol and was to use it as the title of a play. He remembered his feeling of reverence the first time he saw it, the Plough and the Stars. "There it was—the most beautiful flag among the flags of the world's nations: a rich, deep poplin field of blue; across its whole length and breadth stretched the formalised shape of a plough, a golden-brown colour, seamed with a rusty red, while through all glittered the gorgeous group of stars enriching and ennobling the northern skies."[8] He was vexed that Madame only glanced at it, said the design had no republican significance, and returned to oiling her automatic.

Throughout these months of organizing the militant Irish Volunteers and the Irish Citizen Army, Madame continued to urge the women to participate in the national movement. The Manifesto of the Volunteers had expressly stated that there would be work for women to do "and there are signs that the women of Ireland, true to their record, are especially enthusiastic for the success of the Irish Volunteers."

The inaugural meeting of the Irishwomen in support of the Volunteers was held April 2, 1914, at Wynn's Hotel. Some women had met as early as November or December, 1913, and from time to time since to formulate a constitution and rules, but this was the first public meeting. They called themselves the Irish Women's Council for the first month, but by May decided to use its Irish equivalent, Cumann na mBan (pronounced cummon-na-mon). There were four branches, corresponding to the four Volunteer battalions in Dublin. In May, Madame presided at a meeting of the Inghinidhe na hEireann in their rooms at 6 Harcourt Street (Sinn Fein headquarters) and explained the objects of the Cumann na mBan. Thirty members enrolled and elected to be called the Inghinidhe na hEireann Craobh [Branch]. The

Inghinidhe thus merged with the Cumann na mBan and the Irish Volunteers and ceased to be a separate entity. Cumann na mBan branches were soon formed in Killarney, Cork, Limerick, Tralee, Dingle, Enniscorthy, and Wexford. Their consitution was short, definite, and contentious: "Cumann na mBan is an independent body of Irish women, pledged to work for the establishment of an Irish Republic, by organising and training the women of Ireland to take their places by the side of those who are working and fighting for a free Ireland."

Their first job was to initiate a Defense of Ireland fund for arming and equipping the Volunteers. They thought this a necessary step toward regaining for the women of Ireland the rights that belonged to them under the old Gaelic civilization where sex was no bar to citizenship and where women were free to devote to the service of their country their every talent and capacity. There was some muttering about not being represented on the Volunteer Executive, but for the most part the women were devoted to the areas in which it was generally agreed they could be of the most practical use at the time— fund raising and first aid. Some of the women learned to handle guns, but the demonstrations on setting up field kitchens and feeding an army were more popular.

Fund raising was complicated and fairly successful. By mid-May nearly £500 had been collected in Dublin, and a committee in London headed by the historian Mrs. Stopford Green had collected an equal amount. The ladies officially decided that all money they collected would be turned over to the Volunteer's Provisional Committee with the stipulation that it was to be used only for the purchase of arms. To the delight of the members, some of the money actually came from the British Government. The Department of Agriculture and Technical Instruction for Ireland subsidized a course of lectures on first aid. To encourage attendance, each person was paid 4d. an hour for the time spent at lectures, and after twenty hours of instruction received a certificate. The girls were keen to learn first aid and went happily to the classes; even more gleefully, they eventually collected £16 and handed it over to the Volunteers to buy arms. In Ulster, Carson and his unionists had collected one million pounds by the first of the year.

One of the projects Madame particularly enjoyed that spring was an Irish Women's Franchise League fund-raising entertainment at Molesworth Hall on April 24 and 25. The main features of the Great Daffodil Fête were a play written for the occasion by Francis Sheehy Skeffington and a series of feminist tableaux featuring famous women. A. L. Shields and Maire Nic Shiublaigh starred in *The Prodigal Daughter,* which was frankly suffragette propaganda. The tableaux included Mrs. Cogley as Sappho, Miss Maxwell as Florence Nightingale, Mrs. MacDonagh as Maeve the Warrior Queen, Maire Nic Shiublaigh as Brigid, and Sidney Gifford as Anne Devlin. There were two Joans of Arc—Miss Houston as Joan at the Stake, and Madame as Joan in Full Armour. Mrs. Sheehy Skeffington remembered Madame's energy and attention to detail in making her costume: "What fine fifteenth century pieces she contrived out of cardboard silvered over, and what a characteristic Joan she was. And how she toiled over old pictures of the time to get it just right. She posed as Joan, appearing to a suffragist prisoner in her cell. Her alert, gallant bearing was well set off by her silver armour, helmet and uplifted sword. She flung herself with her usual zest into the part, making a magnificent Joan. When years later I beheld her in action in the College of Surgeons, wearing the uniform of the Irish Citizen Army, that earlier vision of Joan flashed upon my mind's eye. They were not so far apart."[9]

On the opening day of the Daffodil Fête in Dublin, April 24, 1914, 35,000 rifles and 2,500,000 rounds of ammunition were landed for Carson's men in Bangor, Donaghadee, and Larne. The guns were Mausers which had been purchased in Germany and passed through the Kiel Canal, so the German and the British governments both knew about them. They were conveyed by Major Crawford to the Ulster coast and were landed and distributed with efficiency and speed, not one gun being confiscated. On the contrary, there was admiration among conservatives in England for the fidelity with which the garrison in Ireland was fulfilling its traditional task. The *Manchester Guardian* later wrote, "The Ulster gun-running won as many titles, honours and offices for its organisers and patrons as if it had been an incident in the first Battle of Ypres."[10] It was an entirely different situation when the Irish Volunteers ran guns into Howth in July. There was no praise then from England, only alarm that such arming was possible. In the meantime, Ulster strengthened itself to fight against being part of any separation from England.

In the south the Irish Volunteers strengthened themselves in numbers but at the same time admitted a wedge that would soon split their own organization. On June 16, 1914, the Provisional Committee of the Irish Volunteers reluctantly agreed to John Redmond's proposal to admit twenty-five representatives from different parts of the country, nominated by the Irish Party. Redmond threatened to create a rival authority to the Provisional Committee and thus disrupt the organization and place it under two competing systems of control if his proposal were refused. This in fact was done three months later, but in June the Committee felt it their duty to accept the alternative which appeared to them the lesser evil: in the interest of national unity, the Provisional Committee acceded to Redmond's demand. They made the stipulation, however, that no person could honorably accept a position of control over or within the Irish Volunteers who was not entirely in favor of a permanent, armed Volunteer organization. An eight-man minority protested that Redmond's proposition was a violation of the basic principles of the Volunteer movement. However, they appealed to all members to sink their personal feelings and persist in their efforts to make the Irish Volunteers an efficient armed force. Six of the eight men who signed this protest were I.R.B. members.[11]

Figures widely circulated by newspapers in Ireland in June estimated the numbers in the Volunteers as of June 1, 1914, at 128,500. Other sources indicated that the Citizen Army was still under 1,000. Membership in the I.R.B. in Ireland, Scotland, and England was estimated at 2,000.

On Sunday, June 26, 1914, the Wolfe Tone Committee organized the annual march from Sallins to the grave of Wolfe Tone in Bodenstown cemetery. Jim Larkin headed two companies of the Citizen Army, the Irish Volunteers were there in number, as were women of Cumann na mBan, and boys of the Fianna, who were led by Madame Markievicz. Tom Clarke addressed the gathering; the honor guard around the grave was formed by alternate members of the Volunteers and the Citizen Army. All obeyed the same commands and demonstrated for the first time that cooperation was possible among all groups dedicated to the cause of Ireland.

The greatest tonic to the Volunteers was their successful gun-running at Howth on July 26, 1914, although the shooting into a crowd of civilians at Bachelor's Walk by English soldiers later in the day was an unforeseen and bitter aftermath. The Volunteers made apparently routine route marches in at least two directions that day, one towards Howth, the little harbor to the north of Dublin Bay. They were accompanied by several Fianna boys with a trek cart. Only the leaders knew their destination and purpose. That same morning Erskine Childers' trim white yacht *Asgard*, crewed by himself, his wife, Gordon Shepherd and Mary Spring-Rice, was cruising off Lamby Island into Howth harbor. The *Asgard* was carrying nine hundred second-hand Mauser rifles and twenty-nine thousand rounds of ammunition which had been transferred from a tug in the North Sea on July 12. One of the Fianna boys described the landing:

"During the week some of the Fianna were told to report at a certain place to-day—that there was important work to be done. This morning we met as we were told, and were given these clubs [200 oak batons Bulmer Hobson had had made]. We piled them in our trek cart, and then were ordered to march with the Volunteers to Howth. Somehow or other we got the idea that we were going to get guns, but none of us knew for a fact how we were going to get them. Only the Volunteer officers, besides ourselves, knew what was in the trek cart, and as we marched all sorts of guesses were made by the Volunteers as to what was in it, while we were guessing how the guns were going to come.

"When we came near Howth two chaps came running towards us and told us to come on the double. The Volunteers were a bit fagged, but when they heard the word 'rifles' they simply raced. When we got to the harbour we saw the rifles being unloaded from a yacht. You ought to have heard the cheers when we first saw them! It was then the clubs were given out to a picked number of men and they were formed across the entrance to the pier. They were to use them if the police attempted to interfere. The rifles were handed out to the men, but there were more rifles than men, so the rest were sent into the city in motor cars. Most of the ammunition was sent in the same way, but our trek cart was loaded with it. None of it was served out to the men."[12]

Hobson paid a great tribute to the Fianna when he said they were the only body with sufficient discipline to be entrusted with ammunition. It was a wise precaution because by the time the Volunteers got back to Clontarf, the Dublin Metropolitan Police had been alerted and two trams full had been sent to meet them. The Volunteers, seeing police blocking the end of Howth Road, attempted to get around them by going right on Marino Crescent, but by the time they got to Malahide Road the police were there as well. The two groups of men stood facing each other, uncertain as to what to do. Assistant Commissioner of Police William Harrel who was at the head of the DMP, ordered the rifles to be seized, and there was a brief skirmish. By that time a company of soldiers, the King's Own Scottish Borderers, had arrived and Harrel waved them forward. The soldiers had guns loaded and bayonets fixed. Fortunately, however, Darrell Figgis, who was with the

Volunteers, stepped calmly between the groups and engaged Harrel in a long palaver. Figgis had spent three months with Erskine Childers securing the rifles in Germany and was not about to let them go. Figgis kept Harrel in conversation long enough for all but the front company to disperse. The Volunteers in the rear ranks slipped away, hid their guns wherever they could in hedges, yards, or outhouses, and disappeared. The encounter on Malahide Road was very near Croydon Park which provided convenient bushes for many rifles. Most of them were later recovered by Volunteers, but some Citizen Army men carried Howth rifles Easter Week.

A number of civilians had gathered near Malahide Road, so word of the landing traveled faster than the soldiers back to Dublin and by the time the troops returned there was a considerable crowd to escort them into town with uncomplimentary remarks and, according to the soldiers' later testimony, with more or less well-aimed rocks. As they moved into the city center and the crowds grew larger, the soldiers' tempers grew shorter. Finally, as the soldiers turned to their right off O'Connell Street to go along the quays to their barracks, on Bachelor's Walk they halted and faced about. Twenty-five or thirty soldiers were drawn in a single file across the road, some knelt in firing position, and twenty-nine shots were fired into the crowd. Thirty-five persons were treated at Jervis Street Hospital for wounds, three were killed outright, and a fourth died several weeks later.

The Royal Commission set up to investigate the day's proceedings was concerned with placing responsibility. First, did Assistant Commissioner Harrel overstep his authority when he asked General Cuthbert to send troops to seize rifles, and second, who gave the order to fire at Bachelor's Walk? There was conflicting testimony from the soldiers whether there had actually been a firing order. The King's Own Scottish Borderers were transferred from Dublin immediately, even before the hearings were over. Soon afterward the Dublin Metropolitan Police filled the position of Assistant Commissioner left vacant by Mr. Harrel's resignation.[13]

Madame first heard of the Howth gun-running at ten o'clock that night when some of the Fianna boys came to her cottage near Three Rock Mountain and triumphantly told their story and the Fianna's part in it. James Connolly's daughters, Nora and Agna, were camping there with some of the Fianna boys and girls, and it was Nora who wrote of their wild excitement. Madame vetoed their suggestion to go off to Dublin that night, but she herself was gone early the next morning. The girls were nearly ready to follow her into town when Joe Robinson came with twenty rifles that had to be unloaded, hidden and guarded. They thought they had been circumspect but apparently their care had not secured them from an observant neighbor who came and told Nora it was wrong to have the rifles there. "There's a retired police sergeant lives up the road a bit," she told them, "and he wouldn't be above telling about them."

Nora did not know what to do so she went in to the Volunteer office for advice. Liam Mellows sent two Volunteers with her back to the cottage in a taxi. The rifles were carried out again, and Nora suggested that no suspicion would be attached to the taxi if it carried a load of girls. "The girls piled in," she wrote, "the discomfort forgotten in the thought that the rifles were safe. When the rifles reached their destination, the girl separated. 'Agna!' whispered Nono, 'we'll go to the Volunteer office and ask Liam does he want us to sit on any more rifles.' Agna and Nono spent the rest of the day sitting on guns, and a rifle each was their reward when the day's work was done."[14]

The Fianna boys with the trek cart full of ammunition were also resourceful in the emergency. One of them later wrote of retreating back along the Malahide Road. All but ten or twelve had stayed at the end of the road to watch the excitement, but a few took the trek cart, wheeled left off the main road, and were soon clear of immediate danger. "We turned up a country lane near a big house and concealed ourselves in a bit of a wood on our right. It was, now, dusk, so we decided to make a pretence of camping out and to conceal the rifles and ammunition until we could have them safely removed after dark. Our commander went up to the house and got permission to camp near the wood. We buried the treasure, which was removed after dark in a taxi, and is now safe."[15]

Sean O'Casey applauded the Fianna and the good account they gave of themselves:

> Oh brave young men, our hope, our pride, our promise,
> 'Tis on you our hopes are set,
> In manliness, in kindliness, in justice,
> To make Ireland a Nation yet.[16]

John Devoy's nephew wrote him that the successful gun-running improved morale: more men were joining the Volunteers; new companies were being formed. "The result of the whole affair," he wrote, "is that the Volunteers are stronger than ever and the controlling factor in the country at present."[17] There was no doubt that the success at Howth made a great impression on the nationalists, while the Bachelor's Walk shooting reemphasized to many people their own helplessness in the face of force.

The funeral for the Bachelor's Walk victims was a display of nationalist sympathy to honor the victims of the British soldiery in Ireland. The services were held in the evening so the workers could attend. The Volunteers marched, as did the Citizen Army, the Fianna, and the Cumann na mBan. All day Madame worked with the girls at Surrey House making wreaths from flowers collected by the Fianna from sympathetic florists and friends. One of the chief mourners was a British soldier whose mother had been one of the three shot dead. A salute was fired over the graves by the Volunteers with Howth rifles. All troops were confined to barracks and that evening not a British soldier was to be seen in the street.

The following week the rest of the arms and ammunition which Childers and Figgis had purchased were brought into Kilcool. The boat bringing them had been delayed by a gale which split the mainsail, but otherwise the second gun-running was without incident.

One week after the funeral for the Bachelor's Walk victims, the United Kingdom of Great Britain and Ireland entered the war which was to guarantee the rights of small nations. The following month, on September 18, 1914, the Home Rule Act received the Royal Assent and was placed on the Statute Book, at the same time a Suspensory Act postponing its implementation was passed. Redmond's supporters hailed the Home Rule Act as a triumph for the Irish Party; the more sceptical view of many nationalists was that it was just a scrap of paper, while Carson saw it as only a postponement of the day when the war was over and he would call upon the Ulster Provisional Government to reject Home Rule for Ulster. The London-Dublin-Belfast triangle still firmly resisted being straightened to a single line.

On August 3, 1914, after Sir Edward Grey's announcement of the Government's decision to declare war, Redmond had said in the House of Commons that if the troops were withdrawn from Ireland the coast "will be defended from foreign invasion by her armed sons, and for this purpose armed Nationalist Catholics in the South will be only too glad to join arms with the armed Protestant Ulstermen in the North. We will ourselves defend the coasts of our country."[18] Throughout August and into September Redmond reiterated his pledge that the Volunteers would defend the shores of Ireland but also insisted they could not be drafted overseas nor should they be required to take the Oath of Allegiance.

However, war fever soon infected Redmond, and in September he was recruiting for the British Army. He had consistently underestimated the passion of the nationalists, and finally on September 20, in a speech at Woodenbridge, he wiped out any sympathy remaining between him and the Irish Volunteers and caused a permanent break in the movement. "This war is undertaken in defence of the highest interests of religion and morality and right," he said to the Wicklow Volunteers, "and it would be a disgrace for ever to our country, a reproach to her manhood, and a denial of the lessons of her history if young Ireland confined their efforts to remaining at home to defend the shores of Ireland from an unlikely invasion, and shrinking from the duty of proving on the field of battle that gallantry and courage which have distinguished their race all through its history. Account yourselves as men not only in Ireland itself, but wherever the firing line extends, in defence of right, of freedom and religion in this war."[19]

This announcement was so fundamentally at variance with the aims and objects of the nationalists that Redmond was in effect expelled. In a public letter dated September 24, the Provisional Committee repudiated him, announcing that he was "no longer entitled, through his nominees, to any place in the administration and guidance of the Irish Volunteer Organisation."[20] The Volunteers, in their convention on October 25, reaffirmed the manifesto adopted at the inaugural meeting, and pledged themselves to resist any conscription attempt.

The Cumann na mBan did not waste any time in declaring its allegiance to the nationalists, who remained with the Irish Volunteers under the leadership of Eoin MacNeill. The Cumann provisional committee met on October 5 and issued a pamphlet to its members reminding them they should abide loyally by the constitution of their organization. "At this time when powerful influences are at work to confuse and obscure the national issue, and when Ireland needs all her sons, we call on Irishmen to remain in their own country and join the Army of the Irish Volunteers—the Army which was founded to gain Ireland's rights and guard those rights when gained."[21]

At a membership meeting October 6, these sentiments were endorsed by an overwhelming majority. By a vote of 88 to 23, Cumann na mBan disassociated itself from the English recruiting movement.[22] Only a few Cumann na mBan members resigned when the results of the voting were announced.

During these weeks of discussion and splintering of the Volunteers into two factions, one, the National Volunteers agreeing with Redmond that Irishmen must still help England, and the other, the Irish Volunteers, holding that their first duty was to Ireland, Sean O'Casey was growing more vehemently opposed to Madame. Sometime after the Howth gun-running he decided to test his strength and popularity against hers. He may have relied on the false assumption that Madame, because of her family background, was sympathetic with Redmond, although how he could have been so mistaken is difficult to understand. In his *Story of the Irish Citizen Army* he several times inaccurately referred to her connection with the National Volunteers, i.e., Redmond's supporters. Or it may have been his inherent suspicion of the Volunteers as a whole which caused his move.

At any rate, O'Casey, as secretary, called a special meeting of the Council of the Citizen Army "to discuss the possibility of members of the Council being allowed to continue an active and sympathetic connection with the Volunteer Movement." In his own account of the hassle, he quietly records his motion: "Seeing that Madame Markievicz was, through Cumann na mBan, attached to the Volunteers, and on intimate terms with many of the Volunteer leaders, and as the Volunteers' Association was, in its methods and aims, inimical to the first interests of Labour, it could not be expected that Madame could retain the confidence of the Council; and that she be now asked to sever her connection with either the Volunteers or the Irish Citizen Army."

The resolution was vigorously opposed by several members of the Executive, including Thomas Foran who had been forewarned of O'Casey's attempt to oust Madame and had enlisted the support on her side of many members of the Executive. A vote of confidence was proposed, and, according to O'Casey, narrowly passed. Years later when he was writing the autobiographical volume *Drums Under the Windows,* he was even more bitter about the outcome of the meeting than he had been when he wrote the *Story.* The thing that bothered him was that Madame had voted for herself. It was "typical, thought Sean, for her to do [so]. Tommy Foran, President of the Union . . . put in an appearance at this [meeting], and, of course, gave his vote of confidence in Madame. Even with Tommy's vote and her own, she had but a majority of one; and had she refrained from voting for herself, as Sean did, like a fool, the vote would have been an even one."[23] The meeting called on O'Casey to apologize, but he refused and wrote his resignation.

Jim Larkin then tried to make peace. He was, if anything, more sympathetic to O'Casey's socialism than to Madame's nationalism, and called a general meeting of members to reconsider the whole question. Although O'Casey's are the only published accounts of the whole controversy, one of the members, Frank Robbins, who was present wrote down what he saw and still remembers the occasion clearly. He agreed that Larkin was closer to O'Casey on this and said that Larkin had advised Foran to keep clear of the quarrel. However, in the course of the meeting the situation reversed theatrically. O'Casey proposed that Madame Markievicz, because of her fraternization with the Irish Volunteers and Cumann na mBan and her general bourgeois tendencies, was not a fit person to be a member of the Irish Citizen Army. How he thought that Surrey House with its rolled up rugs, Fianna boys, and refugees from police showed a bourgeois tendency, he did not explain. Sounding like a minor character in one of his plays, he accused her of being a spy for the Volunteers and requested her expulsion. O'Casey rashly went on and, for some reason known only to himself, said he was afraid of no man and added, pointing dramatically at Larkin, "not even of him." This brought Larkin to his feet with a bellow of indignation and the question was no longer O'Casey versus Madame but O'Casey versus Larkin. It was not an even match. O'Casey "obliged by resigning, and leaving the Army for good."[24]

The entire affair seems petty but probably reflects many suspicions Madame had to overcome because of her birth, background, accent, and sex, as well as underlining the unnecessary but inevitable personality clashes in any movement which relies on passionate feelings for its continued appeal. O'Casey headed this chapter in his *Story* with a comment from *Julius Caesar,* "In such times as these it is not meet that every nice offence should bear its comment." In another context Arthur Koestler said about factional squabbling, "The smaller the group the more it was apt to produce experts in ideological hairsplitting and sectarian monomaniacs."[25]

In the middle of October, 1914, Jim Larkin went to America, where first fund raising and later imprisonment in Sing Sing kept him from the 1916 rebellion. James Connolly became the Acting General Secretary of the Irish Transport and General Workers' Union. He also became the editor of the *Irish Worker,* the October 24 issue of which displayed on its masthead for the first time Connolly's succinct statement of nationalistic position: "We serve neither King nor Kaiser, but Ireland." A linen banner bearing the same sentiment was flung across the front of Liberty Hall.[26]

The Citizen Army immediately began to reflect Connolly's interest in the discipline that could turn the group of men into a fighting unit. Punctuality at drills was stressed; educational lectures as well as practical drill and rifle practice were introduced; route marches and parades had more point; outdoor exercises, sometimes with the Volunteers, were initiated. A Citizen Army man remembers Connolly saying at this time, "I can always guarantee that the Irish Citizen Army will fight, but I cannot guarantee that they will be in time." The Chief of Staff was Michael Mallin who, like Connolly, had had experience in the British Army. Under their control the Citizen Army became what both White and O'Casey had wanted it to be, a tighter, more disciplined force.

Although Connolly later became impatient with the Volunteers because he thought they were letting their opportunity for rebellion pass by, his concern with cooperation among the nationalists is evident during those last months of 1914. The October 17, 1914, issue of the *Irish Worker* started a regular feature of Cumann na mBan notes and for a short time had Irish Volunteer notes as well. Madame may have had something to do with this innovation.

Various attempts were made to weld together the nationalists of different outlooks. One of the early organizations was called the Irish Neutrality League. It had a short life of one public meeting, on October 12, 1914, and was, William O'Brien said, an organization of leaders without members. It was sponsored by the I.R.B. as a possible recruiting ground for the secret movement and for spreading anti-British recruiting propaganda. The meeting was announced "as a set off to John Redmond's recent recruiting meeting in the Mansion House and to define the position of Ireland in relation to the present European war." James Connolly took the chair, and on the platform were Arthur Griffith, who proposed declaration of the objects of the League, Major John MacBride, who seconded the motion, and Madame, William O'Brien, Sean T. O'Kelly, Sean Milroy, and J. J. Scollan, all of whom spoke to the motion. Some lectures were later given under the League's auspices, but British military restrictions soon made the organization impossible. However, it fulfilled to some degree the purpose of the I.R.B., which had sponsored it as a means of agitating through an open organization.

Anti-enlisting campaigns were not new to Ireland. The first regular campaign had been started during the Boer War by the Transvaal Committee, with information sent out by the Cumann na nGaedheal. The Inghinidhe then took over the activities and for several years had the assistance of the Fianna. One of their continual activities was printing bills on their hand press at Surrey House and putting them up around Dublin. Naturally much of the posting was done at night. Madame was credited with introducing the bicycle as a necessary part of the equipment. She soon realized that a bill she could paste up by standing on the road could as easily be torn down by the first policeman to discover it. The bicycle provided not only fast transportation, but she could lean it against the wall, stand on the seat, and paste the leaflet out of normal reach. The bills were printed on gummed paper so that all the anti-recruiter needed to paste them up was a bottle of water and a sponge.

The Fianna boys delighted in after-dark activity of this kind which involved them in all the thrills of the chase. They loved posting such inflammatory sentiments as "Irishmen, Beware, Enlistment in England's Armed Forces is Treachery to Ireland!" Sometimes they included pro-Fianna posters, "Be true to Ireland and do not join the Baden Powell Scouts." The war only increased the importance to Ireland of the work the Fianna and the Inghinidhe had been doing for years.

The Fianna were being turned into a cadet corps specially trained for reconnaissance. The boys were assigned to observe various areas and within a given time report their findings to their commanding officer. A report in the *Irish Volunteer* of September 19, 1914, gives an idea of how the boys were trained. "Two Fianna, Liam Og Murphy and Liam Toomey, whose duty it was to reconnoitre O'Connell Street submitted in a very short time accurate information as to the length, breadth, and manner of paving of the street, also details of number and description of shops, picture theatres, public monuments and electric lights, and an estimate of the pedestrian traffic." And in the same notice, "The Section Leaders and Corporals assembled at Parnell Square 5:30 A.M. Sunday and accompanied the 1st Battalion of the Dublin Regiment of the Volunteers on their march to the Dublin mountains for manoeuvres. During the day the Fianna acted as guides to many of the units."

The value of the Fianna training became more and more widely noted. Fianna boys had rendered good service during the strike by using their knowledge of first aid on victims of batons. The death of one boy, Patsy O'Connor, in 1915, was thought to have been indirectly caused by his batoning in 1913 while he was giving first aid to another victim. The boys had also proved they were trained for other emergencies. At a St. Enda's Fête during the summer, a fire broke out in one of the pavilions. Panic seized the audience, many of them youngsters. Some of the Fianna joined hands and formed a line to stop the rush of people, others drew off part of the crowd in an orderly fashion to the gates, while others cleared the pavilion of its valuables.

On another occasion, when the boys were camped in the field in front of Madame's cottage, word came that one of the local lads had been drowned while trying to swim in an abandoned quarry. None of his comrades could swim, and before help arrived his body had been under water about twenty minutes. Four Fianna boys rushed to the quarry and after more than two hours succeeded in bringing up the boy's body. The policeman who had arrived on the scene was a non-swimmer himself and stood by while the boys persevered. The attitude of local cottagers, who had been suspicious of city boys camping and shooting on the mountain, changed to one of acceptance and admiration.

The flag Madame had designed for the Fianna was a gold sunburst on a blue field, with "na Fianna Eireann" written across it. The badge was a full sunburst with a pike head superimposed. Around the top border was "na Fianna Eireann," and around the bottom border was written in Gaelic "Remember Limerick and Saxon treachery." The fifteen points on the sunburst represented the twelve points of the code of honor and the three of the Fianna motto, "Purity in our hearts, Strength in our arms, Truth on our lips."

In 1914 the first Fianna handbook was issued. Madame's influence is evident throughout. She drew the cover showing Ireland as a goddess in Gaelic dress, standing on a hillcrest with a sunrise behind her. She called it "The dawn of freedom," although it was untitled in the book. She wrote the introduction and arranged for articles from Sir Roger Casement and Padraic Pearse. The articles were both emotional and practical. Visions of past martyrs and future heroes were collected with instructions in first aid, knot-tying, signalling, swimming, camping, and observation.

Madame made a strong emotional appeal: "This year has felt the spirit of Cathleen ni Houlahan moving once more through the land. It will take the best and noblest of Ireland's children to win Freedom, for the price of Freedom is suffering and pain." She appealed to the memories of the Irish heroes, the Manchester Martyrs, Robert Emmet, and Wolfe Tone. She went further afield and enjoined them to emulate the love of country demonstrated by Joan of Arc, by Madar Lal Dingra, by Savarkar, by the nameless heroes of the South African veldt. "Join Na Fianna Eireann, the young army of Ireland, and help to place the crown of freedom on Her head."

Sir Roger Casement's appeal, entitled "Chivalry," was in the same tone. He was proving a helpful recruit to the nationalists since his retirement from the British foreign service. "Chivalry dies when Imperialism begins. The one must kill the other. A chivalrous people must respect in others what they strive to maintain in themselves. The inheritance of chivalry is with us still—a motherland to serve, a fair country to be freed."

In a lively and scholarly essay, "The Fianna of Fionn," Padraic Pearse traced the inheritance of the lads of the third Fianna. The history of the first Fianna "is one of the proudest and saddest of all stories: proud because it tells of such valour and truth and cleanness of life, sad inasmuch as it shows how a goodly fellowship passed away and became only a name on the lips of shanachies because its members quarrelled among themselves and brother turned his arms against brother. For no strength of hand or valour of heart will hold a league or an army or a nation together unless there be peace and gentle brotherhood between all who are of that league or army or nation." Civil war within the decade was to prove this a sadly prophetic statement.

The Fianna handbook was used by the Irish Volunteers as a training manual in the early days, particularly its fifty pages on drill and rifle exercises. It was the best source of training information easily available. Eoin MacNeill, a professor of history, thought that all teachers and managers of boys' schools should have a copy of the handbook. He, among others, urged every boy in Ireland to learn to shoot straight. Joseph McGarrity later asked John Devoy to send a copy of the handbook to Casement when he was in Germany recruiting the Irish Brigade. The combination of high sentiment and practical information made it one of the most useful and widely read pieces of nationalist literature.

After the success of the handbook, the Fianna decided to issue a Christmas paper. It was financed by advertisements from a variety of businesses: McQuillan's who could supply tools, cutlery, scouts supplies, and revolvers; from Monument House which had band instruments and uniforms; from Whelan's who were official outfitters to Fianna na hEireann; from tailors eager to make volunteer uniforms; and from various other businessmen who were willing to clean windows, sell food, typewriters, and guns.

Some of the few surviving letters from Madame before 1916 were about this Christmas paper.[27] Two to Robert Brennan catch some of her breathless activity:

Dear Mr. Brennan

Some of the Fianna are starting a new venture—a Fianna Xmas Annual, & so I am writing to beg a short story off you. Its all been decided on with a terrible rush at the last moment, Percy Reynolds, the boy who came down in the motor with us, is "business manager" & has been out twice for adds, & got a lot; but we have no literature at all as yet. We are going to try & make it bright & funny & not too political, nor too much propaganda, just a good boys Xmas number. We see a good deal of a Wexford member of the Fianna at present, Mr. Devereux. He is a great Nationalist. Miss Molony is tearing up things for bandages & making shirts for soldiers with Mme. Gonne. She writes very little & very seldom. Everything seems to be such an awful mix-up just now, I wish one could see what was coming. With kind regards to Mrs. Brennan.

Yrs, Constance de Markievicz

Dear Mr. Brennan

Many thanks for yours. It is awfully good of you to think of us at all when you are so busy. Sat. 21st is the last moment. I got the promise of a very fine poem today, from George Russel (AE) if he can find two lines to end it in time! By the way do you know where I can get a lttle play "When Wexford Rose" by Kehoe. He gave us leave to act it, & we want to put it on again in a fortnight & I cant find a copy! I remember he came from somewhere in Wexford. We are awfully busy here day & night, meetings, paper, etc. etc. No one knows what to expect next. Kind regards to Mrs. Brennan.

This letter is signed "i gcuis na hEireann" (in the cause of Ireland), which Madame regularly used to close her letters.

AE found two last lines for his poem, "To a Statesman." He asked, "You tell us that you war on war, why do you treat our wit with scorn?" It was in this Christmas paper that Madame first told "How the Fianna was Started." At the bottom of the last page of her introduction was an announcement for a book of national, labor, and other verse by Maeve Cavanagh called "Sheaves of Revolt" which she had dedicated to the Fianna. "Corporal Willie Nelson" (Padraic O'Riain) contributed an account of the Fianna's part in the Howth gun-running. From James Connolly came an often-reprinted article on "Boys and Parents" which called on the boys to work for social progress and learn from the past, at the same time. Seamas O'Sullivan gave a poem on the Donegal Volunteers. There were notes from Colonel Maurice Moore and Bulmer Hobson, a cartoon by Grace Gifford, a poem by Frank G. Reynolds, and three short stories.[28]

"S.M." contributed a boyishly gruesome tale about grave-robbing on an Arctic expedition, perhaps inspired by or told by Madame's father and retold by her to Stanislas Markiewicz, who wrote it for the paper. This was the only item in the issue that did not have some Irish, or obviously anti-English bias. Stanislas' father was somewhere in the Balkans. His stepmother loved him but was busy with the affairs of an alien land in which he had no interest. In a sense, he was one of the first displaced persons of the great war.

The Christmas issue published, Madame continued with money-raising schemes for Cumann na mBan, for the Citizen Army, for the Irish Women's Franchise League. Although her acting days were over, she liked to recite. She nearly always chose patriotic poems such as AE's "Gods of War," or something by Maeve Cavanagh or Seamus O'Sullivan. Sometimes she would recite her own rhymthically thumping poems, particularly her "Battle Hymn," published in 1915. "It isn't great poetry," she said of it, "but it's good propaganda." One of her acquaintances from those years remembers an occasional social evening unconnected with the cause when Madame would read Keats to the piano accompaniment of a friend. These evenings were not many, however. She was usually going to a meeting, a drill, a fund-raising affair, a class, or a lecture. She was wherever she thought she could help the cause.

As Connolly became more confident that the Citizen Army would not only fight but also would be there in time, he occasionally used them in a show of defiance. The ICA became increasingly better trained and equipped, although they never numbered more than 1,000 and it is estimated that less than a third of those were consistently active. Throughout the year and a half between Larkin's departure and the Rebellion, they were seen more and more around Dublin.

The Volunteers and the Citizen Army were both represented at a meeting on November 13, 1914, in St. Stephen's Green held to protest a deportation order for Robert Monteith. Captain Monteith had been dismissed from his job with the Ordnance Department, Island Bridge, on November 12, and ordered to leave Dublin by noon on the 13th. His activity in the Irish Volunteers was the known but unspecified reason for the order. The protest meeting was presided over by William O'Brien and consisted of vigorous speeches by James Connolly, Sean Milroy, W. P. Partridge, P. T. Daly, and, of course, Madame, who would not let an opportunity like this slip by. She announced that the Cumann na mBan were learning to shoot so that they might help resist conscription. On the motion of Connolly, the crowd pledged themselves as fighters for Ireland, never to rest until they were privileged to see Ireland a free and independent Republic among the nations. The sentiments expressed were much the same as the ones shouted in 1911, but now, three years later, the world had changed. The nationalists were organized and armed, Europe was engaged in a mass slaughter, and setting up an Irish Republic was a possibility, rather than an "ideal unlikely to be attained."

The November demonstration at St. Stephen's Green was not interfered with, although a large force of police stood by and watched. The meeting ended with the singing of "A Nation Once Again" and the firing of a number of shots by the Volunteers. A cavalry regiment, the Fifth Lancers, stood to their horses in the Castle Yard for some hours before the meeting and remained there after the meeting ended. Two companies of infantry were under arms in each military barracks. Neither the Lancers nor the soldiers were called out that day. Bachelor's Walk was too close, and recruiting for England too important to risk inflaming public opinion against them.

Some mystery surrounds a trip Nora Connolly made to America just before Christmas that year. Her father telegraphed her to come to Dublin from her home in Belfast. At Liberty Hall he asked her to undertake a very secret and serious job, one so dangerous that five people, including herself, would surely be hanged for treason if it were discovered. The other four were Tom Clarke, Sean MacDermott, Madame, and Connolly. She had to rely on her very good memory because her mission was too dangerous to put on paper.

The job may have been an endeavor to make contact with Germany, as Connolly's biographer, C. Desmond Greaves, has suggested, although Sir Roger Casement was already in Berlin. It may have been an espionage report on British anti-submarine activities, as others have said. Although Sean MacDermott and Tom Clarke were important members of the I.R.B., Connolly did not join until the end of January,

1916, and, of course, there were no women in that organization.[29] It is thus highly unlikely that the message was concerned with a rising or anything connected with a rebellion. It has been suggested that the information concerned some military news that would have been valuable to Germany but it was apparently already known to the German office through other channels. It may have been a gesture of faith in the Germans. However, it was certainly activity which could be considered treasonable by the British, and it was in character for those involved, all of whom were willing to do anything for Ireland.[30]

Nora stayed at Surrey House with Madame until it was time to go to Liverpool where she took the ship to New York. She was met by Jim Larkin and by her friend, Sidney Gifford, and stayed with the Padraic Colums for several weeks until her father deemed it safe for her to return to Ireland. At John Devoy's request she brought back letters from Sir Roger Casement, who was in Germany, and also some money. She made her report to the other four who were involved, and after lengthy discussion went home to Belfast.

A strange foursome of conspirators remained in Dublin. Tom Clarke, with sunken cheeks and slightly seedy, drooping mustache, looked for all the world like the middling tobacconist he was. He was also the grand old man of wisdom who had suffered in prison months of solitary confinement, had endured exile, and had returned to be one of the main strategists in the I.R.B. and their link with the Fenian brotherhood. McDermott was a suave ex-bartender and one of the great Irish charmers. Polio in 1911 had left him with a limp so that he looked the part of the Byron of Irish revolution. It was he who had sent grapes and roses to imprisoned Irish rebel ladies. Connolly, with his owlish, round, serious face, was inventive, brilliant, and practical. And there was Madame. They had in common only a cause and an almost absolute lack of fear. Together they represented all the nationalist groups and were quite capable of anything they thought necessary, as events were to prove.

NOTES TO CHAPTER VI

1. Maud Gonne MacBride, *A Servant of the Queen* (Dublin, 1950), pp. 189–190, reporting her American lecture tour which had been organized by the Clan na Gael. "Parnell was dead and Redmond and Dillon were quarrelling over who should hold the carrot," she told her American audiences.

2. William McMullen, introduction to James Connolly, *The Workers' Republic* (Dublin, 1951), p. 22.

3. March 28, 1914.

4. Captain J. R. White, *Misfit: An Autobiography* (London, 1930), pp. 288–299.

5. Ibid., p. 304.

6. John Devoy, *Recollections of an Irish Rebel* (New York, 1929), p. 394.

7. P. O'Cathasaigh, *The Story of the Irish Citizen Army* (Dublin, 1919), p. 21.

8. Sean O'Casey, *Drums Under the Windows,* p. 342. The flag was taken by a British soldier after the surrender in 1916 but eventually found its way back to Dublin and is now displayed in the National Museum. It is somewhat the worse for wear but has remained inspiringly fresh in the memories of the workers. One of the Citizen Army men called into the Museum to help authenticate it said, "That faded thing couldn't be it, *our* flag was *beautiful.*"

9. *Irish Press,* February 4, 1936.

10. Quoted in Macardle, *The Irish Republic,* pp. 105–106.

11. They were Eamonn Ceannt, Con Colbert, Eamon Martin, Padraic Pearse, Sean MacDermott, and Piaras Beaslai. The others were M. J. Judge, a Captain in the Volunteers, and John Fitzgibbon, who had been one of the eleven men at the initial meeting the previous November 11.

12. Nora Connolly O'Brien, *Portrait of a Rebel Father* (Dublin, 1935), pp. 180–181. Darrell Figgis, *Recollections of the Irish War 1914–1921* (New York, n.d.), pp. 11–58, details his part in securing the arms, their landing, and the subsequent events of the day. Thomas MacDonagh and Bulmer Hobson were in charge of the arrangements in Ireland, Cathal Brugha was in command of the men at the pier. Darrell Figgis, who had been instrumental in obtaining the guns, was also at the pier. Liam Mellows commanded the Fianna.

13. At the hearings a curious distinction was made between the gun running at Ulster and at Howth. "In Ulster the arms were taken away and secreted and brought out after a lapse of time, so that it was impossible to identify them as the arms which had been illegally imported." Royal Commission into the Circumstances Connected with the Landing of Arms at Howth on July 26, 1914. Minutes of Evidence, CD. 7649 (London: H.M. Stationery Office, 1914), p. 62.

14. O'Brien, *Portrait of a Rebel Father,* pp. 183–184.

15. *Fianna,* Christmas issue, 1914, p. 12.

16. *Irish Worker,* August 1, 1914.

17. Letter dated 1 August 1914, in Maloney collection, New York Public Library.

18. Great Britain, *Parliamentary Debates* (Commons), 5th series, LXV, 20th July–10th August 1914, cols. 1828–1829.

19. Quoted in F. X. Martin, O.S.A., ed., *The Irish Volunteers 1913–1915* (Dublin, 1963), p. 148.

20 Ibid., pp. 153.

21. Pamphlet issued by "The Provisional Committee" and dated October 5, 1914, 206 Gr. Brunswick St., Dublin. It was signed by Mrs. Wyse-Power, president, Madame O'Rahilly, vice-president, and eight other members of the Executive.

22. *Sinn Fein,* October 17, 1914. This was a reversal of the numbers of men who remained in the Irish Volunteers. Although it is difficult to get figures, Piaras Beaslai, in his 1926 biography of Michael Collins, estimated that at the time of the split in 1914 the paper strength of the Volunteers was about 200,000, and of these only about 12,000 followed the lead of the Provisional Committee, but their numbers increased while the numbers of the Redmondite Volunteers dwindled rapidly. At their last public appearance, in April, 1915, they mustered 18,000, but by 1916 they had practically ceased to exist. The small nucleus that remained, headed by Colonel Maurice Moore, broke away from Redmond in 1917, and went over to the side of Ireland. Piaras Beaslai, *Michael Collins and the Making of a New Ireland* (Dublin, 1926), I, 52–54.

23. *Drums,* p. 391.

24. Ibid. Frank Robbins, in conversations in Dublin in 1963–64, recounted his version of the meeting he attended.

25. *Arrow in the Blue* (New York, 1952), p. 175.

26. The banner hung across the front of Liberty Hall for several weeks until the defiant announcement was removed during the night of December 19–20, under orders of Brigadier General F. F. Hill, Commanding the Troops, Dublin.

27. These letters are in the National Museum of Ireland, as is one of the few surviving copies of the Fianna Christmas paper. One of the letters was written in August, 1914, to Madge Daly, asking her to thank her uncle for his generosity in taking such a big ad. The back cover of the paper is an advertisement from John Daly, Baker and Confectioner, Limerick. He was the ardent Fenian who was imprisoned with Tom Clarke; his niece married Clarke, and his nephew was Commandant Edward Daly, who was at the Four Courts in 1916 and was subsequently executed.

28. In spite of criticism in the *Irish Volunteer* that it was not educational enough, the paper was a success and its seventeen pages a good buy for a penny. Most of the articles were reprinted from time to time in various national publications and some are still in print. The third edition of the Fianna Handbook which was published in 1964 used Connolly's "Boys and Parents" and the article on chivalry by Sir Roger Casement.

On the strength of the Christmas issue the Fianna started a monthly paper in February, 1915, which survived for five issues. Fianna notes also regularly appeared in the *Irish Volunteer* from July, 1914, until June, 1915.

Some of the senior Fianna boys helped to train the women of Cumann na mBan and to drill the Volunteers. Seamus Pounce, one of the "Surrey clique," remembers with pride that Madame presented him with a token of appreciation for his help in instructing the Inghinidhe branch in stretcher and arms drill.

29. Maud Gonne and one or two other women claimed to have been sworn into the I.R.B., but the affiliation was never recognized by the bulk of the members.

30. O'Brien, *Portrait of a Rebel Father,* pp. 210–217; C. Desmond Greaves, *The Life and Times of James Connolly,* pp. 290–293; Robert Briscoe, *For the Life of Me,* p. 36; Frank Robbins in conversations, 1963–1964.

VII

The Citizen Army Drills

1915–February 1916

Nineteen-fifteen was a year of preparation. As the war in Europe involved larger and larger numbers of men, it became obvious to some of the Irish nationalists that this was the opportunity their generation had been waiting for. Not all of them shared Padraic Pearse's mystic conviction of the necessity of rededication through blood sacrifice. Indeed, many seemed content to talk, march, and wait. But it was clear to some that Ireland's stand for freedom must be made soon. Connolly was the Citizen Army leader of that faction and Madame a lieutenant.

In February the Irish Citizen Army joined the Irish Transport Workers' Union in a ceremony at Croydon Park to honor Madame for her services during the great lockout. She was presented with an elaborately illuminated address bordered in Celtic knots to suggest eternal life and illustrated with sketches of Lissadell and Liberty Hall and a profile photograph of herself taken a few years before in a silk gown and jewels, with her hair tied back in a wide band. It acknowledged her a true aristocrat in the terms of Irish labor:

"At a time when the prisons were full of innocent men, women and girls, and all looked black before us, you came to our aid to organise relief; and for months worked amongst us, and served the cause of Labour by such untiring toil, far seeing vigilance and sympathetic insight as cheered and encouraged all who were privileged to witness it, as well as that great multitude of patient fighters for whose relief it was directed. Inspired and enthused by your example, we were proud to have you amongst us, and now that the fight is over, we desire that you remain one of us, and to that end we unanimously elect you Countess as an Honorary Member of our fighting Irish Union." It was signed by ten men, including Thomas Foran, the President, and James Connolly.

Madame was very proud of the honor, and the address hung in

Surrey House, along with the Count's "Bread Triptych," her own "The Conscript," and other favorite pictures until Easter Week. In the first letter she wrote after the Rising, she was worried about it and her pictures and asked her sister to store them. Miraculously they survived.[1]

Nearly every Sunday night there were concerts or plays in Liberty Hall. One of them was a drama of Fenian rising by James Connolly called *Under Which Flag.* The lead was taken by Sean Connolly who had played with Madame in the Count's melodrama *The Memory of the Dead.*[2] Always there were songs and recitations. A Transport Union man remarked recently, "Connolly was a singing man. The Citizen Army didn't have many guns but they had lots of songs." They always sang on their route marches such stirring Irish songs as "O'Donnell Abu," "Step Together," "Wrap the Green Flag Around Me," and sometimes a recklessly insolent doggerel by Madame called "The Germans Are Winning the War Me Boys."

Under wartime restrictions the *Irish Worker* had been suppressed in November, 1914, at about the same time as other nationalist papers, *Sinn Fein, Eire,* and *Irish Freedom,* had ceased publication. Connolly printed a few issues from Belfast but was forced to abandon the project. However, by May 29, 1915, he was able to start publishing *The Workers' Republic.*[3] Rebellion, however secret, is unthinkable in Ireland without a public journal. This one was printed at Liberty Hall on a rickety second-hand press which was to turn out many seditious paragraphs before its last job, the publication of the proclamation of the Irish Republic in April, 1916.

In the editorial of the first edition of *The Workers' Republic,* Connolly stated that his purpose was "to increase the intelligence of the slave, to sow broadcast the seed of that intelligence, that they may take root and ripen into revolt, to be the interpreter of that revolt, and finally to help in guiding it to victory." Across the masthead he exhorted his readers with Camille Desmoulins' words, "The great only appear great because we are on our knees: let us rise."

Throughout the summer months the new *Workers' Republic* devoted considerable space to Citizen Army education. Connolly used the ICA notes in every issue to summarize various insurrections and draw conclusions about the lessons to be learned from each. They were often more optimistic than the occasion warranted, but his enthusiasm never flagged. Rebels should know the history of revolt. The first lesson was devoted to the Moscow Insurrection of 1905, which he thought succeeded in establishing the fact that even under modern conditions, the professional soldier is, in a city, badly handicapped against really determined civilian revolutionists. About the 1821 defense of the Alamo, he said, "It was one of those defeats which are more valuable to a cause than many loudly trumpeted victories. It gave spirit and bitterness to the Texan forces and more important still gave time to their comrades elsewhere." The insurrection in Dublin, 1916, was to be such a defeat.

The battles he used for examples ranged far afield: the Tyrol in 1809, Belgium in 1830, Paris in the same year and again in 1848, Lexington in 1775. Mallin wrote of guerrilla warfare in India. Again and again Connolly told the Citizen Army to study and prepare, for their own time was coming. The general summary of the series was that "Defence is of almost overwhelming importance in such warfare as a popular force like the Citizen Army might be called upon to participate in." He gave lectures on street fighting to the Citizen Army at Liberty Hall and did his best to prepare the workers to be soldiers in the coming fight. On only one point did Connolly's socialist beliefs lead him to false conclusions: he was convinced that capitalist England would not destroy buildings and property of their capitalist counterparts in Ireland. Considering how often in Ireland real estate had been considered more valuable than human life, this was an understandable error. He was disabused only when the gunboat *Helga* began shelling Dublin on the Wednesday of Easter Week.

The Irish Citizen Army prepared and so did the Irish Volunteers. The annual Wolfe Tone commemoration at Bodenstown was the occasion for a display of nationalist strength and solidarity as it had been the previous year, and the Irish Volunteers and Citizen Army again shared honors. Madame led the Fianna as usual, and the Cumann na mBan were there in numbers. Tom Clarke spoke the graveside address, and Madame said that "the vision of freedom was in his eyes, and looking in his eyes we got a glimpse of the promised land."[4]

But the most important ceremony that summer and the most memorable for the nationalists was the funeral of O'Donovan Rossa on August 1, 1915. The old Fenian, long in exile in the United States, had died there in July. His body was returned to Ireland and lay in state in the City Hall. Funerals for national heroes in Ireland can have an almost ancient Egyptian magnitude and tens of thousands of men and women paid homage to the old man whose life had been spent in the cause of Ireland. The Volunteers and the Citizen Army alternated the honor guard at the lying-in-state. Not since Parnell's funeral had there been such a display in Dublin as there was when Rossa's body was taken to Glasnevin for burial. British authorities were completely absent, neither soldiers nor police were in the streets that day. The Volunteers and Citizen Army took over traffic control, guiding the procession and forming the guard of honor who marched on both sides of the hearse. Madame was a Cumann na mBan representative on the huge committee which planned and carried out the funeral and marched in the procession. It was on that committee she first met Eamon de Valera. In the line of march Padraic O'Riain commanded the large number of Fianna boys.

The Workers' Republic reprinted Walt Whitman's "To a Foil'd European Revolutionaire" and especially recommended its study in connection with the national honor being given to O'Donovan Rossa— one of those whom a cautious but foolish world thinks of as foiled revolutionists. Whitman, "the sworn poet of every dauntless rebel the world over," reminded those who would despair because "the cause is asleep" that "Liberty has not gone out of the place":

> When there are no more memories of heroes and martyrs,
> And when all life and all the souls of men and women are discharged from any part of the earth,
> Then only shall liberty or the idea of liberty be discharged from that part of the earth,
> And the infidel come into full possession.
> Then courage European revolter, revoltress!
> For till all ceases neither must you cease.

To the commemoration booklet issued by the funeral committee, Connolly contributed "Why the Citizen Army Honours Rossa." He affirmed Whitman's theme of the lasting value of ideas and concluded that they were present to honor O'Donovan Rossa "by right of our faith in the separate destiny of our country, and our faith in the ability of the Irish Workers to achieve that destiny." He reiterated this in an address to the Citizen Army as they prepared to take their places in the march to Glasnevin.

Padraic Pearse's graveside oration was short and moving, and he, too, turned the memory of the dead rebel into a battle cry. Pearse stood impassive and serious, almost unmoving until the end. "They think that they have foreseen everything, provided against everything"— here his hand cleft the air three times as if exorcising all enemies— "but the fools, the fools, the fools!—they have left us our Fenian dead, and while Ireland holds these graves Ireland unfree shall never be at peace." In the gloom of the late afternoon of a rainy day, as Irishmen fired three volleys over the new grave and the Last Post was sounded by Bugler Oman of the Citizen Army, men, women, and boys in uniform rededicated themselves to Ireland. The younger generation, particularly, were challenged by the power and pride of the ceremony. "The fools, the fools, the fools." It was an incantation of faith.

A few weeks before the Rossa funeral, the Fianna, at their annual convention, had reorganized under strictly military lines. They no longer tried to be anything but military, and established a G.H.Q. to bring their organization into line with that of the Irish Volunteers. The I.R.B. thought it time to acknowledge publicly its control and its need of the Fianna. Captain Eamon Martin, in proposing the change, said that the anomaly of having a president instead of a military chief at the head of their organization was ludicrous, that the movement was essentially a military one and judging from the resolutions of the Congress it was their desire to have it even more military than ever.

Surprisingly enough, although it may have been prearranged by the controlling Circle to make the change seem less like a foregone conclusion, both Bulmer Hobson and Con Colbert opposed the change and said that character building and training boys to be good citizens of the Irish nation were more important than drill or even musketry. Madame spoke to the question, but she was astute enough to realize the Fianna had not been in her control since the I.R.B. moved in four years before and she did not oppose the change strongly. Although all the other honorary offices were abolished, that of President was kept, and Madame retained the title.[5] This was partly in recognition of all she had done for the Fianna and partly as a placating maneuver. She was still a favorite speaker at meetings, she wrote poems and articles for them, the boys continued to camp near her cottage, and her interest in them continued strong. With this reorganization in July, 1915, the Fianna were even more a direct training school for the Volunteers.

Madame's own interests and energies during 1915 were diverted primarily to the labor movement and the Citizen Army. This was, she thought, the place where her strengths were recognized and her talents utilized without any regard to her sex. In a lecture to the Irish Women's Franchise League in October she deplored the idea that women's role was "not a companion or a friend, but a beautiful houri holding dominion by her careful manipulation of her sex and her good looks." She argued that it would be better for women to "dress suitably in short skirts and strong boots, leave your jewels in the bank, and buy a revolver. Don't trust to your 'feminine charm' and your capacity for getting on the soft side of men, but take up your responsibilities and be prepared to go on your own way depending for safety on your own courage, your own truth and your own common sense, and not on the problematic chivalry of the men you may meet on the way. The two brilliant classes of women who follow this higher ideal are suffragettes and the Trades Union or Labour women. In them lies the hope of the future."[6] Few women in her audience had valuable jewels to leave in a bank, but the appeal is obvious. Although she remained a member of the Cumann na mBan, indeed, was its president, and two weeks after this speech went to Belfast to address a public meeting for them, Madame was critical of the role assigned them. The IWFL's *Irish Citizen* had, since the founding of the Volunteers, complained of the subservient place of women in the organization, and Madame was repeating the assertions made by other militant women when she complained: "Today the women attached to national movements are there chiefly to collect funds for the men to spend. These Ladies' Auxiliaries demoralise women, set them up in separate camps, and deprive them of all initiative and independence. Women are left to rely on sex charm, or intrigue and backstairs influence."

Diplomacy she did not understand, tact merely delayed action. She was direct, forceful, idealistic, and positive herself and had difficulty understanding that some women and men thought their aims could be achieved in other ways. She therefore translated for the suffragettes Connolly's conviction that the time for direct action was at hand.

Fighting was not the only direct action she considered. Miss Molony and Madame were instrumental in starting the Irish Workers Co-operative Society which had a store on Eden Quay next to Liberty Hall. The Co-operative was started to give employment. In the work-room were a dozen sewing machines on which shirts and undercloth-ing were made for sale in the shop where nationalist publications were also sold. It was a small but successful undertaking with stock worth in all about £200.[7] The Irish Women Workers Union, of which Miss Molony was the General Secretary and a motivating force, was organ-ized in November. Madame and James Connolly were elected vice-presidents at the inaugural meeting, the treasurer was Miss Mulhall. James Larkin, though in America, was still technically head of the IT and GWU and was elected president of the Women's Union as well.

Nearly every Sunday and bank holiday the Citizen Army had drills and parades, and as the training progressed there were mock attacks on various buildings in the city. One maneuver around Dublin Castle led to wide speculations about when a real attack would take place and to some extravagant attempts to explain the failure to occupy the Castle Easter Week. The complex of buildings called the Castle, which included a hospital, was unusually well guarded, and there is doubt that an attack on it was ever anticipated.

However, in October, 1915, on a night when a thick, heavy fog hung low over Dublin, the whole Citizen Army, men and women, was mobilized and each section detailed to go from Liberty Hall to the Castle along different routes. They were all nerved up to a high pitch, not knowing themselves whether this was a practice or a real attack. As they waited for their marching orders they asked each other over and over again, "It this it? Is this it?" It turned out to be only a drill but the fog-shrouded figures and the muffled tramping converging from all directions on the symbol of British domination made a lasting impression on the marchers as well as on the officials in the Castle. The men of the G-division, the government's detective force, were out in strength, trying to cover the movements of the various groups.

The companies set out from Liberty Hall at midnight; two hours later the "attack" was over and the attackers and those who had played at defending the Castle all marched to the Emmet Hall at Inchicore for tea and songs. One of the "defenders" remarked, "Imagine going through all this to help the old Castle, when I'd go through twice as much to pull it down." The rest of the night was a social occasion. "At five o'clock," one soldier remembered, "we re-joined the police outside and were pleased to find that it had been raining while we were enjoying ourselves, so that the poor fellows were not dry. We then marched home."

When the Citizen Army did not rattle sabers, Madame did it for them. She made again her appeal for action, as she did on every possible occasion, at a lecture by Francis Sheehy Skeffington to the Irish Women's Franchise League on his impressions of America. Connolly presided at this welcome-home meeting. Connolly thought Skeffington had shown the value of moral courage and demonstrated what he (Connolly) had always held—that it was possible to be an advocate of advanced social reform and at the same time to be intensely national: "It was those who had the strongest desire to secure social freedom who could best be trusted to fight for national freedom."[8] His statement makes a much-debated concept seem clear.

Although a pacifist, Skeffington could be violent-tongued. On this occasion he was flattering and mild. He admired the self-confidence of the American women he had seen, but did not think they were as good speakers as the Irish suffragettes. He though that the American women were not so ripe politically, despite their immense energy and enterprise, as either English or Irish women. They were too much afraid of ideas, particularly of being associated with anything like labor or socialism. It was only at a meeting in Chicago that he found freedom of spirit, breadth of view and grasp of fundamentals strong enough to warrant high praise: "It might almost have been a meeting of the Irish Women's Franchise League."

In the course of his speech the audience applauded his approval of the Ford Peace Crusade and at the conclusion of the meeting cabled an expression of sympathy with the Peace Crusade to the Ford Mission at the Hague.[9] Madame dissented. She said she thought it represented a noble ideal but she did not want the war stopped until the British Empire was smashed. As a result of these remarks, Skeffington, who was appalled at the carnage in Europe, in a letter to *The Workers' Republic* of January 15, challenged Madame to a public debate. Her reply, published the following week, was what he expected:

> Mr. Skeffington has challenged me to prove that Ireland will gain more by the continuation of the war till the British Empire is smashed up than by a speedy peace. I accept his challenge, and unless the Defenders of a certain tottering Realm intervene, I am prepared to meet him when and where he pleases and prove to him—what I believe that he in his heart believes—and what many a person worthier has suffered and even died to prove, that now as ever "England's difficulty is Ireland's opportunity."

The debate was held on February 15, 1916. Two of the audience recorded what went on and interpreted it in diametrically opposite ways. Louie Bennett wrote, "Madame Markievicz has no powers of debate. She reiterated the same few points in various wild, flowery phrases, and talked much of dying for Ireland. The open discussion was ominous. The Countess had the meeting with her. Skeffington's supporters numbered twenty-six. Her supporters spoke in a bitter and sinister vein. I gathered they were willing to watch the war continue, with all its dreadful losses and consequences, if only it led to the over-throw of England and consequent release of Ireland. I broke out at the cowardice of that. I spoke pretty strongly and was listened to with civility. Then Connolly stood up and spoke at some length, claiming extra time from the chairman. As well as I can remember he spoke strongly in favour of seizing the moment to fight now against England."[10]

The debate was much less ominous to Mrs. Skeffington, who wrote: "The topic was 'Shall We Make Peace Now?' He was pro-peace, she for a longer war, as she held Britain was being beaten. After a warmly-contested word-duel, just before the vote was taken, James Connolly, who had been a quiet on-looker, suddenly intervened, on Madame's side, swinging the meeting round. When Skeffington laughingly reproved him for throwing in his weight at the end, he replied, with twinkling eyes, 'I was afraid you might get the better of it, Skeffington. That would never do.' "[11]

At that time, although it was known only to the Military Council of the I.R.B. to which Connolly had been co-opted just a few weeks before, the date of the Rising had been set.

The circumstances of Connolly's joining the I.R.B. are so mysterious that a kind of romance has grown around them. He himself never talked about the matter and parried questions from anxious or curious friends with cryptic remarks that only increased speculation.

From lunchtime on Wednesday, January 19, until late Saturday night, January 22, his whereabouts were unknown to his friends. It was unlike him to leave Liberty Hall without telling anyone where he was going and making the necessary arrangements for carrying on business while he was away. Madame, Michael Mallin, and his other friends were alarmed when he disappeared and at a loss where to find him. As the Citizen Army had become more efficient, Liberty Hall had begun to resemble a fortress of nationalism. Now, quite suddenly, the general of the fortress was gone. Connolly had been critical of what he believed was the "not yet" policy of the Volunteers, and some of his friends thought that he had been taken away by force or guile and held under I.R.B. guard. Others believed that he had gone voluntarily to a secret meeting.[12] Madame was so frantic that she wanted to turn out the Citizen Army. Perhaps she wanted it to troop through Dublin looking for its leader, or to start a rebellion then and there. Probably she was not thinking. Mallin, second in command (after Connolly) of the Citizen Army, perhaps after personal interview with Volunteer or I.R.B. leaders, was persuaded to wait a few days before taking action. He and William O'Brien convinced Madame of the wisdom of patience.

About eight o'clock Saturday night Surrey House was raided by forty plain-clothes men armed with revolvers and under the command of a District Inspector. There were several other raids in the city and suburbs the same night but this was the most formidable. Whether this activity had any connection with rumors reaching the Castle about Connolly's disappearance and with Madame's cry for action has been little discussed, nor was there any indication what they were looking for and why this particular night was chosen. Possibly they were looking for a Fianna boy who had smuggled a huge supply of explosives into Dublin, forgotten where to deliver it, and wandered out to Surrey House to ask for the address. It seems to have been more than just a raid for arms, however, judging from the size of the force, and Madame was told later that a picked body of soldiers had been detained in Portobello Barracks close by to aid the police if necessary.

She arrived home in the middle of the raid, just as her small printing press was being carried out. Unfortunately, her remarks were not recorded. *The Workers' Republic* of January 29 published an impudent account of the raid on the front page:

"No one was in the house except the servants and a few of the boys of the Fianna who make the place their headquarters. While the search was going on these boys and girls kindly entertained the police with songs, music, and comforting remarks. Unfortunately the G men have no ear for music, and hence they did not appreciate such choice items as 'The Peeler and the Goat,' and 'Watch on the Rhine,' 'The Saxon's on the Run,' and 'A Nation Once Again.'

"A large number of American magazines of short stories were taken, a small printing machine, a miniature rifle, a few ballads, and it is understood some teaspoons and a half a pound of carbolic soap. It is believed that the soap was taken because the G man thought the words of the 'Watch on the Rhine' sounded like 'The Wash upon the Line' and was a deeply mysterious message having some sinister reference to soap. We are authorised to state that they can keep the soap as the house was thoroughly disinfected after they left it. Besides the Socialist motto is 'To each according to his needs,' and although Madame is no Socialist she recognizes that the soap is now where it is most needed.

"As the raiders left the building after the Countess had gibed them at their non-success the boys and girls formed up around the piano and sang, 'Will ye no come back again?'

"The Irish Volunteers mobilised immediately word was passed

around, and we understand it was the most successful swift mobilisation yet attempted. And that is significant. Is it not?"

Three hours later Madame and a crowd of her senior scouts were still recovering from the hullabaloo, sitting around the kitchen table drinking tea, when quite suddenly Connolly walked in, quietly greeted them all, and stood calmly by the fire. Miss Molony came in and was astonished to see him, but nothing was said until the boys were sent off to bed. Then she gasped, "Where in Heaven's name have you been?" He took a moment to answer, and then said, "I have been in Hell, but I conquered my conquerors." They waited for what was to follow, but he closed the queries with, "I don't want to speak about it." "Of course neither Madame nor I questioned him further," Miss Molony said, "but proceeded during supper to give him an account of our search during the preceding days, which he listened to with quiet amusement. But he appeared much concerned and touched when we told him of the tearing anxiety that those who were aware of his disappearance had gone through."[13] William O'Brien went to Surrey House Sunday morning. When he told Connolly they had been very concerned about his absence he made an evasive reply and O'Brien did not question him. "He said he had had a very good night's sleep as he was dead tired when he arrived, and that he had walked about forty miles on the Saturday. A lady friend then arrived and, after a few words, she asked him where he had been and he replied with a smile, 'Oh, that would be telling!' "[14]

The detail of the swift mobilization following the raid on Surrey House is particularly significant in the light of future events and knowledge of what Connolly had just been discussing with the Military Council. Adjoining the column with the account of the raid was Connolly's brief statement, the nearest he ever came to clarifying the mystery. With hindsight it is easy to understand. In a regular column called "Notes on the Front" he wrote:

"Our notes this week will be short. The issue is clear and we have done our part to clear it. Nothing we can now say can add point to the arguments we have put before our readers in the past few months; nor shall we continue to labour the point.

"In solemn acceptance of our duty and the great responsibilities attached thereto, we have planted the seed in the hope and belief that ere many of us are much older it will ripen and blossom into action.

"For the moment and hour of that ripening, that fruitful and blessed Day of Days, we are ready. Will it find you ready?"

In case this were not clear enough, Connolly followed it with a poem by Maeve Cavanagh called "Outward Bound(?)" in which the good ship "Ireland" was still moored in the river although the wind and the weather were fair.

> Ah! sweep the frightened ones away
> Or we shall miss this glorious tide
> Put them ashore to plot and play
> For the men who will *act*—Gangway!
> Or else the gallant ship shall stay
> To rest in port till black Doomsday.

Connolly had accepted one of the three main lines of thought concerning rebellion held by Irish nationalists at the time. The Military Council of the I.R.B. wanted a full-scale confrontation with the British forces; they hoped to take advantage of the war. The platitude, "England's difficulty is Ireland's opportunity," had the ring of truth to them. They had been planning rebellion for months and sometime in December, 1915, or January, 1916, had set the date for the Rising as Easter, 1916. Military victory was not an important issue. To Padraic Pearse the Rising had a mystic quality; it was the duty of each generation to rededicate itself to Ireland, even if the Rising became a blood sacrifice. Connolly had accepted this policy for different reasons. He thought a bold military action was dramatically necessary to awaken the people. He hoped that a military revolution would spark a social revolution. His confidence was in historical parallels; one of his models was the American Revolution of 1776. Even if the Rising was put down, he saw the awakened consciousness as victory enough. His was an attitude of faith.

Eoin MacNeill held to a second line of reasoning. He saw the Volunteers under his command as guardians of nationalism and had laid down three conditions under which he would agree to insurrection: (a) attack by the British, (b) an attempt to enforce conscription, (c) a German invasion in force. Under any of these conditions he knew that the Irish would be sufficiently aroused to assure a fighting chance against the British. He did not want to sacrifice a single Volunteer without hope of a military victory.

There was a third line of thought held by a growing number of nationalists who wanted immediate action *and* victory. They thought that guerrilla warfare promised the only hope of success. Robert Monteith, who had fought in the Boer War, was of this school of thought but had no influence in the policy making of the Volunteers. He realized the impossibility of victory over a force superior in arms, training, and numbers, and thought the Irish could win only by taking advantage of superior knowledge of terrain, the element of surprise over a wide area of operations, and the advantages of irregular action. Many of the I.R.B. had long had faith in action, but MacNeill, as Chief of Staff of the Volunteers, had power enough to wreck their plans. It would be more than three years before the value of the third approach became evident. In the early months of 1916 it was a tug-of-war between the "nows" and the "not yets."

Those who wanted immediate rebellion realized they had to work together. The I.R.B. had well-made plans and great influence with the Volunteers but incomplete control over them. Connolly had complete control over his little Army of a few hundred men, but his militarism made many of his union officials squirm with anxiety. Futhermore, his union was losing thousands to enlistment and emigration. Those who remained were, like most of the Irish, indifferent to rebellion. His association with the I.R.B. meant that labor would be represented in rebellion, but would not lead it.

Paradoxically, one of the greatest strengths of the activists was their apparent insignificance. For all their marching and guns they seemed to make nothing happen. Murphy and the employers had been letting men go for enlistment; with great patriotic zeal they sent others to war, and the mailboat from Dun Laoghaire was filled each day with Irish going to English factories and camps. The British had (erroneously) taken to calling all Irish nationalists Sinn Feiners. From the British point of view the Sinn Feiners were clearly divided against themselves and probably incompetent. They were amused when Madame reviewed a handful of men in a park while the rain and the wind ruffled the plumes of her hat. Sometimes she played with live ammunition, and her accent became outrageous with excitement, "Ahland will fight. We'll put these in Ahland's enemies." Clearly she bore watching, but clearly she was mad, quite mad. Why she was any more so than the millions fighting for their nations in France, British officialdom did not inquire.

NOTES TO CHAPTER VII

1. The address now hangs in Dublin's proud new Liberty Hall which rises high on the site of the old Hall in Beresford Place. The two pictures are privately owned.

2. Sean Connolly's sister, Mrs. Barrett, who was also at the City Hall Easter Week was a member of the acting group, as were Emily Norgrove, Molly Reilly, Mary Hyland, and Helena Molony, all of whom were out with the ICA in 1916. Frank Robbins was one of the popular singers; others were Andy Dunne (a Fianna boy whom Madame had helped and encouraged), Sean Byrne, Joe Connolly, and William Oman.

3. This was the second paper of the same name which Connolly edited. For about three months in 1898 he had published a weekly in Dublin as an organ of the Irish Socialist Republican Party he had founded in 1896. Because the original *Workers' Republic* was, in his words, "so weekly it almost died," he undertook, from 1899 to 1903, to publish it irregularly, or as he said, "whenever it was strong enough to get out."

4. *Eire,* May 26, 1923.

5. *Fianna,* n.s., No. 2, August, 1915, had an account of the convention. All of the headquarters staff elected at this meeting were I.R.B. men. They were Chief of the Fianna, Padraic O'Riain; Chief of Staff, Bulmer Hobson; Adjutant, A. P. Reynolds; Director of Training, Sean Heuston; Director of Organization and Recruiting, Eamon Martin; Director of Equipment, Leo Henderson; Director of Finance, B. Mellows.

6. *Irish Citizen,* October 23, 1915.

7. The shop and workroom were wantonly smashed and the contents destroyed or stolen six months later during Easter Week. Through the efforts of Helena Molony and Louie Bennett the shop reopened when the Women's Union was rebuilt in 1917.

8. *Irish Citizen,* January 8, 1916.

9. The telegram was never received. On March 21, in answer to an inquiry from Laurence Ginnell, M.P., he was told by an official in the London G.P.O. that the forms were accidentally mislaid and no further useful inquiry could be made.

10. R. M. Fox, *Louie Bennett: Her Life and Times* (Dublin, [1958?]), p. 48.

11. *Irish Press,* February 4, 1936.

12. In the *Irish Press* from January 14 to March 4, 1937, there were several letters, including ones from William O'Brien, Frank Robbins, Sean Lester, Mrs. Eamonn Ceannt, Denis McCullough, Helena Molony, and Louis N. Le Roux on the subject.

13. *Irish Press,* February 11, 1937.

14. Introduction to James Connolly, *Labour and Easter Week* (Dublin, 1949), p. 10.

VIII

Dressed for Rebellion
February–April 1916

Madame was furious. In February, 1916, British officials decided that she was Russian and ordered her to register as an alien. Their argument was that she held the Count's nationality and that Russia had annexed his area of Poland. She was too deeply involved in getting the foreign government out of Ireland to be amused by the incredible timing of the order. *The Irish Citizen* fumed indignantly, "Irish by birth, descent and residence, she refuses to register herself and ignores the absurd law which makes a woman take the nationality of her husband. The next move is up to the authorities." But this statement was wrong on two counts. Rebel nationalism was a matter of passionate commitment rather than dependent on a place of birth; Madame had been born in England. And it was the rebels who made the next move. The authorities did not act again until April, after Easter Week, when Madame faced more serious charges than non-registration.

Meanwhile Madame's irritation prompted her to make more disloyal utterances than usual. In Cork on March 6 her speech was ostensibly on the subject of "The Sacrifices of Robert Emmet," who had tried to pull the lion's tail a century too soon, but she quickly brought her talk around to contemporary Ireland and the hottest issue of the day, conscription. "They have not dared to have conscription in Ireland [cheers] because the Volunteers have guns in Ireland today. They know we are disloyal and they are afraid of us." More cheers. The response of two G-men, who were among the audience, as they were at every nationalist meeting, is unknown.

Conscription had been made law for Great Britain in January, 1916, but no decision had been made about Ireland. As long as public feeling was strongly against it and voluntary enlistments continued, it seemed unwise to force a draft on an already unsettled country. It was generally recognized that apart from arming and drilling, the most mischievous form of disloyalty practiced by the "Sinn Feiners" was their anti-recruiting propaganda. In some areas they were fairly successful. Sir Morgan O'Connell complained that when he failed to induce the Castle to suppress a seditious anti-recruiting meeting held in Killarney, "recruiting which had been going rather well in the district, came to a sudden stop."[1] The nationalists were well aware of the effectiveness of their campaign, and continued pressing their arguments, hoping that every soldier less for Britain was one more for Ireland.[2]

The hope of success made the nationalists bolder. St. Patrick's day was the occasion for what would be the last peaceful parade of the Volunteers. The day was warm and bright and the Volunteers' new bayonets—never previously seen in the streets—glittered in College Green. Sixteen hundred men lined up opposite the dignified building that had once housed Grattan's Parliament. The Irish Citizen Army of 200 stood by at Beresford Place in case of trouble. Finding none, they marched to Dundrum and Booterstown, where they drilled.

Madame was there fully armed, "so much so that the casual onlooker might readily be pardoned for mistaking her for the representative of an enterprising firm of small arms manufacturers."[3] She was then 48 years old but she took the seventeen-mile hike and drill in her determined stride. A Citizen Army man recalls her on the route marches in a swirl and flash of green. "She was lovely in uniform. I can remember seeing her marching at the head of the Citizen Army with Connolly and Mallin at a parade on Sunday afternoon. My God, she was *it!*"

Exactly a week after the St. Patrick's Day exercises, the Dublin Metropolitan Police, allegedly in a routine search for copies of a seditious paper called the *Gael* (one of several printed by the Gaelic Press), came up against an unexpected show of force by the little army. It was a dramatic mobilization, an unpredicted call to arms with a swift and reassuring response.

Madame was shopping in the vicinity of Liffey Street at noon when she heard of a raid on that street. She saw that the police had entered a printing shop called the Gaelic Press. She rushed to Liberty Hall, up the stairs to Connolly's office, and found his daughter, Nora, alone there. "Where's Mr. Connolly? They're raiding the Gaelic Press, the place is surrounded with soldiers." Nora replied that her father had just gone downstairs where something was going on. Madame ran downstairs to find that several policemen had been in the shop of the

Workers Co-operative Society. Two or three of the girls were there, and Connolly. The policemen were leaving as she arrived. They had come looking for copies of the *Gael,* and Connolly had hurried to the shop. Finding a policeman with a bundle of papers, he demanded a search warrant, although under the Defense of the Realm Act such a refinement was unnecessary. When the policeman said he had none, Connolly pulled out a revolver, "Then drop those papers, or I'll drop you," he said. The police left.

Madame quickly reported her news, and in the belief that this was a prelude to a general suppression of the press as in 1914, Connolly decided to mobilize the Citizen Army to protect the press of *The Workers' Republic* and to prevent the police from entering Liberty Hall, at that time a formidable arsenal of revolt. Madame went back with him to his office, where he told his daughter, "It looks as if we are in for it and as if they are going to force our hands." He took a sheaf of mobilization forms and began signing them while Nora and Madame filled them in. He then gave the orders to several Citizen Army men who were on duty, and they set out at top speed to the railway machine shops, to the dockyard, to the docks, to the barges, to stables, to building sites, to all the working places where there were Citizen Army men.

Madame and Connolly were waiting in the Co-operative Shop when the police returned. Connolly again demanded a warrant. The sergeant saw that the defending forces had been augmented, that several Citizen Army men were there, that Connolly still had his automatic, and that Madame was lovingly toying with a large Mauser pistol. He concluded that retreat was in order. When the second contingent withdrew, Madame and the girls in the shop looked for copies of the *Gael* to see what had been written to cause all the alarm. The new issue had not arrived, none but old copies were on the premises. Ironically, they had been preventing the police from taking papers they did not have. Just as they discovered this, a third group of police arrived. Inspector Bannon produced the original warrant which empowered the police and military to enter all newsagents' shops and seize any copies of the paper they could discover. Knowing that there were no copies of the offending journal, Connolly politely told them to go ahead and search the shop but warned them against stepping over the threshold of the shop into Liberty Hall. The Inspector answered that he would not dream of entering the Hall, and the search consisted of turning over the papers which were on the counter. After that the police departed.

In the meantime, the mobilization order had been answered with enthusiasm, and within an hour one hundred and fifty Citizen Army men arrived at Liberty Hall. They were a curious sight, and "staid middle-class men in the streets, aristocratic old ladies out shopping, well-fed Government officials returning from lunch were transfixed with horror when they beheld the spectacle of working men with grimy faces and dirty working clothes rushing excitedly through the streets with rifle in hand and bandolier across shoulders, on the way to Liberty Hall. Dublin Castle and the Viceregal Lodge were immediately attacked by batteries of telephone calls imploring the British authorities for news."[4]

Building projects had been abandoned, carts left standing at the curb by their drivers, coal bags left where their carriers dropped them. The most spectacular entrance was made by several men who arrived at Liberty Hall dripping wet. They had been working in a yard overlooking the canal when the mobilizer appeared at the door and whistled. "Come on at once, we're needed," one of the workmen shouted, dropping his tools and running out. The others were about to follow him when the foreman, thinking it was a strike, shut the gates in the hopes of reasoning with the rest. But they swarmed the walls, swam the canal, and ran to Liberty Hall.

The Irish Volunteers, who were also alerted, stood under arms until after two o'clock the following morning. Guards were posted at Liberty Hall and were to continue until Easter Monday. All the rest of that Friday, Citizen Army men, the Women's Ambulance Corps, and the boy scouts streamed in, ready for anything. Enthusiasm was high. Crowds collected in Beresford Place and wild rumors were current, including one that military preparations were being made for an attack on Liberty Hall. Nothing happened, however, and the rest of the day passed quietly.

Madame, who was uncomfortable without her own guns (the Mauser pistol was one of Connolly's), had gone to Surrey House in the late afternoon. Connolly sent Nora after her to get a carbine and a bandolier from his room. She found Madame in the kitchen with a crowd of Fianna boys standing by the table with a cup of tea in one hand and a piece of bread in the other.

" 'Help yourself,' she invited. 'What do you think is going to happen?'

" 'Daddy seems to think that anything may happen at any time. He told me not to delay in getting these things down.'

" 'We'll go immediately,' said Madame. 'I'm going to take my turn at standing guard. By the way,' and she stepped back from the table, 'what do you think of my rig-out?' She wore a dark-green woollen blouse with brass buttons, dark-green tweed knee-breeches, black stockings, and huge heavy boots. Around her waist was a cartridge belt; from it on one side hung an automatic pistol, from the other a convertible Mauser rifle; a bandolier and haversack crossed on her shoulders. She stood tall and straight, a fine military figure.

" 'You look a real soldier, Madame,' said Nono, admiringly, and Madame beamed as if she had received a tremendous compliment.

" 'What's your rig like, Nono?'

" 'Something similar. Only I have puttees, and my shoes have plenty of nails in the soles. I was thinking of wearing my Fianna hat, but maybe a tam would be better.'

" 'This will be my hat,' said Madame, putting on her best hat—a black velour with a heavy plume of coque feathers."

Then, having settled the important question of hats and what to wear to a rebellion, Madame and Nora went on to talk about guns and ammunition. Just before they left Surrey House two detectives knocked and asked to see Countess Markievicz. Madame, as she went through the hall, reduced the light to a glimmer. The two detectives entered, but stood just inside.

" 'What do you want with me?' asked Madame.

" 'We've come to serve an order on you.'

" 'What's it about?'

" 'It's an order under the Defence of the Realm Regulations prohibiting you from entering that part of Ireland called Kerry.'

" 'What will happen,' asked Madame, her fingers caressing the butt of her Mauser pistol, 'if I refuse to obey the order and go to Kerry? Would I be shot?'

" 'Ah now, Madame, who'd want to shoot you? You wouldn't want to shoot one of us. Now, would you, Madame?'

" 'But I would,' cried Madame gaily. 'I'm quite prepared to shoot and be shot at.'

" 'Ah now, Madame, you don't mean that. None of us want to die yet, we all want to live a little longer.'

" 'If you want to live a little longer,' said a voice from the dark hall, 'you'd better not be coming here. None of us are fond of you, and you make grand, big targets.'

" 'We'll be going now,' said the detective who had been doing all the talking. 'You'll not be thinking of going to Kerry, Madame, will you?'

" 'Good-bye,' cried Madame, cordially as she closed the door. 'Remember I am quite prepared to shoot and be shot at.' "[5]

Madame was scheduled to give a lecture on "The Fenian Rising of '67" at the second annual Fianna Festival of the Tralee Sluagh of Fianna Eireann at the Rink in Tralee on Sunday. This was the trip she was forbidden to make by order of General Friend. She was willing to defy the order but Connolly advised her not to go; she was risking arrest at a time when she was needed for more important work in Dublin. Madame wrote out her speech for the nimble-tongued Maire Perolz who went in her stead and had a grand time masquerading as Madame, especially when she was questioned about registering as an alien because she was a Russian subject. [6]

One of Madame's duties during this time was making large-scale maps of the city center for use in the rebellion. Nora Connolly remembered her finishing the last one on the day she wrote out the speech for Maire Perolz. Nora wondered at her skill at the drawing board, and asked if no one had been curious about what she had been doing. "Only once," Madame told her, "when an unexpected visitor who has nothing at all to do with the movement walked in one day and caught me at one. I said it was a housing scheme I was interested in." The explanation was accepted without comment, and that, laughed Nora, was "the advantage of being known as a woman of many interests."[7]

Although the Gaelic Press machinery had been dismantled and taken away along with all the loose type, a number of frames of type had been overlooked. Later that Friday afternoon of the raid, some of the Citizen Army men, dressed in their working clothes but carrying small arms, went to the printing office with a hand cart. Several policemen were on guard. The men knocked and were admitted. They loaded the cart with the frames and took them to Liberty Hall without interference. The *Spark* and *Honesty* came out that week as usual.

During the next four weeks prior to the Rising, Liberty Hall was guarded night and day. Some of the Citizen Army men lived there temporarily; when they were not on guard duty they were busy making bombs. One of the men remembers that Madame came in nearly every afternoon with a bag of cakes for tea. One day she remarked, "I have already overdrawn my bank account for my next quarter's allowance to the extent of £45, and if this bally revolution doesn't take place soon I don't know how I'm going to live." Madame was probably exaggerating, but by this time she had sold what she could in order to get money for the cause; nearly all her jewelry and property had been converted to cash. She had always been impetuously generous, particularly when it was to help Ireland. Over and over again stories are told of her taking off a brooch, or, in the early days when she sometimes went to a meeting from a Castle affair, a bracelet or other jewels and dramatically throwing them on the table to add to the funds being collected.

Her long-time friend, an excellent journalist who wrote under the pseudonym "John Brennan," remembered one of the early occasions when she did this at an Inghinidhe meeting. "She had come on to the meeting from some social function and was very beautiful and radiant. We were a despondent company when she came in, for we were suffering from our usual complaint—a lack of funds. There was some essential work to be done in connection with anti-recruiting literature which had to be printed. She took from her hair the diamond band she was wearing and laid it on the table saying, 'Remember you can always have this or any of my jewels for the national work.' I do not remember whether we accepted her offer at that time, but we know that most of her jewelry as well as her money went later to swell the coffers of the revolutionary organizations."[8] Madame never had to work for a living as most of her colleagues did, and this in itself made her different. Her money gave her freedom of action; she never had to consider how a project was to be financed. She could say, "Let's do it" and go ahead unhindered. "All that she got she spent,/Her charity had no bounds. . . ."[9]

Although the Military Council were the only men who knew the date set for the Rising, it was obvious to Madame and other ardent nationalists that a showdown of some kind was imminent. *The Workers' Republic* of April 15 published as its Irish Citizen Army column a poem by Madame entitled "The Call" which began, "Do you hear the call in the whispering wind?/ The call to our race today,/ The call for self-sacrifice, courage and faith/ The call that brooks no delay." Again the following week, April 22, the last issue of *The Workers' Republic* published another of her poems as the ICA

Notes, "Our Faith," which ends, "So we're waiting till 'Somebody' gives us the word/ That sends us to Freedom or death."

Connolly also used pageantry to keep up morale in the trying weeks of waiting for something to happen. On Palm Sunday, April 16, 1916, the Citizen Army was drawn up to form three sides of a square in front of Liberty Hall. Inside the formation were positions occupied by the Women's Section, the boy scouts under Captain Carpenter, and the Fintan Lalor Pipers' Band. A color guard of sixteen uniformed men accompanied a lovely young redhaired girl, Molly Reilly, who carried a green flag, which was placed on a pile of drums in the center of the square. After inspecting the troops, Commandant Connolly, in uniform for the first time, took up his position in front of the drums with Vice Commandant Mallin on his left and Lieutenant Markievicz (in her green uniform, complete with her best black hat with feathers) on his right. After much ceremony, bugles, drums, pipes, and salutes, the young color bearer, radiant with excitement, mounted an inside stairway to the roof, and "with a quick graceful movement of her hand unloosed the lanyard and the flag fluttered out." On a green field was the golden harp—without a crown.

That night James Connolly's play, "Under Which Flag," was produced again in Liberty Hall. Again the hero was played by Sean Connolly in what was to be his final performance. He was one of the first casualties of the rebellion and died Easter Monday night.

On the Tuesday before Easter, the leaders of the Citizen Army were told that the Rising would take place on Easter and their assignments were given to them. Madame wrote that she was proud to be accepted by Tom Clarke and the members of the provisional government as the second of Connolly's "ghosts." " 'Ghosts'," she said, "was the name we gave to those who stood secretly behind the leaders and were entrusted with enough of the plans of the Rising to enable them to carry on that Leader's work should anything happen to himself."[10] Although she was given no definite assignment at that time, the bulk of the Irish Citizen Army was to be at St. Stephen's Green, and it is possible that those were the plans she referred to.

The plans for the Rising were mainly the work of Joseph Plunkett and had been long discussed and finally approved by the Military Council. The strategy was to take and hold several points in the center of Dublin controlling the railway stations and main entrances to the city, and having the military barracks outside the defense line. Detailed plans were made for cutting the telephone and telegraph wires to prevent immediate communication by the British. There was little optimism about the chances of overwhelming success, but the Council hoped that by proclaiming an Irish Republic and remaining in control as a nation for a period of time, they would insure Ireland a place at the peace conference along with other small nations, for whose rights the war was allegedly being fought.

The General Post Office on O'Connell Street was chosen as the General Headquarters. Commandant Padraic Pearse was the Commander-in-Chief of the Army of the Irish Republic, and President of the Provisional Government. James Connolly was in command of the Dublin division. Also at the GPO were three more of the seven signers of the proclamation and members of the provisional government of the Irish Republic: Tom Clarke, Sean MacDermott, and Joseph Plunkett. Thomas MacDonagh, commanding the 2nd battalion of the Irish Volunteers whose headquarters were Jacob's Biscuit Factory, and Eamonn Ceannt, commanding South Dublin Union, were the others who signed the proclamation on behalf of the provisional government.

Roughly, the controlling ring around Dublin consisted of the GPO and the Four Courts on the north; to the west the South Dublin Union; south, Jacob's Factory; southeast, St. Stephen's Green; east, Boland's Mills. From each of these strongholds small groups were to be detailed; the North Dublin Union which controlled the Broadstone Station, for example, was to be occupied by a force operating from the Four Courts. The main body of the Irish Citizen Army was at St. Stephen's Green, with a small contingent at the City Hall which was across the street from a main entrance to the Castle. The Irish Volunteers' four battalions were detailed in this way: 1st battalion, Edward Daly in command, Four Courts (north); 2nd battalion, Thomas MacDonagh, Jacob's Factory (south); 3rd battalion, Eamon de Valera, Boland's Mills (east); and Eamonn Ceannt, South Dublin Union (west). The plans were based on an estimated fighting strength of five thousand in Dublin, with another five thousand rising in the provinces.

The original plan for the St. Stephen's Green area provided for: (1) The occupation of prominent buildings surrounding the Green, including the Shelbourne Hotel, United Services Club, College of Surgeons, and Little's licensed premises at the corner of Cuffe Street; (2) The occupation and organization of the Green for defence and to set up cross-fire against troops coming along any of the several main roads passing the Green; (3) The establishment of an outpost line at Harcourt Street Railway Station, Railway Bridge overlooking the

Grand Canal, Railway Bridge commanding the approaches for the South Circular Road, and Davy's Public House at Portobello Bridge. This outpost line was established to cover the organization of the Green and to prevent British forces from penetrating into the area from Portobello Barracks; (4) Maintaining contact with the garrisons at Jacob's Factory, Boland's Mills, and the GPO. A force of five hundred was expected to be at the Green.

The plans did not presume strong public support; public opinion was against any rising. British propaganda during the war had persuaded most of Ireland to accept the idea of helping England. To many Irish it was emotionally and logically reasonable to help Britain fight her wars as they had for centuries. After all, Home Rule was coming and it was to their advantage to insure a victory for Britain. Opinion makers had been hard at work to make this a religious war for the rights of small nations. The horror of poverty had been somewhat mitigated by the appearance of prosperity brought by the war, the factories and the dockyards were busy, the laborers were getting steady work. There were 150,000 Irishmen fighting in the British army and nearly that many families receiving dependents' allotments from England. For many "separation women," as they were called, it was the first time in their lives money had come to them regularly. They were indifferent to politics and patriotism, understanding only that they were getting so many shillings every week and would as long as their husbands were in the British Army. Liberty Hall with its green flag was an island of nationalism surrounded by hostility, skepticism, and indifference.

The British government leaders in Ireland were sharply divided about the likelihood of insurrection. The nationalists had long been vociferous, but some officials believed them to be all talk and no action. On the other hand, Augustine Birrell, until after Easter Week the Chief Secretary of Ireland, claimed at the Royal Commission on the Rebellion hearing that he had always thought the Sinn Feiners dangerous.[11] His two chief advisers were Redmond, who thought the chances of insurrection were negligible, and Dillon, who thought there was a danger. Neither adviser was in favor of intervention. T. M. Healy, M.P., said that on April 11 there was a Lobby rumor that the Government meant to arrest the militant Sinn Feiners, but that Redmond went to Birrell and objected on the grounds that Carson's Volunteers had been allowed to arm and deploy with impunity.[12]

Justice Shearman, who heard the evidence into the causes of the rebellion, could not understand why the situation was presented in so many shades, it seemed black and white to him. "I cannot understand," he said, "why it did not occur to anybody to say, 'We won't have armed Volunteers drilling while the war is on.' That could have been equally applied to any part of Ireland." Birrell lamely tried to explain. "It seems almost ridiculous [that we did not]. But, on the other hand, the alternative would have been to employ policemen to have done it. You would have attacked these people and disarmed them, and whether it was done north, south, east, or west, it would have resulted in bloodshed."[13]

The government could take no action against any Volunteer without provoking armed demonstrations. It had served deportation orders on three Volunteer organizers, Ernest Blythe, Liam Mellows, and Alfred Monoghan, and immediately precipitated a protest meeting, with armed men moving threateningly and their leaders shouting sedition. Remember what happened at Bachelor's Walk, said the Castle officials, and what a distressing incident that was. Better do nothing for awhile.

The British authorities were not prepared to be brutal and their policy of speaking loudly and carrying a small stick was very nearly successful in isolating the most militant nationalists. The policy threatened to take the edge of anger from the Volunteer forces. To revive that emotion the I.R.B. resorted to a very clever ruse designed by Joseph Plunkett.

On Wednesday, April 20, at a meeting of the Dublin Corporation, Alderman Kelly read a remarkable document purported to have come to him unofficially from the Castle. It had allegedly been in code and when deciphered revealed plans of the authorities for seizing key buildings of the Volunteers and the Irish Citizen Army. There was a long list of premises to be taken, including Liberty Hall, the Sinn Fein building at 6 Harcourt Street, the Volunteers' headquarters at 2 Dawson Street, Surrey House, St. Enda's College, and several other homes and headquarters. More important, the document authorized the arrest of all Sinn Fein members and Volunteers. The authenticity of the document was at once denied by the British military authorities, but for years it had its firm believers among the nationalists.[14] The nationalists were aroused and it seemed evident that a crisis must be near. Following a meeting of the Volunteer Executive that same Wednesday, MacNeill, encouraged by Pearse, had issued an order warning the Volunteers to be on their guard.

From then on preparations for the Rising were bedeviled by all the malignant forces the Irish peasantry had ever believed in. Bad luck and inevitable differences of opinion might have been overcome had it not been for the habits of secrecy ingrained in the I.R.B. Military Council. Although MacNeill was technically head of the Volunteers, he was not a member of the I.R.B. and had not been told that the date had been set for the Rising; Hobson, a member of the I.R.B. but not of the Military Council, was also uninformed. There were wild stories in the provinces. On Thursday Commandant Liam Manahan came from Limerick to the Dawson Street headquarters of the Irish Volunteers to try to find out what the situation was. The publication of the so-called Castle Document and the rumors of impending military action had made him, like many other Volunteer commandants in the various areas, uneasy because they had so little information. He saw Hobson and other officers in Dublin and asked them if a crisis was near. Hobson replied that they expected no exceptional developments.[15]

However, that same evening, Thursday, at the Volunteer headquarters, Hobson and J. J. O'Connell, a Volunteer officer, overheard enough of a conversation to make them suspect that a rising was planned for Sunday. They reported the episode to MacNeill, who was also suspicious, and the three went on to confront Pearse. It was after midnight when they got to his home at St. Enda's College. After Pearse had listened quietly to his determined visitors, he confirmed their assumptions. MacNeill, Chief of Staff of the Volunteers, was furious about the secret proceedings and what he considered suicidal madness in calling out ill-prepared men at a strategically wrong time. He warned Pearse that he would do everything he could short of informing the Castle. His first step was to send out an order cancelling "all orders issued by Commandant Pearse or by any other person heretofore."

Pearse, who was immediately told of the countermand, sent messages to MacDermott and MacDonagh to meet with him, and before nine o'clock Good Friday morning they were at MacNeill's home in Rathfarnham. For the first time then, MacNeill was given the information that Sir Roger Casement was bringing a shipload of arms from Germany and that the fight was definitely to begin on Easter Sunday, at 6:30 P.M. in Dublin, at 7 in the provinces. Realizing that matters had gone too far for him to interfere now, MacNeill acknowledged that the fight was inevitable, authorized the sending of dispatches to the country confirming that the announced maneuvers would proceed as scheduled. Within a few hours, orders to call off maneuvers and countermanding orders to proceed had been issued from Dublin. Confusion was inevitable and was compounded by the failure to land the German arms.

While Pearse and MacNeill were meeting in Dublin, Robert Monteith was trying to find the local Volunteer leader in Tralee to get the arms unloaded. About three o'clock Good Friday morning, he, Sir Roger Casement, and a member of the Irish Brigade named Sergeant Beverley (under the pseudonym of Daniel Bailey) had left the submarine which had brought them from Helgoland and gone ashore to supervise the landing of the arms and ammunition brought from Germany on another ship, the *Aud.* Sir Roger was very ill and had been exhausted by the wet, rough landing. The only place they could find which offered any protection for him was a ruined building locally known as Fort McKenna. Sir Roger, who could not walk further, huddled against the wet stones while Bailey and Monteith made their way to town for help. They were unknown in Tralee and met with considerable delay and suspicion. Eventually, after some hours' delay, the Commandant, Austin Stack, appeared with Con Collins, who knew Monteith and identified him. Stack and Collins drove off, with Bailey as a guide, to get Sir Roger. In the meantime, suspicions of local residents had been aroused; a man saw three strangers on the beach at dawn, a young girl saw them on the road, two or three others had seen two strangers on the way to town. Sir Roger's exposed hiding place was soon discovered and he was arrested. Stack, Collins, and Bailey were also arrested when they went looking for him.[16]

On Good Friday morning another strand of the line which was to bring the arms safely to shore was fraying; by night it too would be broken. Five men, including one who was an expert on wireless installation, left Dublin by train for Killarney. They were to proceed from there to the coast by automobile, and then establish wireless communication with the arms ship which they thought was due Sunday. There were delays in Killarney; eventually they left in two cars. It was dark by this time and one of the drivers made a wrong turn and drove off a pier at Ballykissane. His three passengers were drowned, including Con Keating, the wireless expert. The occupants of the other car, after bluffing their way through a police patrol, waited three and a half hours past the fixed meeting time, then had to abandon the plans and return to Dublin. While they were waiting at the appointed meeting place, and unknown to them, of course, the ship with which they were to have made wireless contact had been taken by British naval forces and was proceeding under escort to Cork Harbor.

One reason for the confusion in Tralee was that the date the arms were scheduled to arrive had been changed in Dublin. By the time the message reached Berlin, the ship carrying arms and the submarine carrying the three men had left Germany and there was no way to radio them about the change. Commandant Austin Stack's orders had been to meet the ship and unload it on Sunday night; apparently there were no alternate plans. Indeed, he seems to have been the only one who knew about the plans at all. When he was arrested, following Casement's arrest, no one knew how to proceed. Montieth's foremost concern was to get a message to MacNeill, as the Volunteer Chief of Staff, that the arms were there but if the Rising were contingent on German help, it was unwise to go further. Monteith, who knew nothing of the Military Council control at that time, directed a Tralee Volunteer to deliver the message to MacNeill, or, in his absence, to Bulmer Hobson. It was, however, delivered to James Connolly at Liberty Hall late Friday night.[17]

Connolly immediately sent for Pearse and others to attend an urgent conference at Liberty Hall and gave them Monteith's message. The Military Council decided to go ahead as scheduled, without the arms, and to make the best fight they could. Pearse and MacDermott saw MacNeill again on Saturday morning and told him of Casement's arrest and as much as they knew of what had happened in Tralee.

Meanwhile the *Aud* and her escort had arrived in Cork Harbor. The *Aud* stopped, lowered her lifeboats, and the crew, now in their German naval uniforms, jumped into the boats. The ship exploded and within ten minutes had gone down with 20,000 rifles, 1,000,000 rounds of ammunition, and ten machine guns.

The Castle had news of the scuttled arms ship at ten A.M.; within an hour the Military Council knew that any lingering hopes they might have had of getting the urgently required guns into Volunteer hands were ruined.

The staggering loss of additional weapons decided MacNeill's next move. On Saturday afternoon he met with Arthur Griffith, Sean Fitzgibbon, Liam O Briain, Joseph Plunkett, Thomas MacDonagh, and several others and told them he intended cancelling all orders for Sunday. Plunkett and MacDonagh, the two Military Council members present, objected strenuously, but MacNeill was convinced that it was his duty to save the Volunteers from hopeless and useless slaughter.

They argued all afternoon, but by night MacNeill was still convinced that his was the correct decision, and he wrote out countermanding orders again. The O'Rahilly set off for Limerick in his car with the latest orders from MacNeill late Saturday night, and by midnight messengers were on their way to every other part of the country to tell the Volunteers the fight was off.[18] MacNeill then cycled with a copy of his orders to the office of the *Sunday Independent* to make sure it would be published the next day. At the same time, he sent a confirming order to the Adjutant of the Dublin Brigade, Eamon de Valera, rescinding all orders given to the Volunteers for Sunday.

Nevertheless, those in Liberty Hall were going ahead with their plans. On Saturday night, William O'Brien, Winifred Carney, and Madame prepared mobilization orders and officers' commissions. O'Brien remembered how pleased Madame was when her commission as lieutenant was typed out by Miss Carney and signed by Connolly.[19] In all the excitement a friend came on business to the hall and noticing the large number of people about and the general bustle, concluded that the Liberty Players were getting ready to produce a play. " 'Rehearsing, I suppose,' she said to Madame. 'Yes,' replied Madame with a knowing smile. 'Is it for children?' inquired the visitor. 'No,' said Madame, 'for grown-ups.' "[20]

The mobilization orders for the Citizen Army were out: they were to be at Liberty Hall at 3:30 P.M. on Sunday, with full equipment. The Citizen Army men and women lived in and near Dublin, it was an easier matter to mobilize them than the Volunteers, who were much larger in numbers and who were scattered throughout Ireland. Meanwhile, Volunteer messengers were off with the latest cancellation orders. Delivering messages was a time-consuming and sometimes uncertain process. They had to be taken by whatever transportation was available; trains, trams, bicycles, and foot were the most common. Automobiles were rare. The messages had to be delivered in secret, to a particular man known to the messenger. By the time the last order had left Dublin, men were already marching in from outlying districts to their Sunday morning rendezvous. In the past few days their leaders had been issued orders to go, counter-orders to stop, orders to go, and now counter-orders again. The men were understandably confused.

The exceptionally complex situation at Tralee was symptomatic of the uncertainty of the Volunteers throughout Ireland. The incredible series of misfortunes in Tralee had resulted in the stranger Monteith being in charge of the Volunteers from the whole district who assembled in the Rink for maneuvers on Sunday. Their commandant, Austin Stack, was under arrest, Monteith himself was on the run. He knew few of the men, little about what training they had had, nothing of the local plans or terrain; the most up-to-date map he could get had been published in 1886. Those who thought the Volunteers were not entirely prepared to fight the British Empire had some reason on their side.

On the other hand, there were those to whom Fintan Lalor's words to Young Ireland were gospel: "Somewhere and somehow and by someone, a beginning must be made, and the first act of armed resistance is always premature, imprudent, and foolish."

NOTES TO CHAPTER VIII

1. *The Times History of the War* (London, 1916), VIII, 410.
2. There were, of course, many factors involved. Lloyd George in his *War Memoirs of David Lloyd George* (Boston, 1933), attributed "the irritation of Southern Ireland to a number of needless follies." John Redmond successfully recruited an Irish Division in which his brother William Redmond, M.P., took a commission. "But Lord Kitchener did his best to damp the ardour of the Redmonds. He refused commissions to educated young Irishmen of the class and type who were being made officers in England, Scotland, and Wales for no conceivable reason, except that he distrusted and disliked their nationalism. The culminating incident will take an invidiously prominent place in the tragic history of Irish relations with Great Britain. Nationalist ladies, fired with enthusiasm for the new Irish Division, for Mr. Redmond and for the cause to which they were devoting themselves, embroidered a silken flag with the Irish harp emblazoned upon it. At the same moment the patriotic ladies of Ulster were embroidering the Red Hand of Ulster on the flag which they designed to present to a division which was being raised in Ulster. In due course the two flags were presented to the respective divisions. One was taken and the other was left. When Lord Kitchener heard of the green flag and its Irish harp, he ordered that it should be taken away. But the Ulster flag was allowed to fly gloriously over the heads of the Orange soldiers of the Protestant North. Ireland was deeply hurt. Her pride was cut to the quick, her sense of fair play was outraged, her sympathy with the Holy War against the military dictatorship of Europe was killed, and John Redmond's heart was broken. . . . From that moment the effort of Irish Nationalism to reconcile England and Ireland by uniting the two peoples in a common effort for the oppressed of another land failed, and Lord Kitchener's sinister order constituted the first word in a new chapter of Irish History" (*War Memoirs of David Lloyd George*, II, 197–198).
   Stephen Gwynn attributed a marked setback in recruiting in Ireland to the fact that in May, 1915, when a Coalition Government was formed, Sir Edward Carson became Attorney-General with a seat in the Cabinet. At the same time

office was offered to Redmond who refused it (the National party being pledged against taking any British office) and expressed a strong opinion that representatives of Ulster should keep out of the administration (*The Letters and Friendships of Sir Cecil Spring-Rice,* London, 1919, II, 273).

In America this quarrel in England between the Nationalist party (Redmond) and the Unionists (Carson) was regarded with alarm, and Ambassador Spring-Rice wrote to Sir Edward Grey on June 10, 1915, of his concern: "It is evidently of very great importance that no action should be taken in England which would arouse a strong anti-British sentiment among the Irish here. . . . It is difficult to exaggerate the importance of the moral factor here, that is, the effect on public opinion of a visible spirit of self-sacrifice among all classes in Great Britain. I consider this aspect of the question even more important than the effect on the Irish party taken by itself" (ibid.)

3. *The Workers' Republic,* April 1, 1916.

4. Details of this incident were given by Nora Connolly O'Brien, *Portrait of a Rebel Father,* pp. 259–265. A full account of the events was given in *The Workers' Republic,* April 1, 1916, under the headline "The Call to Arms" from which the description of the Dubliners is quoted. The author is indebted also to Frank Robbins' memories of the day.

5. O'Brien, *Portrait of a Rebel Father,* pp. 265–269.

6. The substitution was not explained until the meeting on Sunday, when Austin Stack, Commandant of the Tralee Volunteers, introduced her at the meeting. Miss Perolz read the long message from Madame which began with expressions of her regret at not being there, but, she said, "discipline is discipline and I must obey orders." She went on to express her happiness with the Fianna: "Every new branch of the Fianna fills me with joy and hope for I have great faith in our lads and to me each new branch is as one of the foundation stones of the memorial to Robert Emmet" (*Kerryman,* April 1, 1916).

7. O'Brien, *Portrait of a Rebel Father,* p. 272.

8. *An Phoblacht,* July 26, 1930.

9. Part of W. B. Yeats's description of Madame in the first printed version of his poem "Easter 1916." Twenty-five copies were privately printed by Clement Shorter for distribution among his friends.

10. Madame's account of Easter Week given to members of Cumann na mBan some time later was quoted in Esther Roper, *Prison Letters of Countess Markievicz* (London, 1934), pp. 37 ff.

11. It was a fine touch of irony that the Sinn Fein movement, which had followed legal lines, should give its name to the revolutionary aspect of the movement. The Easter rebellion in 1916 was immediately tagged the Sinn Fein Rebellion.

12. Healy, *Letters,* II, 559.

13. *Royal Commission on the Rebellion in Ireland,* testimony on May 19, 1916.

14. Mrs. Skeffington, whose husband had gone to Belfast to post copies of the document for distribution throughout the country, believed it to be authentic, as did Mrs. Eamonn Ceannt. Mrs. Skeffington based her argument on the fact that the Archbishop's House in Drumcondra was referred to as

"Ara Coeli," while that was actually the name of the Cardinal's residence in Armagh. She thought that the British military might conceivably confuse Primate and Archbishop, but such a slip could not be made by Volunteers (*Irish Press*, January 4, 1937). T. M. Healy believed it to be a forgery; in fact, he thought the Countess Markievicz was responsible for the document. She had nothing to do with it, but she was involved in so much that it was a reasonable assumption. At the official inquiry after Easter Week, Justice Shearman testified that he was told that the Countess Markievicz had invented the story. "At any rate," he said, "there was a lot of clever people there."

Within several years after the rebellion, it was generally recognized that the document was indeed written by the Volunteers, specifically by Joseph Plunkett. Although no such document existed in the Castle files, it was thought the officials did have some such intention, and Plunkett chose this dramatic way of presenting it to the Irish people. (Louis N. LeRoux, *Irish Press*, January 7, 1937, and Geraldine Plunkett Dillon, ibid., January 8, 1937, support this view, as does John Brennan in an interview with Alderman Kelly in *An Phoblacht*, April 11, 1936). Whether the address of the Archbishop's house which caused so much speculation was a mistake or a sardonic plant by the ingenious and clever author depended on individual readings of it. A personal letter from Lord Wimborne to Birrell written Easter Sunday urged similar raids and arrests, however, thus verifying the Volunteers' information.

15. Desmond Ryan, *The Rising* (Dublin, 1957), pp. 88 ff. Ryan, who has written many vivid books about Ireland and the Irish, had been a student at St. Enda's College, acted as Pearse's secretary, and fought at the GPO. Much of his information was from personal observation or from other participants.

16. There are varying accounts of the precise chronological order of the arrests. This is Monteith's version. Whatever the exact sequence, Casement, Stack, Collins, and Bailey were under arrest by nightfall. Monteith related his experiences in detail in *Casement's Last Adventure* (Dublin, 1953), pp. 155 ff.

In 1950 Monteith identified a small boat found in the naval technical stores in Haulbowline as the one used by him and Casement. However, the authorities argued it was not the same. See Florence Monteith Lynch, *The Mystery Man of Banna Strand* (New York, 1959), pp. 132 ff.

17. W. P. Partridge (a Citizen Army man) had been in Tralee that day to arrange for the unloading of the arms. He had left for the train to Dublin before Monteith could see him. However, Partridge went with the Kerry Volunteer, William Mullins, to take the message to Connolly, so it seems probable that Mullins saw Partridge on the train and was persuaded by him that Connolly was the proper man to receive the Monteith message.

18. O'Rahilly delivered the cancellation orders in six counties through the night and ended up in Limerick city the following morning. He was still in the country late Monday when news reached him of the Rising. He drove back to Dublin, fought at the GPO, and was killed in action. His death was the subject of a beautiful poem by Yeats which includes these lines:

> He told Pearse and Connolly
> He'd gone to great expense
> Keeping all the Kerry men

> Out of that crazy fight;
> That he might be there himself
> Had travelled half the night
> . . .
> 'Because I helped to wind the clock
> I come to hear it strike.'

("The O'Rahilly," *Collected Poems,* pp. 354–355.)

19. Other officers in the Irish Citizen Army were: Michael Mallin, who was the Chief of Staff and held the rank Commandant; Sean Connolly, Richard McCormack, J. J. O'Neill, and Christy Poole, Captains; Robert de Coeur, Thomas Kain, Michael Kelly, Madame Markievicz, Seamus McGowan, and George Norgrove, Lieutenants; Joseph Doyle, E. Elmes, George Oman and Frank Robbins, Sergeants. Dr. Kathleen Lynn, who held the rank of Captain, was the medical officer. (William O'Brien in his Introduction to Connolly, *Labour and Easter Week* details the activities at Liberty Hall during this time.)

Unknown to any of them, Casement was brought from Kerry that night and was, as the Irish Citizen Army orders were being prepared, passing through Dublin en route to England and his trial and execution.

20. Introduction to *Labour and Easter Week,* p. 18.

IX

The Rising

Easter Week 1916

Easter Sunday was a bright spring day. Trees along O'Connell Street and in the parks were showing new leaves, the sky was cloudless, even the Liffey glittered. Crowds coming from Mass were in holiday mood. But the mood was suddenly dampened for those who knew the plans for insurrection. Placards at the church entrances and the corners, where men and boys were selling the Sunday papers, announced that the Volunteer maneuvers were cancelled for the day. The *Sunday Independent* carried little more news to enlighten them, only a brief paragraph in the middle of the front page. The headlines of the announcement took almost as much space as the text: "NO PARADES. IRISH VOLUNTEER MARCHES CANCELLED. A SUDDEN ORDER." "Owing to the very critical position, all orders given to Irish Volunteers for to-morrow, Easter Sunday, are hereby rescinded, and no parades, marches, or other movements of Irish Volunteers will take place. Each individual Volunteer will obey this order strictly in every particular." It was signed Eoin MacNeill, Chief of Staff. Few readers associated that announcement with news in adjoining columns: "ARMS SEIZED. COLLAPSIBLE BOAT ON KERRY COAST. 'MAN OF UNKNOWN NATIONALITY' "; and "THREE DROWNED. TRAGIC MOTORING AFFAIR IN KERRY. A WRONG TURNING."

Madame arose early that morning, dressed herself for rebellion, then looked at the Sunday paper. The cancellation order seemed to leap out from the front page and was the only paragraph in the paper she saw that day. "I raced down to Liberty Hall heart-broken, and found James Connolly and Sean MacDermott sitting with Tom Clarke at a table in Connolly's bedroom.

" 'What has happened?' said I.

" 'MacNeill has cut the ground from under our feet,' said Tom Clarke.

"I began to lament and question them, he cut me short with, 'It will all be all right, we are going on, it will only mean a little delay.'

"When he said this he must have known that MacNeill's action had taken from us the little chance that we had of winning, or even of holding out for long enough to create that public opinion that might have saved his life and the lives of the other leaders. Postponement of the rising had by now become quite impossible; too many people had begun to smell a rat, therefore, this 'Call off' had created a situation out of which there were only two ways; the one way was to abandon all thoughts of a rising, the other was to go on with it, though, for the leaders, it was going out to certain death."[1]

To those who exonerated MacNeill by saying, "He did not care to take the responsibility of letting people go to their death when there is so little chance of victory," Madame heard Connolly say, "There is only one sort of responsibility I am afraid of and that is preventing the men and women of Ireland fighting and dying for Ireland if they are so minded."[2]

"The busiest day I ever lived through was that day in Liberty Hall," Madame wrote. "Messengers came and went, and the Provisional Government of the Republic sat the whole day in Connolly's little room. I was in there for one moment on business. Tom Clarke presided in the centre of the table facing the door, Connolly was on his left, Sean MacDermott on his right. Pearse was nearer the window on his right. They were all quite cheerful—the cloud had passed."[3]

By one o'clock the Military Council had agreed to go on, and their euphoria spread to their followers. Nevertheless, all plans had to be hastily revised for a smaller, unknown number of men. The rebellion that had taken years to prepare would now be necessarily haphazard and partly improvised.

The wonder is that the insurgents had the day to make any decisions. The Castle had information about Casement. Nearly 2,500 British troops and all the Irish constabulary were at its disposal and the law was on its side. Indeed, orders had been drawn up to arrest all rebel leaders, but not fearing immediate trouble, the officials who were empowered to sign the orders had left town for the holiday weekend. Both sides had blundered in characteristic ways: the nationalists by internal division, the Castle by clumsy bureaucracy.

Since the Citizen Army had been mobilized for Sunday, it was advisable to stage a drill of some kind to give the illusion that all was normal. Shortly after four o'clock the men were on their usual march with Connolly and Mallin at the head. Madame was with them. From Liberty Hall they went via St. Stephen's Green to the City Hall, turned sharply to the left which brought them almost to the upper Castle Gate, and wheeled to the right through Castle Street. The Castle Gates were closed, and the sentry on duty shouted, "Guard, turn out!" But the column marched on across the Liffey, past the Four Courts and back to Liberty Hall where Connolly made his last public speech. It was meant to seem innocuous to outsiders. He referred to the secret session of the British Parliament, which, he was told, was to take place that coming week, and said the Irish question was bound to be under consideration, and also that there was likely to be a question of peace with Germany. He declared it essential that Ireland should be represented at such peace negotiations. He concluded the speech by declaring that the Irish Citizen Army would stand at arms in the name of the Irish Republic until that claim was heard.

To control some of the mounting excitement of the men and women at Liberty Hall, to help pass the weary hours of waiting, and to explain the numbers of people at the Hall to any shrewd-eyed watchers, the usual Sunday night concert was hastily improvised. During the day the Proclamation of the Irish Republic was printed in Liberty Hall. Thomas MacDonagh gave the text to three members of the Dublin Typographical Provident Society who printed it while a Citizen Army guard under William Partridge stood by.[4] "Irishmen and Irishwomen! In the name of God and of the dead generations from which she receives her old tradition of nationhood, Ireland, through us, summons her children to her flag, and strikes for her freedom. . . ."

The day had been so taxing that even Madame's nerves were unsteady. She and Connolly's secretary, Winifred Carney, were staying the night with the William O'Briens. Soon after the family had gone to bed they were all startled by a shot. Madame had forgotten the rules of gun handling she had so carefully taught the Fianna, and in unloading her automatic had sent a bullet through the door of the O'Briens' room. Fortunately, no one was hurt, and the sound attracted no outside attention.

She and Miss Carney went to Liberty Hall early the next day. Thomas MacDonagh had issued orders for the four city Volunteer battalions to parade at 10 A.M. with full arms and equipment, with each Commandant to announce the place for his men. Company E 3 were ordered by Commandant Pearse to parade at Beresford Place. At 11:45 the fall-in for that company and for the Citizen Army was sounded by Bugler Oman.

Madame particularly remembered seeing Tom Clarke in those last few moments. "The hour so anxiously awaited, so eagerly expected, had come at last," she wrote. "Our hearts' desire was granted to us and we counted ourselves lucky. Happy, proud and gay was Tom Clarke on that day. His life's work had borne fruit at last . . . We met for a few minutes just before the time fixed to march out. It seems queer, looking back on it, how no one spoke of death or fear or defeat. I remember saying good-bye to Tom Clarke just at the door of Dr. Kathleen Lynn's little surgery, which we had all been having a look at before we started. We then went downstairs, and each man joined up with his little band."[5]

No one seems to have counted the "little band"; perhaps the neglect was deliberate. The original plans presumed 5,000 rebels in Dublin. Probably less than 1,000 had mustered, though more straggled to the battle during the week. The size of the muster was not lost on Connolly. To William O'Brien he confided, "We are going out to be slaughtered." O'Brien asked if there were no chance of success and Connolly replied, "None whatever."[6] He took his place at the head of the line and moved up Abbey Street to the General Post Office with deliberate, swaying gait. In a little while those still at Liberty Hall could hear the crash and tinkle of broken glass as men broke out the windows and began to barricade their headquarters.

Madame wrote, "I stood on the steps and watched the little bodies of men and women march off, Pearse and Connolly to the G.P.O., Sean Connolly to the City Hall, all marching proudly, confident that they were doing right, sure at last that they had made the subjection of Ireland impossible for generations to come. I went off then with the Doctor [Lynn] in her car. We carried a large store of First Aid necessities and drove off through quiet dusty streets and across the river, reaching the City Hall just at the very moment that Commandant Sean Connolly and his little troop of men and women swung round the corner and he raised his gun and shot the policeman who barred the way. A wild excitement ensued, people running from every side to see what was up. The Doctor got out, and I remember Mrs. Barrett and others helping to carry in the Doctor's bundles."[7]

Maire Nic Shiublaigh had just gone to Jacob's when she looked out towards the Peter Street side of the building near the Adelaide

Hospital and saw "a group of Volunteers letting the remainder of their comrades into the building. Down the street, swaying from side to side, came an open two-seater car. As it drew abreast of Jacob's a figure in Citizen Army uniform stood up in the front seat and waved its hat about its head. It was Madame Markievicz on her way to Stephen's Green. 'Go at it, boys!' she yelled. 'The Citizen Army are taking the Green! Dublin Castle is falling!' "[8] But the Castle stood nervously through the entire Rising, and the Green was in rebel hands only for that day and night.

Dr. Lynn stayed at the City Hall; Madame took the rest of the first aid supplies to St. Stephen's Green. There Commandant Mallin had seized the keys to the lovely Victorian park, set some men to digging shallow trenches beside the shrubbery, others to making barricades by the iron gateways. Attack was expected momentarily from any of the ten streets that feed into those encircling the Green, and the insurgents were making barricades with laundry vans, private cars, stalled trams. Any vehicle that rolled by was commandeered from its astonished driver.

At the Green Mallin gave Madame employment more to her liking than distributing bandages. "He said that owing to MacNeill's calling off the Volunteers a lot of the men who should have been under him had had to be distributed round other posts, and that I must stay and be ready to take up the work of a sniper. He took me round the Green and showed me how the barricading of the gates and digging trenches had begun, and he left me in charge of this work while he went to superintend the erection of barricades in the streets and arrange other work. About two hours later he definitely promoted me to be his second in command. This work was very exciting when the fighting began. I continued round and round the Green, reporting back if anything was wanted, or tackling any sniper who was particularly objectionable." Some outraged British officers at the Shelbourne Hotel and the United Services Club did not wait for orders to shoot their revolvers at the rebels on the Green. Madame returned their fire with frightening accuracy.

It was estimated that in all there were 138 men and women at the Green, of whom probably 103 men and 15 women were from the Irish Citizen Army, plus 20 Volunteers. A dozen or so came in during the week, so the original muster on Easter Monday was around 120. This meant complete abandonment of some plans, such as occupying the buildings around the Green, including the Shelbourne

Hotel. The rebels tried to carry out other plans, but their numbers were too few. For example, Sergeant Joseph Doyle was detailed to take his position in Davy's Public House with seven men (less than half the total in the original plan). They were to stop the approach of troops from Portobello Barracks across the bridge over the canal. That day there were 650 men and 21 officers of the 3rd Royal Irish Rifles at Portobello Barracks. It was an impossible situation; the rebels were helpless to prevent the advance of the troops, and Davy's was soon evacuated. Similarly, Sergeant Robbins was sent to secure the Harcourt Street Station. He had three men to barricade both ends of Hatch Street, instead of sixteen or twenty as originally planned. This detail included seizing cars from a nearby garage to use in the barricades, job enough for twice the men available. They held the railroad station that day but were forced by lack of replacements to retreat to the College of Surgeons later.[9]

The shortage in the Harcourt Street area was nothing compared with what Mallin was contending with at the Green itself. Many women who had been assigned to first-aid stations and the commissary had been pressed into service to patrol the Green and seek out stragglers. From time to time during the afternoon Volunteers would appear at the Green, drifting late into battle. In the general confusion they had received the new mobilization orders late or not at all, and had come into town looking for a point in the fight where they could help out. Strict military discipline was never a strong point with the Volunteers, but during the Rising an easy camaraderie took its place.

Battalion 2 had mustered at the south side of the Green before moving out to Jacob's, and it was to that point that three of the Cumann na mBan girls had taken a tram from their homes in Fairview. After debating what to do and waiting around hoping to get in touch with their own contingent, they saw Madame. She said casually that if they wanted to throw their lot in with them they would be welcome. She led them to the summer house where Miss ffrench-Mullen was in charge of first aid. The girls liked her and decided to stay.[10]

Monday afternoon, a few hours after the Green was occupied, Madame was one of three women and four men detailed by Mallin to cross to the College of Surgeons, secure it, and search it for rifles and ammunition belonging to the Officers' Training Corps attached to the College. There is a gateway to the Green directly across the street from the College of Surgeons, and as Mallin unlocked the gate he told them to veer to the left and pretend that they were going to York Street. The caretaker of the College was trying to get rid of an unwanted visitor, who was completely oblivious to the fact that a rebellion had started and that he was in the middle of it. Just as the caretaker was closing the huge door, Sergeant Robbins leaped up the steps and threw his weight against it. Simultaneously a shot whizzed by him and hit the top of the door. This unnerved the caretaker who failed to throw the lock properly, allowing Robbins to wedge the door open with his foot. Madame and the others rushed in.

The caretaker professed an incredible ignorance of the College and did not know anything about guns or a training corps. Robbins was about to lose his temper entirely when Madame took control. She ordered the caretaker, his wife and son locked in their own quarters out of harm's way and the insurgents proceeded to search the building.

Madame and the other two women then left to report to Commandant Mallin for further instructions. A supply of bombs was sent to the College by a messenger and they were told to go to the roof, take a position there, and stay until further orders. Shortly thereafter Margaret Skinnider brought over a flag, and the tricolor flew proudly over the College of Surgeons. Except for the four men there, the rest of the small force camped the night in the Green.

During the night British soldiers moved into the Shelbourne Hotel, across from the northeast end of the Green, and placed a machine gun on the roof. All of the Green and its surrounding buildings were well within its range. The rebel plans had been to occupy the hotel with a force of fifty men under Lt. George Norgrove, but with the revisions that the Military Council had had to make on Easter Sunday, the taking of this strategic building was abandoned, and Norgrove was detailed to the G.P.O. and later to the City Hall. Mallin never intended to occupy it with the men he had.

Early Tuesday morning the sleepers on the Green were awakened by the sharp rattle of rifle and machine gun fire. Bullets began to spatter gravel on the walks. Hurriedly, the insurgents crossed the street to their new stronghold, the College. The trees in the Green, not yet in full leaf, offered little screening. One young Citizen Army soldier was killed on the way from the Green to the College; even girls wearing aprons and arm bands marked with large red crosses were fired upon. Spectators watched the retreat with disapproval, "Look at them running," one girl said, "with no hats on them."

Walter Starkie was astonished to find the Green no longer safe for sightseeing: "I believed that it was quite safe for me to ride up Grafton Street and pass along the Green to the Shelbourne Hotel. When I arrived at the hotel, however, I received a shock when I discovered that the front entrance had been barricaded with mattresses, tables and chairs, and at every window a British soldier was stationed with a rifle."[11]

Two or three prisoners were taken to the College of Surgeons; others were released, including at least one British officer. Madame was furious because one officer they had taken and later released had, in spite of his word as a gentleman, reported everything he had seen to his superiors.[12]

Once inside the College of Surgeons, the insurgents were well protected by the strong walls of the three story building. On the ground floor of the building were lecture rooms and a museum; upstairs were other classrooms, laboratories, and the library. On the top floor were the caretaker's rooms and a kitchen. One end of a large classroom was curtained off and used as the first aid room. The windows were quickly barricaded with furniture and text books.

Madame was everywhere, searching for anything that might be of use, offering advice and encouragement with her gay smile. The training corps rifles had been found, which added considerably to the stock of the Citizen Army. There was intermittent firing on the College throughout the week and sniping from ICA positions on the College roof. One company was detailed to break through the walls from house to house along the west and north sides of the Green. Then they intended to set fire to houses on the north side since some had been occupied by British forces and the United Services Club there had given them trouble. Just before 10 P.M., when the fires were to be started, Madame crawled through the walls with an order from Mallin to stop; their plans had been cancelled at the last moment. At this point the military usefulness of the rebels in the College of Surgeons became more symbolic than real. Any movement around the College brought a burst of fire which the insurgents returned with fitful sniping. No troops could pass by them, but none tried. Nevertheless, during the week their flag waved insolently over Dublin.

Food was a problem, especially the first few days after the evacuation to the College of Surgeons. Connolly sent three of the girls from the G.P.O. to the College with ammunition, and gave them money to buy what food they could. They managed to get bread, cheese, and Oxo

Countess Markievicz with her daughter Maeve and stepson Stanislas [1904?]

At an Irish Women's Franchise League benefit in 1914, Countess Markievicz as
Joan of Arc (a signed photo)

Countess Markievicz in a Fianna uniform [1914?]

Countess Markievicz being driven in a Red Cross van from Kilmainham Prison to Mountjoy Jail after being sentenced to penal servitude for life, May 6, 1916

The Countess in the uniform of the Irish Citizen Army, 1916 (courtesy of B. Keogh)

Countess Markievicz arriving in Dublin from Aylesbury Prison, June 1917

At Kilkenny, July 1917 (left to right, standing), Daniel McCarthy, Darrell Figgis, Rev. Dr. Patrick Browne, Alderman Tom Kelly, Seamus Murphy, Eamon de Valera, Sean Milroy; (seated) Laurence Ginnell, Countess Markievicz, William T. Cosgrave, Mrs. Laurence Ginnell

Cathal O'Shannon and Countess Markievicz at the burial of Thomas Ashe, hunger striker, Glasnevin, October 1917

Countess Markievicz, 1919 (UPI photo)

cubes into the College and reported that everybody was in the best of spirits.

The only woman casualty was Margaret Skinnider, who was seriously wounded on Wednesday. She was one of the party who attempted to burn a house just behind the Russell Hotel, which was thought to be occupied by British military. The English opened fire on them from the ground floor of a house just opposite, killing Fred Ryan, a seventeen-year-old, and wounding Miss Skinnider three times. William Partridge carried her back to the College. She cried then, not from pain, but because they had to cut away the coat of her fine new uniform to get to her wounds. Madame had ordered it for her and she was inordinately proud of it. Madame, with her usual compassion, stood by, held her hand, and comforted her while Miss ffrench-Mullen was probing the wounds.

Earlier on Wednesday they had heard the whine and boom of shells near the Liffey, and expectations and rumors were high. Some even thought that the Germans had landed. But it was only the gunboat *Helga* firing on Liberty Hall, by that time completely empty except for the caretaker. Later the sounds of shelling became common as artillery was brought against the G.P.O. Incendiary shells were used and at night the sky over O'Connell Street glowed red.

They heard, too, the furious spatter of rifles from the Mount Street Bridge. Later they learned that a British contingent had come under fire from three outposts manned by Volunteers from Boland's Mills headquarters. Troops which had arrived in Dun Laoghaire during Tuesday night to reinforce the British were ordered to advance in two parallel columns to the Royal Hospital, the military headquarters. Marching towards Dublin on Wednesday morning, one column went by the Stillorgan road and reached its destination without incident. The other column was ordered via Ballsbridge. On the other side of the bridge, there is a fork: the right-hand street leads into Dublin center by way of Northumberland Road, the left-hand one to Baggot Street Bridge, which was unprotected by Volunteers. The leader of the column chose to veer to the right, although there is evidence he had reports to expect opposition there. As the troops approached the canal bridge at Mount Street, they ran into cross fire from the three Volunteer positions; two houses on the approach side to the canal were occupied by a total of six men, and one house on the far side was occupied by seven men. The British advance was held up several hours with the loss of six British officers killed and fifteen wounded; twenty-four men killed, 142 wounded. Six Volunteers were killed.

Those in the College of Surgeons later heard of fighting around most of the main positions occupied by the rebels. Outside of Dublin city, in North County Dublin, the Volunteers made successful attacks on four police barracks, anticipating tactics used in the Black and Tan war three or four years later. At three of the Royal Irish Constabulary barracks they met with little opposition, but at Ashbourne the fight lasted five hours. There, about thirty-five well-armed police occupied a strong barracks. Reinforcements of fifty men in ten cars were stopped by the Volunteers at nearby Rath Cross in a bloody battle, and the barracks surrendered. The total strength of the Volunteers in North County Dublin was between fifty and sixty, under the command of Thomas Ashe, with Richard Mulcahy second in command.[13]

Sometimes the insurgents were ingenious but unlucky. In Phoenix Park, just before noon on Easter Monday, a small band of Fianna boys, ostensibly there to play ball, was nearly successful in exploding a British ammunition dump. Unfortunately, the key to the high explosive storeroom was not where it usually was, and in the delay the boys were able only to set fire to the building, called the Magazine Fort. After it burned for several hours, the fire was finally put out and the high explosive store was saved. One soldier was fatally wounded, as was a civilian, and at least one of the Fianna was wounded.

There was heavy fighting in the South Dublin Union (now the Dublin Board of Assistance) area which controlled the Kingsbridge Station, the terminus for trains from the largest military camp, the Curragh. From the Union the rebels also hoped to block approaches to the Four Courts from the south side of the Liffey. There were casualties on both sides in Marrowbone Lane and the Mendicity Institute. Much of the fighting from the Four Courts was in the maze of streets threaded through the slum areas which surround the courts. Heavy British fire was concentrated on the General Post Office. Both sides of O'Connell Street along the two blocks from the Liffey to the Post Office were destroyed.

Although Pearse issued communiqués and an *Irish War News* from the G.P.O. claiming that the countryside had risen with Dublin, outside the city there was little fighting. The dispersal of the Volunteers by the call-off on Easter Sunday made it impossible to mobilize them in time for effective action. There was some action in Galway under the reliable Liam Mellows[14] and in Wexford where there were about 300 men under Commandant Robert Brennan in Enniscorthy. Most of the rest of North Wexford was held under Commandant Paul Galligan, but they were told to remain in Wexford County to prevent, as far as they could, any reinforcements for the British passing through their territory.

Of the week Madame herself wrote little. Reports from visitors to the College of Surgeons, messengers, bearers of food and news, described her as busy, indefatigable, exhilarated, and happy. The Rebellion was a climax in her life, but climaxes cannot last. There was a rumor that they were to evacuate the College and take to the hills to continue the fight using guerrilla tactics. To that end they were advised to outfit themselves in civilian clothes, or, if wearing them, to take off their arm bands. Then, to their disappointment, orders came to surrender.

The British plan for defeating the Rising had been simple. A cordon was thrown around the Irish positions, extending on the north side of the Liffey from Parkgate to the North Wall and on the south from Kingsbridge to Ringsend. The British then struck at the center of resistance in the G.P.O., using their superior strength to capture or isolate the other insurgent positions.

The highest estimate of the rebel strength puts it at 1,800; the lowest at 1,000.[15] Against these the British had in Dublin on Easter Monday a fighting force of almost 2,500 officers and men. Reinforcements during the week raised their strength to about 5,500. All were trained and fully equipped. Furthermore, the British had heavy guns to bring against men with a hodgepodge of equipment, most of it light arms and some homemade bombs.

On Sunday, April 30, Elizabeth Farrell, a Cumann na mBan member who had been at the G.P.O. and who had been the messenger the day before in carrying details of the surrender to the north side garrisons, was driven to Grafton Street. From there she walked to the College of Surgeons carrying a white flag and typewritten copies of the surrender order. Bullets were still whistling around St. Stephen's Green, but she saw no one on the streets. She went to the side door in York Street and asked for Commandant Mallin. She was told he was sleeping and that Countess Markievicz was next in command. Miss Farrell gave the order to Madame who, very surprised, awakened Mallin. Mallin sent an order to the men in the houses around the Green to report to the College of Surgeons immediately. A gloomy company assembled in the College. After Mallin read the surrender order to them, he, Madame, and Partridge each spoke of a job done to the best of their ability and of hope for the future. Their generation had not failed in making a stand for an independent Ireland. Earlier in the week Madame had exulted, "We've done more than Wolfe Tone already." More they could not expect.

At 11 o'clock on Sunday morning, April 30, six days after the Rising began, the College of Surgeons force surrendered. As usual, Madame contributed a bit of theatricalism to the proceedings. She and Mallin led the march out of the side door of the College and surrendered to Captain Wheeler. She smartly saluted the captain, kissed her revolver before giving it up, and said, "I am ready!" She refused Captain Wheeler's offer of a ride to jail, and marched off confidently with Mallin and the men and women with whom she had fought. They marched down Grafton Street, up Dame Street, and in through the Castle gate, which Madame had last seen less than a week before when she left Dr. Lynn and the medical supplies there. On the way Madame and Mallin discussed what seemed to them to be the only doubtful point in their immediate future—whether they would be shot or hanged.

Crowds lined the streets. One woman who dared to wave encouragingly at Madame was immediately arrested and spent over a week in jail for her indiscretion. Most of the crowd waved hats and Union Jacks for the Staffordshire Regiment escorting the prisoners, and yelled, "Shoot the traitors," "Bayonet them," "Mad dogs." To the men and women who had expected other Irishmen to share their dreams of liberty the taunts gave a surrealistic, nightmarish quality to the Sunday morning.

The crowd was not merely intimidated by the victors. During the week all petty annoyances had been blamed on the Sinn Feiners. For example, food deliveries were not made, and although bread was available at the bakeries, Dubliners remember grumbling not a little about having to go there and get it. The city was without newspapers for only two days, Thursday and Friday of Easter Week. What was more important was that Ireland was committed to Britain's cause in World War I. At least 150,000 Irishmen from Ireland were in the British forces. For every rebel who fought Easter Week there were a hundred Irish fighting for Britain. Irishmen living in England brought the total number of Irish in the British army close to half a million. It is not surprising that Dublin crowds jeered the insurgents to jail.

After a short stay in the Castle Yard, the company proceeded to Richmond Barracks. Nora O'Daly had carried the Red Cross flag proudly throughout the line of march but just at the entrance to the Barracks it was snatched from her hand by a soldier, to her bewilderment and annoyance. Madame and Miss ffrench-Mullen were separated from the rest of the women.

Julia Grennan, with the others from the G.P.O., had spent Saturday night in the open, crushed inside a small park near the Rotunda. The next day they were taken to the Barracks where they were joined by Cumann na mBan from the Four Courts who were accompanied by Father Columbus. There Madame saw Julia Grennan for the first time since the muster at Beresford Place. Disdaining the guards, Madame ran over to shake hands and inquire after some of the others. "Remove that woman," a voice shouted, and Madame was taken away. They were marched in the evening to Kilmainham Jail.

It was dark when they reached Kilmainham, and the gloom was intensified by the flickering candles the soldiers were carrying. Nora O'Daly saw Madame again briefly. She was on an upper landing smoking a cigarette when the other women were brought up. The guard shouted, "Put out that fag." When Madame refused to take notice, he violently struck it out of her hand. Mrs. O'Daly wondered at her self-control; she completely ignored him, and smiled encouragement to her friends before she was put in a separate cell. They did not see her again.

The Rebellion was over. It was time to bury the dead, to estimate the wreckage of lives and property. Casualties in the British military, Royal Irish Constabulary, and Dublin Metropolitan Police were thought to be 120 killed, 392 wounded or missing. Sixty-four insurgents were killed in action, but nearly twice as many civilians died, an estimated 116.[16] The high number of civilian casualties was due primarily to the insatiable curiosity of Dubliners who treated rebellion as a spectator sport. Contemporary photographs show men and women idling on the street corners watching soldiers firing from the middle of the street. The inevitable writers were among them. Walter Starkie wrote: "During rebellion week I found my bicycle a godsend, for it enabled me to follow the progress of the fighting in the various zones of the city, and I enjoyed exercising my ingenuity to discover ways of by-passing the cordons, barricades and sentry spots. . . . I managed to push my way through the crowd of spectators standing on Aston quay from which I obtained a ring seat view of the attack on Butler's across the river. Sometimes I pinched myself to prove that I was not dreaming, for the crowd behaved as if they were watching a circus. Even the booming of the guns of the gunboat *Helga* down the river near the Custom House did not terrify them, and they paid no more attention to the bullets whistling over their heads than if they had been droves of starlings."[17]

Vindictiveness caused other civilian deaths. Fifteen civilians were allegedly shot or bayoneted by the British during military operations in the North King Street area in the final days and even after the surrender of the G.P.O. Three civilians were shot under orders of the deranged British Captain Bowen-Colthurst: two Loyalist editors, Thomas Dickson and Patrick McIntyre, and the pacifist Francis Sheehy Skeffington, one of Dublin's favorite eccentrics. He had been pasting up posters to try to organize an anti-looting committee (around the G.P.O. the looting of shops was a scandal) and was on his way home on Tuesday when he was arrested and taken to Portobello Barracks with the two editors. In the middle of the night the Captain suddenly ordered his men to take the three prisoners into the courtyard and execute them. The Captain was also said to have shot three other civilians himself without reason.

Militarily the rebellion was no more than an annoyance to the British, who at most were indignant at the perfidious Irish. General Macready saw it as a fanatical attempt to overthrow British rule in Ireland when the Empire was fighting for its very life. To him it added only a minor anxiety to the heavy responsibilities of the Army Council. This was a typical attitude. The state of Ireland was distracting but was nothing compared to the War Office's main job, getting on with the war in Europe.

The vast gulf between the Irish who took their nationalism seriously but not grimly and the British government who looked at them grimly but not seriously, is nowhere more succinctly illustrated than in a letter from Lord Wimborne, Lord Lieutenant of Ireland, to Chief Secretary Birrell. The letter was written on Easter Sunday when the British had decided to move against the Volunteers and arrest the leaders. "These fellows have enjoyed too much immunity already. After all, it is nothing else than to create a diversion in favour of the enemy and detain three or four divisions here to deal with it—at a critical moment, too."

"Nothing else than to create a diversion . . ." How the nationalists would have hooted or blazed at that. Of all the things most difficult and yet most important in understanding the men and women who went out Easter is their sense of dedication. An old concept of the hero died in that war which the Empire was fighting to save itself, and no longer do people talk with the same enthusiasm of honor, of patriotism, of dedication to a cause. "Patriotism" no longer means dedication, no longer do we have the indefinable sense of communion with people who live in a geographically bound area and who share "the possession of a national history and consequent community of recollections, collective pride and humiliation, pleasure and regret, connected with the same incidents in the past."[18] Patriotism is now more often "the last refuge of a scoundrel" than the mark of the hero.

To think that such a man as Tom Clarke had given his life for more than forty years to the ideal of a free Ireland for the sole purpose of creating a "diversion" was to misunderstand abysmally. It was to disparage all that the nationalists had devoted years of energy, money, and time to—the cause of Ireland. If it was difficult for their contemporaries to realize, it is even harder now to recognize and appreciate their zeal. It was their sustenance through long, sometimes dreary years when without it they could not have gone on. In those days before the horror of mass annihilation was dreamed of, one could still talk of the exaltation of personal sacrifice.

Helena Molony articulated the feelings of many of the Volunteers and Citizen Army men and women: "When we walked out that Easter Monday morning we felt in a very real sense that we were walking with Ireland into the sun." Madame tried to explain their dedication in a verse she wrote as "Easter Memories" the year of her death, but could do little more than suggest her emotion: "Rainbow chasers and fanatics . . . You died for a dream." Yeats saw their enthusiasm as an "excess of love" which "bewildered them till they died." To Miss Gore-Booth their achievement was "their strange heroic questioning of Fate" which did "ribbon with gold the rags of this our life." Although AE did not agree with his friends among the leaders, he appreciated the passion of their dreams which "turned life's waters into wine." The "terrible beauty" Yeats saw and what was "broken glory" to Eva Gore-Booth crystallized nationalist emotions about the rebellion and the feelings of those who became sympathetic to it after the event.[19]

The Easter Rebellion, which started a chain of other disasters for the British Empire, was blamed on a failure of statesmanship. Chief Secretary Birrell took the part of the bureaucratic scapegoat and resigned. But the army had been surprised and annoyed, and as they saw it, the ones to pay were the Irish leaders.

Sir John Maxwell had been sent to Ireland to deal with the rebellion and the country was under martial law to be used at his discretion. He decided to make an example of the nationalists. On May 3, Padraic Pearse, Tom Clarke, and Thomas MacDonagh were shot in the courtyard at Kilmainham; on May 4, Edward Daly, Joseph Plunkett, Michael O'Hanrahan, and William Pearse (Padraic's brother, and apparently executed for that reason); on the 5th, Major John MacBride (Maud Gonne's husband); on the 8th, Eamonn Ceannt, Michael Mallin, Con Colbert and Sean Heuston; on the 9th, Thomas Kent was executed in Cork. On May 12th, Sean MacDermott and James Connolly were shot. Connolly, whose leg had been shattered during Easter Week, was brought from the Castle hospital to Kilmainham, then propped in a chair to face the firing squad. Day after day the handsome, the gallant, the wise, the dedicated, the quixotic, and the honorable were killed. All these leaders had expected death, and their executions set an example, but not in the way Sir John Maxwell expected.

George Bernard Shaw, generally out of sympathy with the Irish but an astute observer always, reflected the changing opinions of many people both in England and in Ireland in a letter to the *Daily News* which was published May 10, 1916: "It is absolutely impossible to slaughter a man in this position without making him a martyr and a hero. The shot Irishmen will now take their places beside Emmet and the Manchester martyrs in Ireland and nothing in heaven or on earth can prevent it."

"We are going out to be slaughtered," Connolly had said on Easter Monday. Could he have known they were also going to be martyred? He was a shrewd man.

The patriotism that was not kindled by rebellion was kindled by the execution of the rebels. Within a few weeks the mood of Ireland, and Dublin in particular, changed. "At that time in Dublin," Douglas Goldring wrote, "no one could be in the city for twenty-four hours without discovering what was the general feeling of the mass of the population about the Sinn Feiners. Picture postcards of the executed rebels were displayed in almost every shop window, and their faces were gazed upon with silent veneration by the passers-by. Up and down O'Connell Street urchins ran selling broad sheets purporting to contain, 'The last and inspiring speech of Thomas MacDonagh.' . . . So far as one could tell, except among the shopkeepers who had not received compensation for their losses and among the upper classes, all resentment against the Sinn Feiners had died away."[20]

A British officer with that objectivity which comes from having sympathy with both sides, summed up the changes: "The overbearing attitude towards the civilian population on the part of the British officers engaged was strongly resented; the very gallant battle fought by some hundreds of badly armed men against tremendous odds won sympathy and admiration; and the savage execution of the heroic leaders of the Rising after their surrender kindled a flame of hatred in Irish hearts which it would take very many years to quench."[21]

By mid-May, H. W. Massingham could report to *The Nation* readers in the United States that Dublin was a whispering gallery full of rumor, and "for one sympathizer with Sinn Fein Easter Monday there are ten today."[22] A current joke was that "the temperature is '98 in the shade." The significant change in public opinion by the end of the first week in May is reflected in references to the Rising in pro-British newspapers. What had been called the Dublin riots was now elevated to the status of rebellion. Shooting a rioter was one thing, a rebel another.

In the meantime, there were wholesale arrests by an increasingly arrogant military, and the tempers of the Irish grew steadily hotter. By July 1, 1916, 3,149 men and 77 women had been taken to Richmond Barracks; 1,862 were interned without trial.[23] Darrell Figgis saw that these arrests gave new vitality to Sinn Fein: "It was the university in which the doctrines, methods, and hopes of the men of Easter Week were folded into the life of men from every part of Ireland. Extraordinary to think with what care men were brought from all over the country (many of whom began by disagreeing earnestly with the Rising) to receive one pattern of thought and to know one another and to learn of one another. Nearly every man who took any kind of part in the events of the years to follow passed through Richmond Barracks, and there for the first time many of them met, leaders and followers together."[24] Several writers noted this aspect of prisons during the following months.

"I never knew such a transformation of opinion as that caused by the executions," that shrewd politician, T. M. Healy, wrote to his brother on June 10, in a letter summarizing the reasons for the transformation. "Besides the looting by the soldiers and ruffianism against innocent people—the ill-treatment of the prisoners, the insolence of the military in the streets, the foul language used to women, and the

incompetence shown by officers, have aroused a contempt and dislike
for which there is no parallel in our day. The small boys are singing,
'Who fears to speak of Easter week!' Pearse achieved his object, and
'builded better than he knew.' His executioners would now give a good
deal to have him and his brother back in jail alive."[25]

When Laurence Ginnell reportedly shouted "murder" as the executions were announced in the House of Commons, Prime Minister
Asquith answered that Sir John Maxwell had used his power with
moderation. He pointed out that so far only thirteen rebels had been
executed and there were two more leaders whose sentences could not
be commuted. There were another 137 sentenced to penal servitude
and 23 to imprisonment with hard labor. To be sure, there were hundreds who were untried. As conflicting reports continued to come from
Ireland, Asquith decided to go and see for himself. The day he arrived
he wrote confidently to his wife, "On the whole except the Skeffington
case—there were fewer bad blunders than one might have expected
with the soldiery for a whole week in exclusive charge." Four days later,
after a trip to Belfast, he had begun to sense the complexity and growing turbulence of the land. "You never get to the bottom of this most
perplexing and damnable country."[26]

In isolation at Kilmainham Jail, Madame knew almost nothing of
Ireland's change of heart. She was also locked away from her fellow
prisoners, who were even then starting to make the new friendships
and reputations that would soon give Sinn Fein strength to fight the
British much longer than a week. She heard little more than the heavy
steps of guards on stone and the all too frequent bursts of rifle fire
from a courtyard below. What news eventually came to her from the
prison was of the prison—who had come or gone, who was shot. She
certainly heard nothing of Irish-American fury over the executions nor
of the attempt of Congress to halt them, though such international
protests on the eve of the United States' entry into World War I
probably helped to save her own life.[27] She had never been more alone,
but she had another faith than Irish nationalism to help sustain her.

For several years she had been moving towards religious conversion.
Her epiphany had come in the College of Surgeons. Protestantism had
been part of her inheritance from Lissadell, one aspect of the Anglo-
Irish establishment. She had been deeply impressed by the reality of
Roman Catholicism to those among whom she had lived, worked, and
fought against that establishment. She had shared with Catholics her

wealth, energy, and all the risks of rebellion. It was probably inevitable that she would some day share their faith.

She was particularly impressed by William Partridge, a man remarkable for his gentleness and care. He had hardly slept while at the College, but had roamed the building and outposts bringing some comfort to those who were fearful, alone, or in pain. Everyone who was there speaks of him with affection mixed with reverence. Under the pressures of the week he had risen to become their spiritual guide.

On the last night Madame knelt with the others in prayer. Suddenly, she later said, she had had "a vision of the Unseen" that made a permanent change in her. From that moment things seen became temporal and things unseen eternal. She tried to express some of her feelings in a poem written when she was in Mountjoy after her court-martial and sentence. The poem was dedicated to William Partridge and called "To a Comrade." It has since been titled "The Rosary—College of Surgeons."

> The great hall fades away into the gloom,
> As tremulous night falls slowly from above,
> Merging us each in each in tender love:
> One shadow marching onward towards one doom.
> On our rough altar white flowers shine and bloom
> Intensifying dusky waves that move
> Around the tall black Cross. One hope, one prayer
> Filled all our hearts, one perfect holy Faith
> Lifted our souls. As we knelt humbly there,
> Your silvery voice, soft as a dying breath,
> Was answered by a hundred strong and clear,
> Craving a grace from her whom all hold dear—
> *'Mary! be with us at the hour of death.'*

NOTES TO CHAPTER IX

Unfortunately, there has never been an official history of the Irish Rebellion and the archives are inaccessible. Anyone writing about 1916 must rely on contemporary reports and memories, and try to distinguish the imaginary from what has the ring of truth.

1. Constance de Markievicz, "Tom Clarke and the First Day of the Republic," *Eire*, May 26, 1923.

2. *Debate on the Treaty Between Great Britain and Ireland* (Dublin, 1922), January 3, 1922, p. 185.

3. *Eire*, May 26, 1923.

4. The Proclamation was printed by William O'Brien, Michael Molloy, and Christopher Brady.

5. *Eire,* May 26, 1923.

6. Intro. to *Labour and Easter Week,* p. 21.

7. Roper, *Prison Letters,* pp. 38–39.

8. Maire Nic Shiublaigh, *The Splendid Years,* p. 168.

9. The Dublin train to Wexford, which arrived there four hours past its usual 10 P.M. schedule, brought confirmation of the Rising, rumors of which had been current all day. Among other news, the railway guard told Robert Brennan, Commandant of the Wexford Volunteers, that they had had to get a permit from Countess Markievicz to get the train out (Robert Brennan, *Allegiance,* Dublin, 1950, pp. 55–56).

10. Mrs. Nora O'Daly, "The Women of Easter Week," *An t'Oglac,* April 3, 1926. Bridget Murtagh and May Moore were with her. Nellie Gifford was another who came along in the afternoon, as well as some Volunteers, among them Liam O Briain and Harry Nicholls. In *The History of The Irish Citizen Army* (Dublin, 1943), R. M. Fox gives the names of those who served with the ICA Easter Week, including the 15 women and 103 men at Stephen's Green.

11. *The Irish Times,* October 11, 1963.

12. Years later Madame's daughter met a man on a train who said he had been taken prisoner at Stephen's Green by her. Maeve took him to where her mother was sitting and introduced them. He remembered Madame with enthusiasm, but she did not recognize him and said only, "I hope we treated you well." He may have been responsible for the stories of gay, very polite and drawing-roomish tea parties on the Green while bullets whizzed by her.

A Colonel in the English army, who was a friend of the Gore-Booths wrote sympathetically to Madame's sister and told her, "An enormous Army doctor was in here yesterday who described being captured by the Countess in person, who deprived him of his belt and allowed him to look after wounded Sinn Feiners. Her pistol was enormous and he was terrified of its going off" (Roper, *Prison Letters,* p. 42).

13. Two R.I.C. officers were killed, and six to nine men. Estimates of wounded R.I.C. men ranged from 14 to 20. Two civilian motorists were caught in the cross fire and killed; one Volunteer lost his life.

14. Mellows, whose arrest had been the occasion for demonstrations in Dublin at the end of March, had been deported to England April 2nd. But since he was needed to lead the Rising in the west, his brother Barney, accompanied by Nora Connolly, secretly met Liam in Staffordshire. The brothers changed clothes, Liam went with Nora to Glasgow while Barney stayed in England, and Liam soon returned to Ireland disguised as a priest. Within two weeks of his deportation he was back in Dublin (*Portrait of a Rebel Father,* pp. 275–278).

15. Estimates of numbers of Irish involved in the Rising have varied during the fifty years since the event. Cathal Brugha at the time thought the total was about 1,000; John Devoy in New York estimated 1,500; Desmond Ryan, who was at the G.P.O., estimated 1,100 (700 Volunteers on Easter Monday with 200 more joining in during the week, and about 200 Irish Citizen Army). Diarmuid Lynch, twenty years after the rising, thought that there were 1,600 men and women, including the Citizen Army's 218. Major Florence

O'Donoghue, in a Radio Eireann talk in 1956, put the number at 1,600 Volunteers plus the 200 Citizen Army. A Department of External Affairs handbook, "Facts about Ireland," published in 1963, brought the number back to "about 1,000."

In May, 1936, Diarmuid Lynch made a résumé of the numbers involved, using those who had signed the Easter Week Roll of Honour that year, and estimating where exact figures were unknown. His table (from which the following was compiled) in *The I.R.B. and the 1916 Insurrection*, (Cork, 1957) is one of the few statistical compilations which have been made:

	Executed	Killed in Action	Deceased by 1936	Sig-natures	Garrison Totals
GENERAL POST OFFICE					
Headquarters	6	9	42	351	408
FOUR COURTS					
1st Battalion	1		45	242	288
JACOB'S					
2nd Battalion	3		35	147	185
BOLAND'S					
3rd Battalion			29	144	173
SO. DUBLIN UNION					
4th Battalion	3		37	180	220
CITY HALL					
Cit. Army & Vol.		5	11	30	46
ST. STEPHEN'S GREEN					
Cit. Army & Vol.	1	6	21	110	138
ASHBOURNE					
No. Co. Dublin Vol.			13	46	59
MAGAZINE FORT					
Fianna				11	11
	14	20*	233	1,261	1,528†

* This is somewhat misleading. Of the known 64 dead, only 20 were listed separately, the other 44 were included in "Deceased by 1936."

†Although there may have been some duplications, e.g., Magazine Fort might have been included in the G.P.O., Diarmuid Lynch knew of others who had been omitted, and he estimated they would bring the total to 1,600.

16. Casualties for the week as reported by *The Irish Times* on May 11, 1916, were:

	Killed	Wounded	Missing	Total
British Military officers	17	46		63
British Military, other ranks	86	311	9	406
Royal Irish Constabulary officers	2			2
Royal Irish Constabulary, other ranks	12	23		35
Dublin Metropolitan Police	3	3		6
Civilians and insurgents	180	614	—	794
	300	997	9	1,306

However, in the 1921 official British government publication *Documents Relating to the Sinn Fein Movement,* Cmd. 1108, p. 14, the figures were much higher, particularly those of "Civilians and insurgents." The total casualties arising out of the rebellion reported there were:

	Killed	Wounded	Missing	Total
Military officers	17	46		63
Military other ranks	99	322	9	430
R.I.C. officers	2			2
R.I.C. other ranks	11	22		33
D.M.P.	3	7		10
Civilians and insurgents	318	2,217		2,535
	450	2,614	9	3,073

With the exception of those in the R.I.C., the only other casualties outside Dublin were eight civilians killed and one military officer and nine civilians wounded.

17. *The Irish Times,* October 11, 1963.

18. John Stuart Mill, *Considerations on Representative Government* (New York, 1882), p. 308.

19. Helena Molony, *An Phoblacht,* November, 1930; Constance de Markievicz, "Easter Memories," *Kerryman,* December, 1938; W. B. Yeats, "Easter 1916," *Collected Poems,* p. 202; Eva Gore-Booth, "Easter Week," *Poems of Eva Gore-Booth,* p. 508; George Russell (AE), "Salutation" (London: Privately Printed, 1917).

20. An Englishman [Douglas Goldring], *Dublin Explorations and Reflections* (Dublin, 1917).

21. Eugene Sheehy, *May It Please The Court* (Dublin, 1951), p. 90. Judge Sheehy, whose brother-in-law was the murdered pacifist Francis Sheehy Skeffington, was an officer in the Royal Dublin Fusiliers and was with his company in Dorset Street by the Tuesday of Easter week. Another brother-in-law, Thomas Kettle, was also a British officer.

22. May 20, 1916, p. 208.

23. Of the 3,149 men who had been in Richmond Barracks, 1,104 were released; 183 were tried by courts-martial (160 were convicted, 23 acquited); and 1,862 were interned without trial. Of the 77 women, 71 were released and 6 were imprisoned.

24. Figgis, *Recollections of the Irish War,* pp. 168–169. Asquith recognized this immediately and warned against it. On May 14, after visiting Richmond Barracks and talking to about seventy-five of the three or four hundred prisoners there at the time, he wrote to his wife: "They were mostly from remote parts of the country, and none had taken any part in the Dublin rising. There were a lot who had much better have been left at home. I told Maxwell and his men to comb them out carefully and only send to England those against whom there was a real case" (J. A. Spender and Cyril Asquith, *Life of Herbert Henry Asquith,* London, 1932, II, 216).

25. Healy, *Letters and Leaders,* II, 568.

26. *Life of Asquith,* II, 215–217.

27. On June 16, 1916, Ambassador Spring-Rice wrote to Sir Edward Grey: "The attitude towards England is changed for the worse by recent events in Ireland. I think we might adopt a benevolent attitude towards the distribution of funds for the sufferers by the revolt. If we are able in some measure to settle the Home Rule question at once, the announcement will have a beneficial effect here, although I do not think that anything we could do would conciliate the Irish here. They have blood in their eyes when they look our way . . . we must remember that our cause for the present among the Irish here is a lost one" (*Letters and Friendships,* II, 338).

And on July 31, 1916: "The only occasions on which Congress has intervened or attempted to intervene in the present war, were to prevent a blockade of cotton and to prevent the execution of Irish rebels. . . . It is becoming a profession now among a certain number of Congressmen to attack the British Government. It is quite like old times. The reason, of course, is that many of the Congressmen are Irish or with Irish connections and the irritation among the Irish here has reached a degree of intensity as great as in the 'eighties" (ibid., II, 340, 343).

X

Kilmainham and Aylesbury
May 1916–June 1917

Kilmainham Jail was the gloomy "Bastille of Ireland," but the nationalists of 1916 had a proud identification with other patriots who had been imprisoned there. Henry Joy McCracken (who was with Wolfe Tone at the founding of the United Irishmen) was in Kilmainham in 1796; so were Thomas Addis Emmet, Henry and John Sheares, Napper Tandy, and General Corbet in 1798; Robert Emmet, Thomas Russell, Anne Devlin, and Michael Dwyer, 1803; William Smith O'Brien, Thomas Francis Meagher (who became a brigadier general during the American Civil War), Terence Bellew McManus, and Patrick O'Donoghue, 1848.

The Fenian leaders of 1867 were there: O'Donovan Rossa, John O'Leary, Charles J. Kickham, and John Devoy. In Land League days it held Michael Davitt, John Dillon, William O'Brien, Father Sheehy, T. M. Healy, and Charles Stewart Parnell. (It was from his cell in 1881 that Parnell issued the "No Rent Manifesto" which called upon the Irish farmers to withhold rents from their landlords.) In 1883 Kilmainham received twenty-six Invincibles, five of whom were hanged there. 1916 added more names to the Kilmainham Roll of Honor. The old building was a keep of lost causes.

Madame, separated from the rest of the women in Kilmainham, was in a cell in a corridor occupied by other leaders of the Rising but was unable to talk with them. She could hear doors opening along the corridor and footsteps outside but could only guess what was going on. It was a lonely week of uncertainty and, rare for Madame, almost of despair. At grey dawn of the third day she heard the crack of rifles from a prison courtyard. Some of her friends had been executed, but who? The following morning came more shots, more friends gone. Madame was convinced that she, too, would be executed, but she kept her own stiff-necked pride. When the prison chaplain suggested that she should wear a dress instead of a uniform, she answered like St. Joan, "I fought in these clothes and I'll die in them."

On the fourth morning, May 4, she was brought out of her cell and thought she was going to be shot without the formality of a trial. Instead she was brought to a hearing presided over by a "fuzzy little officer with his teeth hanging out to dry" as she disrespectfully characterized her judge. A seventeen-year-old page boy at the University Club was one witness for the prosecution. He swore he saw her drive up to the Green in a motor car, blow her whistle, and lean out of the car. She gave orders to a Sinn Feiner after he had shut the gate of Stephens Park [sic]. "She then drove up towards the Shelbourne Hotel—I saw her again about 1:15 P.M. she was then behind one of the monuments in the Green, she had a pistol in her hand which she pointed towards the club and fired. I ran upstairs and saw where the bullet struck. After firing she walked up towards the Shelbourne Hotel dressed in knickers and puttees."

The second witness was Captain Wheeler, to whom she had surrendered her arms on Sunday. Madame, in common with the other accused rebels, was not allowed legal advice but she was allowed to question the witnesses. She later said, "I blew the little boy's evidence to pieces, and showed that he could not have seen what he alleged from the position in which he stated he was standing—it would have been a physical impossibility." The boy's testimony seems innocuous but the fact that he testified at all apparently infuriated her. "I, of course, admitted what the officer swore as I was second in command under Michael Mallin in the Stephen's Green area. I gave the fuzzy little officer beans, and defied him to shoot me.

"I thought," she continued, "that my trial was then over but the formal court-martial was subsequently held [the same day]. The witnesses were the same as at the preliminary investigation. The little boy, however, changed his evidence and burst into tears when I asked if he had been put into the industrial school for thieving.

"I told the court that I had fought for the independence of Ireland during Easter Week, and that I was as ready now to die for the cause as I was then."[1]

The morning of the fifth of May she waited in the dawn, and listened a third time to the English soldiers firing their volleys in the yard below. That night, when she was lonely and sad, an English soldier on guard outside her cell waited until all was quiet, then unlocked her door, offered her a cigarette, and sat down himself to smoke with her. He was kind and sympathetic, telling her the news and answering questions. He told her that Padraic Pearse, Tom Clarke, and Thomas MacDonagh had been shot that first day, that Ned Daly, Joe Plunkett, Michael O'Hanrahan, and Willie Pearse had gone on the second, and that John MacBride had faced the firing squad alone that morning. She was sure she would be next.

The next day, Saturday, she was standing on the table in her cell drearily looking out of the window, when a young officer came in, very correct and formal, but ill at ease. He read the findings of the court-martial:

"Constance Georgina Markievicz (1) Did an act to wit did take part in an armed rebellion and in the waging of war against His Majesty the King, such act being of such a nature as to be calculated to be prejudicial to the Defence of the Realm and being done with the intention and for the purpose of assisting the enemy. (2) Did attempt to cause disaffection among the civilian population of His Majesty.

"The finding and sentence was 'Guilty. Death by being shot. The Court recommend the prisoner to mercy solely and only on account of her sex.' Signed by J. G. Maxwell, Convening Officer, and C. J. Blackrader, Brig.-General, President, 4th day of May 1916." The Confirming Officer (also General Maxwell) noted on the proper space on the Schedule: "Confirmed. But I commute the sentence to one of Penal Servitude for life." The previous year the Germans had executed Edith Cavell and England was making good propaganda of the event. It was politic to commute Madame's sentence.

Something of Madame's irrepressible spirits unexpectedly popped up at the sight of the young British officer so obviously embarrassed at having to read the sentence. He mumbled rapidly through his job, but at the end of it she made him read it through again, clearly this time. When he had stumbled through the ordeal the second time, she remarked with devastating directness, "I wish you had the decency to shoot me."

After she was sentenced, she was moved to a cell in Mountjoy, where she could hear the newsboys calling their headlines from the street. On the 8th of May she heard that more friends had been executed: Eamonn Ceannt, Michael Mallin, Con Colbert, and Sean Heuston. The latter two she had known since they were enthusiastic Fianna boys in the first sluagh formed in the little hall in Lower Camden Street seven years before. At Cork on the 9th of May Thomas Kent was shot. On the morning of May 12th, Madame heard the news she dreaded: two of her closest friends were dead, Sean MacDermott and James Connolly.

At Mountjoy she was allowed her first visitors. Her sister, Eva, who lived in London, had applied for permission to visit her as soon as she heard of her reprieve, and on the night of May 11 she and Esther Roper crossed to Dublin.[2] They visited Madame with a Dublin friend.

Nearly two weeks before, the day the College of Surgeons forces surrendered, there had been reports in London papers that Madame had been found dead on St. Stephen's Green. Miss Gore-Booth had frantically run up and down all day trying to get more information. Now she was able to visit her sister for a few minutes, trying to store up impressions to last for months, not knowing when she would be able to see her again. "Nobody," Miss Gore-Booth wrote, "who has not gone through the ordinary prison visit can realise how unsatisfactory it is, nor what a strain it is, to fling one's intimate conversation across a passage with a wardress in it, to a head appearing at a window opposite."

Miss Gore-Booth found her sister calm and smiling, full of all sorts of commissions she wanted carried out. She asked a great many questions and seemed really puzzled only by the murder of Sheehy Skeffington. "Why on earth did they shoot Skeffy? After all, he wasn't in it. He didn't even believe in fighting. What did it mean?"

One of her first questions was to verify that Connolly had been shot. Her visitors had been warned that on no account must they answer that question. Though no word was spoken, the answer was in their faces. Tears ran slowly down Madame's cheeks. She said, "You needn't tell me, I know. Why didn't they let me die with my friends?" (That terrible moment was the only time she showed grief during her imprisonment; whenever a visitor was present or she wrote to her sister in the months that followed, she was deliberately gay.) Soon she was in control again, "Well, Ireland was free for a week."

"There was much to hear," Miss Gore-Booth said, "her adventures in the Rebellion, details of her court-martial, her anxiety for the wife of a dead colleague [Mrs. Mallin] who was ill, in hiding and without money. Many and very insufficient directions as to how to find her. About her own treatment the prisoner had not much to say. She was a 'convict' and a 'lifer' and that was all about it. And anyway, it was splendidly worth while.

"For one glorious week, Ireland had been free and then back she went to stories of that wonderful time, of the night-scouting and the

trench in Stephen's Green and the machine-gun on the Shelbourne
. . . the College of Surgeons. And how they could have held out for
days, and the shock and grief of the order to surrender. . . . At the
end of twenty hurried minutes of rapid talk we said good-bye for the
next four months, and the oddly becapped head disappeared from the
window, vanishing into what unimaginable scenes of dullness, dingi-
ness and squalor."[3]

An old friend of the Gore-Booths was an Army officer in Dublin
at the time. He had written Madame after the surrender and Miss
Gore-Booth wrote to tell him of her visit to Mountjoy. He answered
from his "Main Barracks" address:

> Dear Miss Eva,—Your letter is painfully interesting. I do hope
> my letter gave your sister a ray of pleasure. It is dreadful to think of
> the charming high-spirited girl I used to know being a prisoner. It
> is wonderful her keeping up her spirits. Perhaps they will find her
> some kind of work that might suit her clever artistic fingers.
> . . . I don't know what the dear child would say if she knew I
> was commanding the garrison here, defending bridges and controlling
> the district.
> Shall we ever have peace and quiet? Anyway, we cannot manage
> without belonging to an Empire.
> Small states seem to be demolished.

At Kilmainham when she was sure she would be executed, Madame
asked Father Ryan to be with her at the end. After she was reprieved
and transferred to Mountjoy, she registered herself as a Catholic. Father
McMahon, the Chaplain there, started to give her instruction, although
the idea of joining the Church formally while she was in jail was an-
tipathetical to her and she was not baptized until she was released in
1917.

Father McMahon was puzzled by her attitude to his instruction and
told Mrs. Skeffington, "I can't understand Countess Markievicz at all.
She wants to be received into the Church, but she won't attend to me
when I try to explain Transubstantiation and other doctrines. She just
says, 'Please don't trouble to explain. I tell you I believe all the Church
teaches. Now Father, please tell me about the boys.' " Mrs. Skeffington
later heard that Madame had shocked Father McMahon by defending
Lucifer as a "good rebel." "But that, I think," Mrs. Skeffington said,
"was part of her habit of leg-pulling of authority."

Mrs. Skeffington mused further about Madame's religion and what it
meant. "I would say that she belonged to the church of St. Francis of

Assisi, rather than that of St. Paul. The ritual and the ceremonies, the music and the beauty of the Catholic Church, its art and cultural background attracted the mystic in her. She defended the socialist Connolly against an attack by a Jesuit, Father McKenna. She held Socialism to be possible with the church. Individual clerics she often sharply disagreed with. Over her bed was a picture of Da Vinci's Christ."[4]

Four days after her sister's visit, Madame was able to write her first letter from Mountjoy. In a poem she wrote at the time she detailed the things she missed—beauty and color, love and friends, hope and work. Her letter is full of concern for others with no histrionics about herself. She missed her dog, Poppet, who was nearly as familiar a sight around Dublin as Madame herself. She gave her sister explicit directions about closing up the house, she was careful about mundane details—mothballs and starch, and how to get into a locked desk without a key. She was not entirely resigned to a lifetime in prison and obviously hoped some day to use her things again, or at least keep them available for her family.

Number B374 Name Constance G. de Markievicz
            H.M. Prison, Mountjoy Female
            Dublin
                                    May 16, 1916
Dearest Old Darling,—It was such a Heaven sent joy seeing you, it was a new life, a resurrection, though I knew all the time that you'd try and see me, even though I'd been fighting and you hate it all so and think killing so wrong. It was so dear of Esther to come all that long way too. Susan too, for I expect lots of people will think it very awfull of her! Anyhow you are three dears & you brought sunshine to me, & I long to hug you all!

Now to business. Hayes & Hayes, 41-42 Nassau St. are agents for Surrey House. They wrote to me re giving up tenancy, & very decently secured house which had been left open. There is no lease. I had one for 3 years & since it finished, I just paid each quarter. House was in very bad condition when I got it. The house is very untidy as I had no time to put it straight after the Police raid. If you could get Bessie Lynch she would be a great help. There is a charwoman called Mrs. Boylon too whom Bessie would know of who is honest.

My valuables are all with a friend (i.e. silver and jewelry). I don't know how much it will cost to store furniture, I dont know if it would be cheaper to pack it into a tiny house & put in Bessie to care it. There is a lot—I dont want anything thrown away. Egan,

Lr. Ormond Quay might store those pictures hanging on the walls & my illuminated address from the Transport Union. He has some pictures of ours already. Don't store furniture with Myers, he was a brute to the men in the strike.

You'll want to insist on their bringing proper boxes for the books as they are awfully careless.

The china too wants care. Then there are the acting things. You'll probably want to buy a tin trunk or two & get them packed with naphtha balls. There are wigs in the bottom of the kitchen press & in the cupboard half-way up stairs, they want to be put by with care. The linen, too, such as it is, wants to have the starch washed out before its put by. If you could only catch Bessie Lynch she knows the house so well & is such a good worker. There are a lot of crewel wools & work in a drawer of the big press on the stairs they want to be put with naphtha balls too. If someone could house the wigs & them I'd be thankful.

On the R. of fireplace Drawing room is a sort of a desk. The same key fits it & the big brown press upstairs. One of my friends has the key. If you have not got it, pull out top drawer & push down & push lock back where it pokes through. Small centre drawer is locked—there is nothing in it—but bank book may be there & in a small drawer to R. there are papers for recovering income tax. Some more of them are in the pocket of my coat that is here. Could Susan get my clothes that are here and look after them for me? I haven't recovered Income Tax for two or three years, Casi has to sign, & its an awful nuisance so I always let it run on till there was something worth recovering. There should be now.

There is a little brown letter case with drawing things that Susan might keep for me.

I told you that Cochrane and Co. are trying to let St. Mary's. It should be put down at Norths Dockrels & a couple of other agencies. I think my name should be suppressed & it should be let in yours.

Of course my household bills are not paid. John Clarke S. Richmond St. is my grocer; Ferguson, Rathmines, my baker, Kehoe, Butcher, Hendrick, oilman both Rathmines. I owe two coal bills: one to Clarkin, Tara St. the other to a man I forget in Charlemont St., on the R-side if you face the bridge but close to the chemist at the corner where the trams cross. I owe also a trifle to Gleeson of O'Connel St. for a skirt, and to the Art Dec. Co., Belfast. But theres no hurry about any of these—they are quite accustomed to waiting. Dont pay anything without being sure the bill is really mine as people have tried on queer tricks getting things on credit in my name before now.

You dear old darling its such a bore for you. I feel rather as if I was superintending my own funeral from the grave.

There is a very old book of music in the D. Room. It might be valuable. If you have time bring it to a Mr. Braid at Pigotts & ask his advice about selling it. I promised to let him look at it. He says its unique. I had no time to leave it with him.

I left a green canvas suit case and a small red dressing case & a brown hand bag with Peter Ennis, Caretaker of Liberty Hall. I've had them there some time. I dare say Peter's arrested, but he wasn't mixed up in anything so he may be out. I left my bike knocking round the Hall too.

I miss poor "Poppet" very much & wonder if he has quite forgotten me. Poor Mrs. Connolly, I wonder where she is, & if you got him from her. Her Belfast address was 1 Glenalina Terrace, Falls Rd. Belfast. I do feel so sorry for her. She was so devoted to her husband. Also she has four children at home, & only the two older girls working. With regard to Bessie Lynch what I had in my mind for her was to start her washing in a small way after the War. She is a beautiful laundress. Of course she would want another girl with her to do accounts etc. but you could let her know I haven't forgotten & that the 10/ a week is only to keep her safe & happy till something can be arranged. Its much better for people to earn their own livings if they can.

Poor Bridie Goff my servant ought to get a months wages at least. She was arrested with me. Bessie would know where she lives, somewhere in Henrietta St. If you cant find Bessie advertise for her in the evening paper.

I do hope you found Mrs. Mallin. I wish I knew it worries me so to think of her.

I nearly forgot the little Hall in Camden St. Mr. Cummins, pawnbroker, S. Richmond St. is the landlord. If things quiet down [7 or 8 words censored] I'd like to go on paying the rent for them as hitherto. A little boy called Smith living in Piles Buildings could find out. The landlord, of course might know. He was quite nice.

I feel I'm giving you such a lot of worries & bothers, & I feel too, as if I had'nt remembered half. Anyhow its very economical living here! & I'm half glad I'm not treated as a political prisoner as I should feel so greatly tempted to eat, smoke & dress at my own expense. In the mean time I live free, all my debts will be paid & I suppose after a time I will be allowed to write again or see a visitor. I don't know the rules but try to get in touch with Mrs. Connolly, Mrs. Mallin & Bessie Lynch for me. I would be sorry for any of them to be hungry & I would be sorry too if they thought I had forgotten them, for they were friends.

By the way the garden seat & tools might be of use to Susan—there are a few decent plants too she can take if she likes, & a couple of nice rose trees.

Now darling dont worry about me, for I am not too bad at all; & its only a mean spirit that grudges paying the price. Everybody is quite kind, & though this is not exactly a bed of roses still many rebels have had much worse to bear. The life is colorless, beds are hard food peculiar, but you might say that of many a free persons life, & when I think of what the Fenian suffered & of what the Poles suffered in the sixties I realise that I am extremely lucky. So darling dont worry your sweet old head. I dont know if you are still here so I am sending this to Susan to forward.

I hope that I shall see you again some day & shall live in hopes.

With very much love to you three darlings. I can see your faces when I shut my eyes.

Yrs
CdM

By this time the house had been looted, first by the military authorities and then by curiosity seekers. Surrey House was in chaos when Miss Gore-Booth and her two friends visited it. The furniture had been broken; papers, ornaments, books, and pictures were trampled and smashed on the floor. There was a box of lanternslides which had been overturned and every slide crushed to bits by someone's boots; a beautiful leather dressing-case was ripped across by a bayonet. The garden had been dug up in search of arms, but nothing had been found. Even the kitchen utensils were gone—they had been tied up in tablecloths and carried off. A few things were recovered and stored, but many more found their way into soldiers' haversacks as war souvenirs. The letters from Canon Hannay about the quantity of underclothes Madame should wear in *Eleanor's Enterprise,* which caused his parishioner such concern, were among the official confiscations.

There were two more letters from Mountjoy, one written partly in pencil and partly in ink on toilet paper, and smuggled out by a sympathetic apprentice warder, an Irishwoman from County Wexford. Madame was still fighting, still encouraging Eva not to be depressed about her, and still agitating to get things done. In a hurried, cramped hand she wrote:

Darling, I am, alas! going into exile. Make a point to try & get in to see me. I believe you could by influence. Do you know Seddon?

& is he an M.P.? He and I were great allies in the Strike, & he might be willing to help. I know he liked me personally. He might get the Labour people to put questions anyhow. Remember, I dont mind being in jail, & if its better for the cause I'm prepared to remain here. My only desire is to be of use to those outside in the long tedious struggle with England. Nothing else matters really to me. I believe by rules I am entitled to write & receive on moving. So if you get no letter in a few weeks write and say that I had previously arranged to always write to you. Quote this rule, & ask why you have not heard. They would do a good deal to avoid any fuss, & to combat the idea that we are being illtreated. This is d'être paper! & written under huge difficulties! Remember it is only by pushing & by sort of discreet threats & making yourself disagreeable that you will be able to do anything for us.

I am going to Aylesbury. Shall be quite amiable—am not going to hungerstrike, as am advised by comrades not to. It would suit the Government very well to let me die quietly. I want to work for the Army, that's all. I look forward to seeing you the whole time. Put on your prettiest hat when you come! Give Esther my best love. I shall never forget her coming. My family must be quite amusing about my latest crimes! I wonder so many things & I'm getting quite clever about noticing trifles & details. I told you to write to Casi & try & get the news through. It would have to be very diplomatically done to evade censor. You might try. Now I must stop. Very very best love. Am going to Aylesbury. Let friends there know.

[unsigned]

The second smuggled letter from Mountjoy was pencilled on the back of an envelope and confirmed her transfer:

Darling. Got your. Ever so much love. If its better for the cause to leave me in just leave me—being sent to Aylesbury! You can probably get in *back door* influence. Duchess of Bedford is a 'visitor' there. I want to get my teeth done, two ought to be stopped. I am glad that M [Maeve?] was amused & not shocked! Best love & many kisses & hoping we may someday meet again.

[unsigned]

Madame was sent to Aylesbury in June. It was an antiquated, rambling building, damp and gloomy, surrounded by a thick, high wall. The entrance was the usual prison arrangement of double doors, the intervening space wide enough for the vehicle bringing the prisoner; the first door was shut and locked before the second was opened. It was familiar enough to the repeating offender but forbidding and final to the novice.

The prison routine did not take long to get used to. Prisoners rose at 6:30, washed and dressed. The early rising was no hardship to most of the women who had too much time to sleep and think and regarded having something to do as a God-send. They ate alone in their cells. The menu was scant and monotonous: lukewarm or cold tea and six ounces of bread at 7:30; at noon two ounces of meat, one potato, two ounces of cabbage or other vegetable, six ounces of bread; supper was at 4:30, a pint of cocoa or tea and four ounces of bread. Once the initial revulsion at the food was over, there was never a day when Madame was not hungry. A few later references to stealing food hint at how desperately hungry they were: "We had a certain community of hatred that gave one mutual interests & the mutual sport of combining to pinch onions, dripping or rags! Doesn't it sound funny and mad? but it kept one going." And again, "For one awful moment I thought I was back at Aylesbury eating a stolen onion." Once when talking to Miss Roper she said, "All prison does for people is to teach them to use bad language and to steal. I was so hungry yesterday that I stole a raw turnip and ate it."

Madame's reputation as a fearless, impulsive, and adventurous aristocrat had arrived before her. The prison authorities were awed and did not know quite what to make of this unusual charge. They were impressed that she had been presented at Court when she was nineteen, that she had spent her girlhood riding to hounds, that she had studied art at the Slade and in Paris, and that she was married to a Count. Their only defense in the face of this background was to deal as harshly as they could with her. For several weeks she was kept under close observation. She was placed in a cell with a door and an iron gate where she could be closely supervised.[5] Madame later told a fellow convict that what she hated most was being constantly spied on, and that for the first week she was there she walked the floor all night trying to exorcise the devilish spyhole in her cell.

After some time in solitary confinement, the prison governor decided she could be employed on some useful work but that she had to continue to occupy the same closely-watched cell. She was sent to the workroom, where she made prisoners' nightgowns and various articles of underwear from coarse unbleached calico.

The prisoners were allowed one book a week from the library, and after several weeks they were allowed to write a letter every month.

It was not enough for a woman of Madame's temperament, who needed activity and opportunities to express herself in writing, in painting, in creating beauty of some kind. From the workshop she stole a needle, from cleaning rags she patiently pulled colored threads to use for embroidery cotton, and, using the best rags she could steal, fashioned some beauty for her enjoyment. She used to get up early and sew for an hour before the 6:30 rising. When she heard the jingle of the officer's keys she carefully folded up her treasures and hid them. If they had been found she would have been liable to a disciplinary report for possessing unauthorized articles. A prized possession of a County Galway woman who was a prison nurse there was a pincushion embroidered by Madame. It said "Easter Week 1916." Madame's initials were worked with her own hair as thread. A picture of the Madonna and Child was found by a prison officer in her library book, after some weeks of this surreptitious embroidering. It was so well done that the matron could not believe it was created from such poor materials and her cell was searched. No disciplinary action was taken, although the needle and rags were confiscated.

After a time Madame's job was changed to scrubbing in the kitchens. The prison governor recognized that she had little aptitude for work of this kind; the officer in charge of the kitchen complained frequently about her work and repeatedly sent her back to do it over again. Madame's thoughts were far away, and she did not appear to be able to concentrate on anything that did not interest her. She never grumbled nor did she try to justify her actions when reprimanded, but simply carried on in her own way.

She kept her promise to her sister to be amiable and not to hunger strike, and except for the clandestine sewing there was only one other instance of her refusing to obey orders. Once when the Germans were making a successful push, the prisoners were ordered to go to the chapel and pray for the success of the British troops. The Irish Countess, a German spy, and an American swindler refused. They could not be forced to pray, they could be forced to do extra work. The American was May Sharpe, a brassy strumpet who wrote the memoirs of her shabby life under the name "Chicago May." To her the Irish lady was the grandest woman she ever met. No kind of hardship fazed her, and when they refused to pray for British success, Chicago May wrote, "For spite, they [the guards] made the three of us women carry enough gruel around the prison to feed the entire two hundred convicts. We had to carry immense, heavy cans, up winding stairs. While we were doing this, the Countess recited long passages in Italian, from Dante's 'Inferno.' The place looked like Hell, all right, with the lights dimmed and musty-smelling bags tacked across the windows, as a precaution against bombing."[6]

Madame never attempted to incite trouble, and she was finally regarded by the staff as a good prisoner. On her part, however, she stored up complaints about the way things were done. She concluded that the whole atrocious system should be done away with and the whole machinery scrapped. She had her own ideas about the sanitary arrangements and standards of the prison: "The dinners were served in two storey cans, used indiscriminately among 200 women, and, more, some of the cans were very old and musty. A great many of the women were known to be suffering from venereal disease, and at the time an attempt was made to keep their tins separate. This was dropped after a while. There was no proper accommodation for washing these 400 tins. I used to do 200 with another convict. We did our best to get them clean in a big terra-cotta bowl on the kitchen table and to dry them on two towels. Sometimes the water would not be hot, sometimes there was no soap or soda, and then you could neither dry nor clean the tins. Many of the tins were red with rust inside. I could give you endless examples of English cleanliness. It may be summed up as follows: Brasses, floors, doorknobs, all that jumps to the eye immaculate, but dirt and carelessness behind the scenes. I have seen vermin found in the baths."[7]

The prison governor said that Madame kept herself scrupulously clean but was not particularly tidy. Her blouse was always out of her skirt band and her skirt was hitched up one side and dropping down somewhere else, showing several inches of grey petticoat. Since she did not see herself in a mirror for months and the prison clothes were ugly, her lack of interest in them is not surprising. She had grown gaunt from bad food and her uniform hung loosely on her.

The rule of silence forbade her talking with her fellow convicts, gamblers, thieves, prostitutes, and murderers. "Even the miserable little grain of comfort you can get from a few minutes' talk with another prisoner can only be procured by endless trickery and deceit," she said later. "The silence rule merely gives people an incentive to underhand intercourse. The old hands are experts at this, and their conversation is often filthy. A few words exchanged are worth any risks that may be run, especially to a new comer, and it is the worst of their comrades that they find it easiest to talk with."

The right of association was one of the privileges the men prisoners of the Rebellion had won and jealously guarded. The lack of congenial companionship was the greatest hardship to Madame. Five other Irishwomen had been deported to England and three were interned with Madame, but as unsentenced prisoners they were confined in a wing with spy suspects.[8] By standing on an outside step and looking over a wall they could see her, and twice a day they were there to give her a surreptitious greeting as she passed on her way across a small yard to the wash-house. They also saw Madame in chapel every Sunday and occasionally were able to pass a note of greeting.

During the early autumn the Irish prisoners had made what must have seemed a quixotic request to the Home Office, a formal, written appeal to be allowed to live as convicts in the convict wing with Countess Markievicz. They agreed to give up all their privileges, letters, visits, food, other than those allowed to the long-term convicts. They included in their request a reminder that during the worst period of prison tyranny of the Russian Czars, the family or friends of political prisoners could accompany them to Siberia if they were willing to submit to the prison regimes. They asked no more than this from the enlightened British Government. They further pledged themselves not to use their prison grievances as propaganda in the future and not to communicate further in any illicit manner with the outside world. The latter they considered was a major concession. It was notorious that since the coming of "the three Irish" to Aylesbury, a constant flow of news and messages got out to the press and to the families and friends of the unfortunate women who were spies or suspected of being spies—German, Greek, Belgian, English. Their request was "disallowed" by the Home Office and the prisoners withdrew their offer.[9]

Madame was too resilient, buoyant, and proud to let the prison break her. It was only after her release that she occasionally gave vent to her indignation at the whole system. Her prison letters to her sister are cheerful, full of vigor and ideas, and reflect her boyish breeziness.

Her first letter from Aylesbury was dated 8-8-16. The paper was an official form, with a fold on the left, so there were two large sheets. Printed rules of letterwriting fill the first page—the prisoners were cautioned they must write only to a "respectable friend," watch the language used, write only about personal business or domestic affairs, no politics, no complaints, no subversive opinions. The letters were, of course, censored.

Dearest Old Darling,—The one thing I have gained by my exile is the privilege of writing a letter, but theres very little to say, as I do not suppose that an 'essay on prison life' would pass the Censor, however interesting & amusing it might be. What you have called my 'misplaced sense of humour' still remains to me & I am quite well and cheerfull. I saw myself—for the first time for over 3 months the other day. It is quite amusing to meet yourself as a stranger. We bowed & grinned, & I thought my teeth very dirty, & very much wanting a dentist, & I'd got very thin & very sunburnt. In 6 months I shall not recognise myself at all my memory of faces is so bad. I remember a fairy tale of a Princess, who banished mirrors when she began to grow old. I think it showed a great want of interest in life. The less I see my face the more curious I grow about it, & I dont resent it growing old. Its queer and lonely here. There was so much life in Mountjoy. There were seaguls, & pigeons—which I had quite tame;[10] there were 'Stop Press' cries, little boys splashing in the canal, & singing Irish songs shrill and discordant, but with such vigour. There was a black spaniel too with long silky ears, & a most attractive convict baby with a squint—and soft Irish voices everywhere. There were the trains 'Broadstone and Northwall' trams, & even an old melodion & a man trying to play an Irish tune on a bugle over the wall! Here its so still & I find it awfully difficult to understand what anyone says to me, & they seem to find the same trouble with me. 'English as she is spoke' can be very puzzling. One thing nice here is the Holy hocks in the garden, they seem to understand gardening. There is a great crop of carrots too that we pass every day, going to 'exercise' round & round in a ring—like so many old hunters in the summer.

I had such a lovely journey over here. My escort never had been on the sea before & kept thinking she was going to be ill. I lay down & enjoyed a sunny porthole & a fresh breeze. There was a big air ship—like the picture of a Zeppelin cruising about when we arrived. I was awfully pleased as I never saw one. I long so to fly! Also I'd love to dive in a submarine. I dreamt of you the other night. You had on a soft looking small blue (dark) hat & it was crooked. You had bought tickets & 3 donkeys & were going to take Esther & I to Egypt of all places! When I woke up I had to laugh, but it was wonderfully vivid. Look it up in a 'dream book.' I dream a great deal ever since I was in jail & never hardly did before.

I'd love to show you all the dogrel I wrote in Mountjoy, though I know you'd only jeer in a kindly way. I love writing it so, & I've not lost it its in my head all right. Whens your next book coming out, & the one with some of my pictures if it ever does. They were very bad. I can do much better now. I was just beginning to get some feeling into my black and white when I left Ireland. I made quils out of rooks tail feathers that I found in the garden, they are much nicer than most pens—you can get such a fine soft line.

Now darling again I repeat dont worry about me. I am quite cheerful & content, & would really have felt very small & useless if I had been ignored. I am quite patient & believe that everything will happen for the best. One thing I should enjoy getting out for, & that would be to see the faces of respectable people when I met them! I dont like to send anyone my love for fear that most valuable offering would be spurned. I expect though Molly has a soft spot for me somewhere. Very best love to Esther & to Susan & to all of the 'rebelly crew,' if ever you come across them. Do go to the Transport Union headquarters if ever you go to Dublin, theyd all think you were me & love to see you & you could tell them about me. Now best love, old darling & send me a budget of news & gossip, when you can write, about all my pals, & my family, & any things amusing at all.

I laugh when I think of Mordaunt! & Mabel—

Yrs.

Con——(vict G.12)

The defiant play on her name and position with which she signed the letter was a typical gesture of her humor and irrepressible spirits.

The book to which she referred was published that autumn and Madame received a copy a few weeks after this letter. It was *The Death of Fionavar* which her sister had written and she had decorated during that busy winter 1915–16. In Miss Gore-Booth's version of an ancient story, Fionavar, the daughter of the warrior queen, Maeve, died on the battlefield as foretold, but she died of pity for the men who lay dead and wounded after the battle. At the moment the prophecy had been made, Christ had been crucified, new and terrible Imaginative Pity had come into the world. At her beloved child's death, Maeve's own interest in the mystical world reawakens and she conceives new ideas of impartial good will. Compassion and understanding take the place of punishment in her ruling. Eventually she casts away her kingdom and ambitions and goes away by herself to meditate and live austerely under the hazel boughs in an island on the Shannon. Thus she finds the way to her own soul.

Madame decorated each page of the poetic drama with borders of primroses (a symbol in the book of beauty hiding truth), of birds, of lilies, of butterflies and cocoons, and drawings of winged horses. The winged horse was a favorite symbol of both Miss Gore-Booth and Madame; it was the figure in the book's patterned end papers. The final words were: "The Winged Horse shall be harnessed to many ploughs, but in the end there is freedom and the aether vibrates to the rhythm of unseen Light." The book was dedicated "To the Memory of the Dead. The Many who died for Freedom and the One who died for Peace." In the context of the drama, Christ could be the one who died for peace, but the dedicatory poem makes it clear that Miss Gore-Booth was referring to the martyrs of Easter Week.

Shortly after Madame received the book, her sister had the first of two or three unauthorized communications, undated and unsigned, written on toilet paper. The first was more or less a test of the effectiveness of the new method of getting messages out:

> Dearest old darling—You see the 'gap' has been thrown & I have found a real friend, & it just makes the whole difference both mentally & bodily. She is taking awful risks for me & both body and soul are ministered to. Tit-bits of news & 'tuck'.
>
> I want you to give her a copy of our book with your autograph. Try to find some person connected with [Notting?] that has not *too* grand an address, who could then just send her a picture postcard with her name and address & whom she could then write & let her know if she was going to town & call for news. Also give her tit bits of rebel news—that must not be sent through the post.
>
> Trust her absolutely, & 'let not your right hand know what your left hand doeth' Esther of course excepted. None of the 'crew' or the family must even guess, for people *will* talk. You had probably better not try & see her again, as most likely you are both under watchful & protective eyes. At present anyhow I see my friend a lot. I am sending you also some things to do for me. No hurry about them. Best love & kisses.

For someone who abhorred secrecy, Madame learned quickly in jail that at times it was the only way.

In the second illicit letter from Aylesbury, written at about the same time, she again mentioned the book. By now Madame had been given sewing in the workroom to do. Typically, she wanted her sister to continue asking questions and agitating; making a real fuss was the way to action in her experience.

> Darling, This will go to-morrow—all my love & for Gods sake be discreet.

I am all right, & not a bit unhappy. I *love* the book. Its a real joy. They have put the rose in the triangle on its side, didn't I put it upright? Ask me all the questions you can think of. The doctor here (Fox) a woman is a devil. She is going to be Governor but rules are so strict that she cant hurt me in any way. It makes all the difference having a friend here. Don't count on my getting out for ever so long. Unless a real fuss is made (Home and America). I don't see why they should let me go. You should get 'questions' asked on anything you can think of & start grievances—company ones in—starvation etc & try & make them publish trials. Youve probably done all this! Im so in the dark. They don't want a continuous fuss.

Let me know the trades union conditions for workrooms *temperature*. The trades unions should have a visitor or Inspector here. They should start jail reform. The people are all poor people & they should see to them.

Best love & kisses to you both.

I love being in poetry & feel so important!

Yrs for Ever

The poem she referred to was the dedication of *The Death of Fionavar,* which contains the verse written after Miss Gore-Booth's visit to Mountjoy with the lines, "Little I thought to see you smile again/ As I did yesterday, through prison bars."[11]

There was a third communication which relates to the second and may have been sent at the same time, or after Madame had been in the workroom for awhile and had a chance to observe the other prisoners. Without heading, date, or signature, it was just a list of questions with a note at the end:

These questions should be asked *me* and *all* political prisoners at a visit:

What do you weigh? What was your normal weight?

What do you get to eat? Can you eat it?

How much exercise do you get per day?

How often do you get clean underclothes?

Are you constipated? Can you get medicine?

What temperature is the room you work in?

What is your task i.e. how much must you do in a week?

If they won't let me or any of the others answer, push to get answers by *every possible* means.

The women I am with are the gutter rats of England—quite different from Mountjoy. Prostitutes & widows for baby murder. Others for abortion. Make capital of this in Ireland and America.

One nice Irishwoman I want you to help when she comes out. Murphy is her name. She has been so nice to me—but be cautious if others find you out. I will always give some token or pass word, but some may try & black mail you!

Madame had her first visit from her sister at Aylesbury in September, after she had been there for three months. They had not seen each other since that awful day in Mountjoy when the future was uncertain and dark. "I did love seeing you and Esther so. I hope she got her hat all right. Yours was very nice & you dont know what a picture the two of you made, all nice soft dreamy colours. (Moral:—Always visit criminals in your best clothes—Blue and grey for choice, if it's me!)"

She was allowed to write every four or five weeks, but as she said, "I could go on babbling for ever, though there is nothing to write about." Since there was little news to tell her sister she remembered old friends and anecdotes; she wondered what her friends and family were doing; she wrote down bits of verse she had thought of; she told of her dreams and her appreciation of any beauty she saw. She was always cheerful when she wrote and neither complained nor mentioned her hard lot.

In a letter she wrote at Christmas, she said, "I was so sorry about Ernest. He was a bit of a genius. Will try & write something. Tell Maev to collect his drawings, originals & reproductions. We'll bring them out some day." She referred to Ernest Kavanagh, a caricaturist of talent, whose drawings had appeared regularly in the nationalist papers. It was his "Battle of the Poles" which had caused such a sensation in 1911, and Madame had known him since she herself had been in the movement. He was killed by British fire on Tuesday of Easter Week as he was working in his office at the front of Liberty Hall opposite the Custom House.[12] It is curious that this was the first Madame had heard of his death and is indicative of the great amount of detail about Easter Week she did not hear until much later.

In the same letter she told what joy the dozens of Christmas cards from friends had brought her. She drew a picture of a woman behind bars, looking out. There were birds flying about and resting on the window ledge and a verse on either side of the picture:

> The wandering winds at Xmas time
> The twinkling of the stars
> Are messengers of hope & love
> Defying prison bars.

> The birds that fly about my cage
> Are vagrant thoughts that fly,
> To greet you all at Xmas time—
> They wing the wintry sky.

"This is supposed to be a Christmas card! for you & all friends," she added. She was wildly curious about a card her sister had sent her; it had arrived, she was told, but she could not have it until the Home Office had been consulted and approved. The card was finally delivered, a week after Christmas. Miss Gore-Booth had drawn a similar card which Madame thought better than her own. She pictured a woman looking out of a barred window at an angelic figure with a harp. Four children surround the singer, the border shows seven or eight women sitting, kneeling, or standing. The verse was:

> Do not be lonely, Dear, nor grieve,
> This Christmas Eve
> Is it so vain a thing
> That your Hearts Harper, dark Roseen,
> Crowned with all her sixteen stars,
> A wandering singer, yet a Queen,
> Outside your prison bars,
> Stands carrolling.

The authorities thought it was a signal for an escape attempt and it had to be closely examined before Madame was allowed to have it. Madame did not attempt escape, and no such effort was ever thought of. Later, when messages about escapes were sent by such greeting cards to other Irish prisoners, Madame realized why it had aroused so much suspicion.

Madame's delight in her sister's visits is always apparent in the letters. Miss Roper usually went with Miss Gore-Booth and remembered her own misery at even visiting that most dreary place. "Constance never grumbled at conditions," she wrote, "and she received great kindliness from some of the officials in prison. No prisoner was allowed to talk in the passages, but the first sound we heard while we waited was always her gay ringing laugh as she came along the corridor from the cells, talking to the wardress in charge of her."

After she had been several weeks in Aylesbury, Madame was allowed a large notebook of cheap, lined paper, about 13½″ by 8½″ for sketching and jotting down her verses. It was carefully controlled, each page numbered so none could be torn out, and it was regularly censored. After a time she got another notebook the same size but with unlined paper of better quality; she used the first for sketching out her ideas for pictures or verse and the second for the finished work.

On the first page of the original book was the sketch of a bookplate for her sister; the following sixty pages contain several verses and many sketches—mainly of figures of Irish heroes and heroines. Her drawings of horses were always the most successful. She had trouble delineating the human face, although her figures were usually graceful and lifelike. The second notebook contained mostly finished pictures from sketches in the first and some illustrated poetry—sometimes a poem of her sister's, sometimes one of her own. Two pictures show Joan of Arc kneeling with sword in left hand, rosary beads in right, and angels hovering over her.

Madame was always a keen gardener. Even during the busy days in Dublin she found time to get out to her garden. She failed, however, when she tried to grow a rose in her cell. When she told her sister about it, Miss Gore-Booth wrote a poem which Madame copied and illustrated in her journal. "There is nothing good, there is nothing fair/ Grows in the darkness thick and blind/ Pull down your high walls everywhere/ Let in the sun, let in the wind." Madame later expanded this idea for prison reform, and reiterated her belief that the prisons only bred criminals.

One of the last pages of the second book was a very successfully decorated one on which she printed another poem by Miss Gore-Booth, "To C.A." [Clare Annesley?]. "You seem to be a woman of the world. . . . I know you for the Umbrian monk you are/ Brother of Francis and the sun and rain. . . ." The picture of St. Francis surrounded by birds and animals was a happy one, and the representations remarkable considering that she was drawing from memory in a dark cell with inadequate materials.

Miss Gore-Booth was active in trying to soften her sister's prison conditions and enlisted the support of friends, organizations, and journals in Ireland and England. Throughout the first months of the year letters were circulated to town councils asking support in bettering her treatment and suggesting that copies of any resolutions passed be sent to the Home Office. Questions were asked in the House of Commons, and in May, Cumann na mBan wrote letters to many foreign countries calling attention to the unjust treatment of the Irish prisoners of war, of whom 122 were still confined in English convict prisons. Special attention was drawn to Madame's case.

The change in attitude toward the Rebellion was clearly indicated in the provincial papers. *The Sligo Champion,* for example, printed only cursory, condemning accounts of the Rising at the time (its editorial Easter Week had been concerned with adulterated milk). Within months its attitude had reversed. For the first time since Madame's initial arrest in 1911, her home-town paper commented sympathetically on her plight. Sligo was among the towns asking better conditions for the prisoners, but perhaps its sympathy was for the family at Lissadell as much as for the Countess at Aylesbury.

Very little information about what was happening in Ireland filtered through to Madame in her lonely confinement. The monthly visits from her sister were forty-five minutes of hurried exchange of personal news; the ever-present warden permitted no discussion of politics. Some bits must have gotten through, but there was no hint in the half-dozen letters written in 1917 that she knew of the changes taking place in public opinion.

Ulster still blocked the few attempts at settling "the Irish problem." These were dictated to some extent by a desire to propitiate powerful Irish-Americans. The British Ambassador, Sir Cecil Spring-Rice, warned his government of their great political importance and their sympathies with the nationalists. There had been changes in the British government. Asquith had resigned in December, 1916, and Lloyd George became Prime Minister on December 6, but Sir Edward Carson remained the First Lord of the Admiralty and a leading influence in the Cabinet. Bonar Law became Chancellor of the Exchequer as well as Leader of the House of Commons. Henry Duke was the Chief Secretary of Ireland.

John Dillon, M. P., had questioned the detention of the Irish prisoners; by December 21, Duke decided it was less risky to release the internees than to detain them, and on the following day six hundred untried prisoners were set free from Frongoch; on the 23rd, others were released from Reading. The two untried women at Aylesbury went home to Ireland on Christmas Eve.

In February, 1917, Count Plunkett, the father of Joseph Plunkett who had been shot on May 4, was elected in Roscommon to fill a parliamentary seat. He had run on a nationalist platform and was strongly supported by Sinn Fein and the Irish Volunteers. He received 3,022 votes, his Parliamentary Party candidate opponent, 1,708. It was a significant indication of the Irish change of sentiment from the non-support of Easter Week to the election of a candidate who had pledged that the freedom to be accorded to Ireland must be the same as that to Belgium, Serbia, Bohemia, Roumania, France, and Germany.

On April 19, less than two weeks after the United States declared a state of war with Germany, Count Plunkett called a convention in Dublin to try to formulate a policy or program to follow towards the agreed-upon end of complete independence for Ireland. He was a moderate, but his son had been a rebel. Had his election been a vote for his dead son and the full Republican program of the insurgents? Or was it for himself and a less aggressive policy? Delegates of over seventy groups were present. Inevitably, but unfortunately, no program was acceptable to all. However, it was agreed that a National Council be formed of the various groups which wanted to put forth Ireland's claim at the Peace Conference.[13]

On May 9 there was another by-election victory. This time the elected man, Joseph McGuinness, was still a convict in Lewes Prison. He won the South Longford election by a thirty-seven vote majority. Small as the majority was, South Longford was a stronghold of the Parlimentary Party, so this was regarded as a great victory. The most popular slogan in that election was, "Put him in to get him out!"

Lloyd George, in order to reassure his allies that the British government was trying to solve Irish difficulties, called for a convention in July to discuss the Home Rule and partition dispute. Since ninety per cent of the delegates were men who had already consented to partition, the chances for arriving at an equitable solution were negligible. Sinn Fein decided to ignore the Convention, and the decision was ratified throughout Ireland by labor organizations. However, the Convention had one important and positive effect. In order to secure a favorable atmosphere for its meetings, Bonar Law announced on June 15 the release of all participants in the Rising who were still imprisoned. The men were freed on June 16 and arrived in Dublin on the morning of June 18, 1917.

Madame's last letter from Aylesbury was dated June 6, 1917. She had been in jail more than thirteen months and there was no hint in her letter that she knew anything of the events taking place in Ireland. She wrote about a book on St. Francis that Father Albert had sent her, of decorating Eva's poem "To C.A.," about horoscopes, the compensations of developing her subconscious self under her "ascetic way of living," of flowers her sister regularly brought on her visits, of spiritual communication with her at their appointed time every day. She was still conscientiously gay, and chided herself for the unhampered way she used to conduct meetings; red tape she thought did nothing but waste precious time and take the place of "the divine inspiration of the moment. I always rather liked taking the chair for the fun of bursting thro all the red tape & when remonstrated with, I could always corner them by saying 'ridiculous English conventions. Surely an Irish committee is not going to be bound by them!' " The nearest she came to a complaint was an objective comment, "I think my handwriting is getting awful. I think the sort of work I do is bad for writing." She ended the letter on a note of longing for the next visit.

On Sunday, June 17, 1917, just a week after Madame's letter had reached her sister, a Home Office employee told Miss Gore-Booth she could go to Aylesbury the next day to get Madame. That same day Madame was told the great news. She tried to express her joy in drawing. This time the cage was open, the bird's wings were outstretched, ready for flight. On Monday Miss Roper went with Miss Gore-Booth to the prison, "armed with all the gay clothes that we could beg or borrow," Miss Roper wrote. "Soon Constance, herself again, thin but beautiful, in a blue dress instead of that twice too large, hideously ugly garment supplied by a paternal Government, left that prison for ever."

The flat at Fitzroy Square was full of flowers and congratulatory messages; there were crowds of journalists and Irish well wishers waiting for her when she arrived from prison. She was in good health and high spirits, delighted with the show of affection for herself and her country. Even those who were not in sympathy with her ideas admired her courage and welcomed her release. Maire Perolz and Helena Molony had gone to London as soon as the announcement was made that the prisoners would be released. They waited at Miss Gore-Booth's flat for Madame's arrival, and stayed to escort her back to Dublin. Madame visited her sister Tuesday and Wednesday, and spent part of Wednesday afternoon visiting some friendly members of the House of Commons and having tea with them on the terrace.

There was an affectionate crowd of women and girls at Euston Station on Thursday morning to see her off for Dublin. Flags flew, the people cheered and sang "The Soldiers' Song" while Madame stood at attention. As the train was leaving, someone called for "Three cheers for the Countess," and with a happy gesture, she kissed the bunch of roses she held in her arms, and scattered them among her admirers.

There was another crowd at Holyhead, where the train passengers board the boat to take them across the Irish Sea. Miss Roper remembered the platform packed with people waving flags, singing and cheering. Madame was trying to get on the gangway to the boat, and her clear voice called out, "Which is the right side for us to get on?" A coal-smeared worker looked out of an engine room and with a broad grin replied, "It's always the right side if you're on it." She acknowledged the salute gaily, and the crowd cheered.

It was late afternoon when they finally arrived at Dun Laoghaire. There were more people waiting to greet her, and a still greater crowd at Westland Row when the train arrived shortly after six o'clock. Boys had climbed up lamp posts to see her. A great cheer and a huge display of Republican flags greeted her as she took her place with Miss Gore-Booth and Dr. Lynn in the doctor's car which was driven by a uniformed Volunteer. She passed throuh the crowds, standing up in the car, holding a great bouquet which had been given her, thrusting out her hand to the Dubliners who had come to greet her.

A pipers' band headed the procession which formed. Contingents of marchers representing the various organizations to which she belonged preceded her car. From the station they drove by way of Brunswick (now Pearse) Street, Tara Street, and across Butt Bridge to Liberty Hall. She appeared at one of the windows there and was received with cheers. "I am going home now to rest in order that I may start work at once," she said. On her way to Dr. Lynn's home, where she stayed for some time, they stopped briefly at the College of Surgeons.

A few days after Madame's return to Ireland she was formally received into the Catholic church. She was baptised at Clonliffe College on June 24, 1917, in the presence of her friends Mrs. Foran and Mrs. Mallin, and took the baptismal name of Anastasia.

Madame had considered herself a Catholic since her epiphany in the College of Surgeons but had waited for her release from prison to join the Church. Although freedom of worship for Catholics in Ireland had long been won and the revolution in which she fought was political rather than religious, as she saw it the purpose of revolution was to bring Ireland into its full national inheritance and that included a faith. Joining the Church was one way Madame identified herself more completely with the cause of Ireland. She joined the Church with wholehearted enthusiasm and brought to it her devotion, her meticulous observance of its forms, and a measure of indifference to the fine points of its theology.

Neither the welcoming crowds nor her conversion was lost on the politicians. Clearly Madame had become a popular symbol in her own land.

NOTES TO CHAPTER X

1. Details of the courts-martial were never made public. Madame gave her sister the documents she had which Miss Roper printed in her introduction to *The Prison Letters of Countess Markievicz*, pp. 22–27. Madame also recounted the story to reporters after her release from Aylesbury (*Freeman's Journal*, June 19, 1917).

2. They were on the same train and boat on which Asquith travelled. Although Miss Gore-Booth and Madame had known his wife, Margot Tennant, in their society days, there is no evidence that they saw each other or communicated in later years. It is unlikely that he was responsible for Madame's reprieve, since this had been granted several days before he took a personal interest in what was happening in Dublin. His intervention, however, did save many lives.

3. Roper, *Prison Letters*, pp. 47–48.

4. H. Sheehy Skeffington, "Constance Markievicz in 1916," *An Phoblacht*, April 14, 1928.

5. Mary Size, *Prisons I Have Known* (London, 1957), pp. 55–58.

6. May Sharpe, *Chicago May Her Story* (London n.d. [c. 1930]), p. 199.

7. *New Ireland*, April 15, 1922. Madame often spoke against the prison system and published three articles on the subject: "Break Down The Bastilles," *The Voice of Labour*, May 1, 1919; "On English Jails," *New Ireland*, April 8, 1922; and "Conditions of Women in English Jails," ibid., April 15, 1922.

8. Maire Perolz and Brigid Foley were released before the others went to Aylesbury; Nell Ryan was released during the autumn; Winifred Carney and Helena Molony were held until Christmas Eve, 1916.

9. Helena Molony, *An Phoblacht*, November, 1930.

10. "She that but little patience knew, / From childhood on, had now so much / A grey gull lost its fear and flew / Down to her cell and there alit, / And there endured her fingers' touch / And from her fingers ate its bit" (Yeats, "On A Political Prisoner," *Collected Poems*, p. 206).

11. Madame was included in many poems after Easter Week, by AE, W. B. Yeats, Dora Sigerson, and others. She took delight in all of them.

12. He and Peter Ennis, the caretaker, were the only ones in Liberty Hall at the time. The British must have thought the Hall was occupied for they went to extraordinary lengths on Wednesday and Thursday to shell it from the Liffey. It would have been a simple matter to occupy the building; a few soldiers could have walked across Beresford Place and in the front door.

13. The organizing committee included Count Plunkett, Arthur Griffith, Father O'Flanagan, Alderman Tom Kelly, Stephen O'Mara, Dr. Dillon, Countess Plunkett, Helena Molony, Sean Milroy, and Sean Brown.

XI

Victories for Sinn Fein
June 1917–1918

During the fourteen months after Easter Week, Ireland saw a resurgence of Republican sentiment. Young men who had paid scant attention to Volunteer marches now began to wear the illegal uniform, to meet in the night and to talk long about the Defense of the Realm Act, Castle government, or separation from England. But they needed a leader who could focus their new patriotism. They were loosely called Sinn Feiners, but Griffith, who had headed the old Sinn Fein party through years of poverty, seemed too moderate, too much the elder statesman. These patriots wanted a rebel for a leader. They found a very interesting one, a thirty-five year old teacher of mathematics named Eamon de Valera.

The occasion that brought de Valera to office was a by-election in East Clare. The representative had been Major Willie Redmond, the amiable brother of John Redmond, leader of the Parliamentary Party. When the Major was killed early in June at Messines, the Rural District Council of Ennis, the largest town in Clare, notified the Redmondites that it wanted no more of their candidates and sent a telegram asking de Valera to run for Sinn Fein. Little was known about him except that he had distinguished himself at Boland's Mills and was the only commandant in the Rising who escaped the firing squad. The telegram was given to de Valera as he stepped from Pentonville Prison, June 16, 1917. No one in Ireland underestimated this trial of Sinn Fein strength, and the Redmondites put up a popular local candidate, Patrick Lynch.

Madame was in Ennis July 7th to speak at several meetings. She was still such a celebrated novelty that she drew large crowds, and somehow she even appeared at a meeting for Lynch where there were many soldiers' relatives. Her inflammatory republicanism made them so angry that leaders of the Labour League of Ennis, stout Sinn

Feiners, had to cluster around her and help her escape down a side street to a friendly home. Her clothes were torn and her hat bent, but she was unhurt and her spirits were high. It was like old times.

The voting on July 10th was a victory for Sinn Fein. De Valera received 5,010 votes against Lynch's 2,035. East Clare had endorsed republicanism and complete separation from Britain. Throughout Ireland the Republicans rejoiced.

Two great compliments were paid to Madame that month after her release from Aylesbury. Both Kilkenny and Sligo added her name to their rolls of honorary citizens, although it was unusual for a woman to be so distinguished. Both ceremonies were used as occasions for party rallies.

She went to Kilkenny on July 19th accompanied by Commandant de Valera, now M.P., W. T. Cosgrave and Laurence Ginnell. Cosgrave had been made the Sinn Fein candidate for Kilkenny the previous night. Ginnell had resigned his seat in the House of Commons a few weeks earlier to join in the struggle for Irish independence. By that gesture he demonstrated Sinn Fein policy that elected representatives should disdain service in the British Parliament and demand their own. The six o'clock train was met by large, cheering crowds; almost everyone was wearing the Sinn Fein colors, green, white, and orange.

The following week Madame went to Sligo. When she wrote to arrange the date, she acknowledged that for once she was speechless. "I have no words to tell you of all I felt when I heard that my own native town of Sligo were conferring such a great honour on me. I long to see Sligo again, I used to think & dream of our hills & rivers & of the sun setting out over the sea & of all the people at home. My thoughts were often with you all this weary year I spent in an English jail." After her signature she proudly added "I.C.A." (Irish Citizen Army) and then, wryly, her Aylesbury convict number, "q 12."[1]

Sligo received her as a returning heroine. The inevitable brass band played nationalist airs, and a torchlight procession paraded to the Sinn Fein Hall on Teeling Street for speeches of welcome by the Mayor, of thanks by Madame, no longer speechless, and by Darrell Figgis, who had escorted her to Sligo.

After Mass at Drumcliffe, Madame spent Sunday addressing various meetings, fourteen in all. On Monday she was joined by others whom Sinn Fein was bringing into power. The ceremony that night, July 23, 1917, was at the Sligo Town Hall, built on the site of a Cromwellian fortress which had figured in earlier Gore-Booth family history. The mayor pointed out that this was the first time the freedom of the Borough had been conferred on a woman and that in honoring her they paid a tribute to a family of which she was the most distinguished member. Madame acknowledged that being a rebel was rather a long jump from where she had started. "I became a rebel," she told the crowd, "because the older I grew and the more I thought and the more I used my eyes and the more I went around amongst the people of Ireland, and particularly Dublin, the more I realised that nothing could help Ireland only get rid of England bag and baggage." She was proud of having been a friend of James Connolly and working with him through the strike. As usual she urged her audience to work for Ireland. "Nothing is too small to be done for Ireland and nothing is too great a sacrifice to be made for Ireland." In concluding she pointed to the hope of Sinn Fein, that Irish independence be recognized at the Peace Conference. "In appealing to the Peace Conference we are appealing not only on the grounds of sympathy but on logical grounds, and on these grounds we are going to have the support of the nations."

However, Sinn Fein did not have the support of all Sligo. Everywhere the visitors went there were separation women, British sympathizers, and anti-nationalists. Sods were thrown, banners attacked, insults shouted. Sinn Fein was gaining strength, but there was a hard fight ahead. The name Gore-Booth was conspicuously absent from the newspaper accounts of the events, and the family of the Joan of Ireland stayed discreetly aloof. Madame and the other guests stayed in Sligo in a hotel; the church at Drumcliffe was as close as she got to Lissadell that weekend. Spiritually and emotionally it was a great distance removed.

Two weeks later Madame spent a speech-filled weekend at Cork. News had just come from Kilkenny that W. T. Cosgrave had been returned. As the train traveled through the country, there were cheering crowds and burning tar barrels on the hills to mark another victory for Sinn Fein.

Cork gave her a gift that touched her, an illuminated "Address from the Remnant of the Irish Republican Brotherhood of Rebel Cork of '65–67 to Countess Markievicz." She prized this with the address from the Transport Union. They survived various raids and looting of her property, and hang now in Liberty Hall.

She gave three speeches that weekend, two in Cork and one in

Clonakilty, and took part in several meetings conducted by transport workers, Cumann na mBan, and Fianna, and demonstrated on behalf of some prisoners arrested under the Defense of the Realm Act. It was a strenuous schedule for a middle-aged woman not long out of prison.

Her speeches were typical of dozens she made during the next several months. She was helping to organize Sinn Fein and exhorted her audiences to work for any of the several Republican societies connected with it. Physical force and moral force would together win freedom; the Rising was only a beginning. She often compared it with the Battle of Bunker Hill, a lost battle in America's struggle against Britain which ultimately led to victory. Sinn Fein defined victory as recognition of Ireland at the Peace Conference. She constantly reiterated that "there was an International Law which said that any nation which in time of war held its capital for a week, or three days, had a right to be present and take part in the discussions after peace, at the Peace Conference." British politicians were paying lip service to President Wilson's proposals for small nations and Sinn Fein hoped its enemies would be caught in their own hypocrisy. Madame reminded her audiences that their movement was constitutional but they were ready to defend themselves against attack and to fight for the right to be at the Peace Conference.

The *Cork Examiner*'s editor, after complete coverage of her weekend in its news columns, cautioned his readers against the views of this Peace Conference school of patriots. Not that they were worth considering, but Madame's zeal might influence the unthinking who did not stop to analyze her proposals. She scoffed at this "wait and see" school, she believed Ireland should "demand and get."

The four by-election victories in North Roscommon, South Longford, East Clare, and Kilkenny City were the first fruits of the Rising. They fed the republican movement as nothing else could have and always remained symbols of the new popular support. With no funds, no central organization, no trained workers, Sinn Fein had won four seats from the Irish Parliamentary Party with its powerful local machines, money, and experience. The victories gave Republicans hope that the first general election would see an end to the party which, as they saw it, for fifty years had directed Irish politics to appeasement.[2]

As the pace of organizing Sinn Fein increased, Madame was one of several speakers who every Saturday and Sunday attended meetings, fairs, concerts, wherever people gathered, and explained what they hoped to accomplish for Ireland. As she saw it, Sinn Fein was being

remarkably law abiding. "No one is preaching rebellion," she wrote
to her sister, "we are all talking of organizing the country into a
strong constitutional movement."[3]

As the Castle saw it, Sinn Feiners were insufferable in jail but intolerable out of it. Their new policy was insidious and worse than a
direct military affront. It denied the right of Castle government to
exist and presumed that all British law in Ireland was illegal. The
Castle responded with increased repression, thereby creating the kind
of situation in which Sinn Fein thrived.

In September there were fourteen men in Mountjoy who had been
arrested for their support of the new constitutional movement. They
denounced the courts, paid no attention to the judges, constantly
resisted being treated as criminals, and demanded to be treated as
prisoners of war. Austin Stack, now a veteran of many prison fights for
rights, acted as the prisoners' Commandant. Sinn Fein speeches through
the month emphasized their support for the prisoners. On September
18, when their demands to be treated as political prisoners were refused, the men went on hunger strike. For fifty hours the ascetic
Thomas Ashe was deprived of bed, bedding, and boots. He suffered
intensely from the cold and in his weakened condition was forcibly
fed. Dr. Lynn, who saw him just before he lost consciousness, was
sure that food had been forced into his lungs. On September 25, during this ordeal, he collapsed and was removed to Mater Hospital,
where he died. The Castle officials had canonized another martyr in
the cause of Ireland.

Madame wrote to her sister about Ashe's "heroic death." She had
seen two of the prisoners on their way to Mountjoy and wrote: "I had
a talk with Liddy and with Brown, during the hour they had to wait,
under arrest at Limerick Station. Both said they knew what they had
to do. I said 'Think it over before you hunger strike, for they will let
you die, and it would be fatal for the Cause if you gave in to save
your life.' I told them that there was no need for them to strike, and
that it was terrible suffering, and in fact tried to persuade them not to,
but the one idea that is in every one of their minds is 'We are soldiers
pledged to Ireland, & we can fight in jail as well as out, & die in jail
as well as out, & it is up to us to do it.' I think the English are trying
to goad us into another rising, to wipe us all out. . . . They have machine guns and armoured cars parading the streets here and in every
corner of Ireland, and masses of soldiers in every district. When I gave

a lecture in Cork they mobilised a regiment, with four machine guns in the neighbouring street."[4]

Ashe's funeral on Sunday, September 30, 1917, was reminiscent of the one two years before when nationalist Ireland had honored O'Donovan Rossa, an assertion of popular force against military force. The body lay in state for two days, in the proscribed uniform of the Irish Volunteers. Thirty thousand people followed the coffin to the grave, led by an advance guard of armed Volunteers and nearly two hundred priests. Men and women were there wearing the forbidden uniforms of Volunteer, Cumann na mBan, Fianna, and Irish Citizen Army. There were delegates from the Gaelic Athletic Association, the National Foresters, the Women's Franchise League, the National Aid Society, Sinn Fein clubs, the labor unions, Gaelic League, and hurling clubs. These thousands of marchers were technically "criminals." They had been drilling, they were carrying arms; when they did not have arms they had hurleys; they were in uniform. The spectators seldom made any kind of demonstration, though there was some smiling and applause when Madame went by in her Cumann na mBan uniform. Except when one of the several bands was playing, the procession was ominously silent. One onlooker, who had been deeply moved by the ceremony and the mood of the crowd and the marchers, was brought up short when he overheard a British officer saying to a companion, "Oh, yes, we do just the same in Indiah. We always give the natives a free hand with their religious rites."[5]

The officer would have been wise to consider the significance of the brief funeral oration. It was delivered by a big, handsome young man in Volunteer uniform who seemed to generate a tumultuous energy. He was unknown to most of Dublin, though he had had an important place in the G.P.O. Easter Week. He was Michael Collins, clearly one of the new leaders who would make a formidable opponent. The Last Post was sounded, three volleys were fired, and Collins spoke: "The volley we have just heard is the only speech it is proper to make above the grave of a dead Fenian."

The annual Sinn Fein convention, the Ard Fheis, in October, 1917, brought together under one name the disparate elements of nationalism. After some debate, it was decided by the nearly two thousand delegates to retain the name of the movement which, although it did not advocate physical force nor a complete political break with Britain, had given its name to the rebellion and the name by which all nationalists were called outside of Ireland, Sinn Fein. The meetings in the Mansion House on October 25, 26, and 27 demonstrated a unity among its members which promised well for the future. The best evidence of the closing of ranks was that Arthur Griffith and Count Plunkett generously withdrew their names as candidates for the presidency. Eamon de Valera, the senior surviving officer of Easter Week, was unanimously elected president.

One issue threatened to split the convention and, typically, Madame raised it. She still resented Eoin MacNeill's cancellation order Easter Sunday. Pearse before his death and de Valera in prison had both wisely resolved not to let MacNeill's action split the Volunteers permanently. In his manifesto to his soldiers written April 28, 1916, the fifth day of Easter Week, Pearse had said: "Of the fatal countermanding order which prevented those plans from being carried out, I shall not speak further. Both Eoin MacNeill and we have acted in the best interests of Ireland."

With a sure instinct for doing and saying the right thing, de Valera had dramatically demonstrated this attitude. One morning when the prisoners in Dartmoor were lined up in the dark Central Hall for morning inspection, a small group of Irish prisoners who had arrived the night before came down the stairs. They were led by Eoin MacNeill. Without hesitation, de Valera stepped out from the ranks and faced his men. His voice rang out, "Irish Volunteers! Attention! Eyes left!" They obeyed the command for the salute to MacNeill, and after "Eyes front" de Valera stepped back into the ranks, leaving his men dazzled by his chivalry and courage. This was rank mutiny by prison regulations, and de Valera had risked, although he did not receive, corporal punishment.[6]

Madame, who understood the dramatic gesture as well as anyone, did not, however, share this desire for conciliation. What is uncompromising integrity in oneself, too often becomes obdurate unforgiveness towards another. She opposed the election of MacNeill as a member of the Executive on the grounds that he had changed his mind many times and that it would not be safe for Sinn Feiners to trust their lives to such a man. She was supported by Mrs. Tom Clarke and a few others. But de Valera spoke warmly in MacNeill's defense, and echoed Pearse's comment when he said, "I am convinced that Eoin MacNeill did not act otherwise than as a good man." MacNeill had not signed the proclamation, nor did he ever pretend to be a revolutionary.

With the exception of de Valera who was elected unanimously, and

Arthur Griffith who was elected Vice-President with Father O'Flanagan, MacNeill received the greatest number of votes and headed the list of the Executive members. Madame had brought the question of Eoin MacNeill into the open, although many had urged that this cleavage not be brought onto the floor of the Assembly. They might not all agree, but nearly half of the delegates had expressed their confidence in him, and the air was cleared on that issue. Madame was elected to the twenty-four member Executive board.[7]

Unity was required if Sinn Fein were to win a general election. A policy was agreed upon and a constitution passed which stated the objectives in two sentences: "Sinn Fein aims at securing the international recognition of Ireland as an independent Irish Republic. Having achieved that status the Irish people may by Referendum freely choose their own form of Government." Freedom first, then decisions about form of government. It was the old aim stated in terms vague enough for all nationalists to accept.

A few weeks after the Ard Fheis, the Irish Volunteers Organization held its Third Convention at Croke Park. On November 19, 1917, Eamon de Valera was elected president and was thus the head of both the civil and the military sides of the Irish Republican movement. Other members of the Sinn Fein Executive were in authority in the Volunteers: the wiry Cathal Brugha, whose body was so riddled that he was left for dead Easter Week, was the Chief of Staff; Diarmuid Lynch was Director of Communications; Michael Collins was Director of Organisation. The last two were I.R.B. members, as was the General Secretary of the Volunteers, Sean McGarry. (De Valera had given up his brief membership in the I.R.B.) The same conditions that had caught MacNeill unaware Easter Week still existed and within the nationalist organization was a secret one of great influence and a law unto itself.[8]

In the interest of party unity, Madame revived her liaison activity. She had been president of Cumann na mBan since 1915 and was re-elected to that office at their convention in the autumn of 1917.[9] She also continued her interest in the Fianna, and often spoke at their meetings. The boys continued to use the field in front of her cottage for campouts and drills. They had anticipated the elections of de Valera as president of Sinn Fein and of the Volunteers when in August, 1917, they unanimously elected him Chief of the Fianna after Madame proposed his name. She was again voted Chief Scout.

She was on the committee of the Irish Republican Prisoners Dependents' Fund; she was on a Sinn Fein committee to determine available food supplies; she continued her association with the Irish Citizen Army (who promoted her to Major). At the first meeting of the Sinn Fein Executive on December 19, 1917, she was appointed to head the Department of Labour along with Cathal O'Shannon, who was co-opted to the Executive. As usual, Madame found time for the children, and at Christmas nearly seven hundred were entertained at Liberty Hall and given dinner and tea with an afternoon of games. For the labor movement she went to Manchester with Cathal O'Shannon early in 1918 to speak at a large Irish and Labour meeting in the Free Trade Hall to raise funds for the James Connolly Labour College which had been established in Dublin. She spoke in Cork on "James Connolly and the Irish Republic" and made several other speeches on the important question of the place of international labor in an independent republic.

Whether Sinn Fein would have continued to grow until it won a general election is a question, but just as it was thoroughly organized, Lloyd George blundered in such a way that Sinn Fein became the dominant political party in Ireland. The large number of Irishmen who had not answered England's appeal to join her army irritated and challenged him. Hundreds of thousands were dying in the trenches and hundreds of thousands were needed to replace them. The situation was desperate in spite of American intervention, and Ireland had a tempting surplus of men over the three hundred thousand who had volunteered for war service with England. As spring came on the need for more men increased. On April 9 the Prime Minister announced to the House of Commons a new Man-Power Bill on which conscription could be applied at any time to Ireland by the signing of an Order in Council.

The Prime Minister had been warned against such an act by almost everyone who knew anything about Ireland. Henry Duke, Chief Secretary of Ireland, advised Lloyd George that it would set Ireland ablaze. Nevertheless, the Prime Minister hoped that the removal of young men would cut the claws of the Sinn Fein movement.[10] The entire Irish Parliamentary Party voted against the Conscription Act, and when it was passed on April 16, in protest they returned to Ireland to cooperate with Sinn Fein in organizing resistance.

On April 18, the Lord Mayor of Dublin presided at a conference at the Mansion House attended by representatives of Sinn Fein, Labour, All for Ireland League, and other parties. The conference declared that

Ireland was a separate and distinct nation entitled to self-determination. The attempt to enforce conscription was regarded as an unwarrantable aggression, a declaration of war on the Irish nation. "The alternative to accepting it as such is to surrender our liberties and to acknowledge ourselves slaves. . . . We call upon all Irishmen to resist by the most effective means at their disposal." This declaration was taken to Maynooth and given the blessings of the Irish Bishops. On Sunday, April 21, two million men and women signed the declaration to resist conscription.[11]

Madame joined with other leaders in arousing public support for their stand. The burden of all speeches was, as Madame said at Longford, at Ennis, and at other towns: "Ireland does not intend to submit to conscription or to compromise in any degree on this question." On April 27, Madame brought the Irish Women's Franchise League, Cumann na mBan, and other women's organizations together to reiterate their opposition: "Denying the right of the British Government to enforce compulsory service in this country, we pledge ourselves solemnly to one another to resist Conscription by the most effective means at our disposal."

On April 23, all Ireland (except Belfast), on the advice of the Irish Labour Congress, stopped work as a mark of its determination to resist conscription. The one day strike was general and effective.

T. M. Healy wrote to his brother on May 11 that machine guns were mounted on the Bank of Ireland in anticipation of another rising. On May 17 he wrote: " 'Anti-conscription' is the most remarkable movement that ever swept Ireland. Your apprentice (Kevin O'Higgins) was handcuffed by police before his father and mother to take him in the train to prison, and all Tullamore turned out to see him off, including the priests and Christian Brothers. His mother kissed his handcuffs. Travellers in the train so put the police out of countenance that the handcuffs were taken off until Dublin was reached, when they replaced them to stow him in Mountjoy. He is to be brought tomorrow to Portarlington for trial. Seeing that his brother was killed in France, and that another brother is in the Navy, the police might have spared his parents such indignity. . . . There is no faction here favourable to Conscription."[12]

Lloyd George was so alarmed by the fury he had raised that at last he listened to advice, bad as it was. His Chief Secretary of Ireland had suggested a daring, yet feasible plan: "The first thing is to get all known leaders out of the way at once; extra troops should be on the spot simultaneously, and everyone, irrespective of who he is, arrested on the first sign of giving trouble."[13] But they would have to be arrested on serious charges. Plotting another rebellion? Consorting with the enemy? Both? In the end Dublin Castle concocted a fiction of "treasonable communication with the German enemy." This so-called "German Plot" was so transparently fabricated that even General Macready, who could usually accept anything against the Irish, did not believe it. However, on the night of May 17–18, 1918, seventy-three prominent Sinn Fein leaders were arrested and deported immediately; more arrests were made in following days.

There had been a time when the Castle could move secretly, but that time had passed. Sinn Fein leaders had had such reliable intelligence reports indicating when they were to be arrested that the Executive met that night and discussed the three possibilities open to them: they could resist arrest and fight; they could go on the run; they could allow themselves to be arrested in the knowledge that there were others who could step into the leadership and that their arrests would solidify the members. Darrell Figgis, writing of that discussion, said, "I am stirred by pride in my comrades and our comradeship of those days. No one thought of himself or herself and all our debate was directed to the effect on the country."[14] They decided on the third action, carefully disposed of records (having duplicates of important transactions hidden elsewhere), bundled up other papers to be taken to safety, put Sinn Fein affairs in order, and dispersed to their homes. They had not long to wait. Many of them, including Madame, were arrested before they reached home.

After she had left the Sinn Fein headquarters in Harcourt Street, Madame had walked to Madame MacBride's on nearby St. Stephen's Green.[15] She prepared her for probable arrest, then walked to Rathmines, where she was living. At Rathmines Road, near the entrance to Portobello Barracks, she was stopped by six soldiers and two detectives. An armed car was at the curb; Madame was told to step into it. (Her dog, Poppet, was with her and jumped up on the seat beside her.) The prisoners were taken first to Dublin Castle, then very early in the morning to Dun Laoghaire, where they were loaded into the holds of a gunboat. All day long more and more prisoners came aboard. It was after four o'clock in the afternoon when they left Ireland, and ten at night when they arrived at Holyhead. The following day the men were taken to Usk Gaol and Gloucester Gaol, and later removed to various other prisons in England.

Madame was kept at the police station in Holyhead and on Sunday taken to London on the train. On the way to London a ticket was demanded for her dog and she paid the required six shillings but not without expressing her opinions about the claim. To her great joy and surprise, when the train reached Euston Station, her sister was there. She rushed to her, flung her arms around her neck and kissed her warmly. Miss Roper later told the curious story of how she and Miss Gore-Booth happened to be there. On the trip across the Irish sea and on the train to London, Madame was filled with a strong desire to see her sister and regretted that she had been unable to let her know of the arrest. Miss Roper, on her part, said she and Miss Gore-Booth were sitting in their flat on that Sunday afternoon, thinking and talking of Constance. "Suddenly, for no reason whatever, I felt I must go to Euston Station to meet the Irish Mail. Eva looked very much astonished but said, 'Very well, then, I will come with you.' In the late afternoon we went wearily enough." The station was hot, the platform deserted except for various policemen and detectives. Miss Roper went to one end of the platform, her friend to the other. "Then the train came in, a number of passengers emerged, none of whom I knew. I got more and more depressed, when suddenly looking up, I beheld coming towards me the strangest little procession ever seen by my astonished eyes. First a brown cocker spaniel, well known in Dublin as 'The Poppet,' then a couple of soldiers with rifles, then Eva and Constance together, smiling and talking hard. Lastly an officer with drawn sword, looking very agitated. I, of course, shouted a greeting as I tried to get near. A detective opened the door of a taxi and Constance got in accompanied by an escort. All information as to her destination was refused. The dog jumped in, too." Miss Gore-Booth heard a detective tell the driver to go to Holloway Prison. An hour after they got back to their flat, the doorbell rang, and the spaniel was brought in.[16] (He later was sent back to Ireland and spent the time Madame was in Holloway with the Robert Bartons at Glendalough.)

Miss Gore-Booth did not see her sister in Holloway; Madame and the other Irish were internees, not prisoners. They were never brought to trial on any charge. Before permission was given to see visitors, they were required to sign an undertaking not to discuss politics, but they refused to do this and saw no one.

Nobody in Ireland believed the allegations of a plot. It was generally recognized that the unprecedented solidarity of the Irish people against conscription had alarmed the government into this rash act.

Even in their own official report of the evidence the case was extremely weak and was based primarily on speeches by Sinn Fein leaders protesting conscription and demanding that their case be heard at the post-war peace conference. The official report made much of a St. Patrick's day meeting in Berlin where "representatives of the German Government declared that they would support Ireland's claims at the Peace Conference." Five weeks before the German Plot arrests, Joseph Dowling, a former member of Casement's Irish Brigade recruited from the German prisoners of war, had come ashore in Ireland ostensibly with a message from German leaders to Sinn Fein leaders. There was no evidence that the Irish knew of his coming, but the British regarded it as sufficient evidence of a plot.

On June 21, at a by-election in East Cavan in Ulster, Arthur Griffith defeated the Parliamentary Party's candidate. Griffith was a prisoner in Reading Gaol. Here was assurance that the arrests of the leaders did not break Sinn Fein as the British had hoped but had strengthened it and the resistance to conscription. Madame was elated: "Such a victory, *our arrests did it,* for we were not at all certain, in fact most doubtful of results. Ireland is always true to those who are true to her, putting us away cleared the issues for us, so much better than our own speeches ever could."[17]

Madame MacBride and Mrs. Tom Clarke had been arrested soon after Madame Markievicz, and they, too, were sent to Holloway. T. M. Healy's indignation at the treatment of Mrs. Clarke reflected the intensity of feeling in Ireland: "The arrests are stupid. The denial of the cloak offered to Mrs. Clarke by a friend on Kingstown pier when she was to cross the Channel, and the taking her away from her five children, days after others had been arrested doesn't improve one's temper. It should have been enough for them to shoot her husband and her brother, without depriving her children of their mother."[18]

The three women were at first kept apart in Holloway, but after considerable protesting they were moved to adjoining cells on an isolated landing and were allowed the right of association. In this way the months at Holloway were in many ways much happier for Madame than the dreary loneliness at Aylesbury had been. Her letters to her sister were cheerful, but the prisoners would not accept the terms under which visitors would be allowed and she missed the visits which had been very important to her at Aylesbury. At one time during her ten months' freedom in Dublin she had written in a moment of longing to see her sister, "Do you know, I sometimes almost regret jail—I loved your visits so? and now you are so far away and life is such a rush. I think the greater the gloom, the brighter the spots of sunlight. That's one of the things that make even the horror of jail bearable."

She tried to explain her position on visits to Holloway: "We are asked, above and beyond the ordinary jail rules of having a wardress present at visits to 'give undertakings in writing not to talk politics etc & our visitor not to carry messages or make reports.' Under these conditions we refuse visits." Miss Gore-Booth tried to convince her to let her visit, but Madame was adamant. "I would not like anybody to submit themselves to such an indignity just for me. *No,* NO, NO. *Either* sign or see me with a wardress present (according to jail rules) but once we Irish rebels pledge our word we are to be trusted, & to be watched & spied on *after* ones word is given is more than I would put up with. Its a nuisance, but unavoidable; & one is not looking for a bed of roses!"

The three political prisoners were allowed to have food, clothes, books, and approved newspapers sent in. One of Madame's first requests was for painting supplies, water colors, for she thought the odor of the oils in the close confines of the cell might offend her friends. Many of the watercolors she did at Holloway survived and are at the National Museum of Ireland. She painted remembered Irish scenes of fields and the sea, and horses, heroic figures from the past, rainbows, visions of freedom. In February she tried her hand at an illumination, choosing for her subject James Connolly's "The cause of Labour is the cause of Ireland." In brilliant, confident colors she crossed the Irish tricolor and the plain red flag, because, as she wrote to her sister: "Connolly was such a prophet. He said war was going to be between the Fat man & his black Flag against the Workers & the Red Flag & now its come! He also saw Victory for the Red." Those were the days when the Russian Revolution seemed simple and wholesome.

Madame took delight in needling the censor who read her letter before it was sent on: "First let me tell you & our common enemy the Censor that there is no German plot!" And again, "One thing I am quite grateful to that diabolic long nose the Censor for: he has taught me a lot of useful things, caution for one. If one had more paper & a less obvious Censor, one might have been tempted to be indiscreet. Not about policies. I shall always stand against secret diplomacy, not in pompous speeches & newspaper articles, but by speaking out myself. Saying things that might get others into trouble is all that I fear." She joked about herself, and said that probably she was accused of taking part in a German plot because she had had the German measles just before she was kidnapped. The first few letters were signed "Auf Weidersehn" but she soon tired of that. She laughed at the restrictions. "We are now only to write on 'domestic & business subjects.' I would like to remind the sweet rulers of this Empire that they have constantly affirmed that 'Ireland is a domestic question.' "

She was seriously concerned about Mrs. Clarke, who was ill. "Poor Mrs. Clarke will never stand this; she frets for her boys & she has never got over the shock of her husband and brothers murders. She nearly died & has been very feeble since." Again, "Mrs. C. loves the fruit & she finds it so hard to eat enough." And later, "She really has a heros soul & makes the best of everything." Nearly every letter comments on Mrs. Clarke's health, which was poor, and her attitude, which was uncomplaining.

Patricia Lynch, who was a frequent caller at Holloway to leave food, flowers, books, and other treats, remembers shopping for an invalid chair for Mrs. Clarke and finding sympathy for the prisoners even in England. She chose a chair at Gamage's, and when she gave the Holloway address for delivery to the department manager, he recovered quickly from his surprise and said, "Is it for one of the Irish prisoners there?" "Yes, it is." "This one is not good enough, we must send the best one we have." He did. Madame frequently asked her sister to thank Patricia Lynch for things she had left. Such friends made prison life bearable.

Knowing that both Madame MacBride and Madame Markievicz were fond of gardening, friends often sent them potted plants. They soon discovered they would not grow well in the cells, and hit upon the idea of leaving them in the exercise yard alternate nights to try to prolong their lives. Each day while the weather was warm enough, they descended to the exercise ground carrying their pots of flowers. They sometimes hung branches of grapes on the bars of their "cage" to bring some color and life to the dreariness, or colored clothes or ribbons, anything bright that would help dispel the gloom. "The worst of prison is its such an ugly place."

For one day in August Mrs. Skeffington was in Holloway with them. She was arrested under the Defense of the Realm Act for having, on her return from the United States, crossed to Ireland without a passport. In spite of the grim surroundings, they were quite happy, even merry, as they exchanged the news. Madame had not seen her friend since Easter Week. Mrs. Skeffington had toured the United States, speaking at over two-hundred-fifty meetings about Ireland's claim to independence. A highlight of her visit had been her reception by President Wilson. She was, she said, the first Sinn Feiner to enter the White House and the first to wear there the badge of the Irish Republic. Her mission was to urge Ireland's claim for self-determination and to appeal to President Wilson to include Ireland among the small nations for whose freedom America was fighting.[19] This was the substance of a petition signed by Madame, as President of the Cumann na mBan, by Mrs. Pearse, by Mrs. Wyse-Power, and by many other distinguished Irishwomen. It had been smuggled to her in New York with a request to deliver it personally into the President's own hands. Thanks to her arrest, she was able to report personally to the president of Cumann na mBan that she had carried out her instructions.

On her release, Mrs. Skeffington spent a few days with Miss Gore-Booth, so Madame's sister had direct news of her. In October, Madame MacBride was released to a nursing home in London, but not until February was the ailing Mrs. Clarke released. Characteristically thinking of her friends first, Madame wrote, "Of course I miss K. very much though for the first time of my life, I was thankful to see the back of a dear friend."

She was hungry for news of Sligo and family ("I love all the local gossip so"), and of Ireland, which the prisoners usually referred to as "Kitty" or "Kathleen" in their letters to pass the censor. She knew only what was in the newspapers they were allowed to have. Unfortunately, her sister's letters to her were burned after Madame's death, so what news of family and friends she sent can only be guessed. Madame had not heard anything from her husband since before 1916, and only indirectly from her stepson. "Poor Staskow, I'd hate him to be killed or wounded; he did love life so. He was attached to the Russian Volunteer Fleet at Archangel, & was interpreting. When you get back [Miss Gore-Booth was in the country recuperating from flu] try & find out through any & all Russian agents. Russia must be an awful place to be in." And in another undated letter, "I often feel so anxious about my Polish relations. Poor Casi hated wars, revolutions & politics & there he is or was in Kiev, or in the Ukraine." In the same letter she asked Eva to go to see "an old Aylesbury comrade" who was in a mental hospital in London, and "give her some money to buy little extras, & my love, & tell her why I can't write & where I am." If her sister could not go herself, Madame asked her to send someone "*not* a duchess!" to see her.

It was from Holloway that she wrote a letter to a young playwright, Frank J. Hugh O'Donnell, in which she expressed her views of the peasant-local-color plays which were so much a part of the Irish theater:[20]

> I still remember your play [*Dawn Mist*] although six long months have passed since I read it, & I recall to mind the pleasure that was mine when I found a young author inspired by the idealism & spirit of self-sacrifice that is the keynote of the true Irish character.
>
> So much prominence has been given by our dramatists to the very attractive local colour that surrounds our peasantry and to the peculiarity & beauties of the 'foreign' English they speak, that a stranger to Ireland might easily think that they were our only outstanding National characteristics, instead of merely picturesque results of our history.
>
> Your play has struck another note—that of the great sacrifice which is no sacrifice to the Gael.
>
> Good luck to it, & to you, & may you write many more, & with each one dig deeper into the true heart of Ireland.
>
> Mise i gcuis na hEireann
> Constance de Markievicz

In Ireland throughout 1918, more and more restrictions were placed on the people and arrests continued. During September and October alone, one hundred sixty-seven sentences were passed for political offences. Between the German Plot arrests in May and the general election in December, there were over five hundred political arrests. In July, 1918, Lord French proscribed all Sinn Fein Organizations and Clubs, the Irish Volunteers, Cumann na mBan, and the Gaelic League. In defiance of the ban on Gaelic games, on one day, August 4, fifteen hundred hurling matches were played in Ireland. On August 15, nearly two thousand Sinn Fein Cumainn held meetings at the same hour.

In February, 1918, the Representation of the People Act became effective. It included provision for extending the suffrage to women over thirty years old. A one-clause act passed November 21, 1918, permitted women to be members of Parliament. As early as September, 1918, Sinn Fein invited Madame to stand; the announcement of her candidacy was made in November. The inaugural meeting of the Sinn Fein election campaign was held November 11, 1918, with jubilant and noisy Armistice Day celebrations sounding in the background. Of the seventy-three Sinn Fein candidates, forty-seven were in jail.

The relationship of Labour and Sinn Fein was causing some discussion in Ireland; the original movement had not been sympathetic during 1913, and some mutual suspicion still remained. Connolly's "The cause of Labour is the cause of Ireland" was often quoted and discussed. The decision of Irish Labour Congress, which met after the 1918 Sinn Fein Ard Fheis, not to contest Irish constituencies tended to cement the bond between the nationalists and labor.

Madame's own feelings on the obvious need for cooperation between the two were well known. She had been advocating cooperation for years. She sent a message to the Ard Fheis from Holloway which included a reiteration of her views: "That, as the first principle of Sinn Fein is to end the connection with England, Sinn Feiners affiliated or amalgamated with English Trades Unions should be recommended when possible to sever the English connection. That where Irish resources are being developed, or where industries exist, Sinn Feiners should make it their business to secure that workers are paid a living wage."

Friends of the imprisoned candidates carried on the electioneering for them. Madame had written, immediately after their arrests, "I think its about the best thing that could have happened for Ireland as there was so little to be done there, only propaganda, & our arrests carry so much further than speeches. Sending you to jail is like pulling out all the loud stops on all the speeches you ever made or words you ever wrote!" To Mrs. Wyse-Power she wrote in December: "My letters lately have been objected to, so I must be very careful what I say to you. People all know me so well in Dublin that it will not matter a bit my not being able to write to them. My present address alone will make an excellent election address."[21]

The Irish Women's Franchise League, Sinn Fein, the Volunteers, and Cumann na mBan all held meetings in St. Patrick's Division for Madame, and her friends spoke for her. Polling day, December 14, 1918, was a great day for the Franchise League as well as for Sinn Fein. The oldest suffragette in Ireland, the ninety-year-old Mrs. Haslam, who with her husband had founded the Dublin Women's Suffrage Society in 1874, voted at the William Street courthouse accompanied by smiling women carrying the green banner of the League.

The issue was clearly put to the people. Those who voted for the nominees of the Sinn Fein Party knew that they were voting for complete independence, for the establishment of a republic, for the repudiation of the British Parliament, and for the policy of active opposition to the British government in Ireland.

Two weeks later the result of the election was announced, and with it the recognition of the overwhelming support of Sinn Fein given by the Irish people, who voted for freedom by a majority of seventy per cent. Out of 105 candidates returned for Ireland, 73 were Republicans and 26 Unionists. The Parliamentary Party had shrunk from eighty seats at the beginning of the year to seven (six in Ireland and one from a Liverpool constituency). The vote in St. Patrick's Division, Dublin, was Madame Markievicz, 7,835; William Field (Irish Party), 3,742; Alderman J. J. Kelly (Ind.), 312. The Irish Unionist Alliance (the pro-English Party in Ireland) said: "The General Election of December, 1918, was the first occasion when the numerical strength of Sinn Fein could be officially known, for they contested all the constituencies against the sitting Home Rule members. They stood boldly on the issue of an Irish Republic, free from all connections with England, and on that issue swept the Home Rule party out of existence."[22]

Frank Gallagher described the excitement at Sinn Fein headquarters as the results of the General Election came in. "Outside the second-floor window a notice board had been fixed and as each result was phoned or wired from the counting rooms first the victory and then the figures appeared on it. For those whose names the people knew well, Harry Boland would come to the window and in the silence that immediately fell would call out: 'Countess Markievicz is in' or 'Sean T. O'Kelly has been elected' or 'Alderman Tom Kelly beats them both in Stephen's Green.' Then the crowd would demonstrate to its heart's desire. To the crowd the results were almost unbelievable. Never had a nation so much reason to make a cautious demand and never had it made a more daring one. As the figures poured in and Sinn Fein won with huge majorities it seemed as if with their bare hands the ordinary men and women had seized the cordon of bayonets around Ireland and thrust them aside to call their sovereignty to the world."[23]

The Republicans read the election results as a clear mandate to take the claims of Ireland to the Peace Conference. There could be no doubt now that the Irish people wanted to govern themselves, no question that they had fulfilled the conditions of self-determination described by President Wilson in a Fourth of July address in 1918: "The settlement of every question, whether of territory, of sovereignty, of economic arrangement, or of political relationship, upon the basis of the free acceptance of that settlement by the people immediately concerned, and not upon the basis of the material interest or advantage of any other nation or people which may desire a different settlement for the sake of its own exterior influence or mastery. . . . What we seek is the reign of law based upon the consent of the governed and sustained by the organized opinion of mankind."

To this, Lloyd George had added his approval the following day when he said to American troops in France, "President Wilson yesterday made it clear what we are fighting for."

"These declarations," wrote de Valera, "constitute a complete estoppel upon any protest from England against the recognition of Ireland's independence."[24]

On January 7, 1919, twenty-six of the elected Republicans met at the Mansion House to make plans for convening Dail Eireann (Assembly of Ireland). Over Count Plunkett's signature, as Chairman of the meeting, invitations were sent to the elected representatives for all the Irish constituencies to attend three weeks later the public opening of the Parliament of Ireland.

NOTES TO CHAPTER XI

1. This letter is in the Sligo Museum.
2. David Hogan [Frank Gallagher], *The Four Glorious Years* (Dublin, 1953), vividly details and discusses these important years 1917–1921.
3. September 26, 1917. Roper, *Prison Letters*, p. 296.
4. Ibid., pp. 295–296.
5. Douglas Goldring, *Odd Man Out* (London, 1935), pp. 197–198.
6. Brennan, *Allegiance*, pp. 103–194. This is an engrossing book of Ireland and of those who fought for her freedom.
7. The election results at that 10th Sinn Fein Convention, the first under its newly reorganized strength, were: Vice-Presidents, Arthur Griffith (1,197 votes) and Father O'Flanagan (780); Honorary Secretaries, Austin Stack (857) and Darrell Figgis (510); Honorary Treasurers, W. T. Cosgrave (537) and Laurence Ginnell (471); Executive Members, Eoin MacNeill (888), Cathal Brugha (685), Dr. Hayes (674), Sean Milroy (667), Countess Markievicz (617), Count Plunkett (598), Piaras Beaslai (557), Joseph McGuinness (501), Finian Lynch (475), Harry Boland (448), Dr. Kathleen Lynn (425), J. J. Walsh (424), Joseph McDonagh (421), Father Matt Ryan (416), Father Wall (408), Mrs. Thomas Clarke (402), Diarmuid Lynch (390), David Ceannt (385), Sean T. O'Kelly (367), Dr. T. Dillon (364), Mrs. Joseph Plunkett (345), Sean McEntee (342), Ernest Blythe (340), and Michael Collins (340).

8. Some former members of the Volunteer Executive were not so gracefully received as MacNeill had been by Sinn Fein. Bulmer Hobson was among those discredited by the Volunteers.

9. A pamphlet outlining some of the history and aims of the women reminded them of their Constitution, which pledged them to work for the establishment of an Irish Republic by organizing and training the women of Ireland to take their places by the side of those who were working and fighting for a free Ireland. The local clubs were urged to continue educating their members by means of lectures, literature, debates, and classes in the conduct of public affairs so that they might be fitted to occupy public positions.

10. Lloyd George, *War Memoirs*, V, 190.

11. Healy, *Letters*, II, 595–596.

12. Ibid., pp. 597–598.

13. Lloyd George, *War Memoirs*, V, 189.

14. Figgis, *Recollections of the Irish War*, p. 211. Darrell Figgis, who was one of the Sinn Fein Executive members arrested, has suggested that the decision of the British to imprison the Sinn Fein leaders and the decision of the Irish to accept arrest had an unexpected result. The arrested leaders were for the most part the nationalists who were working along constitutional lines, while the more radical men, most of whom were I.R.B. members and physical-force advocates, were now in control. Ibid., especially pp. 216–222.

15. Maud Gonne was often called by her maiden name. In Ireland after the execution of her husband in 1916, however, her married name was more frequently used.

16. Roper, *Prison Letters*, pp. 64–66.

17. June 22, 1918 letter to her sister.

18. Healy, *Letters*, II, 599.

19. Mrs. Skeffington recorded her trip in *Impressions of Sinn Fein in America* (Dublin, 1919).

20. Printed as the foreword to O'Donnell's play *The Dawn Mist: A Play of the Rebellion* (Dublin, 1919).

21. *The Irish Independent*, December 5, 1918.

22. *Ireland's Request to the Government of the United States of America for Recognition as A Sovereign Independent State* (n.p., n.d.) [Signed, Eamon de Valera, President of the Republic of Ireland, October 27, 1920, and addressed "To His Excellency The President of the United States"], p. 50.

23. Hogan, *Four Glorious Years*, p. 50.

24. *Ireland's Request to the Government of the United States*, p. 18.

XII

Anglo-Irish War

1919

On January 21, 1919, the first Dail Eireann met, presided over by Cathal Brugha since both the Sinn Fein President and Vice-President were in jail. In the face of steadily increasing British resistance, the creation of such a body was an act of solemn daring. Only twenty-four members answered to their names at the roll call. To the name of Countess Markievicz and to thirty-five others, the answer given was "Fé ghlas ag Gallaibh" ("Imprisoned by the foreign enemy," or, more simply, "In a foreign prison"). The non-Republican deputies did not attend.

In two hours, in a dignified meeting attended by representatives of the press and visitors from many countries, the Provisional Constitution of the Dail was read and passed unanimously; Ireland's Declaration of Independence was read and adopted; three delegates were appointed to the Peace Conference (Eamon de Valera, Arthur Griffith, and Count Plunkett); and the Democratic Programme of Dail Eireann, based on the Easter Week Proclamation, was read and adopted. The Irish Republic had risen from the dead and had been formally established as an independent state within a British state. Each government tried to force the other to recognize its own authority as autonomous while enacting a legal fiction that the other did not exist. The result was an inevitable drift into undeclared war.

The presentation of Ireland's claim for recognition of her independence before the Peace Conference then meeting in Paris was the first task of the Dail. To this end Sean T. O'Kelly was accredited as Envoy of the Government of the Irish Republic and sent to Paris to secure the admission to the Conference of the three delegates. In March he was joined by George Gavan Duffy.

In the meantime, in the United States friends of Ireland were working for support from America. They succeeded in getting Congress to pass a resolution on March 4, 1919, which read, "That it is the earnest hope of the Congress of the United States of America that the Peace Conference, now sitting in Paris, in passing upon the rights of various peoples, will favorably consider the claims of Ireland to the right of self-determination." An Irish-American delegation saw President Wilson in New York as he was leaving for the Peace Conference on March 5, but the man on whom Sinn Fein had built high hopes was going to negotiate with Lloyd George, and the delegation found him disturbingly noncommittal. An American Commission on Irish Independence went to Paris in April to try to help Dail Eireann delegates get a hearing at the Peace Conference. Its three members also visited Ireland in May, but were unable to obtain safe-conduct for the Dail delegates.

Throughout January and February, for ten weeks or more after their election, there were Sinn Fein members of Parliament who remained untried in English prisons. A resolution from the Irish Women's Franchise League in February remonstrating detention of Madame Markievicz was typical of the many protests from Ireland which went unheeded.

Incongruously, a form letter was sent all the deputies to their Irish addresses and subsequently forwarded to their temporary residences. On February 5, from 10 Downing Street, "Yours faithfully, D. Lloyd George" informed each member that on Tuesday, February 11th His Majesty would open Parliament. "I hope you may find it convenient to be in your place." Madame's was addressed to St. Patrick's, Dublin, and was forwarded to Holloway Gaol, London, but for some reason was held in Dublin until a week after Parliament had opened, perhaps to be sure she would not be there.[1] Receipt of the letter enlivened many dreary prison cells and occasioned some choice responses. Madame had a grand time replying to the invitation (which was not gilt-edged but black-bordered) but thought that her masterly reply was held up by the Holloway censor and never delivered to the Prime Minister. Later, on a visit to Westminster she dropped in to the members' vestibule to look at the peg reserved for her top hat and overcoat and was amused to see that it was next to that of Sir Edward Carson, whose politics were so far removed from her own. That was as close as she ever got to the British Parliament, to which she had been the first woman elected.

The politicians might play the game of nonrecognition, but the great influenza epidemic put all confined persons into too real a danger to be ignored. On March 6, 1919, the decision to release the Irish internees was announced, spurred by the death of Pierce McCann, T. D. (Teachta Dála, Member of Dail Eireann) from Tipperary, in Gloucester Gaol from influenza. The next several days saw the evacuation of the untried from English jails. Madame was released on March 10 from Holloway and spent a few days with her sister in London before going home to Dublin on the 15th.

Her reception was even more jubilant than it had been twenty-one months before when she had come home from Aylesbury. "Mme. O'Rahilly and Mrs. Humphries met me at Holyhead, and they had secured sunny seats on the boat. The sun on the rippling sea was divine, and the seagulls gave the finishing touch to the reality of freedom. I was met by deputations of everybody! We motored in to Dublin to Liberty Hall. Last time was nothing to it. The crowd had no beginning or end. I made a speech, and we then formed up in a torchlight procession and went to St. Patrick's. Every window had a flag or candles or both. You never saw such excitement."[2] She was full of energy and constructive plans for a new Ireland. "The best and the last of the long fight is before us, the watchword is 'organise.' Organise politically and economically. Put your trust in God and the spirit of Republican Ireland, and full steam ahead."[3]

Eamon de Valera had not waited for official release from Lincoln Prison but had escaped and been in hiding since early February. Plans were made for his triumphant return to Dublin March 26. He was to be met at the gates of the city by the Lord Mayor and escorted to the Mansion House as the official head of an established and independent state. If the Castle permitted this, it would seem to recognize the legitimacy of Sinn Fein, so it prohibited all meetings and brought in more troops to meet any emergency. Witnessing the preparations that day, the sensitive English writer H. W. Nevinson saw evidence that all hopes of conciliation and arrangement were rapidly fading away: "I watched the English garrison preparing as for another Easter Week. All day long our soldiers paraded the streets of Dublin. Guns and cavalry paraded. Tanks and armoured cars rumbled about, while overhead flights of aeroplanes buzzed, in battle formation."[4] De Valera, hearing of the critical situation, sent word to cancel his reception to avoid bloodshed.

When Dail Eireann met for its second session on the first of April, 1919, fifty-two members were present. On the motion of Cathal Brugha, seconded by P. O Maille, Eamon de Valera was declared elected Priomh-Aire (President). The following day he submitted his nominations for his ministry, which were approved: Secretary for Home Affairs, Arthur Griffith; Secretary for Defence, Cathal Brugha; Secretary for Foreign Affairs, Count Plunkett; Secretary for Labour, Countess Markievicz; Secretary for Industries, Eoin MacNeill; Secretary for Finance, Michael Collins; Secretary for Local Government, William Cosgrave. By her appointment, Madame became the first woman cabinet minister in western Europe.[5]

Madame's first Dail assignment was as a member of a committee appointed by Arthur Griffith to consider prisoners of war and kidnapped children. In Tipperary, on January 21, 1919 (coincidentally the day of the first session of Dail Eireann) Dan Breen, Seumus Robinson, Sean Hogan, Sean Treacy, and three or four other Irish Volunteers had ambushed employees of the South Tipperary County Council who were under Royal Irish Constabulary escort and carried off explosives destined for the quarry at Soloheadbeg. In the fray, the two armed R.I.C. were killed.[6] The gelignite, detonators, and Volunteers disappeared. In its investigation, the R.I.C. thereatened an eight-year-old boy with rifles and questioned him alone for nearly five hours. Matthew Hogan, the fifteen-year-old brother of Sean, and Timothy Connors, an eleven-year-old whose father worked on Sean Treacy's farm, had been held incommunicado for ten weeks. The father of the eleven-year-old had made several fruitless efforts to find out where his child was and had only curt and evasive replies from the English authorities. It took the Dail Eireann inquiry to obtain their release. Madame's committee was able to report their return home.[7]

The ambush at Soloheadbeg was the first sign of the renewed strength of the Volunteers and the first time since the Rising that they struck back at the British. It is regarded by some historians as the beginning of the Anglo-Irish War.

During 1918 arrests had been continual. Nine hundred and seventy-three men, women, and children were sentenced to varying prison terms in Ireland during the single year. Most of their "crimes" were making speeches in public, appearing in public in military formation, or having or issuing papers or documents which, if published, might cause "disaffection."

Arrests were often made on even flimsier grounds. On October 1, a boy was sentenced to one month's imprisonment for carrying a Sinn Fein flag. A week later a young man was sentenced to five months' imprisonment for "being in the company of boys carrying a Sinn Fein flag." On October 17, a youth was sent to jail for one month for "whistling derisively at the police." One man was sentenced to two years in prison for singing a song the R.I.C. did not like.

Each side harassed the other, the British with troops and legal machinery, Sinn Fein with raids, public support, and wit. Before adjourning on the fourth day of the second session of Dail Eireann, President de Valera proposed that members of the police forces acting in Ireland as part of the forces of the British occupation and as agents of the British Government be ostracised socially by the people of Ireland. The motion was unanimously passed.[8] Madame was soon to be arrested for advocating this policy.

Meanwhile, she had organised her Ministry of Labour. The democratic program adopted at the first Dail in January declared, "It shall be the first duty of the Government of the Republic to make provision for the physical, mental and spiritual well-being of the children, to secure that no child shall suffer hunger or cold from lack of food, clothing, or shelter, but that all shall be provided with the means and facilities requisite for their proper education and training as Citizens of a Free and Gaelic Ireland." This summed up Madame's philosophy of the duties of the state to its children and workers.[9] She was a good choice for the ministry, which was concerned not only with labor but also with social welfare. She was acceptable to both Sinn Fein and Labour and therefore effective as liaison between them. "I belong to both organisations," she said, "for my conception of a free Ireland is economic as well as political."[10] The Irish Women Workers Union, of which Helena Molony was a leader, expressed unqualified approval of Madame's appointment. "We rejoice that the first woman elected to Parliament in Ireland is one to whom the workers can always confidently look to uphold their rights and just claims."[11]

To the IWWU, Madame had written from Holloway about a milk supply project she had in mind, based on a cooperative plan AE had successfully introduced in the North. Sinn Fein clubs would supply the milk from the country and send it to a cooperative shop in Dublin which would be set up close to Kingsbridge Station near the slum section which formed a large part of her own constituency of St. Patrick's. Under a cooperative system milk would cost 5d. a quart instead of 8d. "I am sure we should get help all around for such a scheme. Our poor mothers suffer so and our little babies get such a poor chance."[12]

Such a plan presumed more stability than Ireland was allowed. But

Madame occasionally found instability useful. Louie Bennett remembered one of the first of a number of industrial disputes in which the IWWU was involved during Madame's term of office. A conference had been arranged with a Dublin manufacturer of beads to discuss a wage demand. The meeting was held at the Republican offices in Harcourt Street. As it dragged on with apparently no hope of settlement, Madame rushed in with the news that the military were on their way to raid the office. "They will be here in a quarter of an hour," she said. Still no concessions from the employer, or the union. "Ten minutes more," Madame announced. Still no agreement. "Five minutes left." Finally, in the last minutes before the raid, the employer signed an agreement to pay the same wages as other firms.[13]

After her enforced rest in Holloway, Madame's work for the Dail involved a rush of meetings reminiscent of the pre-1916 days. There were Dail Eireann meetings, committee meetings, meetings with workers and employers. She addressed a huge meeting in Glasgow at the end of April, presided at the Fianna Aeridheacht at Croke Park on May 11, and spent the next weekend in Cork at meetings for which she was eventually arrested in June.

Late in May Madame talked with the three members of the American Commission on Irish Independence. The three men (Edward F. Dunne, a former governor of Illinois; Frank P. Walsh from New York; and Michael J. Ryan of Philadelphia) had gone to Ireland from Paris at the invitation of President de Valera and with the approval of the British, who expeditiously amended their passports to allow the trip. What the visitors saw was not what Lloyd George had intended. Their report, made in June, was sent to British government officials and to newspapers, as well as to various American delegates to the Paris peace talks. It formed a part of the official United States government publication on the Treaty talks, included when the three Americans testified at a hearing before the Congressional Committee on Foreign Relations in 1919. Much of the detailed evidence of atrocities committed against women prisoners in Ireland was furnished by Madame. During the course of their investigations the Americans were astonished to realize that she was shadowed by spies and that threats were made against her. Their reactions are best told by themselves:

"Crossing the Irish Sea from Holyhead to Dunleary [Dun Laoghaire] we came upon the first evidence of the military occupation of Ireland. The vessel and wharves swarmed with soldiers, fully equipped for the field, going to and coming from Ireland.

"When we arrived in Ireland [May 3, 1919] we found soldiers everywhere. A careful investigation made on the day before we left Ireland showed that the army of occupation numbers considerably over 100,000 men, to which accessions are being made daily. The troops are equipped with lorries, armored cars, tanks, machine guns, bombing planes, light and heavy artillery; and in fact all of the engines of war lately employed against the Central Powers.

"In addition to this there are approximately 15,000 members of the Royal Irish Constabulary. The constabulary is a branch of the military forces. They are armed with rifles, as well as small side arms, engage in regular drill and field maneuvers. They are never residents of the districts which they occupy, and have quarters in regular government barracks."[14]

The commission met with some opposition from the prison governor but were eventually allowed to visit Mountjoy, where they were impressed by the fact that the well-filled jail, built for 1,000, had only twelve non-political prisoners. They saw first-hand the arbitrary restrictions placed on freedom of movement when they tried to visit Westport, County Mayo. "As we approached the town a company of soldiers met us about three miles out, and the lieutenant announced, in a surly tone, that under no circumstances would we be permitted to enter. We demanded to see the colonel, to whom we showed our passports, repeated the message of Mr. Lloyd George delivered through Sir William Wiseman, to the effect that he wanted us to visit all of Ireland, explained that we were conducting an investigation under the authority of the Prime Minister. The colonel, however, declared that he would take the full responsibility of not complying with the request of even so high a personage as the Prime Minister of England, though he stated that he was acting on order from the Government officials in Dublin.

"During our visit to Ireland we witnessed numerous assaults in public streets and highways with bayonets and clubbed rifles upon men and women known to be republicans, or suspected of being in favor of a republican form of government. Many of the outraged persons were men and women of exemplary character and occupying high positions in the business and professional life of the country."

A special session of Dail Eireann was held on May 9 to welcome Americans so well disposed to the Irish Republic. Afterwards, on their way to a reception held in their honor at the Mansion House, they were stopped by the military and de Valera was not allowed to pass.

The Mansion House was surrounded by troops searching for Michael Collins and Robert Barton. Neither deputy could be found. Later the Americans witnessed a brutal and unprovoked assault by an English colonel and a crowd of soldiers on Eoin MacNeill.

Madame's influence is apparent in their reports of attacks on women and children, the kidnapping of children by the police for interrogation, in information on education, infant mortality figures, and the appalling destitution and hunger. Their labor report bears signs of her indignation: "Ireland has the best organized and most coherent labor movement in the world. It is being thwarted and suppressed by the army and constabulary. Wages of unskilled workers are below a line which means to them, hunger, cold, and privation. The wage of skilled labor is far below the minimum for decent existence.

"In many of the larger cities and towns the trade-unions have a 100 per cent organization. We met and interviewed almost all of the national leaders of labor. The heads of the National Irish Labor Party, which is in control of the situation, are, without exception, ardent republicans, fully alive to their rights and insisting on self-determination for Ireland. They have all been the innocent victims of atrocities against their own persons in the jails of Ireland and England.

"They work along traditional trade-union lines. If their country is not freed of foreign control and exploitation, and quickly, many of them declare that in sheer defense of their own lives, they will be compelled to set up local Soviet governments, and refuse longer to produce wealth for their oppressors.

"There are few who would disagree with the Right Hon. Herbert H. Asquith, former Prime Minister of Great Britain, who said on June 2, 'Lord French is at present viceroy of Ireland, which to-day is the darkest of the dark spots on the map, not of Great Britain, but of the world.' "

The Americans' report, which was signed June 3, 1919, recommended that an impartial committee be appointed by the Peace Conference "to take testimony as to the alleged facts herein set forth." No such committee was ever formed, but certain comments in the report of the three men who had visited Ireland were used as an excuse to deny safe-conducts for travel to Paris for Eamon de Valera, Count Plunkett, and Arthur Griffith.[15]

Seth P. Tillman, in a recent book about the Paris Peace Conference, summed up the official American attitude towards Ireland's claim: "Wilson did not allow the Irish question to come to the surface at the Peace Conference because of the need of British support in the achievement of his primary objectives, particularly in the establishment of the League of Nations, which he believed, would provide permanent processes for the realization of just such aspirations as those of Irish nationality."[16] It was a sad irony to Sinn Fein that because Wilson was interested in such problems as theirs, their case could not be heard. Once more they were thrown back upon their own devices.

Madame kept on with her strenuous schedule of meetings all through the spring. Now and then a gathering at which she was to speak would be prohibited, and this added zest to the appointment. On the 17th of May, for example, when the Americans were in Ireland, the military authorities forbade an aeridheacht at Newmarket, County Cork, where she had been announced as the speaker. The authorities also banned a concert and lecture by Madame at the City Hall in Cork to be given under the auspices of the Irish Citizen Army on the ground that it would be "an assembly calculated to conduce to a breach of the peace, promote disaffection, and make undue demands on the military and police."

It was nearly midnight on Saturday the 17th when Madame arrived in Newmarket to be met by a brass band to give a short speech advocating ostracism of the police. Along with other practical tips on how to accomplish this, she advised her audience to be cautious what they said to their own children lest they unknowingly passed on the information to a policeman's child. After the meeting Madame exchanged her coat, hat, and scarf with a friend who was then followed around by the police. While they were engaged in watching her coat, she was driven out of town to the home of a sympathizer, where she spent the night. Sunday morning a large force of military and police drew cordons across all roads leading into the town and no one was allowed to pass except those going to church. On Sunday afternoon Madame addressed a crowd at Kisheam. She was to hear more about that weekend later. The following week she was in Glasgow and arrived back in Dublin in time to meet again with the American delegation before they returned to Paris. She thought them "splendid types."

On June 5, the Socialist Party of Ireland planned a Connolly Birthday Concert to he beld at the Mansion House. It was widely advertized and promised to be well attended. Shortly before the scheduled hour and after some of the committee in charge were already inside, cordons of police were drawn across Dawson Street to prevent people from going to the concert. Although the move was sudden, nothing in Dublin could come as a complete surprise, and rumors had circulated the night before that this would happen. Those of the Citizen Army who were in favor of supporting the Socialist Party's tribute to Connolly had been mobilized to act as stewards. When they reached Dawson Street, they found the police were forcibly preventing any gathering near the Mansion House. In the vicinity of St. Stephen's Green there was an exchange of shots and in the fray four policemen and two civilians, including a young girl on her way to the concert, were wounded.

When word had been passed the night before that the meeting at the Mansion House might be prevented, the Trades Hall in Capel Street had been reserved as an alternative. In the absence of William O'Brien, who was at the Mansion House, Madame was called to the chair, and the program proceeded with music and speeches. Cathal O'Shannon abandoned his intention of lecturing on "James Connolly, Educationalist" and chose the more relevant subject of "James Connolly, Anti-Imperialist." Madame made a vigorous appeal for funds towards a Connolly Memorial Workers College.

It was perhaps only a coincidence that the report of the American Commission had been publicized in Paris on June 4, the Socialist concert was banned on June 5, and that Madame was arrested on June 13 for her seditious speech in Newmarket four weeks previously. The American delegates accused the British of having arrested her because of the help she had given them, but the police denied it. The warrant, they claimed, had been issued on May 25, although they did not explain why they waited so long to make the arrest. In a letter from Cork jail a few weeks later to her friend, Charles Diamond, in Glasgow, she described her trial:

"You saw about my arrest I suppose, & that I've got 4 months for advising people to avoid the police! The Scotchman in charge of our poor land tries to justify himself my trying to get people to believe that I was urging people to *kill* the Police! The whole thing is absurd. The Military display that accompanied my arrest & that surrounds me here is quite magnificent. I was taken first to Mallow by a special train, accompanied by about 30 soldiers equipped for war, trench helmets, bayonets fixed & all, & about the same number of police equally armed to the teeth! What they call the 'Preliminary Enquiry' was very funny, its for the Police to rehearse their story about you & get it pat, & to make sure that they will be able to identify you at your trial. Both were very necessary, as I spoke at 11:40 P.M. by the light of a burnt out bonfire, & the police mistook a girl for me directly after & followed her all night, while I slipped away; & it was too dark for them to take notes of my speech, so they had to get it written for them & learn how to pronounce it. I had to laugh when one swore he heard me say 'avoid them like leepers.' They corrected his pronunciation to 'lepers' the day of my trial. I then was taken on by special to Cork jail, which is one armed camp of soldiers & police. I was motored back to Mallow for my trial, one armoured car & 3 or 4 huge lorries full of soldiers & police escorting me. It was very uncomfortable as I was in a low roofed wagon on a very high wooden stool my head bumping on the roof & crushed with 2 wardresses & a policeman. Mallow was like a conquered town, hundreds of soldiers every where, bayonets fixed, a brave photographer snapped me at the risk of his life as I came out. On the way back the armoured car & one of the lorries broke down. I often wonder how these English soldiers like being put into a female prison & having to work under the police. I've sentries under my window, & they seem to be everywhere. The Peelers slip about in noiseless shoes & are always spying on them! Its a funny use to put an army to. I'd be very sick if I'd enlisted to fight Huns & had then been sent to oppress a small nation, & guard a patriotic woman in a female prison. Remember me to all the workers & fighters I met. I am quite content here as well as anywhere else as long as I am serving Ireland, & I am getting political treatment."

The local press reports of the trial and the show of force which surrounded it verify Madame's account. The strain of the last several years was beginning to tell on her, however, and she looked pale and worn at the trial, but spirited still. She did not deny saying as reported, "I hear our meeting for to-morrow is proclaimed. Well, that is a good sign that the Government is afraid of Sinn Fein and that we're on the right path." Nor, "I now advise the young men and young women of Newmarket to go on drilling and training and be ready to take the place of your leaders if arrested. Boycott English manufacturers and burn everything English except its coal."

By this time Madame was adept at using a courtroom as a soapbox. She refused to question either of the police whose testimony constituted the case for the prosecution. She denied the authority of that court to judge her and would call no witnesses nor offer any defense. For the benefit of her friends she wished to say that though she accepted in the main the meaning of the rigamarole they had just heard, there were two charges that were false, and she would tell her friends so. In the first place, she would never advocate the persecution of policemen's children—she would leave that to the police. She begged her friends never to hurt or make a child unhappy. She did not think any of her friends at the meeting in Newmarket took her as advocating the annoying or persecution of children, even policemen's children, and she asked her friends in the name of Eamonn Ceannt, who was a policeman's son and who died for Ireland, to respect children. The other charge she denied was that she had urged shops to boycott the police. She had never done so: it was an impossible policy; she did not ask her friends to adopt it; and she did not see what could be achieved by it. Owing to the late hour at which the meeting was held, she was not able to read the notes she had made—she hadn't the eyes of a policeman—but she thought she had said, "Have as little to do as you can with the police for your own sakes—treat them as if they did not exist." She was not afraid of them, she was not afraid of the British Government, she was afraid only of one thing—God and the judgment of the Irish people. There was an outburst of applause at this from the large audience.

After a short deliberation the judge sentenced her to four calendar months without hard labor in Cork female prison. Madame rose and theatrically called for three cheers for the Irish Republic. The crowd responded despite official protestations and loudly approved a girl who called out "Up the rebels." Fifteen minutes later Madame was on her way to Cork jail under the same heavy escort. Cheers for her and derisive shouts for her escort followed their departure from Mallow. Madame had a talent for leaving hectic scenes behind her.

This was the second successive summer she was in jail, the third of the last four years, a great trial for a woman who loved being outdoors in the country. Nevertheless, she was not too unhappy in Cork. She was allowed many visitors, friends sent in her meals, she had all the reading material she wanted, and many letters. There was no evidence of censorship.

To her sister she wrote: "The two policemen, who recognized me & swore to it being me who made the speech had never really seen me. . . . After the meeting I transferred my coat, hat & a long blue Liberty scarf you gave me years ago to a girl. These Police, who swore they knew *me,* followed *her* round Newmarket while I looked on & laughed. So you see what liars they are!" "I wonder whether Gaga [their mother] realised she was talking sedition when she used to abuse Maggie Campbell for walking with a policeman, years and years ago. It was a terrible crime in her eyes, & she sacked Maeve's first nurse for doing ditto! I wonder what her present point of view is! Someone ought to warn her of the risks she runs!"

She regarded herself as a connoisseur of jails by this time and wrote: "This is the most comfortable jail I have been in yet. Theres a nice garden, full of pinks & you can hear the birds sing. I do wish you were in Cork, its so warm & mild, with just a nice sea breeze coming in, it would do you a world of good." She had time to write about what she was reading, history mostly, which she found "more thrilling than any romance." She liked Chesterton's *History of England* for his style and because it was "so human and so unexpected." Thackeray she found very dull; J. A. Hobson she liked, agreeing with his views on nationalism as "a plain highway to internationalism."

She saw her surroundings with an artist's eye, and wrote to Eva about the beauty she saw: "The moths here are so lovely. They come fluttering in through the bars at night, every shade & every shape, such big ones all splotched over with orange & red, great white soft things, & wee ethereal ones, all opalescent & shimmering, moonlight colours. One I got today was like the waves of a pale, twilight sea, another was like a creamy shell. I try to save their lives."

Nora Connolly visited Madame in Cork jail three or four times in August, and found her well informed. She was avidly reading the papers and books, she had recovered from an earlier attack of flu and was well, but lonely, in spite of the attention and gifts she had had from her friends in Cork. Miss Connolly noted, as Madame did several times in her letters, the number of young soldiers on duty, and echoed the remark of a woman who lived near the jail, "Yerra, God help ye, all that turnout for one lone woman."[17]

In September Madame heard that her sister had received word of Stanislas and was hungry for more news of her family: "So delighted to know that Staskou is alive, do, do, write quick & tell me what you know about him. I am so sorry for him, I dont suppose he is a Bolshevick, & I daresay he is in a rather awful position. He hated politics & wars so, poor boy. I wonder so how he'll live, & what he'll do. He was such a child when I saw him last.[18] I've not heard of Casi either for so long, he was in Kiev, rather a bad place just now, & he might just as easily be a Bolshevick as anything else. Fine ideas always attracted him, & he would be quite capable of being enthused into thoroughly enjoying wearing a big beard & waving a red Flag. He was always torn in two between his artistic appreciation of the rich & Princely people, & just as strong an appreciation of the wrongs of the people & the beauty of self sacrifice. Even here he was a bit of an anxiety for he would lunch with the Enemy, & sup with the Enemy, & between the two make a wild rebel speech. He was absolutely sincere all the time, here it was only rather compromising, in Russia both sides would be stalking him with guns. Do try & find out from S. whats happened to them all. I don't like to write. In the Old Russia it would have got them all on to a black list, even to correspond with a rebel like me. Do you remember, that time, you were interested in a Russian society in Manchester? & how serious Casi was about it. He was not exaggerating."

Madame was released from Cork jail on October 16, 1919, and immediately resumed work in Dublin. The *Watchword of Labour* greeted her cordially: "Everyone rejoices to welcome back to the restricted liberty of ordinary Irish life the cheerful and invigorating personality of Madame de Markievicz. Four months of prison life have not damped her spirit or quenched her flaming idealism."

During the time she had been in Cork the Irish Republic had been gaining strength despite thousands of raids on private homes, suppression of newspapers, continual arrests and harrassment. In June, at about the time Madame was arrested, Eamon de Valera had left Dublin for the United States to explain to the American people Ireland's position and hopes. He wanted to gain their support in pressing Ireland's claims for a hearing at the Peace Conference.

The members of the Irish parliament had moved quickly to establish government in Ireland: raising money for the Republic at home and in America; setting up land courts and commissions to investigate industries and commerce to benefit the Irish people; establishing labor arbitration boards; and instituting courts for civil law. The Irish Volunteers became the Army of the Republic. The Irish were, in short, trying to run their country on a sound basis.

This was all done while the British were amassing troops and equipment to discourage the legally-elected representatives of the Irish people from ruling. An editorial in the June 10, 1919 *Freeman's Journal,* written to protest censorship and the increase of troops, described the city: "Last week Dublin quays were jammed with tanks, armoured cars, guns, motor lorries and thousands of troops, as if the port was the base of a formidable expeditionary force." A French journalist wrote, "The British administration could no longer succeed in governing Ireland, it could only prevent her governing herself." President de Valera said, "The British connection was maintained not by Ireland's choice but by England's force," and Count Plunkett tagged it as "Government with the dissent of the governed."[19]

In spite of the British efforts, the Republic was gaining in strength. It needed money urgently, however, and the indefatigable Michael Collins, as Minister of Finance, began to organize a National Loan. The British responded with a national raid. At the same time a proclamation was issued by the Lord Lieutenant which suppressed Sinn Fein, the Irish Volunteers, the Gaelic League, Cumann na mBan, and the Sinn Fein Clubs. "This is the first time in the history of the English in Ireland that they have risen to the height of proclaiming the elected representatives of Ireland a dangerous association and decreeing . . . the suppression of three-fourths of the elected representatives of the Irish people," the editor of *Nationality* wrote in its final issue. The republican papers were abolished after each had printed large ads explaining the Irish National Loan and the proclamation. Even General Macready admitted the folly of the ban: "As a result many moderate men were arrested merely because they were known to be in sympathy with the political views of the party, and consequently under a sense of injustice these men threw in their lot with the extremists."[20]

The Dail met once more that year, on October 27, 1919. By the time it reconvened in June, 1920, the war, which many Irish considered the British to have declared by the proclamation, had been intensified.

In the meantime the departments of the Dail functioned although every deputy was in constant danger of arrest. Madame, who was on the run along with the others, nevertheless continued her work in the labor ministry. Her department was now concerned mainly with setting up Conciliation Boards and arbitrating labor disputes. The Department had made surveys of various areas, and in an effort to promote stability, established guidelines for wages and food prices.

Madame maintained her connection with the Citizen Army, doing what she could to improve the education of the workers. She spoke at a meeting in the Trades Hall held under Socialist Party auspices to mark the second anniversary of the Bolshevik Revolution. Her idea of a Republic of Ireland was "a state run by the Irish people for the people. That means a Government that looks after the rights of the people before the rights of property. My idea is the Workers' Republic for which Connolly died."[21]

Her ideal was partially inspired by the social order of ancient Ireland, as described by AE in his popular *The National Being*, written just before the rebellion and published that year. AE held, with many others, that the basis of the social order of ancient Ireland, when the country flourished, was communal, built around clans. "The clan," he said, "was at once aristocratic and democratic. It was aristocratic in leadership and democratic in its economic basis. The most powerful character was elected as chief, while the land was the property of the clan. . . . It is by adopting a policy which will enable [this] to manifest once more that we will create an Irish civilization, which will fit our character as the glove fits the hand. . . . The communal character is still preserved [in the growing cooperative movement]. . . . A large part of our failure to achieve anything memorable in Ireland is due to the fact that, influenced by the example of our great neighbours, we reversed the natural position of the aristocratic and democratic elements in the national being. Instead of being democratic in our economic life, with the aristocracy of character and intelligence to lead us, we became meanly individualistic in our economics and meanly democratic in leadership. That is, we allowed individualism—the devilish doctrine of every man for himself—to be the keynote of our economic life; where, above all things, the general good and not the enrichment of the individual should be considered."[22]

Looking back on 1919, Arthur Koestler said, "Communism was a new word and it had the sound of a good, just, and hopeful word."[23] Madame may have been what he called himself, a "romantic Communist." She equated the word with democracy, cooperation, and industrious good will. "We're fighting for the working class," she said. "Call us what you like."

During December Madame's house was one of 188 which were raided, resulting in thirty-two arrests on political charges and nine deportations without any charge at all. Alderman Tom Kelly, T.D., who had headed the Labour department while Madame was in Cork jail, was one of the deportees. Two months later he was unanimously elected Lord Mayor of Dublin by Corporation members who were Sinn Fein, Labour, Unionist, and Independent. Dail Eireann headquarters were raided, and the Mansion House, official residence of the Lord Mayor, was occupied by troops. Even the Aonach, the annual Christmas trades fair, was suppressed. The conservative London *Times* admitted that "the authority of the British name in Ireland has come to rest upon military power," while the *Westminster Gazette* agreed, "Ireland is governed under a system of coercion such as there has not been within living memory."[24]

In two letters to her sister written just after the raids, Madame, who was still eluding the police, mentioned Alderman Kelly's arrest. "He always describes himself as a 'Man of Peace' & it is an admirable description." Again, "No one can understand why he was taken. He is a pacifist & never mixed up with anything violent. Housing of the poor, & building up industries was his line."

"Was it not lucky that I was away? I hear that Mrs. Clarke asked to see the warrant, & that the detective in charge said that there was none, she then asked what I was charged with & was told that they did not know, they had orders to arrest me & that was all. There were some police & a lorry load of soldiers. They searched the house to her great amusement—she made them look *everywhere* & waste a lot of time! If you see Cecil[25] you might try & inspire him to find out what awful crime I am charged with this time! Its enough to make any one curious. . . . It was wonderful, when you come to think how few were caught. Of course we are on the run most of the time & no one who respects themselves lives much in their homes.

"Wasn't it a shame to stop the Aonach? It is just a fair, & nothing more—you hire a stall & sell. Shopkeepers & industries count on making a nice few pounds & manufacturers hope to get Irish goods on the market through it. Its political to the extent that it is organized to help Irish Industry and trade to hold their own against English, German or any other foreign industries & agencies. It gets customers for the shops that are willing to put themselves out in their efforts to help their country's struggling industries. Of course this is treason, as the Enemy wish all Irish men & women to emigrate or starve. Mac-Pherson attributes all the trouble in Ireland to the stoppage of emigration during the war.

"I believe the 'English Enemie' are trying to goad us into another rebellion, so as to murder a large number of intelligent & brave patriots. Everything that is done points that way, but I hope that the country is too well in hand for anything of the sort to occur. The people are wonderfully steadfast under the most ridiculous persecution and provocation. No one knows at what moment they will be arrested on some vague charge, & any house may be raided at any moment. They were not afraid, & they have a great sense of humour. It gives them endless joy when they outwit the Hun, & vast & pompous military raids result in the arrest of a couple of harmless pacifists. I am going to keep quiet for a bit & then go about as usual, & dodge them, as there is so much to be done."

Soon after Christmas she wrote again, thanking Eva for a parcel. "I sent a hamper between the two of you I hope you got it alright. I had to get someone to choose the contents, as I was taking no risks before Xmas, I did so want to have one at liberty. . . . I had two Xmas dinners at the two extremes of Dublin, & quite a cheery time, everyone congratulating me on not having been at home."

She was undaunted by her new way of life. "Its awfully funny being on the run. I don't know whether I am most like the timid hare, the wily fox or a fierce wild animal of the jungle. I go about a lot, one way or another. Every house is open to me & every one is ready to help. I fly round town on my bike for exercise, & its too funny seeing the expression on the policemen's faces when they see me whizz by. There are very few women on bikes in the winter so a hunted beast on a bike is very remarkable."

The work of the Republic was progressing, that was the important thing. "Things are going ahead all right. . . . People are subscribing to the Loan in spite, or perhaps, because it has been made a jailable crime by the enemy."

Desmond Ryan, with clever, revealing phrases, drew a picture of Madame in those days: "William Norman Ewer of the *Daily Herald* had asked me to come to the Cafe Cairo to recover from a three days' controversy he had been conducting with Madame de Markievicz over the lunch table in a restaurant attached to Liberty Hall. Madame had attacked the *Daily Herald* as a monarchist sheet because it had mentioned the Prince of Wales and King George in the news columns, and sailed into the paper for not telling its readers to tear up railway lines and plant the Red Flag over the House of Commons. Ewer knit his brows until Madame proceeded to denounce several famous British pacifists and Labour leaders as hypocrites and double dealers. Whereupon to the joy of the whole restaurant Ewer opened fire upon Madame and told her what he thought of herself and her arguments with great force and candour and finally silenced her with his vehemence. This delighted Madame, who arrived the two following days in the hopes of converting so forceful and fiery a pacifist. The argument had somewhat exhausted Ewer so he asked me if I knew of a nice peaceful Cafe where he could smoke his pipe in safety from Madame de Markievicz for a day or so until he had thought of some argument which would silence her for ever. It had been a great battle between Madame and Ewer and he was being invested with a halo all unknown to himself as the only man who had ever laid out the Countess in argument. At first in the Cafe Cairo Ewer thought he had found his peaceful haven and he smoked his pipe so much at peace that he began to miss the fierce rhetoric and persistance of Madame."[26]

She was as sure as ever of her opinions, loved an argument, had no respect for rank or authority, and never gave a thought to tact. "I dont understand diplomacy," she wrote to her sister.

NOTES TO CHAPTER XII

1. In National Museum, Dublin.

2. Roper, *Prison Letters,* p. 297.

3. *The Voice of Labour,* Dublin, March 22, 1919.

4. Henry W. Nevinson, *Last Changes, Last Chances* (London, 1928), p. 168.

5. Alexandra Kollontay had been appointed Commissar for Social Welfare in the Soviet Cabinet on November 8, 1917, and for a short time before that Countess Panina had held the same post under Kerensky's premiership.

6. "They are no ordinary civil force, as police are in other countries. The R.I.C., unlike any other police force in the world, is a military body armed with rifle and bayonet and revolver as well as baton. They are given full licence by their superiors to work their will upon an unarmed populace" (Eamon de Valera in *Dail Eireann, Minutes of Proceedings 1919–1921* [Dublin, 1921], p. 67).

They were also the eyes and ears of the British. They lived in barracks scattered throughout the country and were a constant source of information to Dublin Castle on what was going on in each community—who were Sinn Fein members, who belonged to Fianna or Cumann na mBan, who attended Republican meetings, even who were praying against the English. At the beginning of the conscription fight, many R.I.C. went to the Novena every evening to observe and report what clergy and people were praying against conscription.

7. The committee of inquiry investigated the imprisonment of several other Republicans as well.

8. A brief statement prefacing the report of the Dail meeting for April 11, 1918, was testimony to the effectiveness of the Irish parliament: "The minutes of the Proceedings of this day were destroyed owing to enemy action." The official minutes had to rely on the press report published in *The Irish Independent.* That day the Dail recorded its support of the principles enunciated by President Wilson and the League of Nations, discussed the freedom of the seas, and reiterated Ireland's social policy in cooperating with Labor in trying to remedy the conditions under which the working people were living.

9. In a pre-election letter from Holloway to J. P. Dunne she wrote, "The whole economic position of Ireland has reduced our workers to such a terrible state of poverty and uncertainty that one bows in admiration to the splendid mothers. If ever I am free to come back to Ireland I will see you & consult with labour as to what I can best do to help Ireland do justice to her mothers in their great work" (in National Museum, Dublin).

10. Letter to Eva Gore-Booth, August 16, 1919.

11. *The Voice of Labour,* Dublin, January 11, 1919.

12. Ibid.

13. Fox, *Louie Bennett,* pp. 75–76.

14. *Treaty of Peace with Germany.* Hearing before the Committee on Foreign Relations, United States Senate, Sixty-sixth Congress. First Session. Part 17 (Washington, 1919), pp. 794–795. The information regarding the Commission's trip to Ireland is for the most part taken from this source, esp. pp. 775–800.

15. Failure of all plans for a hearing at the Peace Conference is apparent in a letter to Frank P. Walsh from Secretary of State Robert Lansing, the American Commissioner to Negotiate Peace. The pupose of the letter was to record the futility of efforts to obtain the safe-conducts, but it is also a refusal to recognize Ireland's claims: "Before your return to Paris, reports were received of certain utterances made by you and your colleagues during your visit to Ireland. These utterances whatever they may have been, gave, as I am informed, the deepest offense to those persons with whom you were seeking to deal and consequently it seemed useless to make any further effort in connection with the request which you desired to make. In view of the situation thus created, I regret to inform you that the American representatives feel that any further efforts on their part connected with this matter would be futile and therefore unwise" (letter dated May 24, 1919, ibid., p. 775).

16. Seth P. Tillman, *Anglo-American Relations at the Paris Peace Conference of 1919* (Princeton, 1961), p. 200.

17. Nora Connolly, "In Jail with Madame de Markievicz," *The Irish Citizen,* Dublin, September, 1919.

18. In June, 1915, Stanislas had left Dublin to visit his father, who was then convalescing in Russia. Count Markievicz had fought in the Carpathians the winter of 1914–15 where he had been wounded, and then he had been seriously ill with typhus. It had been a long-standing promise that Stanislas should go to his father's family when he finished school. He subsequently was an interpreter of English and French in the Russian Volunteer Fleet at Archangel on the White Sea.

19. Y. M. Goblet (Louis Treguiz), *L'Irlande dans la Crise Universelle 1914–1920* (Paris, 1921), p. 360, quoted by Macardle, *The Irish Republic,* p. 301; de Valera in Dail Eireann, May 9, 1919, *Dail Reports,* p. 84; Plunkett, quoted by Macardle, *The Irish Republic,* p. 350.

20. Macready, *Annals,* II, 437.

21. Sean McLoughlin presided and Cathal O'Shannon was the principal speaker. Tom Johnson spoke on the value of the cooperative movement, and Madame Markievicz voiced an appreciation of the educational work accomplished by the Bolsheviks and pointed out that an educated working class in Ireland was essential.

22. George William Russell, *The National Being, some thoughts on Irish polity, by AE* (London, 1925), pp. 125–126. Passages from this work are reprinted by permission of Diarmuid Russell.

23. Koestler, *Arrow in the Blue,* p. 63.

24. *Times* (London, December 16, 1919); *Westminster Gazette,* December 16, 1919.

25. Cecil L'Estrange Malone, Socialist M.P. He was their cousin and also the brother-in-law of Sir Josslyn, their brother. He was one of her relatives Madame was proud of.

26. Ryan, *Remembering Sion,* pp. 257–258.

XIII

Tactics of Terror

1920–June 1921

> Now days are dragon-riden, the nightmare
> Rides upon sleep: a drunken soldiery
> Can leave the mother, murdered at her door,
> To crawl in her own blood, and go scot-free;
> The night can sweat with terror as before
> We pieced our thoughts into philosophy,
> And planned to bring the world under a rule,
> Who are but weasels fighting in a hole.[1]

From 1919 to 1921 southern Ireland found itself in an outrageous paradox. In the name of democracy, law and order, the British forces used terrorism against Sinn Fein while the elected Irish representatives scrambled over rooftops and hid in cellars in order to carry on the ordinary business of their state.

Late in 1919 Sinn Fein initiated political action to increase its power through the municipal elections scheduled for January 15, 1920, when the system of proportional representation was to be used for the first time in Ireland. Although the system was introduced into Ireland in an attempt to undercut Republican interests, there was no opposition from Sinn Fein. When the proposal had been discussed at a public Ard Fheis in Dublin the preceeding April, Arthur Griffith, Eoin MacNeill, Madame, and President de Valera had all spoken in favor of it. They felt that the principle on which it was founded was sound and just. Sinn Fein had for years advocated its adoption, although the object for which it now was applied in Ireland was hostile to their interests. Their election campaign went on in spite of constant danger of arrest, raids, and reprisals. Much precious time was spent explaining the complicated balloting procedures.

Madame was interested in getting women to stand for muncipal office, but she found them reluctant, and in her own St. Patrick's she could not get a resident woman to put her name forward in either of the wards. A brief paragraph in a letter suggests some of the danger and excitement: "I spoke five times for various women in the elections & had some very narrow shaves. At one place I spoke they sent an army just about an hour too late. At another I wildly & blindly charged through a squad of armed police, there to arrest me, & the crowd swallowed me up & got me away. The children did the trick for me."

In that election eleven of the twelve cities and boroughs in Ireland declared their allegiance to the Republic: only Belfast remained Unionist. In Sligo, on February 1, 1920, the newly-elected T. H. Fitzpatrick was the first Mayor in Ireland to refuse the oath of allegiance to England or to take his seat as magistrate in the Borough Court.

The British ignored this Sinn Fein victory as they had ignored the result of the general election and continued to harass the Republicans. Madame wrote to her sister: "Its wonderful to have a birthday 'on the run' [she was 52]. Its an awfully funny experience. Mrs. C. will tell you some of it. Of course I dont keep quiet & the other night I followed the army of occupation round the streets, they had a huge covered waggon & they seized some fellows & put them inside & searched them. They charged the crowd with bayonets too, children were knocked down & terrified & women too.

"Shawn and some boys were held up by detectives last night when they were leaving the public library. One of them said that he thought that there was a detective watching the people reading, when two men stepped past them and poked revolvers at them from their pockets, in the American way, & said that they were talking of them, & demanded to know what they were saying. Of course they just humbugged, and the two men finally moved away."

A few weeks later another letter showed, briefly, signs of strain. "It is rather wearying when the English Man Pack are in full pack after you, though I get a good deal of fun out of it. Even the hunted hare must have a quiet laugh sometimes. You dont know what a joke it is to speak at meetings, & get through with it, in spite of their guns & tanks & soldiers & police. I had some very narrow shaves. The other night I knocked around with a raiding party & watched them insult the crowd. I was among the people & went right up to the Store St. Police Bk. where the Military and police lined up before going home. Night after night they wake people up, & carry off some one, they dont seem to mind who. Some of the people that they took lately did not belong to our crowd at all. When they could not find Mick Staines they took his old father (aged 60) & his baby brothers!"

Every day brought news of arrests and reprisals, but every day had its anecdotes and stories of escape and wit. "You had to joke or you'd go mad," the Irish said, so they joked. A favorite disguise of Madame's was that of a fragile old lady. Frank Robbins remembers a meeting of the Irish Citizen Army Council which "was in progress for some time when word came through to Madame Markievicz to leave Liberty Hall immediately as a raid was contemplated that night by the British authorities. James O'Shea and myself were given the job of seeing Madame safely out of the building, no matter what took place. When she was handed over to us we saw a very old woman, dressed in old fashioned clothes and wearing an old Victorian bonnet. Her make-up gave her the appearance of a feeble old lady anywhere between 75 and 80 years of age."

Nora Connolly recalled an excursion with her sister and a friend when Madame was in her favorite disguise. The two children hung on to Granny's arms, and off they went. At the busy corner of Talbot and O'Connell Streets, a policeman was on duty. Nora said, "I was too tense to do or say anything, but Madame played her part wonderfully. First she stepped off the pavement, and then she stepped back again. She dithered, and stepped off again, and again stepped hurriedly back. Finally the policeman took compassion on the poor old lady and started escorting her across O'Connell Street, his hand on her arm. The two young ones followed behind, their eyes wide as saucers. When they got to the other side, the policeman left her outside Nobletts, and he patted her on the shoulder as much as to say, 'You're all right now, Granny.' When I got across the street, I saw the unholy, mischievous glee in her eye, and her foot doing a little jig under her skirt. That was Madame for you."[2]

There are several variants of a story of Madame and a trunk. One version is that hearing of an impending raid, she hastily packed a small trunk full of her most incriminating papers, loaded it into a friendly cab, and with a friend drove around Dublin trying to think of a safe place for it. Finally she hit upon the idea of leaving it with a friend who owned a second-hand shop. He put the trunk on display in the front window with too high a price tag on it and there it remained in full view of the police until Madame deemed it safe for her to take it home again. It is said that the shop was across the street from a Black and Tan barracks.

She had need of her nerve and talent but these would have been worthless were it not for the public support of Sinn Fein. The Republican courts were successfully functioning in all parts of the country despite strenuous efforts of the British to prevent their convening. They had established a reputation for prompt, fair decisions, and all kinds of disputes involving people of all political affiliations (or none) were being brought to the courts for arbitration. Time after time the newspapers published accounts of the paucity of cases in the British courts, such as this description in the censored Irish press on March 3, 1920: "When Mr. Justice Dodd arrived in Longford for the Assizes, military in full equipment reinforced the police armed guard at the Judge's lodgings and sand bags were placed in the gateways adjoining the house and on the public thoroughfare. There were, however, no cases brought to the Assizes. His Lordship declared the county to be absolutely free from crime and was presented with the customary pair of white gloves."[3]

Meanwhile the Republican loan was being heavily subscribed in spite of efforts by the British to prevent it. In a subscription circular Madame stressed its importance and reminded her readers: "The people collecting it are in constant danger of imprisonment; those already arrested ungrudgingly pay the penalty and accept the suffering that comes to them in Ireland's cause. . . . On mutual trust and mutual help our Republic is being built up." The British were unable to find out where the funds were kept, even after they subpoenaed every bank manager in the city. When one of their most able detectives, Alan Bell, was sent to Dublin in March to spy out the location, he was shot within a month by Irish counter-intelligence agents under Michael Collins. Bell's death unleashed an unprecedented reign of terror and revenge which grew in momentum and fury, reprisals and counter-reprisals, suffering and destruction, until a truce was declared sixteen months later.

By January and February of 1920 there had been five thousand raids and over five hundred arrests, including sixty-four of the seventy-three Sinn Fein Members of Parliament elected at the last General Election. One had died in jail the year before, and of the eight who had not been imprisoned since the general release the previous March, six (including President de Valera, who was seeking recognition and funds in America) were in foreign countries, and two had been deported by the British without trial or charge.

In April, 1920, dozens of prisoners in Mountjoy went on a hunger strike which ended successfully after eleven days. Their freedom had been hastened by a general strike in Dublin. Despite popular support for the Republic, General Macready thought Sinn Fein extremists might have been suppressed at that time "if the Government had been able to withstand the clamour against the detention of men against whom no charges could be preferred and had been in a position to reinforce heavily the troops in Ireland."[4] Perhaps he was right. Larger populations than that in Ireland have been held in check by force and fear. But Sinn Fein could usually count on a certain ambivalence in the British attitude towards them. There were even signs of sympathy and some growing respect. By the spring of 1920, the numbers of men in the Royal Irish Constabulary had dwindled. Many of the outlying barracks had been closed for lack of personnel and it was deemed necessary to recruit reinforcements in England. Those available were mostly ex-soldiers who were too unruly or incompetent for humdrum civilian jobs or regular military service. To them the good pay and excitement in Ireland was appealing. The regulation dark-green, nearly black, uniform of the R.I.C. was in short supply, so they were fitted out in Army khaki and the R.I.C. cap and black leather belt. Soon they were known as the "Black and Tans."

General Macready, who arrived in Dublin in April as Commander-in-Chief of the Army, scorned them: "The majority of officers under whom they served belonged to the R.I.C. and had scant experience in handling the class of men who was enrolled, nor where discipline was concerned, had they as police officers the powers necessary to control the more turbulent spirits. . . . The somewhat feeble bonds of police discipline [being] loosened the men took the law into their own hands to an extent which in time gave cause for anxiety both to the Government and to those who were responsible for the force."[5]

Soon another, even more formidable force recruited from the unemployed ex-soldiery came to Ireland wearing rakish berets. For the most part these were former officers, superior in training, intelligence, and courage to the Black and Tans, even less controllable by their officers and given to greater excesses. They formed an Auxiliary force of a dozen companies whose members were called Cadets, inaccurately implying that they were young men in training. They sickened their own commander, Brigadier General Crozier, who wrote, "I held a camouflaged command as a policeman trying to do a soldier's job without the moral support afforded to soldiers in wartime. I resigned when I discovered the deception, for the Crown regime was nothing more or less than a Fascist dictation cloaked in righteousness."[6] General Macready thought they were a discredit to the whole force. Oddly enough, some of the Irish fighters had a grudging respect for the wild daring of the Auxiliaries who left many a mangled corpse behind.

Many of these Auxiliaries and Tans stare out from the old photographs like frightened, sullen boys. In England they might have formed into gangs that would have been the despair of Scotland Yard. In Ireland they were the law armed with rifles, bayonets, and revolvers, and by degrees provided with more motor transport and armored cars than the army. They careened through the countryside spreading terror.

There were in Ireland, in addition to the 20,000 police, another 20,000 regular army personnel (forty battalions and seven cavalry regiments), most of whom had the reputation of being decent professionals. Even this combined force was considered too weak for the work required of it, in spite of unlimited supplies of arms, ammunition, and transport. Therefore the military were empowered to arrest any Irishman without evidence and intern him with impunity.

The Lord Lieutenant thought there were at least 100,000 Sinn Feiners. It is difficult to find exact figures, but there were probably 15,000 at most in active service, though these were supported by hundreds of thousands of sympathizers.[7]

What remained a problem through the War of Independence was arms supply. Against the strength of the British forces in County Cork in May, 1921 (12,600 fully equipped men), Tom Barry said, "The I.R.A. in Cork never had more than 310 riflemen in the field at any time for the very excellent reason that this was the total of rifles held by the combined three Cork Brigades. The only other I.R.A. arms (excluding shotguns) within the county were five machineguns and some 350 automatics and revolvers. Even this small force could hardly be mobilised for a major operation likely to continue for a day, as its ammunition did not exceed fifty rounds a rifle, two fills per revolver and automatic, and a few full drums for each machinegun."[8]

One effective way of hampering the movement of British troops was the refusal of Transport Union members to work on trains carrying armed men or to handle military stores. The boycott started in May, 1920, lasted for six months, and was credited with seriously slowing military activities during the best season of the year. The work at the docks fell upon fatigue parties of soldiers, and much of the motor transport which should have been employed on tactical work had to be diverted to supplying stations which had been cut off by the railway strike.

Sinn Fein also had a superb intelligence system, brilliantly organized by Michael Collins. Although all Ireland still seemed to live under the microscope of Dublin Castle as it had in the past, now there were Sinn Fein spies in the Castle, and very little escaped scrutiny by Collins and his staff. "If they are clever," wrote Madame to President de Valera in May, 1920, "we can always manage to go one better."⁹

It was a strange cloak-and-dagger time. In mid-May Dail Eireann members received letters threatening their lives, perhaps part of a plan designed to pass off as a Sinn Fein outrage the future murder of the leaders. Madame wrote about it to Dr. Patrick McCartan, who had just returned to the United States after a brief trip to Dublin to report on progress in America. Her letter was dated May 16, 1920: "I was sorry not to see you again before you left, but it was wiser to run no unnecessary risks, & I was receiving a considerable amount of attention & once or twice had considerable difficulties in escaping from a too assiduous 'follower.'

"My latest news regarding myself is that I have just received what is commonly called a 'Death Notice from the Black Hand gang in the Police.' On the paper that they had taken the precaution to steal from us they had typed

> 'An Eye for an Eye
> A tooth for a tooth
> Therefore a life for a Life'

I think there is no doubt that they are plotting to murder us, and before doing so they are taking precautions to manufacture evidence to prove that we assassinated each other! No action is too mean & low for the Present government & its officials. Luckily we are not nervous, & have the strength to go on just the same as before. One is a little more careful to try & be ready to die & that is all.

"We held our Fianna aeritact on Sunday, the annual commemoration of our Fianna Martyrs, & it was a tremendous success.

"There are great military preparations going on here. Motor lorries rolling every where full of soldiers, & great loads of bedding etc. being carted off towards the Dublin mountains from Terenure. No doubt they meditate the reconquest of Ireland."

Enclosed with her letter to Dr. McCartan was an account of a bicycle trip and picnic in the Dublin hills, entitled "An Interlude."

It was reminiscent of the gardening notes she wrote for *Bean na hEireann,* where every natural beauty reminded her of perfidious Albion. In the colors of an Irish spring, gold, white, and green, she saw nature flinging defiance at Ireland's enemies and hanging out bravely her floral tricolor. "The hills have watched Dublin bay and seen her enemies come and go, as they will watch over Ireland's peace long after the iron might of the stranger is broken." More than a year of intensified struggle and pain remained before there would be a brief respite from war but Madame's hyperbole held an element of truth. On May 1, 1920, *The Irish Times* reported, "The forces of the Crown are being driven back on their headquarters in Dublin. . . . The King's government has virtually ceased to exist south of the Boyne and west of the Shannon."

Throughout 1920 British politicians in Whitehall discussed a Government of Ireland Bill with solemn and unconscious irony. The bill provided for two parliaments, one for the twenty-six counties of the south and one for the six counties of the north. They would be linked by a joint council but with some important powers reserved for the British Parliament. Ultimately the bill was a weapon with which Sinn Fein could not cope. Passage of the Act in December, 1920, definitely partitioned the national territory and led to the establishment of the Government of Northern Ireland in June, 1921. Asquith said the bill "was passed for the purpose of giving to a section of Ulster a Parliament which it did not want, and to the remaining three-quarters of Ireland a Parliament which it would not have."[10]

While Republicans in Ireland were fighting the proposed bill, with flamboyant bias Madame expressed her views in an article she wrote for Dr. W. J. Maloney in New York: "This Home Rule Bill is surely the climax of all the Hypocritical legislature that the English government have ever devised. It is produced at this moment because England considers it absolutely necessary to try and convince the world that she is sincere in her support of the principle of self-determination. But the last thing she wants is to confer any power on Ireland, that might allow that country to become prosperous, populated and united. So this Bill for the better subjection of Ireland is termed a Home Rule Bill, though it contains little or no powers of ruling the Home.

"All ultimate Powers under this bill are vested in a Viceroy and a Privy council who are merely servants of the English Cabinet. We are not to be allowed to hold our own purse strings, nor have we the power to foster our own industries, trade and commerce. £18,000,000 of our money will continue to go to England for England's debts. The export of money is always followed by the export of the population, so by their huge tribute of money English ministers know that they can maintain the usual flow of emigrants.

"We are not allowed to keep order in our own country. The English army of occupation will continue to terrorise, murder, insult and rob our people. English controlled police will still coerce us. We are still to be judged by English appointed judges. All the objectionable tyrannies that we suffer under will remain in force. Men and women will still get penal servitude for daring to speak out against the military and police government; little boys will still be locked up for 'whistling derisively at the police.'

"The result of our acceptance of this bill, in the event of it being forced on us has been carefully calculated. Under Proportional Representation the Southern Parliament will contain a much larger percentage of Imperialists. The English military authority, who will still continue to be the real ruler of Ireland, would then imprison a large quota of the Republican M.P.'s and by this means secure a majority of Imperialists in both Parliaments. Thus would be brought into being an elected talking house that could be counted on by the English Cabinet to misrepresent the aspirations and deny the rights of the majority of the Irish people.

"To create a so called representative body in Ireland that will seal her doom, acquiesce in her subjection and deny her rights has ever been England's policy. The so called 'Union' was achieved after this fashion. Every board that has been created in Ireland—since the Union has been created on the same lines. To collect taxes for England to spend has ever been our privilege, to work for her and to fight for her the lot of our impoverished People. This Bill is backed by Ireland's bitterest enemies. It is opposed by all lovers of Ireland. The people will never accept it and it is hard to see how it can be forced on us against the united opinions of the whole nation."[11] Her article was carried to New York by a friend; it probably would never have passed the censor otherwise. In her accompanying letter to Dr. Maloney, Madame complained that quite harmless letters to her sister had been stopped, including letters about publishing Miss Gore-Booth's poems in America.

Censorship was widespread, and one of the great difficulties was getting news out of Ireland. An *Irish Bulletin,* mimeographed and sent to newspapers and influential men and women abroad, was the only record of the atrocities being committed. Under huge difficulties the *Bulletin* staff managed to produce a daily sheet containing verified, detailed facts. It was (and is) the major source of information about what was happening in Ireland. "From first to last the people of Great Britain were ignorant of the real facts of the situation as it existed in Ireland from 1919 onwards."[12]

On June 29, 1920, the Dail met for the first time since October. In his opening statement, the Acting President, Arthur Griffith, noted the great difficulties being encountered and supposed that no Ministry ever existed that did so much work under similar difficulties. He thought their greatest achievements had been the establishment of the Land Bank, which had enabled them to settle the land crisis that arose in the West of Ireland; the Land Arbitration Courts, which prevented the use of the land question to divert the energies of the people from the National issue; and work done by the Industrial Commission. The most extraordinary feat of all had been accomplished by the Minister for Finance, Michael Collins. He had issued a loan of £250,000 which was over-subscribed by £40,000 in spite of the most determined opposition of England.[13]

Madame also attended the next two Dail sessions, August 6 and September 17, 1920, at which the Ministers reported continuing accomplishments in the face of increased opposition.[14] Not only were there more arrests and reprisals against individuals, but the British were reviving their ancient policy of striking at the struggling economic life of the country. Co-operative creameries, mills, and bacon factories were systematically burned.

More and more Irishmen were resigning from the police in protest against the outrages. As Minister of Labour, Madame did what she could to help them, appealing to local Sinn Fein clubs to give them every opportunity to live as good Irish citizens in their native districts. In cases of hardship, she tried to find them jobs or assisted their families from a special fund.

On September 26, 1920, a week after the last Dail meeting, Madame was arrested and held in Mountjoy for several weeks before charges of any kind were preferred against her. Near midnight, a car going through Rathmines was forced to halt. It was driven by Sean Mac-Bride and had three passengers: Madame, a French writer, Maurice Bourgeois, and a stranger who had missed the last tram and was walking home when they gave him a ride. All of them were arrested and taken to Bridewell. Robert Brennan wrote about Bourgeois in Ireland:

"Maurice Bourgeois had come over from Paris ostensibly to collect material for the French War Museum and incidentally to write a few articles for a French newspaper. In reality, though we did not know this till later he was an agent for the French Government and his mission was to observe the Irish scene in the interests of France. . . . When he arrived, Bourgeois was rather hostile to Sinn Fein. The memory of 1916 still rankled. The Rising had been a stab in the back for the Allies. I was supplying him with all the material I could get for his War Museum and I saw him constantly." Bourgeois told Brennan that after his arrest "they threw me into a filthy cell and when I protested, several bullies in uniform threatened to beat me up and shoot me. When I produced my diplomatic passport, they said they were about to provide me with a passport to hell and they reviled France and the French people in the most revolting language."

Brennan remarked on the Frenchman's volte-face: "It was two days before Bourgeois managed to get word of his plight to the French Consul and secure his release. When I met him he was still white with rage over the treatment he had received. He had ceased to be anti-Sinn Fein. Indeed, he became one of our stoutest champions."[15]

Madame reported her arrest to Miss Gore-Booth, who was vacationing in Italy: "Just got a postcard from you, forwarded from L[iberty] Hall, which wonders—most appropriately—what I am doing! It must have been written somewhere about the time that I was layed by the heels again. It was very bad luck. I went for a weekend holiday with Sean & the motor car he was driving broke down all the time! We had to spend Saturday night at a place somewhere among the Dublin Mountains, I at a farm house, he & a French journalist at an inn. Coming back the same thing happened. Engines, horn & lamps all being out of order. The Police pulled us up because of the tail lamp not being there, asked for permit—he had none, so they got suspicious, & finally lit a match in my face & phoned for military. All the Kings horses & all the Kings men arrived with great pomp, & many huge guns & after a weary night in Police station, I found myself here on Remand, till to quote their own words, they 'decide' whether they shall bring a charge against me or not! It sounds comic opera, but its the truth."

The ten weeks Madame was on remand were uncertain and gloomy. She could not paint in Mountjoy, she had a limited number of visitors, mail was restricted, she was not sure her letters were getting through. Although she insisted she was well and cheerful, her handwriting during these weeks was small and cramped, only faintly resembling her usual strong and sprawling hand. She was studying Irish but found it difficult without a teacher or anyone to talk with. Eventually this self-imposed duty became a pleasure and she felt she was making some progress, although she complained of the textbooks. "I wish I knew why Grammarians always search the world or dictionaries for the words you want least in a language & give them you to learn, & leave out the words that you want every day. I can talk about hawks & flails, scythes, rye & barley, magicians, kings & fairies; but I couldn't find out how to ask for an extra blanket or a clean plate or a fork. I suppose I shall find out some day."

While Madame was in Mountjoy the tempo of the fight outside increased. Day after day the *Irish Bulletin* published authenticated statistics of British excesses, and foreign journalists began to come to Ireland to see for themselves. Gradually, uncensored information filtered out. Two or three dramatic incidents which symbolized the struggle caught the imagination of the world and focused sympathy on Ireland's struggle.

One of these was the death of Terence MacSwiney, Lord Mayor of Cork, on the seventy-fourth day of a hunger strike, October 25, 1920. MacSwiney had been arrested on August 12 while presiding at a meeting at the City Hall in Cork. His court-martial charge was that he was "in possession of documents the publication of which would be likely to cause disaffection to His Majesty." He and the ten men who were arrested with him went on hunger strike in protest against the continual arrests of public representatives. On the third day of the prisoners' refusal of food, MacSwiney was separated from the rest and taken to England and Brixton Jail.

Two months later, on October 17, Michael Fitzgerald, one of the prisoners in Cork, died. Commandant of the 1st battalion of the 2nd Cork Brigade, he had been remanded time and time again without a trial. MacSwiney somehow lingered on as the world watched with growing respect and compassion—65 days, 66, 67, 68. . . . It seemed incredible that any man could hold so tenaciously to life without food, only strength of will. He starved seventy-four days, until October 25. Within several hours of his death, another of the Cork prisoners died, Michael Murphy, a twenty-two-year-old native of Lynn, Massachusetts.

Thousands of Londoners watched a procession of honor carry MacSwiney's tricolor-draped coffin through the streets accompanied by uniformed Volunteers and other Irish men and women. The day of his burial in Cork, October 31, was one of public mourning.

The day after MacSwiney's funeral, Kevin Barry, an eighteen-year-old medical student, was hanged in Mountjoy. He had been taken prisoner after participating in an ambush of an armed party of British soldiers. In the melee six soldiers were shot, one fatally. Although there was no evidence that Barry had killed him (indeed, one of the I.R.A. men present wrote that Barry's gun had jammed, and that while he concentrated on trying to fix it, the fight ended and he was trapped). He was tortured for information before he was court-martialled but revealed nothing.

General Crozier, whose duty it was to supply a party of Auxiliaries to watch over "the lad in the prison cell" during his last hours, was deeply moved by Barry's courage. He did not whine, he was proud of dying for an ideal, for the freedom of Ireland. "In Ireland, as no hangman could be found to hang Barry, we had to bring one all the way from England, in disguise and in great secrecy. He came three hundred miles across the sea, surreptitiously, to hang a rebel murderer. Or—he came three hundred miles across the sea, surreptitiously, to hang a soldier of Ireland. You see, so much depends on one's point of view."[16]

Three weeks later, on Sunday morning, November 21, fourteen British spies were shot in Dublin. Retaliation was prompt. There was an important football match at Croke Park that afternoon and the grandstands were filled. Suddenly the Black and Tans appeared and began indiscriminate firing at the crowd of spectators. In the panic which followed hundreds were injured, and when the firing stopped twelve men and women had been shot to death (including one of the players), while another sixty were wounded. Accounts of the actual shooting time usually vary from ten to twenty minutes. Madame, who could hear the noise from Mountjoy, said, "The Croke Park affair lasted 40 minutes by my watch, & there were machine guns going, it felt like being back in the middle of Easter week. Croke Park is quite close. Its a miracle that so few were killed."

That night, three I.R.A. men, including the Commandant and Vice-Commandant of the Dublin Brigade, were killed in the guard room at Dublin Castle. According to the official report they were "shot while trying to escape," though their bodies showed they had been beaten to death. This official phrase, commonly used in Ireland at the time, was later taken from the British and used by Nazi Germany. Many of the techniques of Fascist terrorism were developed by the Black and Tans in Ireland.

Considering the hysteria of such warfare, Madame was treated lightly. By the end of November it was decided that the charge to be brought against her was of organizing the Fianna in 1909. Her court-martial was held at the Royal Barracks in Dublin on Thursday and Friday, December 2 and 3, 1920, more than eleven years after the first meeting of the Fianna in Lower Camden Street. Madame Mac-Bride, Dr. Lynn, Mrs. Sheehy Skeffington, and Henry Nevinson were among her friends who were there, but she could not greet them. Photographers were ordered to hand over the plates of pictures they had taken. Madame, as was the custom of the Republicans, refused to recognize the court on the grounds it was "not constituted legally, not being based on the authority and will of the people of Ireland, but on the armed force of the enemies of the Irish Republic." Evidence was based on a box of Fianna literature found in a raid in September at 26 Nassau Street, where Eamon Martin was living.

The second day of the trial was Madame's. "In the interests of justice, and without prejudice to her non-recognition of the court," she put some questions to the witnesses. She was unsuccessful in getting the prosecutor to define "conspiracy," but she closely cross-examined the witnesses. She focused on statements made by the arresting officers which she thought reflected on her good name. She indignantly disavowed the allegation that she was responsible for the shooting of a policeman who arrested her on one occasion. Ever since Easter Week, she said, terrible things had been put into her mouth that she never had an opportunity to repudiate. "I am willing to sacrifice everything to Ireland except my good name."[17]

To her sister in Italy, she wrote simply: "I suppose now that I can tell you that I was tried by courtmartial for conspiracy, & that the conspiracy was the boy Scouts. They have not made up their minds yet what they'll do with me. I think that they dislike me more than most. The whole thing is Gilbertian, for we have carried on for 11 years. Anyhow its a fresh 'ad' for the boys!" Some of her high spirits and impertinence towards officialdom came out when she commented, "Tell me, do the Italians go in for polished brown leather boots & gaiters? The legs of the English army of occupation was one of the things that struck me profoundly at my courtmartial. Such a lot of time must be wasted polishing them!"

At Christmas she was still waiting sentence and remarked again how Gilbertian the British were to pretend that the Fianna, which was always open, was a conspiracy. "I asked them could they point to one 'cowardly attack' on the armed forces of the Crown by little boys. It was an awful performance; after being shut up alone for two months to be suddenly brought before 8 'judges' plus, prosecutors bewigged barristers, enemy witnesses etc., & surrounded by bayonets it was very bewildering. I'm glad you thought I did not do too badly."

Finally at the New Year she was informed that her sentence was two years' hard labor. Her only comment to her sister was, "It rather amused me to see that for starting boy Scouts in *England* B. Powell was made a baronet! . . . I bet he did not work as hard as I did from 1909 till 1913." She signed this letter "Cheerful though captive."

After the trial her letters seemed more spirited; she had recovered her irrepressible optimism. "Don't bother about me here. As you know the English ideal of modern civilisation always galled me. Endless relays of exquisite food & the eternal changing of costume bored me always to tears, & I prefer my own to so many peoples company. To 'make conversation' to a bore through a long dinner party is the climax of dullness. I dont mind hard beds or simple food none of what you might call the externals worry me. I have my health & I can always find a way to give my dreams a living form. So I sit & dream, & build up a world of birds & butterflies & flowers from a sheen in a dew drop or the flash of a sea-gulls wing. Everyone who has anything to do with me is considerate & kind, & the only bore is being locked up when there is so much to be done."

Attacks on civilians had continued with increasing ferocity during those last months of 1920. Of 203 fatalities during the year, 26 were in October, 64 in November, and 50 in December. None of these occurred in any kind of armed conflict. The *Irish Bulletin*'s statistical analysis showed that 98 were killed in indiscriminate or unprovoked firing by the military and constabulary during the year; 36 were assassinated while in prison; 69 were shot in their beds or on the street.

As Madame waited in her cell and dreamed, the public in England began to shudder awake to what was happening across the Irish Sea. "Britishers grew increasingly ashamed, as the facts became known, of the deeds done in their name. Day after day C. P. Scott in the *Manchester Guardian* insisted that Englishmen wished to do justice to Ireland and were 'resolved in the process to keep their hands decently clean and their reputation in the world unsullied. That is where Mr. George is failing us.' "[18] Asquith also opposed the stupidity of the

Black and Tan policy and demanded dominion home rule, declaring that even the Unionists eventually saw that the reprisals in Ireland were useless.[19]

There were to be more errors of judgment in Ireland before the Truce was declared in the summer of 1921. On December 9, 1920, martial law was proclaimed over the counties of Cork, Kerry, Tipperary, and Limerick, and later extended to Clare, Waterford, Kilkenny, and Wexford. "Official punishments" came into force in these areas, including confiscations, fines, and the destruction of houses and property of any persons who might be considered to be implicated in or have knowledge of any attacks against the Crown forces—ambushes, attacks on barracks, or any other action. The soldiers did not have to have evidence; they could destroy and arrest on the flimsiest suspicion.

Such extravagant license immediately prompted the Auxiliaries to set fire to Cork. On the night of December 11–12, most of the downtown shopping area and the City Hall were burned. The fire was attributed to natural causes in the censored press which Madame read in Mountjoy. "I suppose you saw all about Cork, also the explanations. Some men have a wonderful capacity for lying! [The last word is censored but legible.] What puzzles me is why they dont do it better. For instance, it was so silly to assert that the City Hall caught fire from Patrick St. I know the city well, & a broad river & many streets lie between the two areas. An ordinary human being like myself is puzzled when the cleverest liars [censored but legible] in the world state things that are so easily contradicted. The extraordinary policy of lying & perjury surprises me anew every day. I'd no idea people were so bad."[20]

Elections under the Government of Ireland Act took place in May, 1921. Sinn Fein had spoken out against the Act, as had Madame to Dr. Maloney, which was a definite step towards effective partition of Ireland, but it had passed on December 23, 1920. Elections for the Northern Parliament were held on May 24, elections for the twenty-six counties on May 19, 1921. By a decision of Dail Eireann, the latter were declared to be elections to the Dail and no contests took place in any constituency. One hundred twenty-four Sinn Fein candidates and four Unionists (Trinity College) were returned unopposed.[21]

Madame, who was allowed visitors and newspapers at Mountjoy, had a fairly good idea what was going on. She sometimes commented briefly on events at home and abroad in her letters. She saw hope in India: "I see that Volunteers have been 'proclaimed' according to the papers, & they don't do that for nothing. Ours were only proclaimed about a year & 3 months ago." But she was unimpressed by the League of Nations and in that same letter (December 15, 1920) wrote, "How one longs for peace. The silly old League of Nations is talking pompous rubbish (for the benefit of democracy, I suppose) about reduction of armaments, & each one of them is only intent on finding out what his neighbour is going to do in the way of navies etc. & tip his boss to go one better."

In April, 1921, "Italy certainly fills one with hope, Greece too & Poland. We are the only people left in chains. Our people are wonderful & there is little fear of death among them. Heaven is so real to them, that they look forward to meeting their friends there. The present persecutions [censored but readable] seem to have brought the living & the dead into such close touch, its almost uncanny; it all makes one feel that we must win; the spiritual must prevail over the material in the end; we suffer, & suffering unites us & teaches us to stand by each other; it also makes for us friends everywhere, while the policy of our enemies is leaving them friendless, & more ominous still, it is utterly demoralising themselves & setting all the decent of their own people against them as soon as they find out the truth.

"A volley has just gone off somewhere quite close, it has ceased to be a novelty, or to make one jump, but it is a dreadful bore not to be able to go & see whats up. Most nights one hears them, to me its a wonder that more people are not killed. There were aeroplanes over yesterday, which is usually a bad omen."

Madame continued her study of Irish, but her greatest joy was her garden. She was given permission to work on a bit of prison ground and soon transformed it. Her letters in the spring reflect her renewed interest: "I grub away at my plot here, & have got quite a lot of little things in, it was a desert when I began, & I dont think it had ever been honestly dug, few people share my love for digging deep. I have a few sweet peas quite four inches high, which is a triumph, most people are only sowing them. The eating peas are just coming up & the starlings and pigeons make war on everything." Just being able to dig in the Irish soil she loved was a pleasure and she passed some of the prison hours happily. By the first of May she could report that "my garden work is beginning to repay. Peas are 6 inches high, & new seeds are coming up every day. We've had a spell of fearfully dry weather & a scorching sun, but today we had a nice soft rain, & the sun is now shining again, so the garden will be great tomorrow."

In April, Father Sweetman visited Madame bringing a gift from her sister, a green and silver rosary which had been blessed by the Pope, Benedict XV. Miss Roper and Miss Gore-Booth were visiting George and Margaret Gavan Duffy in Rome, where he was the Irish envoy. At the urging of their friends they went to an audience at the Vatican. The Pope passed around the room giving his blessing, and when he came to Miss Gore-Booth she spoke to him in rapid Italian of her sister's danger and asked him to bless the rosary. He listened carefully to all she said and gave the blessing.

To a friend, T. P. Conwell-Evans, Miss Gore-Booth wrote from Bordighera that spring of 1921. "Con is very gay as usual." And a little later: "I just got a prison letter from Constance, all over printed regulations about not using slang and being respectable and keeping up with your respectable friends. Anyway she sent you a long message, which I will give you before I forget. I was to say how glad she was to hear from you, and 'tell Mr. Evans not only do I remember him for himself, but I remember him for Debussy, to whom he introduced me. How I'd love to hear some more, I've never heard any since.' " Miss Gore-Booth went on to say that she thought she was herself under suspicion: "Great international developments. Most mysterious people turned up yesterday, and very rough-looking men smoking large cigars, and lurking on the balcony, listening to our conversations about Con, etc. They had diplomatic passports, and if they weren't politicians doing themselves proud, they were Black and Tans on a peaceful mission, looking for trouble."[22]

Prime Minister Lloyd George had written President de Valera (who had returned to Ireland from the United States in December, 1920) on June 24, 1921, suggesting a conference with a view to peace. During the next weeks several letters had passed between the Mansion House and 10 Downing Street. A truce between the British Army and the Irish Army was effective from July 11, and President de Valera was in London on July 14 for a conference with the Prime Minister. Ireland rejoiced.

Early in July, Madame wrote, "I wish you could see my rock garden, its beginning to be quite interesting with little stairs up & down & paths, & a sort of obelisk at the top. A most obliging warder, who was bringing me stones offered to get a huge rock put on the top of it, so I made a flat 'plateau' with a stairway up to it, & he got the two rocks hoisted up. Unluckily the weather is too dry for anything to be planted, once it begins to rain I shall make heaps of cuttings & cover it with things."

The ferocity of the war had intensified during the nine months she had been at Mountjoy, but explosions, gunfire, and violence had become a way of life in Ireland, and Madame reported calmly to her sister that as she was writing, "There's an ambush going on outside this, we often hear them, & its most tantalising not to be able to see. I never saw one, & I should love to! We heard a great explosion one day & saw dark columns of smoke, it was very exciting!" Then she went on to talk about what she had been reading—Gavan Duffy's *My Life in Two Hemispheres,* about which she was more excited than the unseen ambush. Surprisingly, there was no hint that she knew of the peace overtures being made.

Her release came suddenly. At three o'clock Sunday afternoon, July 24, she was informed by the prison governor that she was free to leave. The next day she met with President de Valera and other members of the Dail. Her rock garden in Mountjoy remained uncompleted.

NOTES TO CHAPTER XIII

1. Yeats, "Nineteen Hundred and Nineteen," *Collected Poems,* p. 233.
2. Nora Connolly O'Brien, *Sunday Press* (Manchester), October 30, 1960. Her disguise also fooled those who knew her. Joe Reynolds remembers a Fianna Executive meeting interrupted by the secret ring of the doorbell. When he answered, he saw only an old woman. He asked "this oul' wan" what she wanted, and an unmistakable voice said gaily, "Tally, didn't you recognize me?" She could not disguise her accent.
3. Quoted in *Irish Bulletin,* March 5, 1920.
4. Macready, *Annals,* II, 459.
5. Ibid., 481.
6. Frank Percy Crozier, *The Men I Killed* (New York, 1938), p. 109.
7. Estimates vary, but the I.R.A. was probably at its largest in the autumn of 1921, when, Major Florence O'Donoghue estimated, the total in all ranks was 112,650. Not all were active (*No Other Law,* Dublin, 1954, p. 219).
8. Tom Barry, *Guerrilla Days in Ireland* (Cork, 1955); also quoted in *Rebel Cork's Fighting Story* (Tralee, n.d.), p. 206.
9. Letter in Sligo Museum.
10. Spender and Asquith, *Life of Asquith,* II, 333.
11. Maloney collection, New York Public Library.
12. Macready, *Annals,* II, 468.
13. Collins was extremely effective in two important jobs, either of which would have tried most men. As Minister for Finance in the Dail cabinet he directed the Republican loan and established Sinn Fein banks. As Director of Organisation of the Republican Army, he set up the remarkable espionage

system which operated with increasing efficiency throughout the War for Independence. Therefore, in his political role under Sinn Fein he was in control of the Republic's money, in his military role under the I.R.A., in control of its intelligence.

The term I.R.A. (Irish Republican Army) was never officially adopted by the Irish Volunteers but it soon came into common usage. The connotations of terminology were important to those who made appellative distinctions. Piaras Beaslai, for example, briefly discussed "the curious title I.R.A." in his biography of Michael Collins. "Strictly speaking this popular name had no justification. The official title of the body so designated was always 'Ogláigh na h-Eireann,' or, in English, the 'Irish Volunteers.' On the election of Dail Eireann, however, which the Volunteers recognised as the lawful authority in the country, and the submission of their control to a Minister of Defense elected by the Dail, 'An tOglách' began to refer to the Volunteers as 'the Army of the Irish Republic,' and this phrase became popularly transmuted into 'Irish Republican Army' (a very different thing), and regularly abbreviated to 'I.R.A.'" (I, 377).

14. Irish cooperation against the British had become so effective that by August, 1920, the wartime Defense of the Realm regulations (D.O.R.A.) were no longer considered sufficient and a special bill just short of martial law was promulgated. Military courts were empowered to try persons for treason, treason felony, felony and other lesser offenses. Military courts of inquiry replaced coroners' inquests, and at the application of the prosecutor the public was excluded from the courts.

The Women's International League for Peace and Freedom was one of many groups which sent investigating committees to Ireland to try to ascertain what conditions there really were. In October, 1920, their report was issued, with figures of lawlessness, murder, arrests, and coercion. Their conclusion was similar to that of many other reports issued at the time: "To a degree never witnessed by any of us, it is possible to say that Dail Eireann governs with the consent of the people. Although members of the Government are proscribed, their Courts pronounced illegal, and their revenue forfeit, one can truly say that without them Ireland would be given over to sheer anarchy."

15. Brennan, *Allegiance*, pp. 274–275.

16. Crozier, *Men I Killed*, pp. 111–112.

17. *The Sligo Champion*, December 11, 1920, had an extensive account of the proceedings.

18. Thomas Jones, *Lloyd George* (London, 1951), p. 189.

19. "These were the darkest days for Liberalism which I have ever known" (Spender and Asquith, *Life of Asquith*, II, 369).

20. The results of the subsequent official inquiry were never made public, although, in General Macready's words, "it was no secret in the town as to who were the culprits . . . the Auxiliary Division R.I.C." (*Annals*, II, 522). An inquiry was made by the Sinn Fein organization and sworn statements were collected from nearly one hundred witnesses, including Americans and Englishmen, as well as many local persons who were not Republicans. Major O'Donoghue said, "This evidence was detailed and specific and was so overwhelmingly conclusive that no doubt could remain in the mind of any reasonable person

but that the city of Cork had been deliberately burned by the British Army of Occupation on that night" (*Rebel Cork's Fighting Story,* p. 126).

21. The mind which saw the 1916 rebellion as a "diversion" still refused to take Ireland's independence aspirations seriously and regarded the situation as a joke. "Where," asked General Macready, "could open rebellion, martial law, peace proposals, and a General Election be all running side by side at one and the same time? And yet no Irishman or politician seemed to see anything funny about it! Perhaps the simple-minded soldier is easily amused, and certainly we were over in Ireland" (*Annals,* II, 548).

22. Eva Gore-Booth, *Poems,* ed. Esther Roper, pp. 92–93.

XIV

The Treaty

July 1921–June 1922

Shortly after she was released from Mountjoy, Madame wrote, "It is so heavenly to be out again and to be able to shut and open doors. It is almost worth while being locked up, for the great joy release brings. Life is so wonderful. One just wanders round and enjoys it. The children and the trees and cows and all common things are so heavenly after nothing but walls and uniformed people." British lorries were rumbling back into their barracks and young I.R.A. men were returning from the hills and sauntering through their villages. Much of Ireland shared her relief. The months of the Truce were generally happy and full of hope.

Freed from the necessity of secrecy and scrambling over rooftops, Madame's Ministry went to work swiftly. From February, 1921, the Labour Department organized an economic boycott of Belfast as a protest against tests of political and religious beliefs which were often made conditions of employment there. The boycott had high moral motives; unfortunately, it emphasized the dichotomy between Belfast and Dublin when north and south should have been working together.

However, her department did excellent work in labor relations, working closely with the unions and hearing disputes through a system of conciliation boards. Among the several arbitrators were Darrell Figgis, Ernest Blythe, Minister of Trade, Tom Kelly, Lord Mayor of Dublin, and Sean Moylan, Commandant of the Cork 2 Brigade, who complained of the increasing paper work: "We started the war with hurleys, and, by God, we'll finish it with fountain pens."

The Ministry's activities covered a broad field, including agricultural disputes involving the harvest bonus on several farms, disagreements in factories, offices, and stores. Even where the authority of the Dail was not officially recognized, cases were arbitrated by the Republican boards. Madame's pride in the accomplishments of her department showed in her December report: "On September 15th the Tyrone Co. Council, which has not yet severed relations with the British Local

Government Board and therefore does not function under the Local Government Department of Dail Eireann, submitted a dispute between itself and the quarry workers employed by it to the arbitration of the Labour Ministry. The question at issue was settled to the general satisfaction on September 26th." This was but one instance "of the popular respect the National Government enjoys," Madame concluded. "All classes of workers thus signified their confidence in the impartiality of the National Government."

Madame was one of those deeply troubled by the religious bigotry which encouraged injustice by both Protestants and Catholics. When patriotism or arbitration failed, she threatened to use military force. She wrote to a Catholic quarry manager in the north: "It has been reported to us by Mr. McCartan that he has received a notice from you ordering him to dismiss a Protestant workman from his employment under the penalty of having his horses stopped. We wish to state that the Government of Dail Eireann cannot stand for intimidation and for the penalising of men because of their religion, and unless this intimidation is stopped we shall have to put the matter into the hands of the Republican Police."[1]

In spite of the optimism of the time, neither side was confident that the Truce would last and both kept their guns oiled. The British repaired their barracks, and like any army in peacetime, the I.R.A. continued to drill. When Lloyd George objected, Griffith replied, "My conception is that the Truce does not mean that your [British] military forces should prepare during the period of the Truce for the end of it and that we should not." In October Madame sent a contribution to the Dublin Brigade as "a small appreciation of the wonderful work they have done for Ireland." Ironically, the check was drawn on an English bank, for which she felt it necessary to apologize, "but my brother pays in some of my money there, & have not been able to transfer it to an Irish bank in time."[2]

Many Republicans were still imprisoned, including forty women.[3] On September 11, according to Michael Collins, there were 3,200 men interned, less than half of whom (1,500) had been tried.

On Halloween, 1921, Eithne Coyle and several other women slithered over a wall and left Mountjoy. A week later she and Eileen Keogh left the house where they had been staying and went to Madame MacBride's in St. Stephen's Green. "Here they were received with open arms, and the first visitor they had there was Madame Markievicz who gave Eithne a £5 note to tide her over until she could communicate with her relatives, at the same time telling her not to worry about paying it back. Eithne paid it back, but she never forgot Madame's open generous way."[4]

One of Madame's joys at this time was a letter from her husband, the first since 1916. Her answer was full of news about friends, "I never go anywhere that some one does not want to know have I heard from you." She was delighted that he was having success with his plays, made affectionate inquiries about the family at Zywotowka, reported that "most of the pictures & some of the furniture is safe up till this. Lots of things were stolen & destroyed in 1916." She ended with the hope that while the Truce lasted he could get over.[5] Her letter, although warm and gossipy, is curiously lacking in sentiment for a communication to her husband from whom she had not heard for more than five years. It is more like a letter to an old friend. Love had cooled to affection as their separate loyalties had sent them in different directions. This change had been clear as far back as 1911, when the Count wrote *Rival Stars,* in which a husband and wife who have different aims drift gradually apart. Long years of separation had made the Markieviczs almost strangers to each other. The Count paid only two visits to Ireland, once in 1924 and again in 1927 when he rushed from Poland to her deathbed. Unfortunately, all of his letters and the memorabilia in her desk were burned after her death.

Madame stayed with friends in Percy Place for a few months during the Truce, then early in the winter moved to the Coghlans at Frankfort House, Rathgar, her first permanent home since the Rebellion. The Coghlans were long-time nationalists, shared her religion, and the house was full of children and life. Madame was happy there. After her fourteenth birthday the oldest child, May, worked in the Department of Labour office. She remembered her mother had told them a "Miss Murray" was coming to stay with them. May soon realized who their new guest really was, but to the younger children Madame was always Auntie Murray who played games with them, told them ghost stories, sang songs, and planned treats for them. She was gay, sympathetic and understanding, and they loved her.

The main problem during this time was deciding the terms of a treaty that would secure the peace. After an exchange of cautiously worded letters between Lloyd George and Eamon de Valera, on September 30, 1921, the President wrote: "We have received your letter of invitation to a Conference in London on October 11, 'with a view to ascertaining how the association of Ireland with the community of nations known as the British Empire may best be reconciled with Irish national aspirations.'

"Our respective positions have been stated and are understood, and we agree that conference, not correspondence, is the most practical and hopeful way to an understanding. We accept the invitation, and our Delegates will meet you in London on the date mentioned 'to explore every possibility of settlement by personal discussion.' "[6]

Trade, defense, and the terms of association with the British Commonwealth were the problems the Irish nationalists were willing to discuss. To Robert Brennan, President de Valera, the mathematician, explained his idea of "external association" by drawing five separate and independent circles, all contained within a very large circle. He completed the design by drawing another circle tangential to the large one. "There you have it," he said, "the large circle is the British Commonwealth, having within it these five circles which are members of the Commonwealth. Outside the large circle, but having external contact with it, is Ireland."[7] His ingenious plan was to reconcile those who believed that England would never concede absolute independence to Ireland with those to whom anything less would be unacceptable.

On October 7, 1921, the five Irish Delegates were given their credentials from President de Valera: "In virtue of the authority vested in me by Dail Eireann, I hereby appoint Arthur Griffith, T.D., Minister for Foreign Affairs; Michael Collins, T.D., Minister for Finance; Robert C. Barton, T.D., Minister for Economic Affairs; Edmund J. Duggan, T.D., and George Gavan Duffy, T.D., as Envoys Plenipotentiary from the elected Government of the Republic of Ireland to negotiate and conclude on behalf of Ireland, with the representatives of His Majesty George V, a treaty or treaties of settlement, association and accommodation between Ireland and the community of nations known as the British Commonwealth." Additional written instructions given to the envoys modified their authority "to negotiate and conclude" a treaty. The ambiguity of their mandates ultimately led to civil war.[8]

The British delegates appointed that same day were Lloyd George, Lord Birkenhead (Lord Chancellor), Sir L. Worthington Evans (Secretary of State for War), Austen Chamberlain (Leader of the House of Commons), Winston Churchill (Secretary of State for the Colonies), and Sir Hamar Greenwood (Chief Secretary for Ireland).[9]

For eight weeks, from October 11 until December 6, the negotiations continued in London. At 2:30 A.M. December 6, under the threat of "immediate and terrible war," the five Irish delegates signed a treaty. Under this ultimatum the Republic established two years before was surrendered in favor of a government having far greater freedom from British interference than any previously enjoyed. The treaty was both a defeat and a victory.[10]

Under the eighteen Articles of the Agreement, Ireland would be known as the Irish Free State, with a Parliament and an Executive, and would enjoy the same constitutional status in the Empire as Canada, Australia, New Zealand, and the Union of South Africa. She would have her own army, but "until an arrangement has been made between the British and Irish Governments whereby the Irish Free State undertakes her own coastal defence, the defence by sea of Great Britain and Ireland shall be undertaken by His Majesty's Imperial Forces." An annex specifically stated that harbor defenses at Berehaven, Queenstown (Cobh), Belfast Lough, and Lough Swilly would remain in charge of British care and maintenance parties. (It was the sailor Erskine Childers who asked in the Dail debates, "How can you separate the coastal defences of an island from its internal defence?") England would have rights of airports and airspace (a vital concession which was not much talked about). Ireland would have religious and educational freedom.

On the thorny question of Ulster, Article 11 read, "Until the expiration of one month from the passing of the Act of Parliament for the ratification of this instrument, the powers of the Parliament and the Government of the Irish Free State shall not be exercisable as respects Northern Ireland and the provisions of the Government of Ireland Act, 1920, shall so far as they relate to Northern Ireland remain of full force and effect, and no election shall be held for the return of members to serve in the Parliament of the Irish Free State for constituencies in Northern Ireland, unless a resolution is passed by both Houses of the Parliament of Northern Ireland in favour of the holding of such election before the end of the said month." If Ulster decided to remain separate from the rest of Ireland, a Commission would settle the boundary question. One member of the Commission would be appointed by the Irish Free State, one by Northern Ireland, and one by the British Government.

A normal injunction was included: the officers and representatives of the Free State, as officials of a Commonwealth country, were required to take an oath of allegiance to the crown.

The Treaty,[11] or more accurately, the response to it, prompted millions of words of debate and when talk failed, violence. Republicans such as Madame wanted a reaffirmation of the Republic; nothing less would satisfy them. But from the point of view of the British cabinet, the war had been a draw and a compromise such as proposed by the Treaty was in order. To be sure, Britain had used the wretched tactics of terrorism and the terrorism had failed, but only a fraction of the military might of Britain had been released against the Irish. Griffith and Collins, the two leading Irish negotiators, were realists. To them politics was the art of the possible and not the implementation of the ideal. When war was threatened unless they signed, they signed and thought they had authority to do so.

The Irish and the British press were jubilant, and many Irish nodded agreement to their leitmotif "TREATY AND PEACE." Other headlines fed the disinclination to a renewal of war, "RATIFICATION OR RUIN," "REJECTION AND CHAOS."

The deputies were divided. Even in the dispassionate diction of official reports their mounting passion comes through. The Dail met for ten long sessions on the Treaty and listened more or less patiently to each member who wanted to speak.[12] Some of the speeches were controlled and logical; others made strong appeal to sentiment. As the sessions wore on, personal recrimination crept in more often, hard as the Speaker and the statesmen tried to avoid it.

Indicative of the emotions gathering force was the amount of time given to the question of oaths: Is an oath of allegiance to a king manifestation of a slave mind? Did the oath constitute a pledge to a superior or an act of faith with an equal? Does an oath really bind or is it an expedient only? Some felt an oath obliged them morally never to resist England's will, never to secede. On the other hand, those who voted for the Treaty said it was binding only so long as neither party desired to renounce it, just like any other treaty. Since it was not the treaty they wanted, they were not responsible for it nor honor bound to regard it as a final settlement.

Even more basically, the debates divided those who trusted the word of the British Prime Minister from those who did not. The ghost of the Act of Union haunted them. The word of the British to Ireland had been broken before, why should it be different this time? Those who supported the Treaty interpreted it optimistically, those who were against it were pessimistic.

Arthur Griffith, in proposing approval of the Treaty by Dail Eireann, briefly summarized its benefits: "We have brought back the flag; we have brought back the evacuation of Ireland after 700 years by British troops and the formation of an Irish army. We have brought back to Ireland equality with England, equality with all nations which form that Commonwealth, and an equal voice in the direction of foreign affairs in peace and war."

In his initial speech President de Valera said he was against it "because it does not reconcile Irish national aspirations with association with the British Government. I am against this Treaty because it will not end the centuries of conflict between the two nations of Great Britain and Ireland." Approving the Treaty was voting away the independence of the Irish people. "It is [acknowledging] British power and authority as sovereign authority in this country."

Madame, dressed in her green Cumann na mBan uniform, eyes flashing, her voice rising to shrillness in her passion, pleaded for the Republic. "I rise to-day to oppose with all the force of my will, with all the force of my whole existence, this so-called Treaty. . . . First, I stand true to my principles as a Republican, and to my principles as one pledged to the teeth for freedom for Ireland. I stand on that first and foremost. I stand, too, on the common sense of the Treaty itself, which, I say, does not mean what it professes to mean, and can be read in two ways." She railed against giving the Southern Unionists representation in the proposed government, arguing that they "have been the English garrison against Ireland and the rights of Ireland," and worse, "crushing, cruel and grinding" capitalists.

"While Ireland is not free I remain a rebel, unconverted and unconvertible. There is no word strong enough for it. I am pledged as a rebel because I am pledged to the one thing—a free and independent Republic. . . . I know what I mean—a state run by the Irish people for the people. That means a Government that looks after the rights of the people before the rights of property. . . . My idea is the Workers' Republic for which Connolly died." As a Republican who believed that the Republic means government by the consent of the people, as one who stood for James Connolly's ideals—the Irish Workers' Republic, the Republican Co-operative Commonwealth, she protested giving special privileges to a class which stood solely for English interests and whose object it would be to block the way in every effort the Irish nation might make towards progress.

"I don't like to kill. I don't like death, but I am not afraid to die . . . I fear dishonour and I feel that death is preferable to dishonour; and sooner than see the people of Ireland take that oath meaning to build up your Republic on a lie, I would sooner say to the people of Ireland: 'Stand by me and fight to the death.' I think that a real Treaty between a free Ireland and a free England—with Ireland standing as a free sovereign state—I believe it would be possible to get that now; but even if it were impossible, I myself would stand for what is noblest and what is truest. That is the thing that to me I can grasp in my nature. I have seen the stars, and I am not going to follow a flickering will-o'-the-wisp. . . . Do not be led astray by phantasmagoria. Stand true to Ireland, stand true to your oaths, and put a little trust in God."

The next deputy who spoke said, "I have a very elastic mind on oaths."

To a large extent the ten-days' debate was a long dispute over the relative virtues of principle and expediency. Public opinion is difficult to assess. The deputies who were pro-Treaty said their constituents were for it; those who were anti-Treaty also claimed public support. On the 7th of January, 1922, the vote was taken and the result was 64 for approval, and 57 against.

De Valera took this vote to signify loss of confidence and at the next public session of the Dail, Monday, January 9, resigned his office of President. His re-election was immediately proposed by Mrs. Tom Clarke and seconded by Liam Mellows, but the resolution was lost by a vote of 58 to 60. President de Valera himself did not vote, nor did Liam de Roiste, who said, "I refuse to plunge my country into fratricidal strife." He was one of the first to see the approaching disaster.

The great emotional pressures they had lived under for years brought them close to hysteria. As the stress of the debates mounted, even Arthur Griffith, who almost never became personal nor lost his coolness, flared out at Erskine Childers, "I will not reply to any damned Englishman." Madame stung Collins with a joke about the country boy's fondness for power. She said she suspected him of wanting to marry an English princess.

On January 10 the debate was devoted to Michael Collins' motion "that Mr. Arthur Griffith be appointed President of Dail Eireann." Just before two o'clock, when the question was finally put, de Valera staged a demonstration. While the vote was taken, as a protest he and his followers left the House in a cyclone of vituperation:

> Collins: Deserters all! We will now call on the Irish people to rally to us. Deserters all!

Ceannt: Up the Republic!

Collins: Deserters all to the Irish nation in her hour of trial. We will stand by her.

Madame: Oath breakers and cowards.

Collins: Foreigners—Americans—English.

Madame: Lloyd Georgeites.

When the House had quieted down, the motion was passed unanimously, 61 deputies answering to the roll. The new President then proposed six Cabinet Ministers whose appointments were ratified: Michael Collins, Finance; George Gavan Duffy, Foreign Affairs; Eamonn Duggan, Home Affairs; W. T. Cosgrave, Local Government; Richard Mulcahy, Defense.

The last appointment raised a key question about the status of the Republican Army, which two years before had placed itself voluntarily under the control of the Dail. General Mulcahy declared that it would function in the same spirit as it had up to that time. "If any assurance is required, the army will remain the army of the Irish Republic." But like all Ireland, the army was soon split between those who had confidence in the Treaty and those who did not.

As new President of the Dail, Arthur Griffith complied with certain formalities laid down by the Treaty, and a Provisional Government was elected which duly took over at Dublin Castle on January 16, without ceremony. One of the departing Castle officials who saw the meeting between the Lord Lieutenant, Lord Fitzalan, and Michael Collins, who six months before had had a price on his head, wrote, "The drama of seven hundred years—was it comedy, farce, or tragedy? —was about to be played out; the curtain was about to fall on the last act and the last scene. When it would rise again it would not be the same play. The characters, the situation, the staff would be different."[13]

Winston Churchill, shortly after the signing of the Treaty, "became a principal in British-Irish affairs." He had been for a year, since January, 1921, in the Colonial Office. Now that the Treaty had been signed, Southern Ireland as a Dominion fell constitutionally within the sphere of the Colonial Office, and Churchill became Chairman of the Cabinet Committee upon Irish Affairs. "Thenceforward I conducted all the negotiations with the Irish leaders, both North and South, and dealt with all the Parliamentary situations in the House of Commons."[14]

Evacuation of British troops, Auxiliaries, Black and Tans, and the disbanding of the Royal Irish Constabulary began at once in accordance with Churchill's advice that "ostentatious preparations to quit should be begun everywhere." Hundreds of untried prisoners were released from detention camps and nearly four hundred prisoners sentenced in Ireland before the Truce were amnestied. It seemed that England was sincere in keeping promises made under the agreement, and many were ready to believe she would continue to do so. Many agreed with Michael Collins that the Empire was loosening its ties and that acceptance of dominion status would be necessary only for a short time. "A new era is dawning," Collins predicted, "not for Ireland only, but for the whole world. . . . The problem of associated autonomous communities can only be solved by recognising the complete independence of the several countries associated."[15]

He was overly optimistic. On January 21, 1922 (just three years after the establishment of the Irish Republic by Dail Eireann) deputies of the now disastrously divided Dail met with Irish men and women from all over the world at an Irish Race Congress in Paris. The Congress had been projected a year before, in February, 1921, at a conference of branches of the Irish Republican Association of South Africa. They had high aims but no power. Their initial purpose was to help Ireland in her struggle for independence; they also hoped to establish a permanent world organization to promote trade in Irish products. The well-organized Congress brought together representatives from seventeen countries, held an exhibition of Irish art, and gave an impressive number of concerts and lectures. Papers were read by Jack B. Yeats on painting, Evelyn Gleeson on arts and crafts, W. B. Yeats on contemporary lyrics and plays, Arthur Darley on Irish music, Douglas Hyde on the Gaelic League, and Eoin MacNeill on history. Andy Dunne was one of the singers at several concerts, where Madame's "Hymn on the Battlefield" was a favorite.

Madame was one of the Republican delegates to the Race Congress, as were Mary MacSwiney and Eamon de Valera. Republican and Free State delegates were so divided that they would not travel together; Robert Brennan had to split the finances so that each group could have its own treasurer at the unity meeting. Madame's departure had been a stormy one but for once she was not responsible for the thunder. Word had gone out (erroneously) that the train from Westland Row Station on which the delegates were traveling was carrying some departing Black and Tans, and a crowd had gathered to hurl insults to speed them on their way. No one paid much attention to the Irish delegates.

Robert Brennan went to Paris later in an attempt to persuade the two factions to present a united front at the Congress. He immediately realized such plans were hopeless. "Already the Congress was a hotbed of intrigue, with each side canvassing the delegates for support of their respective stands on the Treaty. What might have become a great movement was being wrecked on the rocks of party bias. Roughly as matters developed, the delegates from America, Britain, Chile and the Argentine were ranged on one side, while those from the British Dominions were on the other."[16]

The Congress opened with a splendid reception at the Hotel Continental, which Madame found quite out of keeping with the object of the Congress to discuss the help which all the scattered millions of the Irish race could give to the Republic established by the blood and sacrifice of so many gallant lives. She was shocked, as was Madame MacBride, who attended the reception with her, to see a red-draped dais, a gilded throne and a blazoned coat of arms surmounting it. It was occupied by the Duke of Tetuan, whose Irish title was The O'Connell since he was the lineal descendant of Hugh O'Connell, Prince of Tyrconnell, who had left Ireland in 1601. He had come from Madrid to preside at the Congress, and Brennan noted, "He was frankly puzzled at the whole proceedings." Madame MacBride said, "He knew nothing of Ireland, except its horses, and had bought some good ones for the Spanish government. It hardly seemed to me, or to Constance Markievicz, sufficient reason for erecting a throne in his honour."[17] The grand ideals of sacrifice and dedication seemed far away from the gilded throne in the Salle des Fêtes, and from the undercurrents of machinations and distrust at the public meetings and the concerts and lectures.

Before the Congress adjourned it was decided to establish an organization called Fine Ghaedheal, Family of the Gael, to assist the people of Ireland in their efforts to attain their national ideals, political, cultural, and economic, and to secure for Ireland her rightful place among the free nations of the earth; to foster among the people of the Irish race throughout the world a knowledge of the Irish language, literature, history, and general culture; and to promote the trade, commerce, and industries of Ireland. Fine Ghaedheal was intended to be politically nonpartisan. Eamon de Valera was elected President, Eoin MacNeill its Vice-President. However, the fine plan was scuttled when the Dail Cabinet refused to give the necessary loan to support the organization before funds could be collected from the world-wide units.

Having lost their power in the Dail, the Republicans turned their attention to winning it back in the polling booth. On February 5, 1922, Madame was re-elected President of the Cumann na mBan at a convention in Dublin. The meeting was reminiscent of the one in 1914 when the women had declared themselves strongly against Redmond's Volunteers and had elected to stay with the Irish Volunteers. Now they rejected a motion to support the Treaty by 419 votes to 63. The six women deputies in the Dail had all spoken strongly against the Treaty—Mrs. Pearse, Mrs. Tom Clarke, Mary MacSwiney, Mrs. O'Callaghan, Dr. Ada English, and Madame. They had no ambivalence about the Treaty.

The women turned out in force the following week at a Republican demonstration on O'Connell Street. The crowds were so great that three platforms had to be set up. De Valera spoke at all three, with others who were also well known to Dublin. "The Republican flag may have gone down," Madame shrilled, "but it is only temporarily down." Throughout the next months there were dozens of speeches, meetings, demonstrations—from carts, from platforms, from stages—anywhere the Republicans could expound their reasons for opposing the Treaty.

An important Sinn Fein Ard Fheis met in the Mansion House on February 22, with President de Valera in the chair. The meeting was divided but the members were anxious to avoid any irreparable break in their ranks. It was agreed that no elections would be held for three months in order that the Constitution, then being drafted, could be presented to the electorate along with the candidates.

Dail Eireann met for three sessions, on February 28, March 1, and March 2. The Dail departments were functioning "in harmony with the Provisional Government Departments," President Griffith announced in his opening statement. The Belfast boycott had been discontinued with a view to instituting an era of good will; the decision made at the Ard Fheis not to hold an election for three months was ratified; and the ministers were appointed. President Griffith told the deputies, "Every Minister here is a Minister of Dail Eireann. As a Minister of Dail Eireann he is going to see that the Provisional Government works in harmony with Dail Eireann until we have an election." But in answer to a question put by Sean T. O'Kelly, Michael Collins said, "I am responsible as Minister of Finance in Dail Eireann, but I am not responsible to Dail Eireann for things I do in another capacity." In the Dail much of the debate until the final meeting on

June 8 was concerned with questions of defining areas of authority or with the coming elections.

At the February 28th meeting, Mrs. O'Callaghan brought up the question of enfranchising women between the ages of 21 and 30 (older women had been voting since 1918), hoping the younger women could vote in the June election. The plan was balked on the grounds that new registers could not be prepared in three months, although Griffith was sure the women were ninety-five per cent for the Treaty. He was one of the few so assured; the women had a large anti-Treaty bloc. (Preparing new registers would also have enfranchised those men who had become 21 since the previous registers were made. Many of these young men had been active in the I.R.A. and were for the Republic.)[18]

Madame, of course, spoke feelingly to the question. Equality of opportunity was something which always had been dear to her heart. Remembering the Sligo Women's Suffrage Society, she said, "It is one of the things that I have worked for since I was a young girl. That was my first bite, you may say, at the apple of freedom and soon I got on to the other freedom, freedom to the nation, freedom to the workers. The question of votes for women, with the bigger thing, freedom for women and opening of the professions to women, has been one of the things that I have worked for and given my influence and time to procuring all my life whenever I got an opportunity. I have worked in Ireland, I have even worked in England, to help the women to obtain their freedom. I would work for it anywhere, as one of the crying wrongs of the world, that women, because of their sex, should be debarred from any position or any right that their brains entitle them to hold."

To objections that this was not the right time to bring up the question, and why had the women waited so long, she reminded them that when the Dail was held in secret it was impossible to bring forward measures like this. "War measures were the only measures that were attended to, and, naturally, the women did not push forward at the time when asking for their rights might have delayed people in a house where they would be in danger of murder."[19]

Madame supported the February 5th vote of Cumann na mBan against the Treaty: "One Deputy here seems to think that Cumann na mBan would torpedo the Treaty. In the name of Cumann na mBan I thank him for his appreciation of their valour and strength and I can tell him that it will be up to them to do it whether they get the votes or not. To-day, I would appeal here to the men of the I.R.A. more than to any of the other men to see that justice is done to these young women and young girls who took a man's part in the Terror."

The motion for the revision of the voting register was defeated by a vote of 88 for to 47 against.

On April 1, 1922, Madame left Southampton on the *Aquitania* for the United States, where representatives of both factions from Ireland were stating their cases to Irish-American groups throughout the country. Since the nineteenth century America had been the bank for Irish nationalism. Kathleen Barry, the sister of Kevin, traveled with her. They arrived in New York on April 7 and were met by Father O'Flanagan, Austin Stack, and J. J. O'Kelly (Sceilg) as well as a great crowd of sympathizers. To the press she said that her present mission was "to put the truth before the friends of Ireland in the United States who so magnificently supported us in our fight." She stayed in New York for five days, attending meetings, holding many interviews, and greeting ardent supporters. She took a day off to travel to upper New York state to visit Jim Larkin in prison, where she was favorably impressed with the difference between it and English prisons she had known. She found Larkin very well informed about Ireland and wanting news of his friends. She had lunch with him. Afterwards, the warden, pleased to find a connoisseur of penitentiaries, took her on a tour of his jail.

A week after her arrival she was in Philadelphia where again she was met with crowds, including many American Cumann na mBan, and bouquets, the tricolor, and the star-spangled banner. She was shown the monuments of the Americans' freedom struggle and was particularly struck by a phrase on Franklin's grave, "He tore the lightning from the skies and the sceptre from tyranny." It was in Philadelphia she saw again her co-prisoner from Aylesbury, the brassy "Chicago May" Sharpe, and rushed over to greet her, to the surprise of the people in the crowded lobby.

Madame and Miss Barry were escorted to Mass on Easter Sunday by Irish-American Volunteers in uniform, and were accompanied by a bodyguard of 200 Volunteers to the meeting at the Academy of Music later in the day. Austin Stack and J. J. O'Kelly shared the platform with them. The audience enthusiastically cheered the name of de Valera every time it was mentioned, booed that of Lloyd George, but showed a charitable attitude towards Collins and Griffith, and subscribed over $50,000 to the movement for the Irish Republic.

Madame's itinerary indicates where Irish sympathy was strongest. From Philadelphia she and Miss Barry, accompanied by J. J. O'Kelly, went to Detroit, Cleveland, St. Paul, Anaconda, and Butte, where the Irish-Americans had been strong for many years and where the President of the American Association for the Recognition of the Irish Republic lived. "Butte was one of the places that stand out for its reception," Madame wrote, "for they met us with a band and an army. All Sligo seemed to be there! The town is built on the side of a mountain and motor cars cheerfully bustle up and down. One held one's breath and prayed that the brakes would hold. At Anaconda we found a white town and snow over the tops of our boots. In spite of this, the meeting was fine."[20]

Madame was interested in the working conditions of the miners and was outspoken in criticism of what she saw. The manager of the mine, perhaps misguided by her title, took her on a tour. "It was awful! Of course the manager showed us the show parts, the great passages well ventilated and the wonderful machinery, but we saw few men working. I had been put up to things by 'wicked' friends in the I.W.W. and I started to ask awkward questions. I insisted on going into hot places and seeing men working with pick and with drill. I insisted on climbing into a stoop. I saw a man drilling the copper ore without the water appliance to keep the dust down and breathing in copper dust eight mortal hours every day. They told us few men live to be old in Butte, Montana."

Then they went on to the west coast: Seattle (where she was delighted to be met by "one of the Easter Week soldier girls, Lily Kempston"), to Portland, San Francisco, Los Angeles (where Tom Clarke's son, Daly, was among the welcomers), through Arizona and east again to Springfield, Massachusetts, then Cincinnati, Ohio. Sceilg was recalled to Ireland from San Francisco and had left Madame and Miss Barry there to continue their trip.

Everywhere she went Madame addressed large, enthusiastic meetings, and saw old friends from and of Ireland. In many of her speeches she reiterated her disbelief in the sovereignty of the Irish Free State in the words that Liam Mellows, who had many friends in the States, had used in his arguments against the Treaty in the Dail: "The very words 'Irish Free State' constitute a catch-phrase. It is not a state, it is part of a state; it is not free, because England controls every vital point; it is not Irish, because the people of Ireland established a Republic."

After the meeting in Springfield on May 14, she drove to nearby Westfield where she stayed a day with J. J. Hearn, whose home had been open to Irish patriots for years. There she was able to relax, to lie under a blossoming apple tree and refresh herself in a lovely garden. She was enchanted by New England in lilac time. She found a bird's nest, she admired a caterpillar, she revelled in the syringa. At the Hearns she saw chalked on a child's blackboard in Gaelic "Colmcille's prophecy full of hope for Ireland" signed with the transcriber's name, Liam Mellows. She liked American towns and cities, their cleanliness, the gardens surrounding each home, no walls to separate them from their neighbors, the well-planned houses. Nothing escaped her. She even admired the cupboards which were conveniently built into the walls.

She found another garden in Cincinnati, at the home of A. J. Castellini, whom she had met at the Race Congress in Paris and who had long been a friend to Ireland. There she had time to write letters, surrounded by flowering shrubs and roses, and there she found peace.

She was impressed by the vast distances in America, by the changes of season which she met in her crisscrossing of the continent. They had arrived before spring in the east, but found in Michigan and Minnesota early spring, the first pear trees white and pink buds in the apple orchards. Then back into winter, blinding snowstorms and drifts in Montana, spring in Washington and Oregon, summer in San Francisco, the tropics in Los Angeles—palm trees and orange groves where the fruit hung ripe on the trees. They saw the desert in Arizona, and after a five days' journey, spring again in Massachusetts, and back to summer and roses in Ohio. She liked the railroad travel, and thought it a marvel that tracks could have been laid round horse-shoe curves, up and down mountains and over ravines. "I wonder that the engineers are not national heroes. They certainly ought to be."

On May 21 she was back in New York at a large meeting at Madison Square Garden. The guard of honor was composed of members of a Boys Brigade which had been formed by Michael Lonergan, who had joined the Fianna at their first meeting. Madame's final appearances were in Boston the next day, and after a memorable farewell reception in New York—Boy Scouts, two bands, soldiers, friends with flowers and flags—she sailed on May 30 on the *Berengaria* for home. She was happy that she had found "thousands of voices to cheer our little Republic on the hard path to Freedom."

In the generally pro-British press in America, Madame had read of the developing tension in Ireland. There was continual trouble in the six northern counties. (The economic boycott of Belfast, lifted in January, had been soon resumed.) Particularly along the border terror met counter-terror and both Protestants and Catholics suffered. Although the Irish army south of the Boyne had been split by the Treaty vote, the leaders of both factions worked together against the terrorism. On all other issues they pulled in different directions. In the north between June 21, 1920 and June 18, 1922, casualties were estimated at 1,766 wounded and 428 killed; 8,750 had been driven from their employment and 23,000 from their homes.[21]

Madame had known something of the division of the Irish Army before she left for her American tour, but in Philadelphia she read that Republicans had established headquarters in the Four Courts and had moved into other buildings in the city. (The Four Courts is a handsome Georgian monument housing most of the law records of Ireland.) It had been inevitable that the Army should split in the same way that the Dail and the people split over the Treaty. Republican anti-Treaty army men no longer considered themselves allied to a Dail that had disestablished the Republic, and many thought the Army should revert to its original status as a Volunteer force under the control of an elected Executive.[22] With this in mind they had requested the Minister of Defence to hold a convention of the Army to discuss its new status. After some changes of mind, the Dail declared such a convention illegal. Despite this disapproval, the anti-Treaty units banded together.[23] There were now in effect three armies in southern Ireland: the remnants of the British forces; the former Volunteers who were pro-Treaty and under the authority of the Dail (commonly called Free Staters or Beggars' Bush troops from the location of their headquarters); and the anti-Treaty forces which had been reorganized (usually referred to as the I.R.A.).

After the Army split, the Fianna decided to work under the control of its own general headquarters staff and not cooperate with the Beggars' Bush troops. At an Easter Sunday Ard Fheis, while Madame was still in Philadelphia, she was unanimously re-elected Chief of the Fianna, which was now entirely composed of boys with anti-Treaty sentiments who would accept nothing less than a united, independent Republic.[24]

Having two rival political parties seemed normal, but having two rival Irish armies promised explosions. From all sides Irish organizations rushed to re-create the unity they had known during the Black and Tan war. Throughout April and May Eamon de Valera and Michael Collins tried to find some basis for working together but had the eternal problems of responsible leaders who come to power in a crisis. They had to urge moderation on those whose training had been towards excess. The strengths of wartime were hazards in peace.

On May 20 the two leaders presented a scheme for a national coalition panel of candidates for the June elections which would avoid making acceptance or rejection of the Treaty the issue. The panel was to represent both parties in the Dail and in Sinn Fein, the number from each party being their present strength in the Dail, the candidates to be nominated through each of the existing party Executives. After the election the Executive was to consist of the President, the Minister of Defence representing the Army, and nine other ministers—five from the majority party and four from the minority. It was a workable solution to their differences and offered a basis for unity. The Army Council, working under the expectation of a Coalition government, by the first week in June had reached agreement under which the pro-Treaty and anti-Treaty officers could work effectively together.[25]

Ireland began to breathe easier, but the de Valera-Collins Pact which had been signed on May 20 was not allowed to go unchallenged by the Colonial Office. Arthur Griffith and Michael Collins were summoned to London by Winston Churchill, and on the 31st of May the House of Commons debated whether the Pact was in violation of the Treaty.

In Ireland, however, the election campaign proceeded with coalition candidates often appearing on the same platform. Madame was back from America several days before the election, attended her last Dail meeting on June 8, and made several election speeches. On June 9, Collins and de Valera shared a platform at the Mansion House. Four days later Collins yielded to British demands that he come to London, and he met with Churchill on the 13th. On the 14th, two days before the election, he returned to Ireland and at a meeting in Cork said that since he was "not hampered now by being on a platform where there are Coalitionists" he could "make a straight appeal to you—to the citizens of Cork, to vote for the candidates you think best of, whom the electors of Cork think will carry on best in the future the work they want carried on." The Republicans interpreted this as a repudiation of the Pact, but it was too late for them to reorganize for the elections. Confused voters did not even see the new Constitution until election day.

Voting was by the proportional representation system, the electors indicating an order of preference for a number of candidates. Of a House of 128 members, 94 Panel candidates were returned; of these 58 were pro-Treaty, 36 Republican. The Labour Party, one of the parties urging national unity, returned 17, Farmers' Party 7, Unionists (Trinity College) 4, Independents 6. The four South Dublin City deputies represented two from the Panel (both pro-Treaty), one Labour and one Independent candidate. Madame lost.

Taking a long view, the events led to some good. Sinn Fein was still predominant but Ireland was no longer under one party. Where the strength of a single party was vital in a war-torn land, it would have meant totalitarianism in peace. A single-party, united front was a necessity in the spring of 1921 when the Irish were trying to clear out the Black and Tans, but with the end of fighting, those who disagreed with Sinn Fein were no longer reluctant to put their names on the ballot.

In the short view, however, the election made a muddle. How many of the Panel candidates were voted for because of loyalty to the Coalition Pact and how many on the basis of individual conviction will never be known and each side interpreted the results in its own way. Did the election provide a constitutional mandate for ratifying the Treaty and disestablishing the Republic? The provisional government in Ireland and the rulers in Britain answered yes; the Republicans said no. At any rate, the call to form a coalition government never came. To make matters worse, there was no tradition for peaceful opposition. What Ireland had won it had won by violence. Ominously, throughout the land pistols were once again cleaned and hidden rifles were taken out of the thatch.

Walter Macken synthesized contemporary arguments and emotions in his novel *The Scorching Wind,* with a dialogue between two brothers:

> "Look," said Dualta, "we accepted the Treaty because it was the best terms we could get at the time. We regard the Treaty as a steppingstone, the freedom to achieve freedom."
>
> "You signed an ignoble document," said Dominic. "You betrayed your oath to the Republic."
>
> "If the Treaty was not signed," said Dualta patiently, "we would have been faced with an immediate and terrible war. These were their words."

"What had they been doing up to that, playing tiddlywinks?" Dominic asked.

"In comparison," said Dualta. "We didn't defeat them. We made it impossible for them to rule."

"If they had a pillbox every five yards of the country," said Dominic, "we would have found ways to beat them. We were all one, people and Volunteers, and you destroyed that with your pens."

"Listen," said Dualta. "I know it's nearly impossible to make you see. The people were tired of war. They wanted peace. The very people that voted for peace were the ones that nurtured us in their houses on the hillsides. These were the ones. They were tired and they wanted peace, and you won't give it to them."

"Not all of them," said Dominic. "Not all of them, brother. You had the slanted press and the power of the pulpit behind you, and voting registers from which not even the men who fought them to a Truce could put their names to a vote. You bound no fighting man to you, Dualta, only opportunists and people mad for power and all the tradesmen and sycophants who would have as cheerfully voted for the Union Jack."[26]

The issues were too pressing to neglect, too extreme for compromise. Soon the brothers would be trying to kill one another.

NOTES TO CHAPTER XIV

1. *Irish Bulletin,* November 29, 1921.
2. In the National Museum, Dublin.
3. A list of women in prison in April, 1921, is an interesting catalogue of reasons for incarceration and length of sentences. As of April 8, there were 26 imprisoned, 15 being held without charges or trial; 11 had been courtmartialed, some in secret, and included Linda Kearns, a nurse: arrested while driving a car without a permit in Sligo; Mary Bowles, 14, Co. Cork, 5 years: she "endeavoured to save from capture the machine gun of one of the Republican flying columns operating in that county"; Madame Markievicz, T.D., 2 years: Fianna; L. Hawes, Cobh, one year: in possession of documents dealing with a British courtmartial and some nationalistic literature; Miss Coyle, Roscommon, one year: Cumann na mBan literature and part of a plan of a Constabulary barracks; Miss Ryney, Clontarf, two years: possession of ammunition; Dr. Ada English, T.D., Ballinsloe, Co. Galway, 9 months: Cumann na mBan literature; Miss Anita McMahon, Westport, Co. Mayo, 6 months: literature and documents of Dail Eireann and Republican Courts; Miss Alice Cashell, 6 months: Dail correspondence re local government; Miss Hicks, 3 months: seditious literature. Most of the women arrested purely on "suspicion" spent one or two months in jail.

Later, Mrs. Margaret Buckley wrote about the untried women at Mountjoy with her, including three little girls from Cork, two sisters named Cotter and their cousin: "These children were weeding turnips in a field when a lorry-load of Black and Tans was blown sky high at the end of the field; the only people the survivors saw when they came to were the three little girls; they arrested them, and they were tried and sentenced to penal servitude for life. They were released during the Truce." Neither the young nor the old escaped; Mrs. Buckley also wrote about two sisters, one seventy and the other eighty years old, arrested in Athlone and taken to Dublin in a military lorry. "They were released after a few days, all efforts to extract information from them having proved unavailing" (Margaret Buckley, *The Jangle of the Keys,* Dublin, 1938, pp. 7–8).

4. Ibid., pp. 12–13.

5. In National Museum, Dublin.

6. Dail Eireann, *Official Correspondence Relating To The Peace Negotiations June–September, 1921* (Dublin, 1921), p. 23.

7. Brennan, *Allegiance,* pp. 311–312.

8. The Envoys Plenipotentiary were given written instructions which read:

   1. The Plenipotentiaries have full powers as defined in their credentials.
   2. It is understood before decisions are finally reached on a main question, that a despatch notifying the intention to make these decisions will be sent to members of the Cabinet in Dublin, and that a reply will be awaited by the Plenipotentiaries before final decision is made.
   3. It is also understood that the complete text of the draft treaty about to be signed will be similarly submitted to Dublin, and reply awaited.
   4. In case of a break, the text of the final proposals from our side will be similarly submitted.
   5. It is understood the Cabinet in Dublin will be kept regularly informed of the progress of the negotiations.

Eamonn Duggan and George Gavan Duffy were the legal advisers to the treaty delegation. The secretaries appointed were Erskine Childers, T.D., Finian Lynch, T.D., Diarmuid O'Hegarty, and John Chartres (Macardle, *The Irish Republic,* p. 528).

9. Sir Gordon Hewart, British Attorney-General, was appointed to act as a member of the Conference whenever constitutional questions were being discussed. The two Secretaries were Lionel Curtis and Thomas Jones, the Prime Minister's private secretary.

Much has been written about the Anglo-Irish negotiations. Memoirs of or about the principals give various viewpoints. One of the most detailed, lively, and scholarly books on the subject is *Peace by Ordeal* by Frank Pakenham (London, 1935); a more recent one is Frank Gallagher's *The Anglo-Irish Treaty* (London, 1965).

10. The question of renewal of the war was greatly debated. How far would Britain have gone at that point had the Treaty not been signed under that threat? General Macready said that if negotiations had broken down "and a renewal of the policy of coercion become necessary, a force of probably 150,000 men would have been essential, because during the five months which intervened between the truce and the treaty the rebel forces had been recruited and

reorganized, quantities of arms and ammunition imported, and, above all, the military and police Intelligence services had been reduced and had lost touch with their objectives" (*Annals,* II, 562).

11. Officially, "Articles of Agreement," but in general discussion nearly always called simply the Treaty.

12. The Treaty debates were published in a separate volume of the Dail reports by the Dublin Stationery Office and is still in print. Quotations and details which follow are from this source. Analysis of the debates and of public opinion is brilliantly covered in Dorothy Macardle's *The Irish Republic.*

13. Periscope, "The Last Days of Dublin Castle," *Blackwood's Magazine,* CCXII (Aug. 1922), 188–189.

The new cast included some of the Ministers of the Government of the Republic, Dail Eireann, who now became Ministers in the Provisional Government; other men held office in one or the other. Among those who played a double role were P. J. Hogan, who was Minister for Agriculture in the Dail, and Joseph McGrath, who had replaced Madame as Minister for Labour. Others who were members of both the Dail and the Provisional Government were William Cosgrave, Eamonn Duggan, Kevin O'Higgins, and Michael Collins, who was Minister of Finance in the Dail and Chairman of the Provisional Government. Finian Lynch and Eoin MacNeill were members of the Provisional Government but not of the Dail Ministry.

14. Winston S. Churchill, *The Aftermath* (*The World Crisis, 1918–1928*) (New York, 1929, p. 333). In an outline for the guidance of the departments concerned, Churchill had on December 21, 1921, suggested several points to be considered, including "The Auxiliary Division will be disbanded at once at the cost of the Imperial Government, advantage being taken at the same time of the decision provisionally arrived at to raise a gendarmerie for Palestine" (ibid., p. 330).

15. Quoted by Pakenham, *Peace by Ordeal,* p. 281.

16. Brennan, *Allegiance,* pp. 335–336.

17. Maud Gonne MacBride, *A Servant of the Queen,* p. 165

18. Some of the deputies who spoke to the question, although not feminists, thought themselves duty bound by the Easter Week Proclamation to keep their promise. Cathal Brugha, in particular, paid tribute to the part played by the Cumann na mBan and other women during Easter Week and to the women who afterwards kept the spirit of rebellion alive.

19. When she had arisen to speak, another delegate also stood up. She claimed the right to speak because she was on her feet first, and he replied with centuries-old resentment which the bitter debates had increased, "An O'Keefe will never yield to a Gore Booth."

20. Roper, *Prison Letters,* pp. 287–288. *Poblacht na hEireann,* April 27, 1922 to June 15, 1922, carried Madame's accounts of her trip. The local newspapers in each city she visited have on file publicity about her lectures. For her visits in Springfield, Massachusetts, and Cincinnati, Ohio, I am grateful for information from the children of the Irish-Americans who were her hosts, Mary Hearn, daughter of J. J. Hearn in Westfield, and John Castellani, son of A. J. Castellani.

21. In February, 1922, Churchill remarked, "[With the Great War] the mode and thought of men, the whole outlook on affairs, the grouping of parties, all have encountered violent and tremendous changes in the deluge of the world, but as the deluge subsides and the waters fall we see the dreary steeples of Fermanagh and Tyrone emerging once again. The integrity of their quarrel is one of the few institutions that have been unaltered in the cataclysm which has swept the world. That says a lot for the persistency with which Irishmen on the one side or the other are able to pursue their controversies." He was presenting the Irish Free State Bill implementing the Treaty and concluded, "Ulster must have British comfort and protection. Ireland must have her Treaty, her election, and her constitution. There will be other and better opportunities of dealing with the difficult boundary questions" (*Aftermath*, p. 336).

22. O'Donaghue, *No Other Law*, p. 249. This biography of Liam Lynch is the most complete source of information on the I.R.A. during these years.

23. In spite of the ban, the Convention met at the Mansion House on Sunday, March 26. It was attended by 211 delegates. Liam Mellows presided at the meeting which unanimously resolved:

> "That the Army reaffirm its allegiance to the Irish Republic;
>
> "That it shall be maintained as the Army of the Irish Republic under an Executive appointed by the Convention;
>
> "That the Army shall be under the supreme control of such Executive which shall draft a Constitution for submission to a Convention to be held on 9th April."

The Convention met again on the agreed date with 217 delegates present. They adopted the constitution which reverted the Army to the control of an Executive of sixteen who were to be elected annually at a convention of the Army. The Executive were given power to appoint an army council of seven and a chief of staff who would appoint his own staff. Liam Lynch was named Chief of Staff by this Executive. The Constitution declared the objects of the Army to be:

> (a) To guard the honour and maintain the independence of the Irish Republic.
>
> (b) To protect the rights and liberties common to the people of Ireland.
>
> (c) To place its services at the disposal of an established Republican Government which faithfully upholds the above objects.

(O'Donaghue, *No Other Law*, pp. 223–224.)

24. The Fianna Ard Fheis, under the leadership of Barney Mellows, took place on April 16, three days after the Four Courts Headquarters had been established. At that time Fianna strength was generously estimated to be about 26,000; perhaps 17,000 would have been more nearly accurate. For years the Fianna had operated under the organization of the Army, with most attention being given to training the 14 to 16 year olds. It was thought that within the previous two years four to five thousand boys had transferred from the Fianna to the Army. They had provided a valuable stream of recruits for the I.R.A. and by autumn of 1920 it had been determined that closer cooperation between the two organizations was necessary. In January, 1921, a composite council had been set up consisting of three H.Q. officers of the Irish Volunteers and three of

the Fianna. Although the boys were still mainly concerned with dispatch carrying and intelligence, they took an increasing part in all actions, in some cases under the command of their own officers. After the Truce, in the autumn of 1921, a training camp was established at Loughlinstown, South Dublin, and large numbers were transferred to the Volunteers.

Madame also missed attending the Easter Week Anniversary Commemoration at St. Enda's a few weeks later. There the Fianna were addressed by Liam Mellows and Rory O'Connor, who paid special homage to two of their heroes of Easter Week, Con Colbert and Sean Heuston. There was no doubt on which side the Fianna stood. They started a paper again in June, but only one issue appeared before the leaders were called into action for what they termed "the second defense of the Republic."

25. The Council consisted of Richard Mulcahy, E. O'Duffy, Liam Lynch, Sean Moylan, Gearoid O'Sullivan, Liam Mellows, Rory O'Connor, and Florence O'Donoghue.

26. Walter Macken, *The Scorching Wind* (New York, 1964), pp. 290–291.

XV

Civil War

June 1922–December 1923

When the elections divided the Irish once again, the control of events moved largely from the politicians to the soldiers. Wherever cooperation could have been resumed, nothing was done, and soon Ireland was, in Pakenham's words, "torn with conflict between cruel exacting loyalties, and so preserved for a space for the British Commonwealth with an economy of British lives."[1] It is a general rule that when Irishman fights Irishman, an Englishman wins.

The final crisis began on June 22, when Sir Henry Wilson was killed in London. This Ulsterman, former Chief of the Imperial General Staff, had been Military Adviser to the Six County Government since February. It was under his direction, and allegedly with two million pounds earmarked for whatever measures of repression he might recommend, that the terror in the north had been so effective. He was shot and killed by two members of the London Battalion, I.R.A., both former British soldiers, who were thought to be acting under orders issued from Dublin before the Treaty negotiations and never cancelled. He was a fanatic for the union with Britain and it was believed he had used his influence to maintain the Black and Tan terror in Ireland before the Truce and to continue terrorism in the north.

General Macready was still in command of the remaining British troops in Ireland, which were in Dublin and the Six Counties. At the time of the assassination he was in London and found "the Prime Minister and certain members of the Government in a state of suppressed agitation in which considerations of personal safety seemed to contend with the desire to do something dramatic as a set-off against the assassination of Henry Wilson on the previous day." General Macready was asked if the Four Courts could be captured at once by the British troops. To do so was simple from a military point of view; indeed, he said, "Plans for such a contingency had been long prepared in case the Four Courts should at any time molest the troops." He thought it highly probable, however, that such an operation would unite the Irish and was surprised on his return to Dublin to receive orders to put the scheme into effect at once. However, since some of his officers lived outside the controlled area and he feared for their safety, he delayed the attack, and then word came from London to take no action.[2] "At this darkest hour in Ireland," Churchill later recalled, "came daybreak." It was not seen west of the Irish Sea.

Before the daybreak, in an effort to turn aside the anti-Irish fury of the House of Commons over the death of Sir Henry Wilson, Churchill directed the storm of his eloquence against the Republicans. Although there was not a hint of evidence that they had anything to do with the shooting, they served as his enemy—"a band of men styling themselves the Headquarters of the Republican Executive." If this sort of thing did not come to a speedy end, he threatened, "we shall resume full liberty of action in any direction that may seem proper, to any extent that may seem necessary to safeguard the interests and the rights that are entrusted to our care." What precisely would "seem proper" he did not say. Lloyd George endorsed Churchill's statement and said their views had been communicated to the Provisional Government. He wanted any action against Republicans to look as if the Provisional Government "acted upon their own initiative, rather than with the appearance that they are doing it under compulsion from the British Government."

The daybreak which Churchill so cheerfully greeted came on Monday, June 26, when a motorcar agency on Baggot Street was emptied of sixteen cars by Republican troops which like every army often "requisitioned" what they needed. The officer in charge of the operation, Leo Henderson, was arrested by Beggars' Bush troops, and in reprisal the pro-Treaty Deputy Chief of Staff J. J. O'Connell, was kidnapped and detained in the Four Courts.[3] To the Provisional Government and the British the seizure of the cars and the arrest of an officer seemed to justify firing on the Four Courts, although such an action would obviously signal the start of civil war. Churchill wrote, "Michael Collins, under the pressure of this event, and having doubtless learned that if he did not march, we would, determined to attack the Four Courts at dawn."[4] Collins had an unhappy choice; if he did not order his own troops to fire on the Republicans he would in effect sanction British warfare against Irishmen once again. Collins ordered the triggers pulled.

During all the discussions between the two Irish armies there had never been a question of the Republicans evacuating Four Courts. In fact, Commandant Rory O'Connor claimed that they were there with the approval of the Free Staters, because as long as they were in possession of the buildings all activity directed against the British in northeast Ulster could be attributed to them.[5]

All day Tuesday, June 27, there were reports and counter-reports that action was to be taken against the Republicans. Until after midnight the quays were quiet, but soon government troops began moving through the streets around the Four Courts. The garrison waited. At 3:40 A.M. Rory O'Connor received a demand to surrender within twenty minutes.

Shortly after four o'clock on Wednesday morning, June 28, 1922, Dublin was awakened by the boom of heavy guns firing from the direction of the Liffey. Madame recognized immediately what it was. "Listen!" she shouted to the others in Frankfort House, "They must be firing on the Four Courts." The eldest girl, May, went off to scout the situation and to see if the bridges across the Liffey were blocked. She sent back word that Charlemont Bridge was open, then went to Sinn Fein headquarters on Suffolk Street where some of the Cumann na mBan were already mobilizing. They sent her home, much to her disappointment, and when she got back she found that Madame had gone to find her own place in the defense.

The firing of the 18-pound field guns at the massive stonework continued all day. At first there were two; later General Macready lent two more. The banks of the Liffey on both sides were lined with spectators during the entire episode, and General Macready saw to it that there was a good performance. He gave General Dalton, the officer in charge of the Free Staters, "fifty round of shrapnel, which was all we had left, simply to make a noise through the night, as he was afraid that if the guns stopped firing his men would get disheartened and clear off." (There were stories of Provisional Government soldiers refusing to fight against fellow-Irishmen and certainly there were many who doubted the wisdom of the attack.) "Accordingly, about every quarter of an hour during the night a shrapnel broke up against the walls of the Four Courts, making much noise but doing no harm."[6]

Through the next day and night the shelling went on. On Friday morning the Four Courts caught fire and the buildings were shaken by an explosion. At 4 P.M. the garrison of about 150 men surrendered. The fire, which destroyed centuries of records, is usually blamed on the Republicans, but their commander, Rory O'Connor, gave an account of the surrender that has the ring of truth. This is dated from "The Joy [Mountjoy Jail], July 2, 1922": "1. We had only 25 rounds left per man. 2. Our armoured car was put out of action the previous day. 3. There was not a man or woman who was not asleep on their feet. 4. Several armoured cars were patrolling and snipers posted all around. 5. The fire. It is very important to publish the truth about the fire. The Sunday Independent published Beggars Bush statement that we blew up the place. It was set on fire by the bombardment, as was inevitable, and when the fire reached one of our chemical works naturally there were fireworks. The building which blew up was occupied solely by the Constitutionalist Forces of whom I understand 30 are dead. It is important to fix the responsibility of the loss on Collins & Co. Our total casualties were 6—1 fatal. We did not surrender our arms (we threw them in the flames) and were not asked. They never forced any entrance in the way reported. A few entered and retreated. The reported capture of 33 of our men is wrong. They captured all our Orderlies—youths of course (another British victory) whom we put all together in 1 place."[7]

In the meantime, the Dublin Brigade, under Oscar Traynor, had established position on the east side of O'Connell Street, in a number of buildings, mostly hotels, which lined the street from Nelson's Pillar to the Gresham Hotel. Liam Lynch, Seumas Robinson, and other officers of the Southern Division left Dublin by train early on Wednesday morning to direct operations in the south. Cathal Brugha, Eamon de Valera, Austin Stack, and Robert Barton were among those reporting for duty under Traynor, and Madame was one of several Cumann na mBan who mobilized for action.

The Republicans had learned much about street fighting since Easter Week and could not be cornered easily. After the surrender of the Four Courts the major fighting shifted to O'Connell Street, where the plan was to hold on as long as possible to give the Republican Army in the country time to mobilize. As the garrisons in the chief I.R.A. posts were formed into columns for guerrilla tactics, the positions on O'Connell Street were gradually evacuated. The headquarters were moved several times, eventually to the Grenville and then to the Hammam Hotel. Gradually men and women in the final garrison went out, leaving, according to plan, only about twenty, including three women nurses, to hold out as long as possible, then to surrender. On Wednesday evening, eight days after the Four Courts attack, they finally gave up in obedience to Cathal Brugha's orders. He was the last to leave the burning building, and came out through smoke and flame, gun in hand, a fighter to the end. He had been so badly shot Easter Week that his recovery had been a miracle. The miracle was not repeated. He died in Mater Hospital two days later from his wounds.[8]

The nurses and the Cumann na mBan occupied the big basement of Moran's Hotel, using the large kitchen for cooking and several smaller rooms for dressings. During the four days there they had little sleep, lying down from time to time, but disturbed by the constant firing.

One of Madame's colleagues remembers her effectiveness as a sniper: "Coming on towards evening the fighting was mostly a snipers' battle. There was a sniping post on the roof-tops at the top of Henry Street. It was a well-placed, well-manned post. The snipers in it—there were two or three of them, taking over from one another so that their fire was continuous—made my position in the shelter of the cornice as dangerous a one as you could find.

"I was due for relief, and I wasn't sorry for that. But when my relief came, who was it but Madame. Played-out as I was after two or three hours up there under continuous fire, I didn't like the idea of a woman taking over that position. But Madame just waved me to one side with that imperious air she could put on when she wanted to have her own way. She slipped into what little shelter there was, carrying with her an automatic Parabellum pistol—the kind we used to call a Peter the Painter.

"I couldn't rightly say how long she was up there, for I was so tired that I drowsed off to sleep. But when I woke up, the first thing I noticed was something different in the sound of the firing. The steady, continuous rattle of fire that I had learned to pick out from the sound of rifle and machine gun fire up and down the street had ceased; the snipers' post in Henry Street was silent."[9]

On Sunday they left Moran's and went to the Gresham, but that too was soon evacuated. Sometime early that week, Monday or Tuesday, Madame left the Hammam Hotel and for a time sheltered in a nearby church, then went to a friend's home. Later in the week she was at Whelan's Hotel in Eccles Street and from there dispatched a group of Red Cross nurses to the West.[10]

On July 7, Churchill sent Collins a message of congratulation and appreciation for saving them both. "I feel this has been a terrible ordeal for you and your colleagues, having regard to all that has happened in the past. But I believe that the action you have taken with so much resolution and coolness was indispensable if Ireland was to be saved from anarchy and the treaty from destruction. We had reached the end of our tether over here at the same time as you had in Ireland. I could not have sustained another debate in the House of Commons on the old lines without fatal consequences to the existing governing instrument in Britain, and with us the treaty would have fallen too. Now all is changed."[11] Perhaps Madame remembered her ancestor who in 1608 had set the Irish to fighting among themselves on Tory Island so they could be subdued "with an economy of English lives." The Irish victors were then massacred. Churchill was more humane, but no less shrewd.

The Republicans carried the fight to the country, to the south and west. On August 11 their last town, Fermoy, fell and they went back to the guerrilla tactics which had been successful against the Black and Tans. The Civil War burned like a ground fire, bursting here and there into flames painfully hard to extinguish.

Ireland was further maimed in August by the deaths of three outstanding men: Harry Boland, shot in Skerries by Free State troops, died on August 2; on August 12, Arthur Griffith, shattered by the strain of events, died in a Dublin private hospital; and on August 22, Michael Collins was ambushed by Republican troops not far from his birthplace in County Cork.

The Provisional Parliament, five times prorogued, finally was called to Leinster House in Dublin on September 9. The Republicans who had been elected in June did not take their seats, with the exception of Laurence Ginnell who had recently returned from Argentina where he was Envoy from the Irish Republic. However, when his turn came to step forward and sign the roll, he questioned under what authority they were meeting. After several unsuccessful attempts to get his question answered, he was forcibly ejected from the meeting, just as a few years previously, when a Member of Parliament, he had been forced to leave the British House of Commons for his outspoken position on Irish freedom.

Since the fighting in O'Connell Street, Madame had been "on her keeping." She spent most of the time dodging in and around Dublin, staying with friends until she thought their house no longer safe and then moving on. She wrote publicity articles for sympathizers in America, and did what she could to keep Republicanism alive. She assisted her friend, Madame MacBride, to secure better conditions and release of prisoners and to ease the lot of their dependents.

The main avenue of publicity open to the Republicans was a weekly journal, *Poblacht na hEireann, The Republic of Ireland* which was then being published in Scotland to avoid the Free State censorship.[12] Madame was on the directing committee and wrote for it from the first issue. In a front page article in the first issue she expressed calmly and reasonably, with little of her usual emotional appeal to sacrifice, her belief that the English would not face a renewal of the Irish war and that a peace "in which there will be no attempt to impose subjection on the people of Ireland" was possible. She presented no details of how such a peace would be implemented, relying only on her confidence in Ireland and the Irish. Her article was entitled "Peace with Honour."

But civil war and arrests continued. By the end of 1922, twenty-one Republicans had been executed by their countrymen. Civil war takes a heavy toll of the dedicated, the talented, and the famous. The most shocking executions, because the men were the best known, were those of Erskine Childers in November and a few weeks later the four men who had surrendered the Four Courts and had since been imprisoned in Mountjoy without trial: Liam Mellows, Rory O'Connor, Joseph McKelvey, and Richard Barrett. Madame was particularly saddened by the deaths of Liam Mellows and Rory O'Connor. Both had been Fianna boys, and Mellows had done great service to the scouts from the time he set out as an organizer in 1912. By May 2, 1923, another fifty-six men were shot in prison yards.

The Irish Free State, Saorstat Eireann, was proclaimed on December 6, 1922, the first anniversary of the signing of the Treaty by the delegates in London. William T. Cosgrave was the first President, T. M. Healy, Parnell's old adversary, was named Ireland's first Governor-General. The last British troops left the Free State on December 17.

In January, 1923, Madame went to Scotland on an extended propaganda tour. Ironically, only in Scotland and England was she safe when she appeared publicly. May Coghlan went with her, and remembers Madame's surprise and amusement to see her supposedly secret arrival headlined in the Glasgow papers. "The Red Countess" they called her. Under the auspices of the Irish Republican Organisation of Scotland and the Irish Self Determination League, she spent the next ten weeks addressing meetings, visiting Sinn Fein Clubs, going to receptions and fêtes. Everywhere she went she talked. She was in and around London for a month, where she aroused great enthusiasm. The nature of her speeches was reflected in a brief report of a meeting in London on the first of March. "Her meetings have all been largely attended and her speeches have done much to bring home to the Irish people of the English capital the appalling treachery and tragedy of the so-called Treaty and the brutal warfare of King George's Ministers in Ireland and the Republic."[13]

The tour was tiring (she averaged two meetings every Sunday and two or three more during the week). It was also exhilarating. One of her joys was spending time with Eva in London, the first visit of more than a few days she had had with her sister for years. She walked through the city, past the homes of former friends, past the church where she was married, through streets once familiar in her youth. Once she and May Coghlan visited the House of Commons. She was getting old and full of memories and reminisced much to her young friend. The past occasionally seemed more amiable than the present. No doubt part of her ached to be a grandmother puttering about rose-beds, spoiling grandchildren, having servants who made her habits comfortable.

Poblacht na h-Eireann had continued publication in Dublin until the firing on the Four Courts, then in August had resumed publication in Glasgow. In January, 1923, publication under that name ceased but was immediately succeeded by *Eire, The Irish Nation,* which was published in Glasgow until April, then in Manchester. During these months Madame often contributed to these papers and was ready to write for any journal that would spread her views. Some of her articles were reminiscences, some were on contemporary subjects, but they all contained harsh criticisms of the current government in Ireland and aimed at clearing the minds of her readers of much of the anti-Irish propaganda she found in the daily press.

In April Madame was back in Dublin where she heard of the decreasing strength of the Republican Army. Fighting had continued throughout the winter and early spring against increasing odds. According to Major O'Donoghue, jails and internment camps held an estimated 13,000 Republican prisoners. Against the 8,000 of all ranks still in the field, the Free State Government could muster 38,000 combat troops.[14]

When de Valera met with the Army Executive in April to consider their situation, there were esentially three things the Republicans could do. The first was unrealistically optimistic: go on until the Government was forced to negotiate with them. The second was to negotiate a peace and find some way for Republicans to participate in the Government without taking an oath to the King. The third possibility was to dump arms.

With a view to trying the effectiveness of the second course of action, negotiated peace, Eamon de Valera for the Republican Government and Frank Aiken for the Army signed a proclamation ordering the suspension of all offensive operations as of April 30, 1923, and Aiken sent the necessary orders to his command. However, neither side was able to reconcile its position on the oath, and de Valera's proposals were rejected.

The only possibility now was to cease fire and dump arms, and the order was given by the Chief of Staff on May 24. Accompanying the order was a message from de Valera to "Soldiers of the Republic, Legion of the Rearguard" admitting that "the Republic can no longer be defended successfully by your arms. Further sacrifice of life would now be in vain . . . other means must be sought to safeguard the nation's right. . . . Seven years of intense effort have exhausted our people. . . . If they have turned aside and have not given you the active support which alone could bring you victory in this last year, it is because they saw overwhelming forces against them, and they are weary and need a rest. A little time and you will see them recover and rally again to the standard."[15]

Madame had returned to Scotland at the end of April as an unofficial secretary of propaganda for Irish Republicanism to explain to sympathizers that Republican defeat was not disaster. From Labour platforms she recalled the help Dublin had received in 1913 to feed the children. During June she delivered several addresses entitled "My Experiences Easter Week." She said very little about her own experiences, and much about the bravery of others. She reminded her audiences that the spirit of Easter Week had been kept alive by those who were still defending the Republic against her foes, foreign and domestic.

She went back to Dublin in July when the Free State government announced that a General Election would take place on August 27, 1923. The Republicans had reorganized Sinn Fein and were able to put forward eighty-seven candidates, though most of them were on the run. To appear in public to make an election address was to invite arrest. The Republican forces had ceased fire and dumped arms, but arrests and imprisonment still continued. On the 1st of July, a month after the cease fire, over 11,000 men and 250 women were still imprisoned. A Public Safety Act had been passed through the Dail in June giving the appearance of legality to the arrest and detention of Republicans without trial.

In his note recalling her home, de Valera said he supposed she had heard that he was to come out publicly and speak at Ennis and that he believed the time had come when they should all come out in the open. At Ennis on July 15 he was arrested and imprisoned for nearly a year.

Sixty-four per cent of the electorate went to the polls on August 27. The returns showed approximately the same division of popular strength as before the civil war; the Republicans thought they were slightly stronger. There were now 153 seats in the Free State Parliament, due to rearrangement of constituencies. The Government party returned 63 (5 more than in 1922) while the Republicans won 44 seats (8 more than previously). Madame was returned from South Dublin City once more. Again, however, as in 1918 when she had been elected the first woman Member of Parliament, she barred herself from the Dail by her adherence to the Sinn Fein policy of refusing to take an oath to the King of England. The Dail went on functioning in the absence of the Republican deputies.

In September a series of three articles by Madame which had been published by the British Labour *Forward* were reprinted in pamphlet form under the title "What Irish Republicans Stand For." The essays summarized her views. "I offer this little leaflet humbly," she wrote, "to the memory of Wolfe Tone, of Mitchell, of Lawler, and of James Connolly to whom I am indebted for the faith and the knowledge that inspired it." She presented no abstract argument but used examples of the achievements of the Dail during the Black and Tan days as contrast between the Republican idea of the Gaelic State and the present one. It was a reiteration of her confidence in the efficacy of cooperation, one of the ideals of her youth in Lissadell which she had continually advocated. The Free State she saw as "devised by the British Cabinet of Imperialists and Capitalists and accepted by their would be counterparts in Ireland, whom they supply with money, arms, and men for the purpose of breaking up the growing movement of the Co-operative Commonwealth in Ireland."

She tried to clarify what they had accomplished before the Treaty: "As step by step the Republican Government became the de facto Government of Ireland it began slowly to reorganise the national services on more democratic and Gaelic lines. Of course, we had to go very slowly and carefully, for not only were we faced with the difficulties which inevitably face the development of any country on any lines, but we faced also the fact that an enemy army was in occupation of our country and that the whole nation was individually 'on the run.'

"The Home Office under Austin Stack began its work by remodelling the machinery of the law. The Republican Justices were to be elected in compliance with the old Gaelic custom. . . .

"During my term of office as Minister of Labour for the Republic, very difficult situations were constantly cropping up, especially in rural districts where both sides were often armed and belonging to different sections of the Republican forces. The threat of economic war cropped up again and again. But the people, both employers and workers, believed in the justice of their own Republican Government, and of our desire to act fairly, and to secure the best for the worker without ruining the employer, so they ignored the British Ministry and brought their disputes to us and accepted our decisions. . . .

"The only sane course for Ireland is Co-operation. . . . This was the economic policy of the Republic. . . . The English Government understood it, for the record of Co-operative creameries wrecked and burnt was largely by the Black and Tans. . . . [Cooperative Fisheries and farming] are the obvious ones to start with in Ireland."

Madame devoted half of the pamphlet to giving examples of the non-cooperative nature of the new government in Ireland, which "is not the 'Halfway House' to any Republic, much less to the Republic visioned by those who died for it.

"We Republicans ask: Why encourage the 'Peaceful penetration' of Ireland by English Capitalists, instead of trying to develop trade and industry ourselves on Co-operative lines?" She concluded that she and other Republicans would continue "to work and strive for the establishment of what the people desire—a Commonwealth based on Gaelic ideals."

Ultimately, the Republican prisoners made the best propaganda when they resorted to the last device of the desperate. Four hundred prisoners in Mountjoy started a hunger strike on October 13. The strike spread to other prisons and camps, and within two weeks nearly 8,000 prisoners were refusing food.[16] Republican prisoners would not give any declaration of loyalty to the Free State, but they were convinced that they could bring about the recognition of Ireland's independence without continuing a civil war. The Sinn Fein Ard Fheis in

October had declared its confidence in the weapons of self-discipline, education, and organization and was replacing armed resistance with passive, non-military resistance. There seemed to be no justification for the continued detention of Republicans.

Nevertheless, on November 20, 1923, Madame was arrested a final time. She and Mrs. Sheehy Skeffington had spent the day, as they had several days previously, canvassing for signatures on a petition for the release of the prisoners. They were accompanied by two younger women and had held several meetings throughout the day, mostly in Madame's constituency. Late in the afternoon, three detectives stepped in front of their lorry which was then collecting a crowd in Kevin Street, and Madame was quickly removed in a car to Pearse Street police station. Mrs. Sheehy Skeffington, who was refused permission to go with her, then proceeded to hold two more meetings without interference. Madame was held without charges; her captors were uninformative but polite. When they offered her tea she refused it, saying she would hunger strike with the other prisoners. Later in the evening, Mrs. Skeffington and Madame MacBride went to the station to see if she needed warm clothing and food, but Madame declined their offer.

The day of her arrest, Dennis Barry, a hunger striker in Newbridge, died after 34 days without food. His was the first death of a hunger striker under the Free State regime. On November 23, the strike in all the prisons was called off, and two of the leaders, Tom Derrig and D. L. Robinson went to each of the camps and jails to spread the word. They themselves had been striking for 41 days but refused food until they had visited the prisons.

Madame, as usual playing down hardships when she wrote to her sister, said, "I only did 3 days, & was quite happy & did not suffer at all. I slept most of the time & had lovely dreams & time went by quite quickly. I think I would have just slipped out quite soon. Tom Derrig came in & called off the strike & woke me up!" If she belittled her own suffering, she was always sympathetic with others. "One girl is very bad, she nearly died, it only stopped just in time. She is in Hospital outside now."

Madame was in the North Dublin Union, a detention camp for women which had been opened in June. Used as a poorhouse, then as barracks by the Black and Tans, it had no cells but large, drafty dormitories, communal kitchen and canteen. Bathing and washing facilities were extremely limited. "Its a vast and gloomy place, haunted by ghosts of brokenhearted paupers." Madame made the best of the situation, however, and painted a good deal. She did dozens of water colors of her fellow prisoners, of the wards, of scenes in her mind. At least here she had company to share the long hours.

"I don't know how long they mean to keep me," she wrote to her sister after she had been there three weeks. "There can be no charge against me, that is, anything more than a police court charge for 'impeding the traffic.' Its just spite & fear of my tongue and brain! My real democratic principles, I expect." The Sinn Fein *Daily Sheet* was indignant that Madame was interned and suspected that "Madame's chief offense is the popularity she enjoys with her constituents."

The day before Christmas Madame was freed. She was a little thin and pale but in her usual high spirits. During December, 3,481 political prisoners had been released, including all of the women. It was a happy Christmas in many Republican homes. But in January, 1924, the Free State Government issued another Public Safety Act by which a person could be held in jail without trial. Once again Republicans began filling the busy Irish prisons.

NOTES TO CHAPTER XV

1. Pakenham, *Peace by Ordeal*, p. 335.

2. Macready, *Annals*, II, 652–654. Winston Churchill's version is brief and shifts the emphasis slightly. He wrote, "The Cabinet, supported by the House of Commons, were resolved that whatever happened Rory O'Connor must be put out of the Four Courts. The only question was when and how; and this must be promptly settled. Orders were actually sent to General Macready. However this officer prudently, and as it turned out fortunately, counselled delay" (*Aftermath,* p. 363).

3. The motivation for the raid on the automobile agency is vague. Some say that retaliation against the Northern nationalists was expected for the murder of Sir Henry Wilson and the southerners were determined to send reinforcements. Others say it was simply part of the continuing plan of harassment along the border.

4. *Aftermath,* p. 363. General Macready agreed, "The hand of Michael Collins was now forced, and he was obliged, much against his will, to assert his authority" (*Annals,* II, 654).

5. *Poblacht na hEireann,* August 31, 1922.

6. General Macready, not confident of the outcome of the fight, sent a company of infantry to the Castle in case the attack failed and the Republicans became aggressive.

7. *Irish War News* (New York), July 18, 1922.

8. Whether Cathal Brugha came out firing, as is generally believed, or whether he did not but advanced boldly as a martyr to the sacrifice, as his

friend Sceilg would have it, Brugha's final fight remains one of the great and beloved stories of that terrible time.

9. *The Sunday Press* (Manchester), October 30, 1960.

10. They included Annie M. P. Smithson who told her story in *Myself—and Others* and used her experiences as background for some of her novels.

11. *Aftermath*, p. 366.

12. The paper had started publication on January 3, 1922, as a platform for anti-Treaty views. Liam Mellows was its editor for several weeks, then Erskine Childers. Frank Gallagher, who had done such brilliant work on the *Irish Bulletin* during the previous years, was the assistant editor.

13. *Eire* (Glasgow), March 17, 1923.

14. O'Donoghue, *No Other Law,* p. 300.

15. Macardle, *The Irish Republic,* p. 858.

16. There were 462 in Mountjoy, 70 in Cork Jail, 50 women in the North Dublin Union, 200 in Dundalk, 350 in Kilkenny, 3,300 in Tintown, 1,700 in Newbridge Prison, 711 in Gormanstown, and 1,000 in Hare Park.

XVI

The Last Years

1924–1927

The Republicans were die-hards. Year after year they had endured imprisonment, contempt, division of their ranks, and defeats from the British as well as from their own countrymen. But Irish Republicanism thrived on the repression that its own intractable idealism invited.

In 1924 they were once more rebuilding their shattered organization and planning to carry on with the work of achieving a Republic. Madame's first effort was to help the Cumann na mBan devise a plan "whereby the organisation would continue its military training and at the same time fit itself for other spheres in the national life." By April they were ready for a general meeting to discuss their plans.

Madame set its tone with a statement of her own elastic spirit and provocative energy: "In a time like this when there comes, as it were, a pause, we cannot afford to sit still and do nothing." She presented the new plans which sound much like the work undertaken by the women when they first organized in 1914: there were to be regular lectures on historical, social, and economic subjects; and first aid classes. Disarmament had not served, so they were planning to fight once again, preparing for the day by monthly military and physical drill training. Irish games were encouraged, and members were urged to study and master the Irish language. In her conclusion she touched on the problem of unemployment in Ireland and again suggested co-operatives as an effective method of coping with this chronic problem.

Madame worked hard at several by-elections that year. The first was in Limerick, where the Republican strength showed considerable improvement since the previous August. She found the populace depressed, generous, and uninformed. To a friend she wrote, "I never saw worse slums or met nicer people. Dont talk to me about politics tell me how to get bread for the children was a very general cry. If one could only get the people to understand that politics ought to be nothing more or less than the organisation of food, clothes, housing & transit of every unit of the nation one would get a lot further. Also if they would only learn to watch and heckle their leaders, aye, and distrust them, fear them even more than their opponents. Do you remember how Connolly quotes Debbs somewhere to this effect, 'I would not lead you to freedom, even if I could, for if I could, someone else could as easily lead you back into slavery.' If the people would only read, study and make up their mind as to where they wanted to go and as to how to get there, we would easily win out, but alas, its always their impulse to get behind some idol, let him do all the thinking for them and then be surprised when he leads them all wrong."[1]

If Madame's ideas of politics were simplistic, she never lost her belief in the power of education, organization, cooperation, and chivalric virtues to solve problems. In an autograph book she wrote at the time "Truth, honour, & courage are the corner stones on which the Irish Republic is built." To complete that building seemed ever more difficult, but still possible.

In the summer a pamphlet on which she had been working for several months was published by Sinn Fein. She titled it "James Connolly's Policy and Catholic Doctrine" and made much use of scissors and paste in an attempt to reconcile two orthodoxies that had long sustained her. Its 45 closely printed pages are her most ambitious writing. She described the project to Charles Diamond in Glasgow: "I give all Connolly's most important points in his own words and justify them from The Encyclical and from Dr. Coffey's articles."[2] Half the pamphlet was devoted to "Connolly's Socialism and Catholic Doctrine." "Socialism properly implies above all things the co-operative control of the machinery of production." Dr. Coffey had discussed this point at length and concluded that "State Socialism," wherein the State would be sole owner of all productive wealth and all the citizens would be paid or salaried employees of the State, was condemned by both Connolly and by Leo XIII. She then continued with a discussion of what Dr. Coffey had called "Connolly's anti-clericalism," but felt he had misunderstood Connolly on this point. She quoted from several of Connolly's writings, including an article in the *Catholic Times* of 1912, "The considerations which compel the Holy See, as such, to recognise the de facto government and the de facto social order are not binding upon individual Catholics, and we, therefore, retain to the full all our rights and prerogatives as citizens and workers for social betterment, without abating necessarily one jot of our Catholicity." The next few pages were given to Connolly's views on the principle of confiscation, on industrial unionism, and on strikes.

The second half of her pamphlet detailed "Connolly's Programmes and Catholic Doctrine." Madame used his program of the Irish Socialist Republican Party published in 1896 as his statement of first points to be aimed at, first battles to be won. "The fundamental idea of Ireland as an independent Republic built up on Gaelic ideals, never changed, and he distrusted and denounced any reforms that were calculated to stabilize any status short of this. Hence, though at all times making clear his ultimate objective, he emphasizes the importance of having a progressive policy that develops with the changes of tactics that must ensue with each new invention or discovery, and with each further development in the policy of those against whom he was fighting."

Connolly's ideas on education and on state banks constituted a large part of this section, and Madame concluded with a few pages on the relationship between Connolly's Nationalism and his Internationalism, "The Free Federation of Free Nations." In her final paragraph, Madame summed up, "It was his pleasure to sign himself 'Yours fighting and hoping, James Connolly,' and to us, his friends, who shared his hopes and who fought under his leadership, and who loved and who trusted him, the writings he left will always be the Gospels of our Nationality. It is under his leadership that we continue to march forward fighting and hoping, even as he would have had us to do. His spirit leads us on, Liberty Hall, the G.P.O., Kilmainham, Arbour Hill, will never allow us to forget him, and the writings that he has left us are the marching orders of a risen people."

Count Markievicz paid a visit to Dublin that summer, and his wife welcomed him like a dear friend from whom she had long been separated. He found she had aged during the crowded years since he had been able to travel to Dublin, though she still had her energy and high spirits. He himself had been wounded and ill, for several weeks near death, and hoped for the gaiety of a Dublin that no longer existed. There were affable evenings and long hours of talk, but he found the postwar city dreary and most of his old friends scattered. He was an elegant Edwardian by nature and no longer felt at ease in troubled Ireland. The country was economically depressed, the Republicans particularly had difficulty finding and keeping jobs, and although his wife always had enough money herself, she felt her friends' hardships keenly. "The whole world is so tragic since the war," she wrote. The

Count was having a small success with his plays in Poland and returned to them.

Madame continued speaking for Sinn Fein, for Cumann na mBan, for labor, for the Women's Prisoners Defense League, for Fianna, wherever she could help. She went to Sligo October 26, shared a platform with Eamon de Valera and Sean Lemass, and told the crowd that she was happy to be back home, but that much needed to be done for the poor, the laborers, the children, the old, and the Republic. Sligo could not hold her long. She stayed only long enough to throw out the ball to start a challenge football match between ex-internees of Dublin and Sligo, and to attend a Ceilidh that night.

Madame presided at the Cumann na mBan convention on November 3, and attended the Sinn Fein Ard Fheis the next day at which 1300 delegates re-elected de Valera, at that time in jail in Belfast for crossing the border to speak in Derry. They were publishing a paper again, called by its old name, *Sinn Fein, An Phoblacht. The Republic* was also a platform for Republican views.

Electioneering continued during the new year, and in March 1925, when there were nine by-elections, two Sinn Fein candidates won seats from the Government party.[3] Madame was on the Standing Committee of Sinn Fein and regularly attended the weekly meetings, in addition to Cumann na mBan Executive and Fianna Executive meetings. It seemed to her friends that she was always going to meetings or making election speeches.

Perhaps inspired by the Count's visit the previous summer, Madame had revived her interest in the theater and in September had organized the Republican Players Dramatic Society. Their object was fund raising, and Madame characteristically threw herself into the new enterprise with gusto.[4] Within a year the Republican Players had produced a dozen plays, including two one-act plays that she had written, *The Invincible Mother,* set in Kilmainham Jail in the '80's, and *Blood Money,* set in 1798, which were first produced at the Abbey on March 1, 1925.

That spring she also wrote a full-length play about her own time. "I don't know what started me," she told her sister, "but somehow a situation came into my head and I wrote a scene and then I simply could not stop. Wherever I went I had an old copybook and whenever I was not actually using my hands I wrote. I had to go and drive for an election in the middle—such hard work—and one day I got my car out at 7.0 and never stopped driving round until weary and sleepy

I rang up a house at 2.30 to beg for a bed. But every minute I had to wait for someone outside a house—out with my old book, and anyhow the play is finished at last. Of course it is not literary, only just a story during the Tan war and in Sligo, but I think it is human and natural."

Her preoccupation sometimes made her seem old, crabbed, and fussy, even a bore. Mary Colum met her at AE's one evening during the time she was engrossed in her writing and thought it strange that Madame talked so much about her play "as if it were her one interest in life." Mrs. Colum wrote. "After the life she had lived she was now thinking of how she might dramatize or symbolize some of those ardors and endurances of hers. But her vitality was too low to do anything more; her fight, her imprisonments, the prison fare had depleted her and dimmed her personality. She had been a fighting Irishwoman, a woman of high aristocratic courage, who was afraid of nothing— that, at least, the aristocratic training at its best really can give, moral and physical fearlessness—but how rarely is it at its best!"

Mrs. Colum had known Madame "in her vibrant maturity. . . . At that time [c. 1910–1914] she had not been devoid of feminine coquetries or unconscious of her looks, though her ordinary attire, then, was a tweed suit and a mannish felt hat, but she would on occasions get herself up in a Paris frock and, when few others in Dublin used cosmetics, put powder and rouge on her face. A remark of hers to me when I was a young girl, I always remembered, for it had a real feminine vanity: 'I am not interested in men, for I have had the pick of too many men.' But now no trace of beauty remained; she was like an extinct volcano, her former violent self reduced to something burnt out. [She was] haggard and old, dressed in ancient demoded clothes . . . the familiar eyes that blinked at me from behind glasses [were] bereft of the old fire and eagerness."[5]

Madame called her play *Broken Dreams,* and it was described as "an incident in the Black and Tan War" when it was produced after her death.[6] It is melodramatic and the style is a little old-fashioned for the 'twenties, but if Madame seemed tired to Mrs. Colum, she still had the energy to shape the action of her play so that it shows some of her discontent, pain, and loss during civil war. The heroine, Eileen O'Rourke, is a Cumann na mBan officer, and her description might have been Madame's conception of the perfect woman, or an idealized projection of herself when young. "Tall, slim, goodlooking, with short brown hair softly and naturally curling round a striking face.

There is little suggestion of sex in her, she is more like a young boy in her manner, even with the men who love her. She wears well made, short, tweed skirt and coat, with shirt blouse or jumper, simple hat and good, strong walking shoes with low heels. She does not give the effect of either marcel wave or manicured hands, nor does her face give the effect of being powdered."

Eileen marries Seamus Gillen, an I.R.A. officer who drinks too much. They are on the run and living in a mean cottage after the Tans burn their home. In a drunken, jealous hassle with Eileen, Seamus is shot by someone unseen. Stupefied, Eileen picks up the gun just as the Tans and R.I.C. rush in. She is taken to the Sligo Jail on a murder charge, but is rescued by I.R.A. men who think that she had been arrested on political grounds. She is going to America, broken-hearted, when it is revealed that Seamus had been a spy and an informer, court-martialed and convicted by the I.R.A. A Republican had actually fired the shot which killed him. Seamus's death is her liberation.

The play insists that Seamus's egoism and pride, not love of Ireland, led him to fight in the G.P.O. After his Frongoch incarceration he had come home to be received as the conquering hero. But one of the characters says in the third act, "There was a traitor even among the twelve apostles, and if you get a traitor even among the twelve chosen men, chosen by the Son of God himself, you may expect to find them in a mere human movement."[7]

Nevertheless, honor should be expected even from political enemies. In an earlier scene Eileen repeats what she has told an English soldier who offered to carry a letter for her husband: "I said that we Irish were honourable and true, and that we despised those who were not, and that in making that offer to me, he was either ready to betray the trust his government put in him, or he was playing a dirty trick on me by trying to trick me into betraying the address of my husband."

The other man who loves Eileen, the honorable one, is significantly called Eamon. In his curtain speech he concludes: "Weak and vain men trying to exalt themselves only lose themselves. He [Seamus] lost himself in treachery. With self-respect went hope and faith and courage. Love became a delusion and a mockery. All that made life worth while to him was gone. Men like him are their own slayers. God only gives happiness to those who give all, it is only where there is no self there is God."

Even as Mrs. Colum was commenting on Madame's demoded clothes, Madame herself was writing to her sister and to her stepson that she had bobbed her hair in the modern fashion; she thought it more becoming and was certainly much more comfortable. She still had some interest in clothes and to Stanislas she wrote about boots: "Every one here is wearing Russian boots, and it will amuse you to hear that the red pair that your aunts got made for me at Zywotowka had survived the looting and that I fished them out and am wearing them every day, and they are far the smartest pair in Dublin."[8]

The delight of her life in these later years was her car, which gave her great freedom of movement. Whenever she had spare time she would rattle out into the country to paint, her dog on the seat beside her. Usually the car was full of children or other friends. Her "Tin Lizzie" was as familiar a sight as Madame and her bicycle had been in earlier days. The car was forever disintegrating, and Madame did the repairs herself. May Coghlan says that whenever she took it out "we always made sure she had a ball of twine. It was held together with twine."

Madame was given the Coghlans' garden to do with what she would, and many days she would come in from hours of meetings and speaking still energetic, would whip off her skirt, get into her knickerbockers and spend several hours in the garden.

She saw her mother quite often, whenever she came to Dublin for shopping, and her daughter Maeve was in and out of the city. Her visits were a great joy to Madame; her daughter had grown tall and pretty, full of life and charm.

The time she could give to friends or family was always limited. In June, 1925, Madame was co-opted to the Rathmines and Rathgar Urban District Council and she was regular in attendance at the Rathmines Council meetings. She was on the Housing, Public Health, Old Age Pensions, and Child Welfare Committees, as well as others. She was as conscientious in going to meetings concerned with the problem of keeping pigs within one hundred feet of dwellings as she was in trying to prevent discrimination in government jobs. Her presence made many of the meetings stormy. She fought against the necessity of oath-taking as a requisite for employment, she bristled against allowing the Boy Scouts to use public grounds when the Fianna were not permitted to do so, she protested against all displays of unionism and imperialism. Vehemently she worked for public swimming baths at Williams Park and fought for the poor, or those who were too sick, too young, or too old to work for themselves.

The Fianna began to take more of her time and attention as it had in the early days when it was reorganized in the autumn of 1925 to carry on "the training the youth of Ireland to be honourable, disciplined, self-reliant, healthy Irishmen." The organization reverted to the old sluagh (troop) system, with each sluagh leader in direct touch with General Headquarters. The emphasis was away from rifle and revolver practice, towards physical training and education. An ambitious intellectual program was planned, with Gaelic language, literature, history, archaeology, art, music, and games. In addition there would be physical drill, scouting, first aid, signalling, swimming, woodcraft, botany, and natural history. The Fianna did not have its own paper but *An Phoblacht* was generous with space for news of their activities. Madame was the Chief Scout.

But, perhaps remembering the effectiveness of the Fianna in their work with the Volunteers and the militant movement in previous years, the Free State Government was not willing to believe that the Fianna were rejecting guns for books. On December 3, 1925, twelve boys were arrested in Wexford under the Treasonable Offences Act, 1925, on charges that they "did assemble together for the purpose of being trained and drilled." One 15-year-old was released but the others were brought to trial two months later.

Madame delighted in being a witness for the boys and in reporting the trial for *An Phoblacht.* When she was sworn she added to the formal oath, "I will swear the truth on my allegiance to the Irish Republic." The judge reprimanded her, "You must act with propriety." To which the irrepressible Chief Scout, not averse to playing to a grandstand full of admiring boys, and with a flash of the old harum-scarum bravado, replied, "I always behave with propriety, for I am a most proper person, I assure your honour." The audience hooted and applauded vigorously.

The defense based much of its case on the fact that the Baden-Powell Scouts were not only allowed to drill in peace but also went in for revolver and musketry practise, while the Fianna had forbidden the use of firearms throughout the organization. The judge said the Boy Scouts had nothing to do with the case. The defense insisted that the boys had been drilling to prepare to march to the grave of Liam Mellows on December 13, and if everyone who marched in a funeral procession was accused of drilling, the jails would be overflowing.

The jury returned a verdict of not guilty and the prisoners were discharged. Madame concluded her version on a triumphant note: "A wildly enthusiastic crowd had gathered in the pouring rain and ankle deep mud outside. The Fianna had scored a victory. Cries of 'Up the Republic!' and 'Up de Valera!' echoed from every side and followed us as we walked back to the hotel." But it was by no means the last arrest of a Fianna boy.

The Treasonable Offences Act, under which the Fianna boys had been arrested and tried, proved a strong weapon against the Republicans. Some of its provisions were so drastic that even the government supporters protested, but raids, searchings, beatings, and arrests continued. "They raid this place an odd time and get nothing," Madame wrote, "but I suppose they want to keep their hand in." Republicans, of whom there were now 48 elected deputies, were barred from the Dail by the oath of allegiance. Persons who refused to make a declaration of allegiance to the Free State Constitution were refused employment in the public service. Republicans who found work were constantly arrested for a few hours or a few days for the purpose of making them lose their jobs and forcing them to emigrate. Unemployment, poverty, and the harrying tactics of the Free State Government forced young Republicans to emigrate in thousands. By the beginning of 1926 it was apparent that a new political approach was urgently needed if the Republicans were to be effective.

At the Sinn Fein Ard Fheis which met at the Rotunda in Dublin March 9 to 11, 1926, Eamon de Valera urged that the time had come to work to have the oath of allegiance removed, and once this was done, "it becomes a question not of principle but of policy whether or not Republican representatives should attend the [26 County and the 6 County] Assemblies." This suggestion caused what Madame called "an unholy row." The delegates were divided almost in half on the question and in a wild scene it was defeated by a vote of 223 to 218. After this turbulent poll, de Valera resigned as President of Sinn Fein and formed a new party, Fianna Fail. The name was, according to legend, that of the first standing army of Ireland, and was usually translated Soldiers of Destiny.

Madame expressed her approval of his position to her sister, "Dev, I say like a wise man, has announced that he will go into the Free State Parliament if there is no oath."

Madame presided at the inaugural meeting of Fianna Fail at the La Scala Theatre in Dublin on May 16, 1926. In her introduction she referred to the principal speaker as "President de Valera." After the enthusiastic applause had quieted down, he said, "I am sorry that my first words must be to correct the Chairman. I am not here as president of anything." Madame interposed, "You will always be President to me," and he continued, "I came here simply as a private and with a private's liberty. Is it necessary to say that I come as a Republican?" He then proceeded to outline his plan, to attack the oath and "once the oath was destroyed . . . cutting the bonds of foreign interference one by one. . . . To-day we are making a new start for another attempt to get the nation out of the paralysing 'Treaty' dilemma."

Headquarters for the new party was opened on O'Connell Street, office expenses were paid by contributions from friends, and chapel-gate meetings were held throughout the country to explain policy and enlist support. More than five hundred delegates attended the first Ard Fheis on November 24 and unanimously elected Eamon de Valera President. Madame was one of the sixteen member National Executive.[9] "I don't think we'll get the oath removed," she told Eva, "at any rate for a long time, but anyhow it is something to go for with a chance of success."

The letter in which she expressed her hope for the future and re-iterated her confidence in de Valera was the last one Madame wrote to her sister. Quite suddenly, on June 30, 1926, Miss Gore-Booth died. She had been ill for two days only. Madame was at the seashore for a few days and did not get the telegram until she came back to Frank-fort House. She had been depressed for several days, not knowing why, and then she received the news.

"Everything seemed to go from under me," she wrote to Miss Roper, "I simply can't realise it. There was no one ever like her. She was something wonderful and beautiful, and so simple and thought so little of herself. Her gentleness prevented me getting very callous in a War. I once held out and stopped a man being shot because of her. I had always had a funny habit, since Aylesbury, of referring anything I was doing to her. Every sketch I made I wondered how she would like it, and I looked forward to showing it to her. If I saw anything beauti-ful, I thought of her, and wished she was there to enjoy it. I was always dreaming and planning to take you both along to some beautiful places in the car. I was writing a play and doing a copy to send her, and so on, through everything, though I didn't write often. And then everything seemed to be cut off all at once. But lately I've begun to feel and see her often. When I'm painting she seems to look at me and help me from the clouds. I wake suddenly and it is just as if she was there. Last Sunday at Mass, when I wasn't thinking of her at all, she suddenly seemed to smile at me from behind the priest, and I know it is real and that she, the real Eva, is somewhere very near."[10]

It was an unhappy summer for Madame, who felt her loss deeply. She went to London in September to see Miss Roper. "I feel very sad leaving this house, probably for the last time," she said. "Every corner in it speaks of Eva, and her lovely spirit of peace and love is here just the same as ever."

Madame kept active with the new party, with the reorganized Fianna, with the Republican Dramatic Society, with the Prisoners Defense League, and continued to speak out and protest against injustice with her old courage and conviction, but it was now a strain. Mrs. Skeffington and other friends noticed she often looked tired; her marvellous physique showed signs of breaking down. Some spark had gone out of her life with her sister's death that was never rekindled, but she drove herself on.

During that winter of 1926–27 there was a severe coal shortage in Dublin that particularly affected the poor. Madame's kindness and help to them in this last winter of her life is remembered in countless stories. She arranged for fuel for many who would otherwise have been without. A friend, Lady Albina Brodrick sent turf up from Kerry when she could; other times Madame would go off to the mountains, pile her old car with bags of turf, and take them around to houses where she knew fuel was needed. In her enthusiasm she would lug the bags up the long flights of stairs herself if there was no one immediately available whose aid she could enlist, although there was no one who would not gladly have carried it for her.

One friend remembers her little brother went along in the car while Madame distributed bags of turf one day. She stopped in front of a house and while she visited, Sammy waited in the car. He was in tears when she came back; people had been taking the turf and he had not been able to stop them. The answer was typical, "It's all right, Sammy. It's for them. If they didn't need it they wouldn't take it." She remembers Madame as "the best-hearted person who ever lived." "She was the kindest person I have ever known," echoes another friend. "I remember her carrying the great big bag of turf up a high stairs, hauling it up to a poor little room where there was an old lady living alone. And I remember Madame lighting a fire and fixing up things. But she didn't like people to know much about things like that."

Seven months after her sister's death, their mother died at her home, Ardeevin, Co. Sligo, not far from Lissadell. Madame was in Sligo that dark January when her mother was buried in the Lissadell churchyard.

Age had resolved their differences. She had seen her mother regularly, even though her political convictions had cut her off from the rest of the family. She had not seen her brother since her return from Aylesbury in 1917, although she corresponded with him about business matters. In her more charitable moods she could see his point of view; "I suppose its very embarrassing to have a relation that gets into jail and fights in revolutions that you are not in sympathy with." Lady Gore-Booth often came to Dublin, and between trips Madame did errands for her. The last letter her daughter had had was to ask her to select a suitable cup for the Perpetual Challenge Cup for the Sligo Feis Ceoil of which she had been president since its founding in 1902.

Madame occasionally gave way to her depressed spirits during that winter. Once a friend entered her room without knocking because she thought Madame had gone out, and found her as no one had ever seen her before, sitting quietly looking out at the rainy twilight with tears running down her cheeks.

There was a general election in June, 1927, the first for the new Fianna Fail party, so there was the endless round of campaigning. Another of the favorite stories about Madame concerns this last campaign. She broke both bones in her lower arm while she was cranking her car. All she said while they were being set was, "Glory be, it's not my jaw, I can still talk." With her arm in a sling she went on to her meeting and made her speech. Madame stood in her old constituency, South Dublin City, and was one of 44 Fianna Fail candidates elected to the Dail. The seats of the party in power fell to 46.

The picture taken in June of the new Fianna Fail deputies shows her arm in a large black sling. She was still wearing it on June 23 when she walked with de Valera and the others to Leinster House to demand admission to the Dail. They got inside Leinster House, but the doors of the chamber were locked and they could go no further without taking the abjured oath. After failing to gain admission, the Fianna Fail T.D.'s returned to their headquarters and the leaders addressed the crowds that assembled there.

It was fitting that Madame's last meeting was one of the Fianna Executive in early July. One of the young men noticed that she seemed unwell and wanted her to go home, but, as he said, "She was a peculiar woman. She'd sit a meeting out even if she dropped dead." However, he slipped word to the chairman to shorten the agenda without her knowing it, and took her on the tram home to Frankfort House. Dr.

Lynn was called and Madame was sent immediately to Sir Patrick Dun's Hospital. Dr. William Taylor performed an appendectomy the next day and at first she seemed to be recovering. He joked with her about the great streak of reddish antiseptic painted across her abdomen, "Well, Madame, I never thought I'd see you painted orange." When she flared up with her old spirit, her friends were reassured.[11]

On July 7, however, a message broadcast on the radio summoned Madame's family. There had been a second operation and her condition was serious. Her daughter went immediately to the hospital and was with her for several hours. Miss Roper arrived from London. Madame was in a ward in the hospital, among the poor where she wanted to be.

To her great joy her husband rushed from Warsaw to Dublin and was with her the last two days. With him was her stepson to whom she had written since the war but whom she had not seen for years. She was cheerful and happy; although she was allowed only a few visitors, she knew that all over Dublin those who loved her were praying for her. There was a suggestion of the old buoyancy on the last day when she proudly showed May Coghlan how she could lift her tea cup with her right hand; the broken arm had healed. It had annoyed her because it slowed her down in dressing and in combing her hair. She could not rattle out to the country in her car and could not paint. Now, too late, it was sound again.

The Count was staying in Dublin with the Starkeys, artist friends from the old days. At ten o'clock on July 14, the House Surgeon sent a message to him, "Madame Markievicz became suddenly ill at about 8:30 and is in danger. Sir William Taylor has been here and has told us to inform you." Her husband was with her when she died at 1:30 A.M., July 15, 1927. There were friends by her side, too, including de Valera, Mrs. Sheehy Skeffington, and May Coghlan.

In the Bible her grandmother had given her in 1876, from which she had often read aloud at Surrey House and which was with her in the hospital, was a typewritten verse on which she had written "To Mother and Eva, 1927":

> They are not dead, they do not sleep;
> They have awakened from the dream of life,
> They have outsoared the shadow of our night.
> Envy and calumny and hate and pain,
> And that unrest which men miscall delight,
> Can touch them not, nor torture them again.[12]

Although Madame herself was free from the unrest, the calumny, the hate and pain, even in death she was the center of controversy. Both the City Hall and the Mansion House were refused for her lying-in-state. Since civic property was closed to her, her body was taken to the Rotunda, and there, guarded by Fianna boys, long streams of Dublin friends passed to say goodbye and God bless.

The funeral procession on Sunday, July 17, was huge, and thousands more lined the route to see it pass. The Irish have a sensitivity to funerals that honor a life as well as lament a death. In the mourning coaches were her family: the Count, his son, Sir Josslyn and Lady Gore-Booth. Eight motor tenders were required for the wreaths and flowers her friends had sent, wreaths from all the organizations to which she had given her vitality, from girlhood friends, from Castle society friends, from rich and poor in Dublin. There were even, it was reported, three fresh eggs which a countrywoman had promised to Madame when she came out of the hospital.

The advance guard of uniformed Fianna boys was followed by a band, by a detachment of the Citizen Army, by members of the 1916 club, another band; more Fianna and clergy preceded the tricolor wrapped coffin. One of the priests was Father Ryan, chaplain at Kilmainham in 1916 when Madame had asked him to be with her at the end, thinking it was to be then. He kept his promise eleven years later. The Fianna Fail and Republican deputies followed, three or four more bands, several contingents of Volunteers, members of the Workers' Union, Cumann na mBan, the Clan na nGaedheal, the Women's Defence League headed by Madame MacBride and Mrs. Despard. Miss MacSwiney and J. J. O'Kelly headed the Sinn Fein representatives.

In the crowds lining the streets were "old veterans of the Citizen Army, poorly clad, hungry, worn. Mothers from the slums crowded together, silent, fiercely sad. A champion was passing." Nora Connolly said no one would ever combine "her gaiety, her friendliness, her courage, her philosophy, her generosity, her love of the people which had grown out of her understanding of their problems, and amazed appreciation of their powers of endurance. It was a love which was returned a thousandfold while she lived, and lined the streets through which her funeral passed with sorrowing hearts. She was a great woman of great heart."

At three o'clock when the advance guard reached Glasnevin a hundred Free State soldiers with rifles had already taken up positions a short distance from her grave. Thousands of people had already assembled. Among them were several detectives. It is fitting that they too were represented, peering suspiciously at the faces in the crowd. Just when the hearse reached the cemetery gate the soldiers were drawn in a line fifty yards from the graveside and six Fianna boys marched in single file from the gateway to the plot to stand in formation at one side while other young men formed a square around it.

At the chapel the Rosary was recited in Irish and the coffin taken to the vault. The burial was postponed because the gravediggers did not work on Sundays.

The funeral oration was delivered by Eamon de Valera who said: "Madame Markievicz is gone from us, Madame, the friend of the toiler, the lover of the poor. Ease and station she put aside, and took the hard way of service with the weak and the down-trodden. Sacrifice, misunderstanding and scorn lay on the road she adopted, but she trod it unflinchingly.

"She now lies at rest with her fellow-champions of the right— mourned by the people whose liberties she fought for; blessed by the loving prayers of the poor she tried so hard to befriend. The world knew her only as a soldier of Ireland, but we knew her as colleague and comrade.

"We knew the kindliness, the great woman's heart of her, the great Irish soul of her, and we know the loss we have suffered is not to be repaired.

"It is sadly we take our leave, but we pray high heaven that all she longed for may one day be achieved."

There was another brief ceremony on Monday morning when the coffin was borne from the vault and interred. Again the Free State military were out in force, and large numbers of detectives and uniformed police were stationed at the cemetery. They remained on duty throughout the day.

The Last Post was sounded by buglers of Fianna Eireann, followed by a decade of the Rosary in Irish. The uniform Madame wore at the College of Surgeons in 1916 was lowered into the grave with her coffin.

A wild, kind girl had given her life in the cause of Ireland.

NOTES TO CHAPTER XVI

1. In National Museum, Dublin.

2. *Rerum Novarum,* May 15, 1891 (Condition of the working classes), Pope Leo XIII, and Rev. P. Coffey, "James Connolly's Campaign against

Capitalism, in the Light of Catholic Teaching," *Catholic Bulletin,* 20 (1920).

3. Oscar Traynor in North Dublin and Samuel Holt in Sligo-Leitrim were elected. Madame had gone to Sligo to speak for Holt at a meeting in Ballymote where she urged an enthusiastic meeting to rally to the cause of Ireland free.

4. She had had a one act play produced in 1921, during the Truce, and one at Liberty Hall just before Easter Week, but after 1913 she never acted.

5. Mary Colum, *Life and the Dream* (New York, 1947), pp. 278–281.

6. It was acted at the Theatre Royal by the Republican Players for a Four Martyrs Commemoration on December 11, 1927.

7. Interestingly, almost these same words were used by Jim Larkin in his version of an internal union fight which he described in the *Irish Worker* in June, 1914.

8. Letter in National Museum, Dublin.

9. Other members of the Executive included P. J. Ruttledge and Sean T. O'Kelly, Vice-Presidents; Sean Lemass and Gerald Boland, Honorary Secretaries; Dr. J. Ryan and Sean McEntee, Honorary Treasurers.

10. Roper, *Prison Letters,* pp. 311–312.

11. Dr. Taylor had won the respect of all the Irish when, during the Black and Tan regime, although no nationalist himself, he had refused to comply with a British order to report gunshot wounds he treated. As a fighting Irishman admiringly said, "He was a doctor first, last, and all the time, not a police tout."

12. Adapted, probably by Madame, from Shelley's *Adonais,* XXXIX and XL. She titled it "In Memoriam."

Bibliography

Bibliography

BOOKS

An Englishman [Douglas Goldring]. *Dublin Explorations and Reflections.* Dublin: Maunsel & Co., 1917.

Barry, Commandant General Tom. *Guerilla Days in Ireland.* Cork: Mercier Press, 1955.

Beaslai, Piaras. *Michael Collins and the Making of a New Ireland.* London: George G. Harrap & Co., 1926.

Beaverbrook, William Maxwell Aitken, baron. *The Decline and Fall of Lloyd George.* New York: Duell, Sloan and Pearce, 1963.

Birmingham, George A. *Pleasant Places.* London: Wm. Heinemann, 1934.

Boyd, Ernest A. *Ireland's Literary Renaissance.* New York: John Lane, 1916.

Brennan, Robert. *Allegiance.* Dublin: Browne and Nolan, 1950.

Briscoe, Robert. *For the Life of Me.* London: Longmans, Green, 1958.

Bromage, Mary C. *De Valera and the March of a Nation.* London: Hutchinson, 1956.

Buckley, Margaret. *The Jangle of the Keys.* Dublin: James Duffy, 1938.

Caulfield, Max. *The Easter Rebellion.* London: Frederick Muller, 1963.

Churchill, Winston S. *The Aftermath (The World Crisis, 1918–1928).* New York: Charles Scribner's Sons, 1929.

Colum, Mary. *Life and the Dream.* New York: Doubleday, 1947.

Colum, Padraic. *Arthur Griffith.* Dublin: Browne and Nolan, 1959.

Connolly, James. *Labour and Easter Week 1916.* Edited by Desmond Ryan. Introduction by William O'Brien. Dublin: Three Candles, 1949.

————. *Labour in Ireland.* Vol. I: *Labour in Irish History.* Vol. II: *The Re-Conquest of Ireland.* Introduction by Cathal O'Shannon. Dublin: Three Candles, n.d.

————. *Socialism and Nationalism.* Introduction by Desmond Ryan. Dublin: Three Candles, 1948.

————. *The Workers' Republic.* Edited by Desmond Ryan. Introduction by William McMullen. Dublin: Three Candles, 1951.

Creel, George. *Ireland's Fight for Freedom.* New York: Harper, 1919.

Crozier, Brigadier General Frank Percy. *The Men I Killed.* New York: Doubleday, Doran, 1938.

Davitt, Michael. *The Fall of Feudalism in Ireland.* London: Harper, 1904.

Denson, Alan, ed. *Letters from AE.* London: Abelard Schuman, 1961.

Devoy, John. *Recollections of an Irish Rebel.* New York: Chas. P. Young, 1929.

Dickinson, P. L. *The Dublin of Yesterday.* London: Methuen, 1929.

Dublin's Fighting Story, 1913–1921. Tralee: Kerryman, n.d.

Dunraven, W. T. W. Quin, 4th Earl of. *Past Times and Pastimes.* London: Hodder and Stoughton, n.d. (c. 1922).

Dunsany, E. J. M. D. Plunkett, 18th Baron. *Patches of Sunlight.* London: Wm. Heineman, 1938.

Figgis, Darrell. *A Chronicle of Jails.* Dublin: Talbot, 1918.

———. *A Second Chronicle of Jails.* Dublin: Talbot, 1919.

———. *Recollections of the Irish War.* New York: Doubleday, Doran, n.d.

Fingall, Elizabeth M. M. B. Plunkett, Countess of, and Pamela Hinkson, *Seventy Years Young.* London: Collins, 1937.

Fox, R. M. *Green Banners: The Story of the Irish Struggle.* London: Secker and Warburg, 1938.

———. *History of the Irish Citizen Army.* Dublin: Duffy, 1943.

———. *Louie Bennett: Her Life and Times.* Dublin: Talbot, n.d. (c. 1958).

———. *Rebel Irishwomen.* Dublin: Talbot, n.d.

Gallagher, Frank. *Days of Fear.* New York: Harpers, 1929.

———. *The Anglo-Irish Treaty.* London: Hutchinson, 1965.

Goldring, Douglas. *Odd Man Out: The Autobiography of a "Propaganda Novelist."* London: Chapman and Hall, 1935.

Gore-Booth, Eva. *The Death of Finovar from the Triumph of Maeve.* Decorated by Constance Gore-Booth (Countess Markievicz). London: Erskine Macdonald, 1916.

———. *Poems of Eva Gore-Booth.* Introduction by Esther Roper. London: Longmans, Green, 1929.

Greaves, C. Desmond. *The Life and Times of James Connolly.* London: Lawrence & Wishart, 1961.

Gregory, Isabella Augusta (Persse) Lady. *Our Irish Theatre.* New York: Putnam's Sons, 1914.

Gwynn, Stephen, ed. *The Letters and Friendships of Sir Cecil Spring-Rice.* London: Constable, 1929.

Hackett, Francis. *Ireland A Study in Nationalism.* New York: Huebsch, 1920.

Hammond, J. L. *C. P. Scott of the Manchester Guardian.* New York: Harcourt Brace, 1934.

Hayes-McCoy, G. A., ed. *The Irish at War.* Cork: Mercier, 1964.

Healy, T. M. *Letters and Leaders of My Day.* London: Butterworth, 1928.

Hobson, J. A. *Imperialism: A Study.* New York, James Pott, 1902.

Hogan, David [Frank Gallagher]. *The Four Glorious Years.* Dublin: Irish Press, 1953.

Holt, Edgar. *Protest in Arms: The Irish Troubles 1916–1923.* London: Putnam, 1960.

Hone, J. M. *William Butler Yeats, The Poet in Contemporary Ireland.* Dublin: Maunsel, n.d. (c. 1915).

Hone, Joseph. *W. B. Yeats, 1865–1939.* London: Macmillan, 1962.

James, Robert Rhodes. *Lord Randolph Churchill.* London: Weidenfeld and Nicolson, 1959.

Jones, Francis P. *History of the Sinn Fein Movement and The Irish Rebellion of 1916.* New York: P. J. Kenedy, 1917.

Jones, Thomas. *Lloyd George.* London: Oxford University Press, 1951.

Joy, Maurice, ed. *The Irish Rebellion of 1916 and its Martyrs*. New York: Devin-Adair, 1916.

Kearns, Linda. *In Times of Peril*. Dublin: Talbot, 1922.

Kettle, L. J. *The Material for Victory, Being the Memoirs of Andrew J. Kettle*. Dublin: Fallon, 1958.

Koestler, Arthur. *Arrow in the Blue*. New York: Macmillan, 1952.

Lloyd George, David. *War Memoirs of David Lloyd George*. Boston: Little, Brown, 1933.

Lynch, Diarmuid. *The I.R.B. and the 1916 Insurrection*. Cork: Mercier, 1957.

Lynch, Florence Monteith. *The Mystery Man of Banna Strand*. New York: Vantage Press, 1959.

MacBride, Maud Gonne. *A Servant of the Queen*. Dublin: Golden Eagle, 1950.

Macardle, Dorothy. *The Irish Republic*. Dublin: Irish Press, 1951.

MacDonagh, Michael. *The Irish at the Front*. London: Hodder and Stoughton, 1916.

Macken, Walter. *The Scorching Wind*. New York: Macmillan, 1964.

Macready, Sir Nevil. *Annals of an Active Life*. London: Hutchinson, n.d. (c. 1933).

Markiewicz, Casimir Dunin. *The Memory of the Dead: A Romantic Drama of '98 in Three Acts*. Dublin: Tower, 1910.

Martin, F. X., O.S.A., ed. *The Irish Volunteers 1913–1915*. Dublin: Duffy, 1963.

Maxwell, Constantia. *Dublin under the Georges*. London: Faber and Faber, 1956.

McCartan, Patrick. *With De Valera in America*. Dublin: Fitzpatrick, 1932.

Mitchel, John. *Jail Journal*. Dublin: M. H. Gill, n.d.

Monteith, Robert. *Casement's Last Adventure*. Dublin: Moynihan, 1953.

Moore, George. *Confessions of a Young Man*. London: William Heinemann, 1926.

———. *Parnell and His Island*. London: Swan Sonnenschein, Lowrey, 1887.

Nevinson, Henry W. *Last Changes, Last Chances*. London: Nisbet, 1928.

Nic Shiublaigh, Maire. *The Splendid Years*. Dublin: Duffy, 1955.

O'Brien, Conor Cruise, ed. *The Shaping of Modern Ireland*. London: Routledge & Kegan Paul, 1960.

O'Brien, Nora Connolly. *Portrait of a Rebel Father*. Dublin: Talbot, 1935.

O'Brien, William and Desmond Ryan, eds. *Devoy's Post Bag, 1871–1928*. Dublin: Fallon, 1953.

O'Casey, Sean. *Drums Under the Windows*. New York: Macmillan, 1947.

O'Cathasaigh, P. [Sean O'Casey]. *The Story of the Irish Citizen Army*. Dublin: Maunsel, 1919.

O'Connor, Frank. *Michael Collins and the Irish Revolution*. Dublin: Clonmore & Reynolds, 1965.

O'Donnell, Frank J. Hugh. *The Dawn Mist: A Play of the Rebellion*. Dublin: Thomas Kiersey, 1919.

O'Donnell, Peadar. *There Will Be Another Day*. Dublin: Dolmen, 1963.

O'Donoghue, Florence. *No Other Law (The Story of Liam Lynch and the Irish Republican Army, 1916–1923)*. Dublin: Irish Press, 1954.

O'Faolain, Sean. *Constance Markievicz or The Average Revolutionary*. London: Jonathan Cape, 1934.

O'Hegarty, P. S. *The Victory of Sinn Fein*. Dublin: Talbot, 1924.

O'Malley, Ernie. *On Another Man's Wound*. London: Rich & Cowan, 1936.

O'Rorke, T. *The History of Sligo: Town and County*. Dublin: James Duffy, 1889.

Pakenham, Frank. *Peace by Ordeal*. London: Jonathan Cape, 1935.

Paul-Dubois, L. *The Irish Struggle and Its Results*. Translated by T. P. Gill. London: Longmans, Green, 1934.

Phillips, W. Alison. *The Revolution in Ireland 1906–1923*. London: Longmans, Green, 1926.

Rebel Cork's Fighting Story from 1916 to the Truce with Britain. Tralee: Kerryman, n.d.

Redmond-Howard, L. G. *Six Days of the Irish Republic: A Narrative and Critical Account of the Latest Phase of Irish Politics*. Boston: John W. Luce, 1916.

Robinson, Lennox, ed. *Lady Gregory's Journals*. London: Putnam, 1946.

Roper, Esther, ed. *Prison Letters of Countess Markievicz*. London: Longmans, Green, 1934.

Russell, George William. *The National Being, Some Thoughts on an Irish Polity by A.E.* London: Macmillan, 1925.

Ryan, Desmond. *James Connolly: His Life, Work and Writing*. Dublin: Talbot, 1924.

————. *Sean Treacy and the Third Tipperary Brigade I.R.A.* Tralee: Kerryman, 1945.

————. *Remembering Sion*. London: Arthur Barker, 1934.

————. *The Rising, The Complete Story of Easter Week*. Dublin: Golden Eagle, 1957.

Ryan, Mark F. *Fenian Memories*. Dublin: Gill, 1946.

Sharpe, May Churchill. *Chicago May: Her Story*. London: Sampson Low, Marston, n.d. (c. 1930?).

Sheehy, Eugene. *May It Please the Court*. Dublin: C. J. Fallon, 1951.

Shorter, Dora Sigerson. *Sixteen Dead Men and Other Poems of Easter Week* New York: Mitchell Kennerley, 1919.

Size, Mary. *Prisons I Have Known*. London: George Allen & Unwin, 1957.

Skinnider, Margaret. *Doing My Bit For Ireland*. New York: Century, 1917.

Smithson, Annie M. P. *Myself—and Others*. Dublin: Talbot, 1944.

Spender, J. A. and Cyril Asquith. *Life of Herbert Henry Asquith, Lord Oxford and Asquith*. London: Hutchinson, 1932.

Stephens, James. *The Insurrection in Dublin*. New York: Macmillan, 1917.

Taylor, Rex. *Michael Collins*. London: Hutchinson, 1958.

Tillman, Seth P. *Anglo-American Relations at the Paris Peace Conference of 1919*. Princeton: Princeton University Press, 1961.

The Times History of the War. Vol. VIII, London: The Times, 1916.

Tréguiz, Louis. *L'Irlande dans la Crise Universelle (3 Août 1914–25 Juillet 1917*. Paris: Librairie Félix Alcan, n.d.

Tynan, Katharine. *Twenty-five Years: Reminiscences*. London: Smith, Elder, 1913.

————. *The Years of the Shadow*. London: Constable, 1919.

Wade. Allan, ed. *The Letters of W. B. Yeats*. London: Rupert Hart-Davis, 1954.

With the I.R.A. in the Fight for Freedom. Tralee, Kerryman, n.d.

White, Captain J. R. *Misfit. An Autobiography*. London: Jonathan Cape, 1930.

Wright, Arnold. *Disturbed Dublin, The Story of the Great Strike of 1913–14*. London: Longmans, Green, 1914.

Wynne, Maud. *An Irishman and His Family, Lord Morris and Killanin*. London: John Murray, 1937.

Yeats, W. B. *The Collected Poems*. London: Macmillan, 1952.

————. *Easter 1916*. Privately printed by Clement Shorter, London: 1916.

SELECTED ARTICLES IN PERIODICALS AND BOOKS

Aknefton, "Thoughts at Markievicz Memorial," *Irish Times* (Dublin), April 7, 1956.

Bodkin, M. McDonnell, "The Father of the Land League," in *Famous Irish Trials*. Dublin: Duffy, 1928, pp. 129–143.

Connolly, Nora, "Easter," *Atlantic Monthly*, October 1916, 118, 682–685.

Coyle, Eithne, "The History of the Cumann na mBan," *An Phoblacht*, Dublin: April 8, 15, 22, 1933.

Donnelly, M., "With the Citizen Army in Stephen's Green," *An Phoblacht*, April 19, 1930.

"Elizabeth O'Farrell," *Catholic Bulletin*, April–May, 1917.

Gore-Booth, Eva, "For God and Kathleen ni Houlihan," *The Catholic Bulletin*, May, 1918.

Gore-Booth, Sir Henry, "The Basking Shark," *Longman's Magazine*, November, 1891.

Grennan, Julia, "Recollections," *An Phoblacht*, May 17, 24, 1930.

Hammond, J. L., "The Terror in Action," *The Nation & The Athenaeum*, April 30, 1921.

"Ireland's Joan of Arc," *The Literary Digest*, July 15, 1916.

"Julia Grennan," *Catholic Bulletin*, June, 1917.

Kelly, Anna, "The Rebel Countess," *Sunday Express*, November 3, 10, 17, 24, December 1, 1957.

Markiewicz, Count Stanislas, "Memories of Countess Markiewicz," *Irish Press*, Jan. 26 and Feb. 8, 1938.

————. "Memories of My Father," *Irish Times*, December 2, 9, 17, 1937, and January 6, 1938.

————. *Kerryman*, December, 1938.

Moore, Maurice, "History of the Irish Volunteers," *Irish Press*, began January 4, 1938 and daily installments followed.

Murphy, Major H. L., "Constance, Countess de Markievicz," *An Cosantóir*, June, 1946.

Murray, May, "A Girl's Experience in the G.P.O.," *Poblacht na hEireann,* April 20, 1922.

———. "More Memories of 1916," *An Phoblacht,* May 17, 1930.

Nevinson, Henry W., "Sir Roger Casement and Sinn Fein," *Atlantic Monthly,* August, 1916.

O'Daly, N., "For Stephen's Green," *An t-Oglach,* April 3, 1926.

O'Farrell, Elizabeth, "Recollections," *An Phoblacht,* April 26, May 3, 10, 1930.

Periscope, "The Last Days of Dublin Castle," *Blackwood's Magazine,* August, 1922.

Reynolds, M., "Cumann na mBan in the G.P.O.," *An t-Oglach,* March 27, 1927.

Ronan, Niall, "Irish Portraits," *The Outlook,* August 2, 1922.

Sheehy Skeffington, H., "Constance Markievicz in 1916," *An Phoblacht,* May 5, 12, 19, 1928.

———. " 'The Countess' Some Memories," *Irish Press,* February 4, 1936.

Symons, Arthur, *The Savoy,* November 1896.

Official Papers, Handbooks, Pamphlets, Monographs

The American Commission on Conditions in Ireland: Interim Report. No place or date of publication indicated, although probably 1921. This is an initial report of the Committee of One Hundred called together by the New York *Nation,* which included Jane Addams, Frederick C. Howe, James H. Maurer, Oliver P. Newman, George W. Norris, Norman Thomas, and others. The report has statistics on Black and Tan destruction and many photographs.

Brayden, William H. *The Irish Free State.* Chicago Daily News, 1925.

Colum, Mary. *A Call to Irish Women in America From the Women in Ireland* [c. 1914]. (n.p., n.d.)

———. *The Volunteers, the women, and the Nation, Cumann na mBan.* Dublin: 1914.

Dail Eireann. *Minutes of Proceedings of the First Parliament of the Republic of Ireland, 1919–1921.* Dublin: Stationery Office. n.d.

———. *Official Correspondence Relating to the Peace Negotiations June–September, 1921.* Dublin: October, 1921.

———. *Official Report Debate on the Treaty Between Great Britain and Ireland signed in London on the 6th December, 1921.* Dublin: Stationery Office, n.d.

———. *Official Report. For Periods 16th August, 1921, to 26th August, 1921, and 28th February, 1922, to 8th June, 1922.* Dublin: Stationery Office, n.d.

Defensive Warfare, a Handbook for Irish Nationalists. Belfast, n.p. 1909.

Devoy Memorial Committee, Michael Smyth, Chairman. *John Devoy.* Naas: 1964.

Documents Relative to the Sinn Fein Movement, Cmd. 1108. London: H.M. Stationery Office, 1921.

Facts About Ireland. Dublin: Department of External Affairs, 1963.

Fianna Handbook. Dublin: 1914.

Fifty Years of Liberty Hall. Dublin: Three Candles, 1959.

Ghosts of Kilmainham. Dublin: Kilmainham Jail Restoration Society, 1963.

Ireland's Request to the Government of the United States of America for Recognition as a Sovereign Independent State. No place or date of publication given. The opening statement addressed to the President of the United States is signed Eamon de Valera, President of the Republic of Ireland, and dated October 27, 1920.

Irish Rebellion 1916. A collection of depositions in typescript in the National Library of Ireland.

Kilmainham, The Bastille of Ireland. Dublin: Kilmainham Jail Restoration Society, 1961.

Macardle, Dorothy. *Tragedies of Kerry 1922–1923.* Dublin: Irish Book Bureau, 1924.

———. *Without Fanfares.* Dublin: Gill, 1946.

Maguire, Hugh. *Ireland Since the Treaty.* Dublin: Republican Pub., 1961.

Manifesto of Leaders of the Intellectual Life of Great Britain on Ireland and Report of the British Labour Commission to Ireland. No date or place of publication given, probably 1921.

1913 Jim Larkin and the Dublin Lock-Out. Dublin: Workers' Union of Ireland, 1964.

O'Higgins, Brian. *Salute to the Soldiers of 1922.* Dublin: 1962.

Parliamentary Debates. 5th Series. House of Commons. August, 1914 and April–June, 1916.

Proceedings of the Irish Race Congress in Paris, January, 1922. Dublin: 1922.

Reports of American Committee for Relief in Ireland and Irish White Cross. New York: n.d. (c. 1922).

Rolleston, T. W. *Ireland and Poland a Comparison.* London: Fisher Unwin, 1917.

Royal Commission into the circumstances connected with the Landing of Arms at Howth on July 26th, 1914. Minutes of Evidence, Cmd. 7649. London: H.M. Stationery Office, 1914.

Royal Commission on the Rebellion in Ireland, Cmd. 8311. London: H.M. Stationery Office, 1916.

Sceilg [J. J. O'Kelly]. *A Trinity of Martyrs.* Dublin: Irish Book Bureau, n.d. (c. 1947).

Sheehy Skeffington, Hanna. *Impressions of Sinn Fein in America.* Dublin: Davis, 1919.

Sinn Fein Rebellion Handbook Easter 1916. Dublin: Irish Times, 1916.

Spalpin. *Sinn Fein and the Labour Movement.* Dublin: n.d. (post-1916).

The Story of Fianna Fail, First Phase. Dublin: 1960.

The Struggle of the Irish People. Address to the Congress of the United States Adopted at the January Session of Dail Eireann 1921. Washington: Government Printing Office, 1921. Appendices include detailed statistical information on the 1918 election, population, economic, and taxation figures, as well as details of British aggression in Ireland during the four years 1917–1920. Presented by Mr. Borah and on May 2, 1921 referred to the Committee on Foreign Relations and ordered to be printed. Document No. 8. 67th Congress, 1st Session, Senate.

Treaty of Peace with Germany. Hearing before the Committee on Foreign Relations, United States Senate. Part 17. 66th Congress, 1st Session. Washington: Government Printing Office, 1919.

Workers' Union of Ireland, *Silver Jubilee Souvenir*. Dublin: 1949.

The Young Guard of Erin, The Fianna Handbook. Dublin: 1964.

NEWSPAPERS AND OTHER PERIODICALS

An t-Oglac. Official Organ of the Irish Volunteers. Dublin: August 15, 1918 to April 25, 1922. New series, February 24, 1923 to December 25, 1926. [Continued as *An t-Oglac. The Irish Army Quarterly* October 1, 1927.]

An Phoblacht. Dublin: June 20, 1925–October, 1927. [Successor to *Sinn Fein* (new series)]

Bean na hEireann, Dublin: April, 1909–February, 1911.

Beltaine, Dublin: May, 1899–February, 1900.

The Catholic Bulletin, Dublin: H. M. Gill. The magazine from 1916 on contains interesting articles about the rebellion, the people involved, and subsequent events.

Dublin News, Dublin: November 23–December 16, 1923.

Eire, The Irish Nation, Glasgow: January 20, 1923–April 21, 1924; Manchester, April 28–October 25, 1924. [This was successor to *Phoblacht na hEireann,* and became *Sinn Fein* (new series).]

The Harp, January, 1908–June, 1910. Published in New York until 1910, then in Dublin.

Honesty, Dublin: October 16, 1915–April 22, 1916.

Irish Bulletin, Dublin: November 11, 1919–December 13, 1921.

The Irish Citizen, Dublin: May 25, 1912–August, 1920.

Irish Freedom, Dublin: November 1910–December 1914

The Irish Nation, Dublin: January 2, 1909–December 3, 1910.

Irish Opinion, Dublin: December 1, 1917–April, 1918. [Became *The Voice of Labour.*]

The Irish Volunteer, Dublin: February, 1914–April 22, 1916.

Irish War News, July 18, 1922. (New York, American Delegation Irish Republican Party.)

The Irish Worker, Dublin: May, 1911–November, 1914. [Succeeded by *Workers' Republic* in May, 1915.]

The Irishman, Dublin: May 14, 1927–October 25, 1930. [Successor to *The Voice of Labour.*]

Nationality, Dublin: June, 1915–April, 1916; February, 1917–September, 1919. [Successor to *Sinn Fein* and *Scissors and Paste.*]

New Ireland, Dublin: May, 1915–September 20, 1919; December 10, 1921–July, 1922.

Poblacht na h-Eireann. The Republic of Ireland, Dublin: January 3, 1922–June 29, 1922; July 29, 1922; Scottish ed., Glasgow: August 26, 1922–January 13, 1923. [Succeeded by *Eire, The Irish Nation.*]

The Republic, Dublin: June 21–September 20, 1919.

Samhain, Dublin: October, 1901; October, 1903; December, 1904; November, 1905; November, 1908.

Scissors and Paste, Dublin: December 12, 1914–February 27, 1915. [Successor to *Sinn Fein* and was succeeded by *Nationality.*]

Sinn Fein, Dublin: May, 1906–November 28, 1914. A weekly, except for a brief period when it was published as a daily, August 23, 1909–January 21, 1910.

Sinn Fein (new series), Dublin: December, 1923–June 13, 1925. [Became *An Phoblacht.*]

The Sinn Feiner, New York: June 12, 1920–December, 1921.

The Sligo Champion, Sligo: January, 1879–December, 1927.

Spark, Dublin: February 7, 1915–April 23, 1916.

United Irishman, Dublin: March 4, 1899–April, 1906. [Succeeded by *Sinn Fein.*]

The Voice of Labour, Dublin: December, 1917–September 20, 1919. [Successor to *Irish Opinion,* became *The Watchword of Labour.*]

The Voice of Labour (new series), Dublin: October 22, 1921–May 7, 1927. [Successor to *The Watchword of Labour;* continued as *The Irishman.*]

The Workers' Republic, Dublin: August 12, 1898–October, 1898; May 12, 1899–May 11, 1900; May, 1915–April, 1916; October, 1921–December, 1922; February–November, 1923; March–December, 1927; May 12, 1929.

Young Ireland (Eire Og), Dublin: April 21, 1917–January 26, 1918; January, 1919–December 23, 1922. [Successor to *Nationality.*]

ARTICLES AND MONOGRAPHS BY CONSTANCE DE MARKIEVICZ

These are listed in chronological order and include most of Madame's signed articles. I have omitted some motion picture reviews she wrote in the 1920's.

Women, Ideals and the Nation. A lecture delivered to the Students' National Literary Society, Dublin: Inghinidhe na hEireann, 1909.

"The Women of '98," in *The Irish Citizen,* Dublin: November 6, 13, 20, 27, December 4, 1915. A lecture given October 12, 1915 at a meeting of the Irish Women's Franchise League.

A Call to the Women of Ireland. Dublin: Fergus O'Connor, 1918, a reprint of *Women, Ideals and the Nation.*

"Break Down The Bastilles," *The Voice of Labour,* Dublin: May 1, 1919.

"On English Jails," *New Ireland,* Dublin: April 8, 1922.

"Conditions of Women in English Jails," *New Ireland,* Dublin: April 15, 1922.

"Peace With Honour," *Poblacht na hEireann,* Dublin: January 3, 1922.

"Stop Thief," *Eire,* Glasgow: February 17, 1923.

"An Open Letter to the Independent Labour Party," *Eire,* Glasgow: April 28, 1923.

"DeValera's Oath—The Truth," *Eire,* Glasgow: April 21, 1923.

"Tom Clarke and the First Day of the Republic," *Eire,* Glasgow: May 26, 1923.

"The Fianna," *Eire,* Glasgow: June 9, 1923.

"Larkin, The Fianna, and the King's Visit," *Eire,* Glasgow: June 16, 1923.

"Madame Markievicz Challenges O'Higgins," *Eire,* Glasgow: July 7, 1923.

"The King's Visit," *Eire,* Glasgow: July 14, 21, 28, 1923.

"Going To Jail," *Eire,* Glasgow: August 4, 1923.

"Mr. Arthur Griffith, The Sinn Fein Organisation," *Eire,* Glasgow: August 18, 1923.

"Mr. Griffith," *Eire,* Glasgow: August 25, 1923.

"Mr. Griffith and Mr. Tim Healy," *Eire,* Glasgow: September 1, 1923.

"A Comment on the Folly of Dr. Fogarty," *Eire,* Glasgow: September 1, 1923.

"The Bitter Fraud," *Eire,* Glasgow: October 13, 1923.

"A Note on Eamon de Valera," *Eire,* Glasgow: October 13, 1923.

What Irish Republicans Stand For. Glasgow: Forward, 1923.

"Definite Reply to Mr. O'Higgins," *Sinn Fein,* Dublin: November 15, 1924.

James Connolly's Policy and Catholic Doctrine. n.p., 1924.

"Wolfe Tone's Ideals of Democracy," *An Phoblacht,* Dublin: June 26, 1925.

"Liam Mellows—Pioneer," *An Phoblacht,* Dublin: May 28, 1926.

"James Connolly as I Knew Him," *The Nation,* Dublin: March 26, 1927.

"1916," *The Nation,* Dublin: April 23, 1927.

"Free State Failure," *The Nation,* Dublin: May 14, 1927.

"Return of de Valera to Ireland," *The Nation,* Dublin: May 24, 1927.

"Citizenship," *The Nation,* Dublin: August 13, 1927.

POEMS BY CONSTANCE DE MARKIEVICZ

These are listed in approximate chronological order of their writing.

"Who Fears to Wear the Blood Red Badge," *Irish Worker,* Dublin: October 11, 1913. This was one of the most popular ballads of the lockout, sung to the tune of "Who Fears to Speak of '98." It has been reprinted many times and usually anonymously although when first printed in *The Irish Worker* it was signed "Maca." It was the fashion of the women of the Inghinidhe to adopt Irish pseudonyms and Madame's *Women, Ideals and the Nation* was signed Constance de Markievicz (Maca of Inghinide na hEireann) so it seems reasonable to assign the authorship of this ballad to her. The style and the sentiments are hers.

"To The Citizen Army," *The Workers' Republic,* Dublin: June 26, 1915. This also was signed "Maca."

"Hymn On The Battlefield," *The Workers' Republic,* Dublin: November 13, 1915. This was dedicated to the Citizen Army and is the best known of Madame's poems. The title is now commonly "A Battle Hymn" (To The Irish Citizen Army, 1916).

"The Manchester Martyrs," *The Workers' Republic,* Dublin: November 27, 1915.

"Dreams," *Fianna,* December, 1915.

"The Germans Are Winning the War, me boys," a popular bit of doggeral printed in Margaret Skinnider, *Doing My Bit For Ireland,* pp. 221–225.

"The Call," *The Workers' Republic,* Dublin: April 15, 1916.

"Our Faith," *The Workers' Republic,* Dublin: April 22, 1916.

"To A Comrade, The Rosary—College of Surgeons," written Easter Week or shortly thereafter and reprinted several times, including *An Caman*, Dublin: April 14, 1934.

"In Kilmainham," *New Ireland,* Dublin: February 9, 1918.

"In Mountjoy," *New Ireland*, Dublin: February 16, 1918.

"Her Hero," July 1916. Unpublished.

There are several poems in the Aylesbury Journals, 1916–1917, which are in the National Museum of Ireland. The ones Madame wrote in letters to her sister are included in Esther Roper, *Prison Letters of Countess Markievicz*, pp. 154, 156, 159, 164–166, 170–171.

"The Mass," May, 1917[?], unpublished.

"Heroes and Martyrs," *An Phoblacht,* Dublin: April 19, 1930. Written November 23, 1917.

"Kevin," c. November, 1922, unpublished.

"Let Ireland Pray for the Volunteers," c. 1922, unpublished.

"Easter Memories," *Kerryman,* Tralee: December, 1938, written April, 1927.

A list of authorities consulted would be incomplete without mention of the Irish men and women who aided with their memories. Almost without exception I found willing help and encouragement from all of those to whom I appealed for information and advice. I particularly wish to thank Robert Briscoe, Joseph Clarke, W. T. Cosgrave, Sidney Gifford Czira (John Brennan), President Eamon de Valera, Geraldine Plunkett Dillon, Seamus Doran, R. M. Fox and his wife, Patricia Lynch, Lady Gore-Booth, Gabrielle Gore-Booth, Sheila Greene (who started it all), Professor G. A. Hayes-McCoy, May Coghlan MacMahon, Eamon Martin, Helena Molony, Nora Niland, Angus O'Daly, J. J. Pounch, Justice Kenneth Reddin, Joe Reynolds, Mrs. Jim Russell, Dr. Bethel Solomons, and Frank Robbins, who not only was generous with his time but also let me read his informative memoirs.

The staff of the National Museum of Ireland were of great assistance; my gratitude to Dr. William O'Sullivan and Oliver Snoddy. Those in the National Library were unfailingly patient and knowledgeable. I had much help in getting needed books from the Smith College Library, and would like to express my appreciation to Dr. Herbert Hitchen, formerly of Northampton, for sharing his excellent personal library. Donald Sheehan and Denis Johnston of the Smith College faculty read the manuscript and offered valuable suggestions although not always sharing my interpretation of events in Ireland. My husband, who added life and commas to the book, and our children, who cheerfully accompanied me on pilgrimages to Kilmainham Jail, to the ruins of Madame's cottage, to Bodenstown, Howth, Glasnevin and such meaningful places, know how much they have helped with their patient interest.

Index

Index

ST. STEPHEN'S GREEN